CHANGING CONTOURS OF CRIMINAL JUSTICE

CHANGING CONTOURS OF CRIMINAL JUSTICE

EDITED BY
MARY BOSWORTH, CAROLYN HOYLE, AND LUCIA ZEDNER

CENTRE FOR CRIMINOLOGY
UNIVERSITY OF OXFORD

OXFORD
UNIVERSITY PRESS

OXFORD
UNIVERSITY PRESS

Great Clarendon Street, Oxford, OX2 6DP,
United Kingdom

Oxford University Press is a department of the University of Oxford.
It furthers the University's objective of excellence in research, scholarship,
and education by publishing worldwide. Oxford is a registered trade mark of
Oxford University Press in the UK and in certain other countries

First Edition published in 2016

Impression: 1

Published in the United States of America by Oxford University Press
198 Madison Avenue, New York, NY 10016, United States of America

British Library Cataloguing in Publication Data
Data available

Library of Congress Control Number: 2016943365

ISBN 978-0-19-878323-7

Printed and bound by
CPI Group (UK) Ltd, Croydon, CR0 4YY

To our students—past, present, and future

ACKNOWLEDGEMENTS

We are grateful to all the contributors for their excellent contributions and their gracious and patient responses to our editorial suggestions. We thank Emma Burtt for her outstanding research assistance and Lucy Alexander, Franziska Bröckl, and Jack Webb at OUP for their continued support and seamless production of this volume.

CONTENTS

PART III PUNISHMENT, POLICY, AND PRACTICE

PART IV VICTIMS IN, AND OF, THE CRIMINAL JUSTICE SYSTEM

LIST OF CONTRIBUTORS

EDITORS

Mary Bosworth is Professor of Criminology and Fellow of St Cross College at the University of Oxford and, concurrently, Professor of Criminology at Monash University, Australia. She works on immigration detention and punishment. Mary is currently heading a five-year European Research Council Start Grant (313362) on 'Subjectivity, Identity and Penal Power' and a three-year International Network on 'External Border Control' funded by the Leverhulme Trust. She is Director of Border Criminologies (http://bordercriminologies.law.ox.ac.uk), the UK Editor-in-Chief of *Theoretical Criminology*, a co-editor of *Routledge Studies in Criminal Justice, Borders and Citizenship*, and a member of the editorial board of the Clarendon Studies in Criminology.

Carolyn Hoyle is Professor of Criminology and Director of the Centre for Criminology and Fellow of Green Templeton College, at the University of Oxford. She is currently conducting research into applications to the Criminal Cases Review Commission concerning alleged miscarriages of justice, for a forthcoming book (with Mai Sato) to be published by Oxford University Press (*Last Resorts: Decisions and Discretion at the Criminal Cases Review Commission*, 2017). She has recently completed a study of those falsely accused of abuse while in occupations of trust (with Ros Burnett and Naomi Ellen Speechley). She also conducts research on the death penalty.

Lucia Zedner is Professor of Criminal Justice, Senior Research Fellow, All Souls College, and a member of the Centre for Criminology, University of Oxford. She is also a Conjoint Professor, Faculty of Law, University of New South Wales, Sydney, where she is a regular visitor. She is a Fellow of the British Academy and an Overseas Fellow of the Australian Academy of Law. Recent publications include *Prevention and the Limits of the Criminal Law* (OUP, 2013), co-edited with Andrew Ashworth and Patrick Tomlin and *Preventive Justice* (OUP, 2014) with Andrew Ashworth. Her research interests include criminal justice, criminal law, security, and counter-terrorism.

CONTRIBUTORS

Ana Aliverti is Associate Professor at Warwick Law School, University of Warwick. Before joining Warwick, she was the Oxford Howard League Post-Doctoral Research Fellow (2012–13) at the Centre for Criminology, University of Oxford. Her work examines the intersections of immigration and criminal law regulation in Britain, in particular the functioning of criminal law in the policing of non-citizens.

Her research has focused on the criminal courts. Her book *Crimes of Mobility* (Routledge, 2014), an empirical and theoretical examination of immigration crimes, was co-awarded the 2014 British Society of Criminology Book Prize.

Andrew Ashworth held the Vinerian Professorship of English Law, University of Oxford from 1997 to 2013 and is now Professor Emeritus and an Emeritus Fellow of All Souls College, Oxford. He is also an Adjunct Professor of Law, University of Tasmania. He has been associated with the Centre for Criminology since 1979, and served as Acting Director of the Centre 1982–83, 2003, and 2004–05. He was a member of the Sentencing Advisory Panel from its inception in 1999, becoming its chair in 2007 until its demise in 2010. His research interests include sentencing practices, sentencing theory, and criminal law theory.

Ben Bradford is a Departmental Lecturer in Criminology at the Centre for Criminology, University of Oxford. His research interests include procedural justice theory, and issues of trust, legitimacy, cooperation, and compliance in policing and the wider criminal justices system. Along with Ian Loader, Beatrice Jauregui, and Jonny Steinberg he is editor of *The SAGE Handbook of Global Policing* (SAGE 2016,). Ben has worked with a range of police and other organizations on projects aiming to enhance understanding of public perceptions, needs, and priorities in the arena of policing.

Rachel Condry is Associate Professor of Criminology at the Centre for Criminology, University of Oxford and a Fellow of St Hilda's College. Her work focuses on the intersection between crime and the family, including research on families of offenders, families of victims, and the family as a site of crime. She has previously been a lecturer in criminology at the University of Surrey, and a lecturer and British Academy Postdoctoral Fellow at the London School of Economics. She is currently working on a book on adolescent to parent violence having recently completed a three-year Economic and Social Research Council (ESRC)-funded project on this topic.

Stephen Farrall is a sociologist who works in the Centre for Criminological Research at the University of Sheffield, where he is a Professor of Criminology. He was a DPhil student and a research officer at the Oxford Centre for Criminology from 1996 to 2000. He is best known for his work on why people stop offending, the fear of crime, and the legacy of 'Thatcherite' social and economic policies for the criminal justice system. His research has attracted funding from the ESRC (seven grants), the Leverhulme Trust (three grants), the British Academy, The European Commission, and the Ministry of Justice.

Lyndon Harris is currently reading for a DPhil in Criminology at the University of Oxford. He is the editor of the *Criminal Appeal Reports (Sentencing)*, *Current Sentencing Practice* and *Thomas' Sentencing Referencer*. He also writes monthly case commentaries for the *Criminal Law Review* and recently advised the Law Commission in relation to their sentencing procedure project.

Roger Hood was the first student to be awarded the PhD at the Cambridge Institute of Criminology (1963), and was awarded the DCL (Doctor of Civil Law) at the University of Oxford in 1999. He is now Emeritus Professor of Criminology at

Oxford University and an Emeritus Fellow of All Souls College. From 1973 to 2003 he was Director of the Oxford Centre for Criminological Research (now the Centre for Criminology). His research has had four main strands: the death penalty; race and sentencing; the parole system; and the history of the emergence of penal policy. He has received the Sellin-Glueck Award of the American Society of Criminology for 'Distinguished International Contributions to Criminology' (1986); he was elected a Fellow of the British Academy in 1992; he was awarded the Cesare Beccaria Medal from the International Society of Social Defence (2011) and the ESC European Criminology Award 'for a lifetime contribution as a European criminologist' (2012). He was consultant to the United Nations on capital punishment, leading to publication of *The Death Penalty: A Worldwide Perspective* (OUP, 1st edn 1989, 5th edn with Carolyn Hoyle, 2015). Since retirement he has held visiting professorships at the University of Virginia, Hong Kong University, and the City University of Hong Kong. He was appointed CBE for services to the study of criminology (1995), Honorary QC (2000), and Hon LLD by Birmingham (2008) and Edinburgh Napier (2011) Universities.

Ian Loader is Professor of Criminology at the University of Oxford and Professorial Fellow of All Souls College. He is editor (with Ben Bradford, Beatrice Jauregui, and Jonny Steinberg) of *The SAGE Handbook of Global Policing* (SAGE, 2016) and Editor-in-Chief of *The Howard Journal of Crime and Justice*. He was Director of the Oxford Centre for Criminology between 2005 and 2012.

Michelle Madden Dempsey is Professor of Law and Associate Dean for Faculty Research at the Charles Widger School of Law, Villanova University, USA. A former domestic violence criminal prosecutor, she was a Lecturer in the Oxford Law Faculty and a doctoral student at the Oxford Centre for Criminology before moving to Villanova. Her book, *Prosecuting Domestic Violence: A Philosophical Analysis* (OUP, 2009) was awarded second prize in the UK's Society of Legal Scholars Peter Birks Award for Outstanding Legal Scholarship. She is an editor of *Criminal Law & Philosophy*. She is an elected member of the American Law Institute and an elected Fellow of the American Bar Association.

Caroline Miles is a Lecturer in Criminology in the School of Law at the University of Manchester. Her research areas centre round the understanding of and responses to domestic violence and homicide. Caroline previously worked as a Research Officer at the Centre for Criminology, University of Oxford on a project investigating child to parent violence and is currently involved in an ESRC project on understanding and improving risk assessment in domestic abuse.

Ian O'Donnell is Professor of Criminology at University College Dublin. Previously, he was Director of the Irish Penal Reform Trust, Research Officer at the Oxford University Centre for Criminological Research, and Research Assistant at the University of London. He served as a member of the Board of Visitors for HMP Pentonville and as a magistrate on the Oxford bench. An Adjunct Fellow of Linacre College, Oxford, a Member of the Royal Irish Academy, and a Member of the Academia Europaea, his latest book is *Prisoners, Solitude, and Time* (OUP, 2014). His current research focuses on capital punishment and clemency.

Alpa Parmar is Senior Research Fellow at the Centre for Criminology, University of Oxford and an associate director of Border Criminologies. Her research interests include: race, racism and criminalization, borders and policing migration, and the policing of minority ethnic communities. Alpa has published on ethnicity, racism and criminal justice, policing and race, and perceptions of crime amongst the Asian community.

Daniel Pascoe is an Assistant Professor at the School of Law, City University of Hong Kong. He is an MSc, MPhil, and DPhil graduate of the Oxford Centre for Criminology. Daniel's research interests include comparative and international law perspectives on capital punishment, law and society in Southeast Asia, criminal law, and Islamic law. Daniel recently testified before Australia's Joint Parliamentary Standing Committee on Foreign Affairs, Defence and Trade regarding an official Inquiry into Australia's Advocacy for the Abolition of the Death Penalty.

Jill Peay is a Professor of Law at the London School of Economics and Political Science and a member of the Mannheim Centre for Criminology. She is the author of *Decisions and Dilemmas: Working with Mental Health Law* (Hart Publishing, 2003) and *Mental Health and Crime* (Routledge, 2011). Her life as an employed academic started at the Oxford Centre for Criminological Research in 1980, where she was a Research Fellow until 1987.

Julian V. Roberts is a Professor of Criminology at the University of Oxford. He is Associate editor of the *European Journal of Criminology*. Books include: *Popular Punishment* (OUP, 2014, ed. with J. Ryberg); *Exploring Sentencing Practice in England and Wales* (Palgrave, 2015); *Sentencing Guidelines: Exploring the English Experience* (OUP, 2013, ed. with A. Ashworth); *Sentencing for Murder* (Hart Publishing, 2012, with B. Mitchell); *Mitigation and Aggravation at Sentencing* (Cambridge University Press, 2011); *Punishing Persistent Offenders* (OUP, 2008); and *The Virtual Prison* (Cambridge University Press, 2004).

Gwen Robinson is Reader in Criminal Justice at the University of Sheffield's Centre for Criminological Research. She has published widely in the areas of community sanctions, offender rehabilitation, and restorative justice. Her recent publications include *Community Punishment: European Perspectives* (Routledge, 2016, ed. with Fergus McNeill) published in 2016, and *Restorative Justice in Practice: Evaluating What Works for Victims and Offenders* (Routledge, 2011, with Joanna Shapland and Angela Sorsby). She is co-chair of the European Society of Criminology Working Group on Community Sanctions and Measures. Gwen worked as a Research Officer at the Oxford Centre from October 1996 to December 1997.

Joanna Shapland is the Edward Bramley Professor of Criminal Justice and Director of the Centre for Criminological Research at the University of Sheffield. She worked at the Centre for Criminology from 1978 to 1988. At Oxford she researched victims' experiences with the criminal justice system, as well as community views about policing and crime, and comparative criminal justice. She is Executive Editor of the *International Review of Victimology*. Recently she has been researching restorative justice, desistance from crime (with Tony Bottoms), quality in probation supervision (with Stephen Farrall, Gwen Robinson, and Angela Sorsby), and the informal economy.

Richard Young is Professor of Law and Policy in the School of Law, University of Birmingham. He was formerly a Reader in Criminal Justice and Assistant Director of the Centre for Criminology at the University of Oxford until 2006, when he moved to a chair in Law and Policy Research at the University of Bristol. He specializes in empirical research on criminal justice.

MAPPING THE CONTOURS OF CRIMINAL JUSTICE

AN INTRODUCTION

Lucia Zedner, Carolyn Hoyle, and Mary Bosworth

This volume has been produced as part of the Oxford Centre for Criminology's 50th anniversary celebrations in 2016. All the contributors have a connection to the Centre, either as current members of staff or former faculty and students. Their essays demonstrate the breadth and ambition of enquiry characteristic of the research carried out by those at the Centre. They explore the ways in which that research has engaged with, shaped, and been shaped by changes in criminal justice policy over the last half century.

However, this collection is very much more than a *Festschrift* or tribute to the work of the Oxford Centre. Rather, it is a sustained exploration of how criminal justice scholarship relates to criminal justice practice over time. To this end, the authors reflect on the changing nature of criminal justice over the last 50 years, examine the challenges it faces today, and its possible futures. They explore shifts in its scope, dominant concerns, values, and aims. Together their essays reveal a landscape in flux, in which certain issues or institutions have disappeared from view, some remain constant, and a host of new problems, practices, and challenges have arisen. They also hint at the changing contours of the academic habitus, as criminology's working relationship with the government waxes and wanes, and the academy becomes subject to other institutional demands, not least for demonstrable impact beyond the university.

Some developments spring from substantive changes in crime, policy, and practice, whereas others owe their origins to innovations in academic thought or the findings of pioneering research. Just as criminal justice practice has changed significantly, so too has criminal justice scholarship. Teasing out the complex interactions between academic research, policy development, and practice is a daunting task. Taking the Oxford Centre as a microcosm of that interaction permits a closer enquiry into the interface between the work of one founding centre of criminological research and the wider world. Since its inception, the Oxford Centre has had a particular focus on criminal justice (Ashworth 2011; Zedner 2003). So exploring its contributions makes possible larger reflections on the emergence and expansion of criminal justice scholarship as a distinctive and increasingly dominant aspect of criminological research.

CRIMINAL JUSTICE SCHOLARSHIP—A BRIEF HISTORY

At the risk of compressing a complex history, this section sets out the main trajectories, crossroads, and key junctures in the development of criminal justice scholarship in the UK. Criminal justice as an object of sustained and systematic academic enquiry is a relatively recent endeavour: little more than half a century ago, it was only emerging as a topic of serious enquiry (Ashworth 1988: 111–12; Rock 1994: 131). Even the establishment of the larger field of criminology as an academic discipline in the UK can only be traced back to just before the Second World War. Central to this story is the impact of a powerful triumvirate of distinguished European émigrés, Max Grünhut and Hermann Mannheim, who had fled Nazi Germany, and Leon Radzinowicz, who had left Poland a little earlier. Radzinowicz went to Cambridge (where he later founded the Institute of Criminology); Mannheim secured a lectureship at the London School of Economics; and Max Grünhut finally escaped in 1939 to All Souls College Oxford, which made it possible for him to pursue his studies.[1] Once there, Grünhut formed a close relationship with Oxford's Department of Social Policy and Social Work at 'Barnett House', which was also temporary home to the Howard League for Penal Reform, allowing for the development of a relationship with that organization that continues to this day.

Although Radzinowicz, Mannheim, and Grünhut were very different in character, outlook, and interests, all three shared a common view of criminology as scientific, practical, and purposive. Its role, they believed, was to ensure that policy formation was informed by expert knowledge and scientifically rigorous empirical studies. Grünhut's *Juvenile Offenders before the Courts* (1956) was one such ground-breaking study of the court process. Its novelty at the time was captured by one review that observed, 'the experience accumulated by the courts in the course of the years is enormous but it has been allowed to remain inchoate and has never been so organised that it has become available knowledge' (James 1956: 617). Yet making such knowledge 'available' was severely limited by the tiny numbers of scholars then engaged in criminological research. In recognition that the penal process was little studied and poorly understood, the 1959 Government White Paper *Penal Practice in a Changing Society* sought to promote criminological research as a basis for a better informed penal policy. It committed the government not only to fund long-term research within the Home Office and universities (Home Office 1959: 7–9) but also to the creation of institutional structures that would provide an enduring basis for scientific inquiry (Zedner 2003: 207).

This commitment was pivotal in the history of British criminology, funding not only the Home Office Research Unit, but also the Institute of Criminology in Cambridge in 1959 (Martin 1988: 35) and, in 1966, the Oxford Penal Research Unit—the precursor to the present Centre for Criminology at Oxford—by Grünhut's succes-

[1] This discussion of Max Grünhut draws on Roger Hood (2004). Grünhut was appointed to the first University Lectureship in Criminology in 1947 and made a University Reader in 1951, a post he held until his retirement in 1960.

sor as University Reader, Nigel Walker. As these developments make plain, the 1959 White Paper brought into being a close, if highly co-dependent, relationship between the academy and government. It ensured that what was then termed 'the penal system' remained a central subject of enquiry while insisting that criminological scholarship was policy relevant.

Although a number of studies of sentencing and punishment had already been published by 1966, including, for example, Roger Hood's authoritative *Sentencing in the Magistrates' Courts* (1962) and *Borstal Re-assessed* (1965), and Nigel Walker's classic textbook *Crime and Punishment in Britain* (1965), research into the criminal process was in its infancy. Ground-breaking studies into the operation of the criminal process and, in particular, the role of the jury (e.g. McCabe and Purves 1972, 1974) prompted one reviewer, struck by the innovative quality of this early research, to observe, 'field research into a province so lawyerly as the criminal trial is important and unusual' (Cornish 1973: 102). The relative scarcity of academic inquiry into the criminal process before the 1960s is partly explained by the fact that government funding was previously motivated more by an instrumental commitment to promote 'useful knowledge' (Zedner 2003: 206ff). It valorized empirical investigation of sentencing and punishment as means to tackle the increase in reported crime rather than the normative and legal challenges of criminal process and trial.

Whereas in the 1960s the Home Office tended to fund external academic research, in the 1970s, the number of researchers working within the Home Office began to grow faster than any university department. It was propelled by the drive toward policy relevance, which was only compounded by the stricture imposed by the Rothschild Report (1971) that all externally funded study must have a firmly identified governmental 'customer'. Remarkably, Roger Hood, who had been appointed to the Oxford Readership in 1973, managed to secure a five-year 'rolling grant' from the Home Office, giving the newly renamed Centre for Criminological Research[2] a welcome measure of intellectual freedom, at least in that its projects could be proposed by academics rather than set according to government agendas.

These institutional developments might at first appear to be of little more than local historical interest. But as David Garland has observed, '[i]ntellectual history can never be detached from the social and cultural settings in which ideas and sentences occur, and this is particularly true in respect of criminology which is so deeply marked by its institutional location' (1992: 414). These institutional structures produce and nurture but also mould and constrain the discipline's intellectual development over the post-war period. There may, nonetheless, be a hazard in overplaying this structuralist account: the development of criminal justice research was informed not only by its institutional settings but also by the rapidly changing world of criminal justice policy and practice and by ruptures within the academy itself.

Perhaps the most radical challenge to the discipline's sense of self was to come from outside the established circles of Oxbridge and London. In 1968, the first National Deviancy Conference in York gathered together a group of scholars who were attracted by the ferment of ideas coming out of the US sociology of deviance, including

[2] So named in order to reflect the broader range of interests and research activities of its members.

subcultural theory, social disorganization, and labelling theory (Downes 1988). These new theories consciously challenged the status quo within both criminal justice practices and scholarship and paved the way to radical, new left realist, and feminist critiques of what became known, disparagingly, as establishment or administrative criminology. The history of the discipline in the 1970s and 1980s can be characterized as riven by 'two irreconcilable conceptions of itself' (Zedner 2003: 197) as the chief protagonists waged verbal war on one another (for exemplars of these opposing views see e.g. Cohen 1988 and Radzinowicz 1999).

In the longer term this rivalry was largely overcome as new left realists found themselves carrying out research for radical local councils that made their oppositional, state-sceptic stance difficult to maintain (Walton and Young 1998); while those in the supposed mainstream were influenced by what were no longer radical agendas, such as realist exploration of the human costs of crime that fell disproportionately on the vulnerable. So, for example, studies of victimization were carried out by left realists at the behest of the London boroughs of Islington, and Hammersmith and Fulham, as well as Merseyside (e.g. Jones et al. 1986), at the same time as researchers at the Oxford Centre conducted pioneering research into victims' experiences of crime and the criminal justice system (e.g. Shapland et al. 1985). Such studies made apparent the benefits of large-scale victimization surveys that had been used in the US since the 1960s, challenging the ideological schism over methodology and introducing a more pragmatic 'mixed methods' approach that continues today. A rapprochement of sorts is also suggested by the fact that engagement with theoretical criminology[3] became a mainstream activity no longer the preserve of 'rebels'.

In the 1990s, the location of many criminology departments within law faculties[4] made possible what was to become a central strand of enquiry addressed to jurisprudential questions of how best to 'do justice' in the context of criminal justice (notable work by Oxford academics included Ashworth 1994; Sanders and Young 1994). Major series like *Oxford Monographs on Criminal Law and Justice*, founded and edited by Andrew Ashworth in 1992, and the *Clarendon Studies in Criminology*,[5] inaugurated with Roger Hood as the first general editor in 1994, became important vehicles for cutting-edge scholarship in this period. Other drivers include the interplay between legal, socio-legal, and criminological scholarship (e.g. Hawkins 2002), and exploration of human rights as means of defending the liberties of individuals caught up in the criminal process (Ashworth 2001, 2002). If the resulting works did not always provide immediately policy-relevant recommendations or proposals for reform of the sort once demanded by the Home Office, by drawing on moral, political, and legal philosophy and rights theory, they offered sophisticated conceptual frameworks on the basis of which a better criminal justice could be conceived and elaborated.[6]

[3] Witness the founding of the journal *Theoretical Criminology* in 1997—current General Editors Mary Bosworth and Simon Cole.

[4] The Oxford Centre was made an integral department within the Oxford Law Faculty in 1991.

[5] A collaborative venture between criminologists at Oxford, Cambridge, and LSE.

[6] For example, the elaboration and endorsement of 'just deserts' by scholars like Andrew Ashworth and Andreas von Hirsch directly informed the principled framework for proportionality in sentencing introduced by the Criminal Justice Act 1991. More recently, former Director and present Professor of the Oxford Centre, Ian Loader, together with his colleague Richard Sparks, have sought to establish how we might advance 'a better politics of crime' (2010, ch. 5).

CRIMINAL JUSTICE AS ACADEMIC DISCIPLINE

Criminology, itself an interstitial discipline, draws on sociology, social administration, law, politics, psychology, and economics. Despite its continuing eclecticism, criminology now has an established place in the academy, stable institutional structures, a wealth of conferences and meetings, numerous dedicated journals, and its own professional bodies (Garland 2011). Yet although much of what is done under the banner of criminology is in fact criminal justice (the study of policing, probation, criminal process, the trial, sentencing, and punishment), criminologists—particularly in Britain—seem curiously unwilling to acknowledge this fact (Ashworth 2011; Zedner 2011). Perhaps one reason for this reticence is that, whereas those engaged in broader criminological endeavour have developed a strong sense of the vitality of their collective enterprise (Bosworth and Hoyle 2011), criminal justice scholarship has always been a less cohesive venture. It has found such intellectual coherence as it possesses in its common substantive focus on the legal system by which the state seeks to prevent crime and respond to alleged infractions of the criminal law, rather than any unity of disciplinary approach. Its territory is the agents, institutions, procedures, and practices by which the state governs offending and maintains order.

One metric suggested by the sociologist Andrew Abbott for determining the status of a field of academic inquiry is whether 'departments hire Faculty almost exclusively from their disciplines' PhDs' (Abbott 2016: 64). Partly in recognition of this need to foster the next generation of scholars, many centres of criminological research have established graduate and even undergraduate teaching programmes. Following the lead of other universities, Oxford launched a Masters in Criminology and Criminal Justice and a Criminology doctoral programme in 2001, explicitly drawing on its extensive research experience to teach the substantive and also the quantitative and qualitative methodological tools of the trade. The renaming of the Oxford Centre as the 'Centre for Criminology' in 2005 reflected the contribution that its members now make in teaching as well as criminological research.[7] Today the Oxford Centre is a vibrant home to twenty-eight doctoral and thirty-three Masters students, as well as many visiting students and younger, as well as established, scholars.

Like many other criminology departments, the Oxford Centre has long been integrated into the Oxford Law Faculty, and its members teach criminology and criminal justice to undergraduate and postgraduate lawyers. As we observed above, such proximity with legal scholars not only provides mutally beneficial opportunities for intellectual exchange that fosters interest in the role of rules in the legal process, but also directs criminological research towards questions of justice, rights, due process, and legitimacy. Legislative developments, resultant changes in criminal justice policy and practice, and shifts in normative framework thus have a particular importance for the academic study of criminal justice. At the same time, generations of law students graduate from university with an understanding not just of 'law in the books' but also of law in practice—of the impact of political pressures, professional cultures, and the exercise of discretion—that they take forward in their work within the legal system.

[7] In July 2005, Professor Ian Loader joined the Centre as its new Director, and in 2012, Professor Carolyn Hoyle took over as Director.

Criminal justice research, in Oxford as elsewhere, also has a particularly close relationship to the external world of politics, policy, and practice. In addition to funding from the main research councils (Economic and Social Research Council, Arts and Humanities Research Council, the British Academy, the Leverhulme Trust, European Research Council, the Independent Social Research Foundation), members of the Oxford Centre, for example, have carried out a range of projects funded by the Home Office, the Royal Commission on Criminal Justice, the Youth Justice Board, the Legal Services Commission, the Nuffield Foundation, among others. By responding to important contemporary issues as they perceive them, these various funders can influence the research agenda, shape the way academics do research, and the questions they seek to answer. This effect has perhaps been most apparent in funding from the EU, which has broadened the scope of research from domestic to European and international criminal justice matters, coinciding with the growing importance of international law and transnational criminal justice institutions.

Examining the development of criminal justice scholarship reveals how the social sciences respond to, interact with, and influence the world beyond the academy. This book does so at a cusp point at which the emergence of 'impact' requirements and 'knowledge exchange' partnerships alter incentive structures and approaches to scholarship. The growing nexus between funding and the 'impact' of academic research risks creating perverse incentives that may affect the issues academics choose to address and how they go about doing so. Likewise, academic recourse to communications technologies and social media as research tools and means of disseminating findings stand set to alter criminal justice scholarship, indeed all social scientific endeavours, beyond recognition. So it is timely to reflect on the development of criminal justice scholarship and to consider its future.

The hazards entailed in ensuring that research has 'policy relevance' (Hogg 1998; Laster 1994; Petersilia 1991) have long bedevilled criminal justice scholars in need of access and funding to pursue their research. Today it is no longer sufficient simply to be relevant—only demonstrable impact will suffice. Although criminal justice scholars have never enjoyed the luxury of being truly dispassionate observers and have long struggled with the tensions arising from their complex relationship with the penal state (Bottoms 1987; Downes 1978; Hood 2001), they are now vested, as never before, with a responsibility not merely to inform but positively to effect change. Criminal justice scholars need to be alert to the possible distortion of their priorities and reflect critically on what they are doing and, importantly, for whom.

Wider engagement with society is now a core strategic objective among all the research-active universities, including Oxford. The Oxford Centre, like many other institutions, engaged in knowledge exchange before it was fashionable. Its researchers have regularly shared learning, ideas, experiences, and expertise through collaborative work with individuals or organizations from beyond the academy at the start, during, and following research projects. They have also maintained partnerships with external bodies, promoted the application of social science outside of the academic community, and sought to maximize the impact of their research findings, as current work on immigration detention, policing, family violence, and the death penalty demonstrates (Bosworth 2014; Bradford et al. 2016; Condry and Miles 2016; Hood and

Hoyle 2015). They have done this by applying for funding from organizations that are less prescriptive than government; funders that trust academics to achieve the right balance between academically led, but policy relevant, scholarship. The discernible shift away from Home Office funding is perhaps indicative of a fear of being pushed too far down the road of policy-led research towards projects that may, in any case, be hidden on a high shelf in government if the findings do not meet with the approval of whichever Justice Secretary holds the power on the day of publication.

STRUCTURE AND THEMES OF THE BOOK

In line with the aspiration to explore the interactions between criminal justice as academic study and the shifting practices of criminal justice through the microcosm of the Oxford Centre for Criminology, the contributors to this volume all have, or have had, a close connection with it. Several are former colleagues (Farrall, Robinson, Young, Peay, O'Donnell, and Shapland), some are current or former students (Aliverti, Harris, Pascoe, Madden Dempsey), and the remainder present members (Loader, Bradford, Parmar, Roberts, Zedner, Bosworth, Condry, and Hoyle) or distinguished emeritus professors (Ashworth, Hood) of the Centre.

Invited to consider the changing contours of criminal justice over the last half century, contributors were encouraged to examine key critical issues within their area of expertise in order to explore the intellectual and methodological foundations of, developments in, challenges to, and tensions within it. Some consider their role as scholars in researching criminal justice, punishment, and state institutions (e.g. Hood, Pascoe) Others write about research primarily designed to improve, evaluate, or implement policy (e.g. Condry, Young). Still others reflect on the normative frameworks, principles, and values that underpin criminal justice (e.g. Zedner, Parmar).

Roughly reflecting the organization of the criminal justice process, the essays are structured into four sections: 'Politics, Legitimacy, and Criminal Justice', 'Justice, Courts, and Security', 'Punishment, Policy, and Practice', and 'Victims in, and of, the Criminal Justice System'. The essays range across criminal justice agents, institutions, and practices from police and policing (Loader, Bradford, Parmar), probation (Robinson), access to justice (Young), sentencing (Ashworth, Roberts and Harris), youth justice (Condry), to the pains of imprisonment (O'Donnell), and even the death penalty (Hood, Pascoe). All these topics would have been familiar enough to those studying criminal justice half a century ago. Other topics are newer—victims (Hoyle, Condry, Dempsey, Parmar), adolescent to parent violence (Condry), wrongful convictions (Hoyle), restorative justice (Shapland), and mental health (Peay). Some would have been unfamiliar to post-war criminologists (Zedner, Bosworth), while others, such as the legacy of Thatcherism (Farrall) or legitimacy (Bradford), might well have been regarded as the province of political scientists or political theorists, not criminal justice scholars. Topics now high on the criminological agenda would no doubt have been regarded as beyond the disciplinary horizon, for example migration control (Aliverti, Bosworth) and security and counter-terrorism (Zedner).

This collection makes clear that criminal justice scholars still value scientifically rigorous empirical studies that are able to inform policy but no longer believe, if they ever did, that quantitative approaches to data collection are the only appropriate method. There is an increasing appetite for comparative research (Pascoe), for intersectionality (Parmar, Condry, Zedner, Aliverti) and for more experimental methods, including visual (Bosworth). The intellectual resources now drawn upon include anthropology, migration studies, and postcolonial studies, and concepts such as citizenship, which were rarely invoked, have become integral to our sense of justice (Aliverti, Bosworth). At the same time, some aspects of the field have not changed much. Despite the important work at the Centre by Roger Hood on race and sentencing many years ago, for instance, race and ethnicity continue to be marginalized in criminal justice scholarship (Bosworth, Parmar, Loader).

Not only do the contributions to this volume recognize the need to frame research within a broader political landscape and culture (Farrall, Loader), but they also critique those criminal justice agencies and actors that work in silos (Robinson). Criminal justice scholars carry out empirical research with normative questions in mind to consider, for example, how legitimacy may be achieved in the criminal justice system (Bradford, Robinson). They are not satisfied with studying only at the local level, but, against the context of rapid globalization, look beyond geographical as well as disciplinary borders (Bosworth, Parmar, Aliverti). They also try to include 'hard to reach' populations, access to whom challenges our methodological resources as well as our peace of mind as researchers (Hood, Pascoe). In moving beyond the familiar territory of criminal justice, academics reach out to partner agencies not only with noble knowledge-exchange goals in mind, but also to obtain data that necessitates engagement with those on the ground, whether they are human rights NGOs (non-governmental organizations) or government agencies that are not always human rights compliant (Hood, Pascoe).

While academics may resist the idea of undertaking 'service' research, many have been willing participants in the endeavour to demonstrate the impact of scholarly research, notwithstanding the challenges posed by a fluid criminal justice landscape (Young). Despite their best endeavours, experts on the sentencing process are adamant that research has had little impact on policy and legislation (Ashworth, Roberts and Harris). Although O'Donnell expresses the view that the Oxford Centre is particularly well placed to have a positive impact in an increasingly punitive climate (Loader), Ashworth makes clear that criminological findings have been persistently ignored by governments more persuaded of the need to institute politically attractive measures for public protection against 'dangerous offenders'. As Zedner points out, governments have introduced increasingly restrictive laws to try to ensure public protection against terrorist threats but pay little regard to the concerns of legal scholars about the expansion of the security state and the growth of coercive legal powers.

The significant changes to the criminal justice system over the past 50 years also reflect shifting political landscapes including concerns about mass migration and globalization and, importantly, new fears about terrorism and the radicalization of Western Muslims (Parmar). From these contemporary concerns have emerged new sites of detention, new forms of coercive measure like deportation, and supposedly non-coercive but nevertheless intrusive practices such as monitoring, data retention, and surveillance. These developments pose a challenge to our existing intellectual resources and require us to think not only about race and ethnicity but also about religion, culture, and what it means to be a citizen (Bosworth, O'Donnell, Zedner). Even within the long-established criminal justice system of the UK significant changes, including the privatization of some forms of punishment, have caused us to think differently about who controls us and how they do so (O'Donnell, Robinson). Challenges to the structures of policing, including the rise of Police and Crime Commissioners, could not have been imagined five decades ago (Loader, Bradford). Scandals in policing have come and gone, interest in crime has grown only to recede, and yet the police, in the UK at least, continue to attract significant public support and legitimacy (Loader, Bradford). Such findings suggest the need for further research to understand why some organizations remain stubbornly resilient to public criticism, whereas others do not.

Changing philosophies of justice that today prioritize risk and danger over care and rehabilitation also call for new intellectual resources (Peay, Robinson). The significant increase in services to protect the interests and rights of victims (Shapland, Madden Dempsey) has gone hand-in-hand with decreasing concern for offenders, and in particular for suspects' right to a fair trial (Hoyle). As Shapland's essay makes clear, there are grounds for concern that victims' voices do not take precedence over the public interest. Though criminal justice, like the world around it, has changed significantly over the past 50 years, O'Donnell reminds us of continuities, for example, dramatic changes have 'hardly penetrated the penal realm' and prisoners' lives today are broadly similar to how they once were. Researchers are, however, busily developing new resources with which to understand the harms caused by penal confinement of all types, by drawing on psychological research on trauma, pain, and resilience (O'Donnell, Bosworth, Hoyle).

While researchers have sought to keep up with the changing contours of criminal justice, some things have apparently slipped through the net. For instance, despite the work of Sarah McCabe and her colleagues many decades ago (McCabe and Purves 1972, 1974), there has been little research on the court process since the work of Mike McConville and his colleagues (McConville et al. 1994). Aliverti's chapter is therefore a welcome contribution, particularly given its exploration of the contemporary court through the lens of citizenship (see also Shapland). Similarly, although the Centre for Criminology once had within it a Probation Studies Unit run by Colin Roberts and Ros Burnett, today there is little academic attention to probation and non-custodial punishments (Robinson, Roberts and Harris). The dearth of empirical research on sentencing makes difficult the task of bridging the 'undoubted gap between theory and research on the one hand and penal policy and politics on the other' (Ashworth). Criminal justice scholars have not always immediately comprehended the political and ideological context within which they research (Farrall). They sometimes fail adequately to map the contours of a problem or to propose a normative framework for state responses (Hoyle) and do not always realize that the past might be an unreliable guide to the future (Loader). Today terrorism and counter-terrorism are considered new and exciting areas for research, which attract the attention of doctoral students in particular. This leads Zedner to wonder why, despite 30 years of sectarian 'Troubles' in Northern Ireland and the IRA bombing campaign in mainland Britain, the securitization of criminal justice remained largely beyond criminological notice at the time and why we have failed to appreciate the profound implications of the growing convergence between police and security services. Of all the gaps in criminal justice scholarship, perhaps the most egregious oversight is the enduring insufficient attention paid to race (Parmar).

Although seismic shifts in the cultural and political landscape of criminal justice are a continuing challenge for those who study it, researchers also took too long to appreciate the damaging harms being done within the home. They finally caught up with this in the 1980s and 1990s, when they started to focus on violence in the family, and on children as victims of violence, both in the home and beyond its walls. Even then, however, little attention was paid to children's violence against their own parents (Condry). Furthermore, criminal justice policy on abuse in the home seems to have gone full circle during this time, at least in the US, with changing views of the efficacy of 'private' and 'public', 'formal' and 'informal' responses to violence (Madden Dempsey). Some of this has been in response to new academic studies, but often policy and practice change regardless. As Roberts and Harris note, in the context of sentencing in the UK, 'Successive governments have legislated in a way that reflects little awareness of, or alternatively an indifference to, the lessons from the academy.' How do academics influence a criminal justice system in flux (Young)? We can remember the past, understand the present and imagine the future. Doing so 'will be the key to mapping the contours of imprisonment over the next 50 years' (O'Donnell).

CONCLUSION

The question of how any social science discipline develops and changes does not invite easy answers. But the task is made all the more difficult where the subject under scrutiny is highly politicized, its own institutions are unstable, its practices are volatile, and its targets are rapidly evolving. Criminal justice is just such an area of study and it has changed almost beyond recognition over the past 50 years.

Topics that are now accepted as central to the study of criminal justice—victims, restorative justice, security, privatization, terrorism, citizenship, and migration (to name just a few)—were unknown to the discipline half a century ago. Indeed, most criminologists would once stoutly have denied that they had anything to do with it. Likewise, some central topics of past criminological attention, like probation, have largely receded from academic attention and some central criminal justice institutions, like Borstal and corporal punishment, have, at least in Europe, been abolished. Whereas criminal justice scholarship was once fairly parochial and confined to local, regional, or at most national studies, much is now global in its reach. Although the rapidity and radical nature of change make it quite impossible to predict what criminal justice will look like in 50 years' time, reflection on its changing contours furnishes a better understanding of how it arrived at its current form and may also hint at what the future holds.

Crime, once an enduring staple at the top of the agenda, has been knocked from pre-eminence and replaced by other concerns like restorative justice, transitional justice, terrorism, security, and migration. Whereas these were once deemed to be beyond the remit of criminological scholarship, such matters are now firmly within the field. Recognizing just how much the world has changed over the past 50 years invites further discussion of where and how we draw, and re-draw, the boundaries of criminal justice. It might also make us more alert to future shifts and receptive to emergent challenges to our conception of what criminal justice is and what it is for. At the same time, the contributions to this volume make abundantly clear that some issues are enduring and remain unresolved, like the influence of class, race, and gender, and the effects of their intersection on the justice process.

In sum, this volume is simultaneously a reflection on the troubled tangled pasts of criminal justice, its accumulated present, and its possible futures. It serves also, therefore, as an invitation to reflect on where we might anticipate the next major shifts will occur in the institutions and practices of criminal justice, in the nature and scope of the discipline, and in the concerns and preoccupations of criminal justice—and their possible resolutions.

REFERENCES

ABBOTT, A. (2016), *Processual Sociology*, Chicago, IL: Chicago University Press.

ASHWORTH, A. (1988), 'Criminal Justice and the Criminal Process', *British Journal of Criminology*, 28, 2: 111–23.

ASHWORTH, A. (1994), *The Criminal Process*, 1st edn, Oxford: Oxford University Press.

ASHWORTH, A. (2001), 'Criminal Proceedings after the Human Rights Act: The First Year', *Criminal Law Review*, 855–72.

ASHWORTH, A. (2002), *Human Rights, Serious Crime and Criminal Procedure*, The Hamlyn Lectures, London: Sweet & Maxwell.

ASHWORTH, A. (2011), 'Criminal Justice, Not Criminology?', in M. Bosworth and C. Hoyle (eds), *What is Criminology?* Oxford: Oxford University Press: 335–45.

BOSWORTH, M. (2014), *Inside Immigration Detention*, Oxford: Oxford University Press.

BOSWORTH, M. and HOYLE C. (eds) (2011), *What is Criminology?* Oxford: Oxford University Press.

BOTTOMS, A.E. (1987), 'Reflections on the Criminological Enterprise', *Cambridge Law Journal*, 46: 240–63.

BRADFORD, B., JAUREGUI, B., LOADER, I., and STEINBERG, J. (eds) (2016), *The SAGE Handbook of Global Policing*, London: SAGE.

COHEN, S. (1988), *Against Criminology*, New Brunswick, NJ: Transaction Books.

CONDRY, R. and MILES, C. (2016), *Uncovering Adolescent to Parent Violence*, London: Palgrave.

CORNISH, W.R. (1973), 'Review of *By-Passing the Jury* and *The Jury at Work*', *The Modern Law Review* 36, 1: 102–4.

Downes, D. (1978), 'Promise and Performance in British Criminology', *British Journal of Sociology*, 29, 4: 91–101.

Downes, D. (1988), 'The Sociology of Crime and Social Control in Britain 1960–1987', *British Journal of Criminology*, 28, 2: 45–57.

Garland, D. (1992), 'Criminological Knowledge and Its Relation to Power', *British Journal of Criminology*, 32, 4: 403–22.

Garland, D. (2011), 'Criminology's Place in the Academic Field', in M. Bosworth and C. Hoyle (eds), *What is Criminology?* Oxford: Oxford University Press: 298–317.

Grünhut, M. (1956), *Juvenile Offenders before the Courts*, Oxford: Oxford University Press.

Hawkins, K. (2002), *Law as Last Resort: Prosecution Decision-Making in a Regulatory Agency*, Oxford: Oxford University Press.

Hogg, R. (1998), 'Crime, Criminology and Government', in P. Walton and J. Young (eds), *The New Criminology Revisited*, Basingstoke: Palgrave: 158.

Home Office (1959), *Penal Practices in a Changing Society*, Cmnd 645, London: HMSO.

Hood, R. (1962), *Sentencing in the Magistrates' Courts* London: Tavistock.

Hood, R. (1965), *Borstal Re-assessed*, London: Heinemann.

Hood, R. (2001), 'Penal Policy and Criminological Challenges in the New Millennium', *The Australian and New Zealand Journal of Criminology*, 34: 1–16.

Hood, R. (2004), 'Hermann Mannheim (1889–1974) and Max Grünhut (1893–1964)', in J. Beatson and R. Zimmermann (eds), *Jurists Uprooted, German-Speaking Émigré Lawyers in Twentieth-Century Britain*, New York: Oxford University Press: 709–38.

Hood, R. and Hoyle, C. (2015), *The Death Penalty: A Worldwide Perspective*, 5th edn, Oxford: Oxford University Press.

James, T.E. (1956), 'Book Review of *Juvenile Offenders before the Courts* by Max Grünhut', *International and Comparative Law Quarterly*, 5, 4: 617–18.

Jones, T., Maclean, B., and Young, J. (1986), *The Islington Crime Survey*, Aldershot: Gower.

Laster, K. (1994), 'The Lure of Relevance', *The Australian and New Zealand Journal of Criminology*, 27, 1: 3–4.

Loader, I. and Sparks, R. (2010), *Public Criminology?* London: Routledge.

Martin, J.P. (1988), 'The Development of Criminology in Britain 1948–60', *British Journal of Criminology*, 28, 2: 35–44.

McCabe, S. and Purves, R. (1972), *The Jury at Work*, Oxford: University of Oxford Penal Research Unit, Occasional Paper no. 4.

McCabe, S. and Purves, R. (1974), *The Shadow Jury at Work*, Oxford: University of Oxford Penal Research Unit, Occasional Paper no. 8.

McConville, M., Hodgson, J., Bridges, L., and Pavlovic, A. (1994), *Standing Accused: The Organization and Practices of Criminal Defence Lawyers in Britain*, Oxford: Oxford University Press.

Petersilia, J. (1991), 'Policy Relevance and the Future of Criminology', *Criminology*, 29, 1: 1–15.

Radzinowicz, L. (1999), *Adventures in Criminology*, London: Routledge.

Rock, P. (1994), 'The Social Organisation of British Criminology', in M. Maguire, R. Morgan, and R. Reiner (eds), *The Oxford Handbook of Criminology*, Oxford: Oxford University Press.

Rothschild, Lord (1971), 'The Organisation and Management of Government R&D', in *A Framework for Government Research and Development*, Cmnd 4814, London: HMSO.

Sanders, A. and Young, R. (1994), *Criminal Justice*, 1st edn, Oxford: Oxford University Press.

Shapland, J., Willmore, J., and Duff, P. (1985), *Victims and the Criminal Justice System*, Aldershot: Gower.

Walker, N. (1965), *Crime and Punishment in Britain*, Edinburgh: Edinburgh University Press.

Walton, P. and Young, J. (eds) (1998), *The New Criminology Revisited*, Basingstoke: Palgrave.

Zedner, L. (2003), 'Useful Knowledge? Debating the Role of Criminology in Post-War Britain', in L. Zedner and A. Ashworth (eds), *The Criminological Foundations of Penal Policy*, Oxford: Oxford University Press: 197–235.

Zedner, L. (2011), 'Putting Crime Back on the Criminological Agenda', in M. Bosworth and C. Hoyle (eds), *What Is Criminology?* Oxford: Oxford University Press: 271–85.

PART I

POLITICS, LEGITIMACY, AND CRIMINAL JUSTICE

1

CHANGING CLIMATES OF CONTROL: THE RISE AND FALL OF POLICE AUTHORITY IN ENGLAND & WALES

Ian Loader

INTRODUCTION

My aim in this chapter is to describe and analyse the changing contours of police politics in England and Wales over the last 50 years. By 'police politics' I mean the ways in which political actors, contests, and processes have affected police organizations and practices. This is the standard referent in the literature—what is meant when someone claims that policing has been 'politicized' over the period (Reiner 2010). But I also intend the notion of police politics to refer to the involvement of the police as actors in political contests and processes seeking to influence the terms of debate, governmental decisions, or public opinion (Loader and Mulcahy 2003: ch. 7). My concern, in short, is with how political culture has shaped policing and how the police have shaped political culture.

My claim is that these two faces of police politics can helpfully be understood using the metaphor of 'climates'—or what I term 'climates of control'. Drawing on work conducted with Richard Sparks (Loader and Sparks 2010), I examine how from the 1970s onwards, the police were simultaneously affected by, and active agents in, the 'heating up' of the climate around questions of crime and social order. This process resulted in the police assuming a symbolically powerful place in public life and popular culture. I then argue that since 2008 it has been possible to discern important shifts in that climate—signs at the very least of milder weather, but possibly of a more enduring climactic 'cooling'. One notable effect of the hotter climate that emerged in the 1970s was the priority given to the police in the control of crime and the regulation of marginal or disaffected populations—a priority reflected in greater funding and powers, and often fulsome support. Control came to mean control *by* the police. But the process of heating also gave rise to forms of contestation in which previously settled questions to do with control *of* the police came to assume public and political salience. As the climate started to cool, the practice of calling into question, and subjecting to scrutiny, what was once a taken-for-granted, culturally resonant police authority became more pervasive, placing the police on the back foot.

Given the time span under consideration, I have to paint in broad brushstrokes. My hope is that doing so will illuminate the significant shifts (and certain continuities) in police politics over the period—especially with regard to what I shall argue is the rise and fall of the symbolic power of the English police. The story starts in the mid-1960s. This was not a time in which policing was entirely free of either wrongdoing or political attention. A series of minor scandals had led up to the Royal Commission on the Police that reported in 1962. The Commission's Report was largely implemented by the Police Act 1964 which introduced a tripartite structure of accountability involving the Home Secretary, chief constables, and local police authorities (Walker 2000). This legislation has to be situated in the wider context of crime governance that prevailed at the time—what I have elsewhere described as rule by 'platonic guardians' (Loader 2006a). This term refers to a liberal elite of senior officials and criminal justice practitioners whose operative assumptions were that crime was an issue to be managed through expert deliberation in ways that sustained the delicate balance between order and decency. The key policing component of this ruling orthodoxy was the doctrine of constabulary independence, enshrined in the Police Act 1964 and tested in, and reaffirmed by, the Court of Appeal in 1968.[1] This doctrine rested on and protected a vision of English policing as impartial and independent. It made chief constables subject to the law but free from external political interference. It held that policing should be guided by the professional judgement of senior officers who, it was assumed, had an 'organic' relation to the people and were able to discern their wishes. By 1966, these notions had acquired a sacred status—the ideals underpinning the claim that English policing was 'the-best-in-the-world' (Weinberger 1995). This chapter tells the story of how these governing certainties fell apart.

POLICE POLITICS IN A 'HOT' CLIMATE

The cluster of settled assumptions about English policing started to crumble during the 1970s, as did the wider political culture that had nurtured and sustained them. They were undermined by a set of social and cultural changes in British society that have been well described by David Garland (2001: ch. 4): the rise of the mass media, individualization and ethnic diversity, the spread of the mass media, and declining deference toward elites, which led to a collapse in uncritical acceptance of authority. This was coupled with a mounting economic crisis (runaway inflation, faltering growth, rising unemployment) and the emergence of the idea—pressed by the political right—that Britain had become 'ungovernable' (King 1975). The broad political consensus through which Britain had been ruled in the post-war period was coming apart. Industrial and social conflict returned to the streets. Against the backdrop of rising levels of volume crime, questions of order began to acquire renewed political

[1] *R v Metropolitan Police Commissioner, ex parte Blackburn* [1968] 2 QB 118.

significance. The police found themselves embroiled in industrial turmoil, notably during the miners' strikes of 1972 and 1974, and escalating racial tension, for example in the Notting Hill Carnival riot of 1976 and protests prompted by the rise of the National Front in the late 1970s (Loader and Mulcahy 2003: ch. 1).

The 1979 general election was a key symbolic turning point in this process and in the heating up of the political debate about crime. The election was the first in the post-war period in which law and order had featured prominently in the campaign. The decision of the Conservatives to break with political convention and highlight the issue was considered to have played a part in persuading especially working-class voters to elect Margaret Thatcher as Prime Minister (Downes and Morgan 1994). It is now well established that the Thatcher administrations (1979–90) were characterized as much by continuity as by change, especially in respect of criminal justice and penal policy (Farrall and Hay 2010; Loader 2006a; see Farrall this volume). During this time, two Conservative Home Secretaries (first Willie Whitelaw, then Douglas Hurd) avowedly pursued the aim of reducing the prison population and the period culminated in the Criminal Justice Act 1991, a legislative attempt to supply penal policy with a new coherent 'just deserts' rationale (Faulkner 2006). Yet the period was marked by important changes, both in the style of rule (much less reliance on fora of expert consensus-building) and in political symbolism. Much of that symbolic shift concerned the police. The Thatcher government moved in its first few days in office to meet in full the police pay claim, settling a dispute that had mired the Labour administration's final years in office. This was a prelude to several years in which the police were placed by government at the forefront of the 'fight against crime' and buttressed by greater funding, more powers, and vocal support. Government backing for the police was especially pronounced during the urban disorders of 1981 and 1985 in London, Birmingham, and Liverpool and the bitter and protracted national miners' strike of 1984–5. It was also evident during the disputes that occurred in the early 1980s between chief constables and Labour-controlled police authorities. The Labour Party was caught off-guard by the return of crime and disorder to the political agenda and struggled for over a decade to find a distinctive or persuasive stance on the issue (Miller 2016: ch. 3). Against a backdrop of rapidly rising crime, while in opposition Labour focused on police accountability, notably by seeking to bring police policy under the direction of democratically elected local police authorities. In the conflicts that ensued, the Conservative government very publically supported chief constables and stood firm in defence of the still-revered doctrine of constabulary independence.[2]

The next significant moment in the heating-up of the crime question occurred in 1992–3 at the conjunction of two apparently separate events—the ejection of the UK from the European Exchange Rate Mechanism in September 1992 (on what became known as 'Black Wednesday') and the murder of 2-year-old James Bulger by two 10-year-old boys in Liverpool in February 1993. Faced with crumbling political authority, and mass-mediated anxiety about 'Lawless Britain', the Conservative Home

[2] In the midst of the public foregrounding of police authority the first signs emerged of a shift in Conservative orientations towards policing. Home Office Circular 114/1983 quietly made increases in police funding conditional upon forces being able to demonstrate that they were delivering 'economy, efficiency and effectiveness'.

Secretary Michael Howard abandoned the philosophy underpinning the Criminal Justice Act 1991 and declared that 'prison works'. There followed in the next five years a series of new police powers (e.g. to tackle 'raves' and trespassing) and penal measures (e.g. minimum mandatory sentences) designed to improve public confidence in the justice system and, arguably, shore up the government's waning legitimacy. But this was accompanied by some notable shifts in Conservative thinking on policing and an emerging emphasis on exerting control over the police. The Police and Magistrates' Courts Act 1994 introduced national police performance targets for the first time—a small incursion into the idea that the police should be free from external political interference. Moreover, as crime levels continued to rise during the 1980s, senior Conservative politicians began to ask what dividends increased investment in the police had delivered (Baker 1993). This gave rise, inter alia, to an enquiry led by Sir Patrick Sheehy, chair of British American Tobacco, into police organization which reported in 1993. The Conservative government sought to implement the Report's 'modernizing' recommendations on police pay, rank structure, promotion, and pensions. The measures generated angry, organized defiance from rank-and-file police including a rally of an estimated 23,000 officers at Wembley Arena. Lacking the political strength needed to 'take the police on' the government retreated.

The murder of James Bulger also prompted the Labour Party to rethink its stance on crime. Tony Blair was Shadow Home Secretary at the time of the killing and he actively responded to it in ways that moralized the crime question and sought to reclaim it as Labour territory (Blair 1993). Subsequently, as Labour leader, Blair sought to reposition Labour on crime, as on several other issues. The 'New Labour' approach (as this reorientation was termed) combined a traditional leftist focus on social causation with a novel emphasis on individual responsibility and an accommodation with retributive punishment—a position captured by the slogan 'tough on crime, tough on the causes of crime'. What followed in the mid-1990s was the emergence of a new fractious, unstable consensus as the Conservatives and New Labour sought publically to display their anti-crime credentials (Lacey 2008; Newburn 2007). Partly as a result of its realignment around the crime question, New Labour was returned to office in 1997. It governed for the next 13 years. During that period, crime assumed a more prominent place in political life—partly because it was a public policy issue in respect of which Tony Blair's personal morality aligned closely with what he felt was required to hold together the broad but shallow coalition of support that had returned New Labour to office. The period was marked by a *mix* of social programmes (such as early years education) and criminal justice/penal measures designed to reduce crime and address public fears about crime and social disorder; something Lisa Miller (2016: ch. 3) has demonstrated in an important corrective to what has become criminological orthodoxy about New Labour's penal populism (e.g. Tonry 2004). But Miller's correction does not quite capture the shift of emotional register (in my terms, the turning up of the heat) that attended New Labour's approach: its hyperactive preoccupation with showing that it empathized with victims and was on the side of law-abiding citizens.

Nowhere was this more emphatic than in New Labour's approach to the police. On the one hand, New Labour consistently gave the police public backing, massively increased funding for the police throughout the period between 1997 and 2008, and extended the police new powers to tackle crime and anti-social behaviour. The national neighbourhood policing programme made visible police authority pivotal to the production of order and reassurance. In all these respects, the New Labour period was marked by practices of 'ambient policing' (Loader 2006b). On the other hand, New Labour posited the police as a remote and recalcitrant bureaucracy unresponsive to the experiences and demands of its 'consumers'. Having cast the police in these terms, the government appointed itself consumer watchdog-in-chief. The New Labour years were marked by a proliferation of national directives and performance targets monitored and enforced by a regime of external audit, monitoring, and inspection that many saw (for good or ill) as the attempt to control the police from Whitehall. In the aftermath of the police failure to investigate the murder of black teenager Stephen Lawrence in 1993, and the conclusion of the ensuing Macpherson Inquiry that the Metropolitan Police were 'institutionally racist', this general orientation was brought to bear in getting the police to take action around endemic problems of racial injustice, both inside and outside the force. Indeed, one wider indicator of the hotter climate was the struggles waged by social movements and campaign groups around police discrimination with respect to issues such as stop and search of young black men, violence against women, and the treatment of lesbians and gay men. Much of the critique focused on police over-regulation and under-protection of marginalized populations, something that the Lawrence case encapsulated.

This, then, is a sketch of the main elements of the hot climate of control that emerged during the 1970s and lasted—I shall argue shortly—until the global financial crash of 2008. In this climate the police assumed a materially and symbolically central place as a solution to the problem of order. But it was also a climate in which previously settled questions pertaining to how to control the police came to prominence and became contested. What though can specifically be said about police politics during this period? Three points can usefully be made.

First, the police enjoyed and took-for-granted political support from both major parties throughout the period. When this was not true of the Labour Party—in the early 1980s—that lack of support was often represented by their opponents as a sign of Labour's unfitness to govern. There were also indications during the period of both Conservative and Labour unease about the police's bureaucratic rigidity and remoteness and an emergent concern to bring the police under greater external oversight. But these were a backdrop to what remained the headline features of a hotter climate of control: that of the political necessity to back the police and of policing taking centre stage in the fight against rising crime and social disorder. Few politicians during this period wanted to fall out of favour with the police, or were willing to argue with them in public. The political price to be paid was too high.

Second, the police emerged as active players in public life with the power to 'legitimately name' crime and related social problems (Loader and Mulcahy 2003: ch. 7). This was strikingly true of a number of maverick police chiefs (such as Robert Mark, David McNee, John Alderson, James Anderton, and Kenneth Oxford) who, in the 1980s, broke with the tradition of 'police silence' (Mark 1978) and became high-profile commentators on crime and policing issues (typically demanding greater powers), and on occasions on wider aspects of morality, politics, and social change. For a time, these figures became household names. During the 1990s, the senior police voice became more collective under the auspices of the Association of Chief Police Officers and tended to operate behind-the-scenes, although Sir Ian Blair was to buck this trend during his controversial tenure as Metropolitan Police Commissioner from 2005–8 (Blair 2009). The police officers' 'union', The Police Federation, also came to great prominence during this period. The Federation considered itself as a power-in-the-land and expected to be treated as such. It not only organized high-profile campaigns for higher pay and to defend existing working practices (McLaughlin and Murji 1998); it also at times offered vocal support to conservative law and order politics, campaigning in the 1970s and 1980s for the return of the death penalty (Reiner 1980). The police, in sum, emerged as influential players in British public life—part creatures and part creators of a hotter climate of control.

Third, the police benefited from a deep reservoir of popular attachment. For significant numbers of citizens the police were a reassuring signifier of authority, community, and nationhood (Hall et al. 1978: ch. 6) and such citizens evinced an affective identification with the police that bordered on faith (Loader and Mulcahy 2003: chs. 3–4). This period of British policing was not without conflict, abuse, or malpractice—recall, to name but the most notorious cases, the killing of anti-racist protestor Blair Peach, disbanding of the West Midlands Serious Crime Squad, the Guildford Four and Birmingham Six miscarriage of justice cases, the Hillsborough Stadium disaster, the Stephen Lawrence case, and revelations of rogue activities by undercover police squads. Part of the puzzle of the last half-century of British policing is why the police have been unable to find systemic remedies for these failings, getting trapped instead in a recurring cycle of scandal and reform (Loader 2014). A further puzzle is why, in the face of these scandals, public support for the police has remained in certain quarters so *high* (Loader and Mulcahy 2003: 35; see also Harkin 2015; Bradford this volume)? The answer lies in part in an entrenched element of the organizational culture that holds the police to be all that stands between order and chaos and as requiring unconditional backing, a culture that treats oversight as an obstacle to effective crime-fighting. The answer is also to be found in a structure of lay feeling that is willing to lend the police support of just this kind and quick to dismiss scrutiny and criticism as the motivated postures of those who are 'anti-police'. These cultural dispositions towards police authority reached their zenith in the years between the 1970s and the global financial crash of 2008.

POLICING AND CLIMATE CHANGE

We no longer inhabit a political culture in which crime and policing dominates public discourse or is central to government action. The fact that previously heated political debates about law and order have cooled over the last decade has not yet been fully recognized by criminologists. Nor have its lessons been absorbed. We too often still treat seminal texts such as Garland's (2001) *The Culture of Control* or Jonathan Simon's (2007) *Governing through Crime* as if they remain reliable guides to the present. But these texts emerged from, and were attempts to make sense of, what Simon calls 'the years of fear' (Simon 2014: 156) and it is by no means certain that they can account for what at least seems to be milder weather, and may even constitute more enduring climate change. So what has happened?

The first thing to have happened is the crime drop. It is now well established that from the mid-1990s onwards levels of volume crime have been falling across Western democracies (Roeder et al. 2015; Tonry 2014). To be sure, debate continues about the scale and evenness of that decline. There is also uncertainty about whether crime has not simply fallen but also migrated into forms of criminal behaviour (such as internet fraud) that do not appear so clearly on police and criminological radar screens. It is not my task here to enter these debates. What is pertinent is that crime has slipped down the hierarchy of public concerns. An *Economist*/Ipsos MORI poll conducted in March 2015 found that only 12 per cent of those interviewed named 'crime/law and order' as the 'most important issue facing Britain today'—the corresponding figure when the same question was asked in 2010 was 25 per cent.[3] We can relatedly observe the waning attention afforded to crime and policing issues in recent elections. In the 2015 British General Election the issue barely featured at all. It may of course be that—in the aftermath of 9/11, 7/7, and the Paris and Brussels attacks—public concerns are focused on terrorism. It is also possible that the symbolic work once performed by crime in condensing wider social fears and racialized anxieties (Girling et al. 2000) is now being done by migration and border control (see Bosworth this volume). Yet the evidence continues to mount that crime is no longer the structuring presence in social relations and political life that it was during the period from the 1970s to the early 2000s. British society no longer seems animated by what Garland (2001: ch. 6) calls 'crime consciousness'.

The second thing that happened was the global financial crisis of 2008 and, more significantly, the ideological transmogrification of that crisis into a period of sustained austerity. The financial crisis had the immediate effect of elevating concerns about the economy, employment, and public finances to the top of the political agenda where they have remained. But it also meant that money was no longer available for continued expansion of the police and penal system of the sort experienced in Britain since the early 1990s. In the case of policing quite the reverse has occurred. The Coalition government elected in 2010 introduced sharp and sustained cuts to police funding. By 2014–15, the police experienced a real terms budget cut of 20 per cent, an estimated loss of £2.1 billion across forty-three forces. An overall loss of around 15,000 officers took place by 2015. Further reductions of 'up to 6%' were announced by the Treasury in the Spending Review for 2016–17, though following the terrorist attacks in Paris in November 2015 the Chancellor spared the police from further budget cuts. Notwithstanding this partial *volte face*, fiscal austerity is likely to be part of the structuring context of policing in England and Wales for the foreseeable future.

A third relevant contextual change concerns the political and cultural ascendancy of two variants of liberalism. In the immediate aftermath of the global financial crash,

[3] https://www.ipsos-mori.com/researchpublications/researcharchive/3542/EconomistIpsos-MORI-March-2015-Issues-Index.aspx.

it appeared that the game was up for economic liberalism and that the crisis had fatally exposed the limits of the philosophy that had dominated British politics since the 1980s. This turned out to be a false dawn (Crouch 2011). Since the return of the Conservatives to power (in Coalition in 2010, governing alone from 2015) that ideology has cemented its place as the governing orthodoxy of the age. What has followed is a quest to forge a new political settlement that not only makes temporary cuts to public spending, but seeks permanently to shrink the size and scope of the British state. A key element of this settlement is a further extension of market principles and practices to domains of public provision. One sign of this was the contracting out of probation services to 'community rehabilitation companies' in 2015. Another is likely to be further outsourcing of police functions of the kind pioneered in the 'partnership' between Lincolnshire Police and G4S (White 2014). The triumph of economic liberalism has been accompanied by the less noticed, but also now less contested, rise of social liberalism. I mean by this the mainstream acceptance of orientations, lifestyles, and cultural differences that were previously censured, especially around questions of sexuality. This has not ushered in a world free of discrimination. But it has resulted in cultural and legislative change with respect to a range of issues sparked by the identity politics of the 1960s. The result of this dual ascendancy of economic and social liberalism was captured neatly by the late Jock Young (1999) in his account of an 'exclusive society' marked by intolerance of *difficulty* (unemployment, poverty, ill-health, and the like) and celebration of *difference*. It is a change that has had profound implications for police authority and priorities.

So what impact has this changed climate had upon police politics? What realignments can be discerned? The most important such realignment is to be found in the changing disposition of British Conservatism towards the police. Since being returned to office in 2010, the Conservatives have embarked on a police reform programme the scale and speed of which took many commentators—and the police themselves—by surprise. In addition to radical budget cuts (just mentioned) and the introduction of elected Police and Crime Commissioners (PCCs) (on which more shortly), the government has set about cutting national targets and wasteful bureaucracy, encouraged cooperation with the private sector, and established a new College of Policing. It also largely implemented the report of the 2011 Winsor Review which recommended a far-reaching programme of internal modernization, including rewarding specialist skills and high performance rather than length of service, and concentrating pay on front-line officers; developing more robust appraisal systems and routine fitness testing of officers; establishing a compulsory severance scheme; and enabling direct entry to inspector and superintendent levels from outside the police service.[4] The former Home Secretary Theresa May, moreover, publically took the police to task for what she regarded as the excessive and discriminatory use of stop and search.

These are weighty reforms. But the analysis of the police that informs them and the tone in which the government has pursued them are equally telling indicators of change. The government often appears to treat the police as the last unreformed public

[4] See https://www.gov.uk/guidance/police-pay-winsor-review. In 2012, the Report's author—Sir Thomas Winsor—was appointed Her Majesty's Chief Inspector of Constabulary. He was the first-ever holder of this post not to have previously been a police officer.

service: bloated, inefficient, run in the interests of its producers, and unresponsive to public concerns. A great deal of the reform agenda seems in this regard to be considered unfinished business from the Sheehy Report of the early 1990s; only this time the government is determined to prevail. The Conservative government has also been prepared publically to take on the police and defend their proposals in the face of opposition from within police ranks. On occasions this has spilt over into disdain, especially in respect of what the government dismisses as repeated scaremongering by senior officers and the Police Federation about the likely effects of cuts to the police budget. Seldom has a government seemed so *unfrightened* of the police, so relaxed about challenging police interests and postures in a very public fashion. So much so that Theresa May sometimes neglected to utter the platitudes about the 'police doing a great job', and 'how grateful we all are for their bravery', that had become compulsory preludes to official speeches and statements for the past 50 years. Seldom, conversely, has there seemed a time in that period when the police's cultural authority has been at such low ebb.

Further realignment can be detected in a radical reordering of the arrangements of police governance and the thinking that informs them. The key plank of the Conservative government reform's agenda was the creation in the Police and Social Responsibility Act 2010 of elected PCCs, replacing local police authorities. They were given powers to set the policing plan and precept for their force and to hire and fire chief constables, as well as budgets to spend on victim and community safety provision. PCCs are constitutionally unique figures: nowhere else in British governance is a directly elected individual in charge of a single public service. The stated rationale for their introduction was to replace invisible police authorities and bureaucratic control from Whitehall with local democratic accountability. In the face of widespread opposition to the whole idea of politicizing the police, and deep disquiet within the police, the first cohort of forty-three PCCs were elected in November 2012 on a notoriously low overall turnout of 15.1 per cent. Having subsequently been accepted by all political parties and by most senior officers, the second round of elections took place in May 2016. PCCs have become entrenched and increasingly influential actors in the policing landscape.[5]

Situated in the overall context of the 50-year period under consideration here, PCCs take some explaining. They give practical effect to the idea of democratic accountability that was championed by Labour local authorities in the 1980s. As we have seen, that idea was strongly resisted by the then Conservative government on the grounds that enabling elected politicians to determine policing policy was incompatible with the doctrine of constabulary independence. So what accounts for the *volte face*? Some critics have seen the Conservative administration's conversion to local accountability as a cynical attempt, against a backdrop of stringent budget cuts, to shift blame from central government to PCCs. It is more likely that the Conservatives intended PCCs to be a remedy for what they saw as cosy, unaccountable relations between chief officers and police authorities. On this view, PCCs are meant to be 'big

[5] At the time of writing, the Home Office and Ministry of Justice are giving active consideration to extending the remit of PCCs to include, inter alia, juvenile justice and establishing and overseeing schools for young offenders.

local figures with a mandate to drive the fight against crime and anti-social behaviour' (Herbert 2010; cf. Loader 2013). PCCs also make more sense when one remembers that localism has deep roots in Conservative philosophy. Indeed, the future of police governance (in respect of PCCs and city mayors with responsibility for policing, as in London and Manchester) seems likely to be embroiled in a wider debate about devolved governance in England and Wales.

Given all this, two noteworthy effects of the advent and first term of PCCs stand out. First, while great emphasis has been placed on protecting the operational independence of chief officers (and there have been no notable examples of PCCs interfering with operations), there remains little doubt that PCCs exercise democratic control over policing in ways that have downgraded the practical significance and cultural force of what was once *the* structuring ideal of British policing. Constabulary independence simply lacks the potency it once carried. Second, something similar can be said about the cultural authority of chief constables who now for the most part play second fiddle to PCCs as the public face of their force. Throughout much of the last half-century a *chief* constable was an authoritative and almost un-dismissible individual holding a powerful independent office. Today, they have morphed into public officials managing a police force for so long as they retain the confidence of an elected politician.

CONCLUSION: UNSETTLED PROSPECTS

What though of the future? The shifts in cultural authority described in this chapter are the backdrop against which the police have to interpret and respond to changing patterns of crime and new configurations of public demand. We are here in poorly mapped territory. It is apparent, however, that the police are increasingly required to address forms of criminal behaviour and victimization that take place in private (rather than the more familiar public) spaces, from internet fraud, to domestic violence, to child sexual exploitation. It also seems clear that the police have to think more—in determining how to spend scarce resources, or deciding with which agencies they can best partner—about protecting the vulnerable from harm, whether they be children, or people with mental illness, or trafficked women, or refugees fleeing war-zones (Thornton 2015). These challenges have to be met in a context of reduced budgets that seems set to persist. They also take place in a climate in which the practices, performance, and legitimation claims of the police are routinely subject to external scrutiny and public contestation: from politicians, journalists, civil society groups, and across social media (Goldsmith 2010).

Seasoned observers of the police over the last half-century will have been taken aback by the way in which investigating and preventing sexual exploitation of children has become so pivotal to contemporary police activity and legitimacy, whether in respect of historic cases that failed in the past to secure police attention or the current imperative to protect children from abuse. This focus seems genuinely new and is a far cry from the days when domestic violence was dismissed by the police as 'rubbish work'. But at least some of this work has become entangled with the policing and politics of race, notably in cases where white teenage girls have been targeted and abused by groups of Pakistani men, as in Oxford, Rochdale, and Rotherham. Indeed, for the foreseeable future the police appear likely to remain preoccupied by a group that has become its principal suspect population: namely, British Asian/Muslim communities (see Parmar this volume). This preoccupation is not only or mainly driven by issues of child protection. It is fuelled, under conditions of globalization, by a volatile mix of tensions and fears pertaining to migration, security, and belonging (Phillips and Webster 2013).

These altered demands and priorities coexist with some striking continuities. Foremost among them are the legacies of a hot climate in which the clamour for order too often trumped the rights of minorities and the requirement to exercise vigilant oversight of police behaviour—a climate in which control by the police prevailed over control of the police. Hence the unfinished business of the miners' strike (1984–5), the Hillsborough disaster (1989), the Stephen Lawrence case (1993), and repeated episodes of misdirected spying and deceit by undercover police units. These past events all actively impinge on the work and standing of the police today. Just over half a century on from the Report of the 1962 Royal Commission, the British Police, shorn of cultural authority it once took for granted, are haunted by ghosts and beset by future uncertainties to which the past may not prove a reliable guide.

REFERENCES

BAKER, K. (1993), *The Turbulent Years: My Life in Politics*, London: Faber and Faber.

BLAIR, I. (2009), *Policing Controversy*, London: Profile Books.

BLAIR, T. (1993), 'Why Crime is a Socialist Issue', *New Statesman*, 25 January 1993.

CROUCH, C. (2011), *The Strange Non-Death of Neo-Liberalism*, Cambridge: Polity.

DOWNES, D. and MORGAN, R. (1994), 'Hostages to Fortune?: The Politics of Law and Order in Post-War Britain', in M. Maguire, R. Morgan, and R. Reiner (eds), *The Oxford Handbook of Criminology*, Oxford: Oxford University Press.

FARRALL, S. and HAY, C. (2010), 'Not so Tough on Crime?: Why Weren't the Thatcher Government More Radical in the Criminal Justice System?', *British Journal of Criminology*, 50, 3: 550–69.

FAULKNER, D. (2006), *Crime, State and Citizen*, Winchester: Waterside Press.

GARLAND, D. (2001), *The Culture of Control: Crime and Social Order in Contemporary Society*, Oxford: Oxford University Press.

GIRLING, E., LOADER, I., and SPARKS, R. (2000), *Crime and Social Change in Middle England: Questions of Order in an English Town*, London: Routledge.

GOLDSMITH, A.J (2010), 'Policing's New Visibility', *British Journal of Criminology*, 50, 5: 914–34.

HALL, S., CLARKE, J., CRITCHER, C., JEFFERSON, T., and ROBERTS, B. (1978), *Policing the Crisis: Mugging, Law and Order and the State*, Basingstoke: Palgrave/Macmillan.

HARKIN, D. (2015), 'The Police and Punishment: Understanding the Pains of Policing', *Theoretical Criminology*, 19, 1: 43–58.

HERBERT, N. (2010), *Who Runs the Police?*, Speech to IPPR, available at: http://www.nickherbert.com/media_centre.php/438/Who%20runs%20the%20police.

KING, A. (1975), 'Overload: Problems of Governing in the 1970s', *Political Studies*, 23, 2–3: 284–96.

LACEY, N. (2008), *The Prisoners' Dilemma*, Cambridge: Cambridge University Press.

LOADER, I. (2006a), 'Fall of the "Platonic Guardians": Liberalism, Criminology and Political Responses to Crime in England and Wales', *British Journal of Criminology*, 46, 4: 561–86.

LOADER, I. (2006b), 'Policing, Recognition and Belonging', *ANNALS of the American Academy of Political and Social Sciences*, 605, 1: 349–67.

LOADER, I. (2013), 'Why Do the Police Matter?: Beyond the Myth of Crime Fighting', in J. Brown (ed.), *The Future of Policing*, Abingdon: Routledge.

LOADER, I. (2014), 'Police Scandal and Reform: Can We Break Out of More of the Same?', *Left Foot Forward*, available at: http://leftfootforward.org/2014/03/police-scandal-and-reform-can-we-break-out-of-more-of-the-same/

LOADER, I. and MULCAHY, A. (2003), *Policing and the Condition of England: Memory, Politics and Culture*, Oxford: Oxford University Press.

LOADER, I. and SPARKS, R. (2010), *Public Criminology?*, Abingdon: Routledge.

MARK, R. (1978), *In the Office of Constable*, Harmondsworth: Penguin.

MCLAUGHLIN, E. and MURJI, K. (1998), 'Resistance through Representation: "Storylines", Advertising and Police Federation Campaigns', *Policing & Society*, 8, 4: 367–400.

MILLER, L. (2016), *The Myth of Mob Rule: Violent Crime and Democratic Politics*, New York: Oxford University Press.

NEWBURN, T. (2007), '"Tough on Crime": Penal Policy in England and Wales', in M. Tonry (ed.), *Crime, Punishment and Politics in Comparative Perspective*, Chicago: University of Chicago Press.

PHILLIPS, C. and WEBSTER, C. (eds) (2013), *New Directions in Race, Ethnicity and Crime*, Abingdon: Routledge.

REINER, R. (1980), 'Fuzzy Thoughts: The Police and Law-and-Order Politics', *Sociological Review*, 28, 2: 377–413.

REINER, R. (2010), *The Politics of the Police*, 4th edn, Oxford: Oxford University Press.

ROEDER, O., EISEN L.-B., and BOWLING, J. (2015), *What Caused the Crime Decline?*, New York: Brennan Center for Justice, New York University School of Law.

SIMON, J. (2007), *Governing Through Crime*, New York: Oxford University Press.

SIMON, J. (2014), *Mass Incarceration on Trial: A Remarkable Court Decision and the Future of Prisons in America*, New York: The New Press.

THORNTON, S. (2015), 'We Must "Reimagine" Policing in the UK', 2015 John Harris Memorial Lecture, The Police Foundation, 20 July, available at: http://news.npcc.police.uk/releases/npcc-chair-sara-thornton-we-must-re-imagine-policing-in-the-uk

TONRY, M. (2004), *Punishment and Politics: Evidence and Emulation in the Making of English Crime Control Policy*, Cullompton: Willan.

TONRY, M. (ed.) (2014), 'Why Crime Rates Fall and Why They Don't', *Crime and Justice*, vol. 43, Chicago: University of Chicago Press.

WALKER, N. (2000), *Policing in a Changing Constitutional Order*, London: Sweet & Maxwell.

WEINBERGER, B. (1995), *The Best Police in the World: An Oral History of the English Police from the 1930s to the 1960s*, London: Scolar Press.

WHITE, A. (2014), 'Post-Crisis Policing and Public-Private Partnerships: The Case of Lincolnshire Police and G4S', *British Journal of Criminology*, 54, 6: 1002–22.

YOUNG, J. (1999), *The Exclusive Society: Social Exclusion, Crime and Difference in Late Modernity*, London: SAGE.

2

WHAT IS THE LEGACY OF THATCHERISM FOR THE CRIMINAL JUSTICE SYSTEM IN ENGLAND AND WALES?

Stephen Farrall

> Ideas can move mountains.
>
> (Margaret Thatcher)

> Extrapolation from a governance philosophy so strongly rooted in market thinking to other areas of policy can make neo-liberalism work too hard as an explanatory framework. We need to understand the dynamics of adoption in different policy fields, which involve distinct sets of policy entrepreneurs in different arenas and at different levels of government.
>
> (Macauley 2007: 39)

In this chapter, I explore English and Welsh criminal justice legislation of the 1980s and some of the criminological responses to that period of history and its legislative agenda. I argue that 'Thatcherism', whilst radical in many sectors of social and economic policy, did not affect criminal justice as much as it did other policy arenas. However, both criminologists and criminal justice scholars were quick to associate Thatcherism with punitive sentiments, and have, along with other branches of the social sciences become too focused on neo-liberalism as the explanatory framework, ignoring the neo-conservative elements of Thatcherism. Finally, I will argue that several criminological critiques of the recent past have failed to engage with the criminogenic elements of precise social and economic policies in specific countries and have shied away from naming some of the key social and political processes associated with crime trends, hiding behind terms like 'late modernity'. I start by outlining what Thatcherism was, before reviewing the standard criminological approach to it. I then describe how I operationalize the concept of punitiveness, before charting six trends in the criminal justice system between 1982 and 1998. I conclude with a discussion of recent thinking in political science and reflect on the lessons this holds.

WHAT WAS THATCHERISM?

Margaret Thatcher's tenure as Prime Minister from mid-1979 until late 1990 was one of considerable social and economic turbulence. During her 11 years in office, her governments' policy and legislative agendas changed and developed. Initially there was a focus on the economy, housing, and industrial relations. In anticipation of the loss of the 1983 general election, the manifesto was 'de-radicalized' leaving some to refer to the second administration as the 'lost term of office' (there were some notable Acts, however, such as the 1986 Social Security Act and several key state-owned utilities were privatized). Following re-election in 1987, education and health were focal points for activity along with further privatization of state-owned utilities. During her period in office, de-industrialization accelerated, with the result that manufacturing declined by about a half, increasing unemployment, decimating whole communities, and leading to a stark rise in economic inequality. Her electoral platform had been one of controlling inflation, limiting the influence of trade unions, cutting income tax, upholding the rule of law, the 'liberation' of families from an 'unhealthy' dependence on the state, and strengthening Britain's defences. Accordingly, local government's control of schooling, housing, and other public services was challenged, and trade union powers were reduced (Walker and Walker 1997). The social security system was also modified (Walker 1993). Perhaps unsurprisingly, officially recorded crime and self-reported victimization rates rose significantly and consistently (Farrall and Jennings 2014; Taylor 1990). Culled from a range of sources (Crewe 1988; Gamble 1988; Hay 1996; Hayes 1994; Levitas 1986; Russell et al. 1992), the following have all been cited as some of the values which distinguished Thatcherism from the stances taken by both Conservative and Labour politicians which came before her: a distrust of 'big' government, local governments, trade unions, and the welfare state; hostility towards comprehensive education, wealth redistribution, and taxation; the support of 'traditional' values (especially 'traditional' families, discipline, self-reliance, obedience, and respect); a nationalistic mindset associated with an anti-immigration stance; hostility towards gay-rights, pornography, and abortion; a pro-free trade agenda; and a 'resolute' approach to matters of law and order.

Indeed, law and order was a central plank of Thatcherite discourse. In her final 1979 general election broadcast, she referred to citizens as needing to feel 'safe in the streets' (Riddell 1985: 193). She repeatedly stated that she was in favour of capital punishment (Thatcher 1993: 307), and also claimed that the country wanted 'less tax and more law and order' (Savage 1990: 89). In March 1988 she expressed the opinion that social workers were to blame for the recent rises in crime as they 'created a fog of excuses in which the muggers and burglars operate' (Riddle 1989: 171). Despite such 'law and order' rhetoric, Thatcher's successive governments actually passed few draconian Acts (Faulkner 2014: 68, 132; Hurd 2003: 349–72, 377–8); an omission all the more surprising given the rise of crime in the 1980s. In 2014 Lord Hurd reflected that to his surprise, 'because she had a reputation for poking her nose into everything; she really left me alone as Home Secretary'.[1] The economy and the Treasury, he continued, 'were

[1] Interview with author.

her two priorities really, and it [meant] that she didn't really have the time or the instinct to go too deeply into crime and the causes of crime'. Why then, have others argued that there was a distinct 'Thatcher effect' in criminal justice?

WHAT IS THE STANDARD CRIMINOLOGICAL POSITION ON THATCHERISM AND THE CRIMINAL JUSTICE SYSTEM?

Possibly the clearest summary of the criminological *doxa* on Thatcher's impact on the criminal justice system is to be found in the work of Cavadino and Dignan, who write that 'In the early 1980s, the Conservative government of Margaret Thatcher injected a heavy dose of [punitiveness] into penal policy. This meant being deliberately harsher in punishing offenders' (2007: 6).

Others have linked her government's policies with criminal justice matters in much greater depth. Terrill (1989), for example, explores four Acts: the British Nationality Act, the Criminal Attempts Act (both 1981), the Police and Criminal Evidence Act (1984), and 1986's Public Order Act. For Terrill, the British Nationality Act was an attempt to make it harder for immigrants to enter the UK and as such was aimed at reducing the pool of young black males who would form part of the traffic of the welfare and criminal justice systems. Likewise, although the Criminal Attempts Act abolished the notion of 'loitering with intent' from the 1824 Vagrancy Act, it gave the police more discretion over such matters, which, Terrill implied, although did not demonstrate, would increase the arrest of young black men. The Police and Criminal Evidence Act was reviewed in terms of the policing of black people and the discretion of police officers in terms of their rights to stop and search individuals. Terrill provides little evidence as to the actual effects of the Act. The 1986 Public Order Act is cast as increasing the discretion of the police, but, as Terrill notes, 'it is too early to tell what impact the Act will have on an actual public order incident' (p. 452). Norrie and Adelman's review of Thatcherite criminal justice legislation (1989) is similarly weakened by a focus on what *might* happen without the evidence of what *did* happen. Their review is inspired by the work of Hall (1980) and in particular his notion of authoritarian populism. Although they refer to the Police and Criminal Evidence Act and the Public Order Act, their focus is on the policies adopted with regards to policing, and hence they do not develop much analysis of the legal instruments. Wiles' review focuses on the Public Order Act (1986), particularly in the context of industrial disputes, and is unable to present any firm conclusions as to the effects of the Act on crime, debates about crime, or policing.

The degree to which the Thatcher governments were able to produce the changes they wanted has been the subject of much debate within political science. Foremost amongst this body of work is Marsh and Rhodes' contribution (1992). As they note, the contemporary literature on Thatcher was deficient in a number of ways. It largely focused on the first term, and tended to overstate the Thatcher effect (p. 3). To this one could add that the policy changes initiated in the early 1980s might not produce substantive outcomes in terms of the redistribution of tangible goods or access to services for some considerable time. In effect, the insights afforded by a consideration of long-term impacts were absent. The existing literature in this field is therefore limited in that it was written before the full impact of the Acts could be assessed. It did not deal with many of the criminal justice Acts after the mid-1980s, and hence misses a large portion of Thatcher's (and Major's) periods in office. It also dealt with a small number of Acts and hence was very selective in nature.

One of the goals of my wider project on Thatcherism and the criminal justice system has been to remedy this gap in the literature, and in so doing to explore not just whether England and Wales saw a trend towards punitiveness during the 1980s and 1990s, but also to examine why this might have been (Farrall et al. 2016). I wish to question why one would expect neo-liberals to be concerned with crime (a question that was raised some years ago by Matthews, 2005) and then to chart some of the trends in punitiveness since the 1980s.

WHY WOULD A NEO-LIBERAL CARE ABOUT CRIME ANYWAY?

In a wide-ranging essay on the nature of punitiveness, Matthews questions why neo-liberal governments like Thatcher's would care about locking up minor offenders 'rather than just leave them to their own devices in deprived inner city areas?' (2005: 187). Indeed why would they? One only has to look at texts outlining the New Right of the 1980s (such as those by Gamble 1988; Hayes 1994; or Levitas 1986) to be reminded that what we call 'neo-liberalism' today was understood 30 years ago in a more nuanced manner. Neo-conservativism was as strong a part of 1980s New Right thinking as was neo-liberalism. As O'Malley reminds us, some of the recent trends in penality owe rather more to *neo-conservativism* than they do neo-liberalism (1999: 187). It was the neo-conservative strand of thinking which brought 'wrongdoing' and hence criminal justice into the ambit of Thatcherism. Like O'Malley (1999), I find it hard to attribute the 'toughening' of criminal justice to neo-liberalism. Rather, the explanatory model I and colleagues have developed points to the influences of *both* neo-conservatism and neo-liberalism, although each played a slightly different role (Farrall and Jennings 2014). Criminologists, in their haste to write about the next big idea, have not taken stock of some of the earlier thinking about the 1980s New Right which spawned local variants in the form of Reaganism, Thatcherism, Rogernomics, and (my favourite) Ruthanasia.[2] Macauley's observation at the start of this chapter seems especially pertinent—neo-liberalism has become the plaything of the critical, 'informed' left, without, it appears, much reflection on whether it is the most appropriate lens through which to view developments in criminal justice.

[2] Reaganism refers to the economic and social policies of the Reagan administration in the US (1980–8), Thatcherism to those policies associated with the UK administrations from 1979 until 1990. Rogernomics refers to the economic policies enacted by Roger Douglas, Minister of Finance in New Zealand (1984–8), whilst Ruthanasia refers to those of his successor Ruth Richardson (1990–3).

OPERATIONALIZING PUNITIVENESS

Of course, how authors define punitiveness is crucial in shaping the extent to which they will find it in any body of legislation. As Hamilton (2014) notes, empirical studies on punitiveness have either focused on collecting social attitudinal data towards sentences (measured at the individual level using surveys) or have sought to catalogue 'state punitiveness' (levels of imprisonment, length of terms of imprisonment, etc.). This chapter adopts the second of these two approaches, in that I am interested in the Acts which shaped the sorts of sentences which were available, and which regulated various branches of the criminal justice system. I follow Hamilton in using a range of indicators to measure punitiveness. These include but are not limited to: the use of mandatory sentences; support for increased police powers and resources; increase in post-prison release and community disposal controls; reductions in the control of police activities; increases in the possible length of prison terms; and limits to the decision-making of the judiciary and parole boards.

LOOKING AFRESH AT SOME OF THE KEY CRIMINAL JUSTICE SYSTEM DEVELOPMENTS OF THE 1980S

Let us now turn to some of the changes in the criminal justice system between 1982, the first major criminal justice Act under Thatcher's period in office, and 1998, the first under New Labour. Table 2.1 summarizes key aspects of each of the Acts explored and indicates whether or not they exhibit some of the important aspects of punitiveness. The Acts explored, many of which have also been listed by David Faulkner (2014: 68) in his list of 'legislative landmarks', are:

- The Criminal Justice Act, 1982
- The Police and Criminal Evidence Act, 1984 (hereafter PACE)
- The Prosecution of Offences Act, 1985
- The Drug Trafficking Offences Act, 1986
- The Criminal Justice Act, 1988
- The Criminal Justice Act, 1991
- The Criminal Justice Act, 1993
- The Criminal Justice and Public Order Act, 1994
- The Criminal Procedure and Investigations Act, 1996
- The Crime (Sentences) Act, 1997
- The Crime and Disorder Act, 1998.

In selecting these Acts, I concentrated on those which were 'key' to establishing new approaches to sentencing or levels of proof, or ways in which 'ordinary' members of the public or defendants were treated by the criminal justice system, rather than just 'tidying up' the legal system. Additionally, the Acts addressed the nature and length of the sentences which could be given, or the ways in which the criminal process could unfold. Further details on the rationale behind the choice of these Acts and some of their finer details can be found in Farrall et al. (2016).

Table 2.1 lists, by year of enactment, the eleven pieces of legislation passed between 1982 and 1998 which I shall focus on. A tick symbolizes that the measure listed in the first column was included in that Act. So, for example, the 1982 Criminal Justice Act replaced borstals with youth custody which had stronger post-custodial supervision (Burney 1985: 1). Willie Whitelaw, the Home Secretary of the day, wanted to avoid custodial sentencing for youths wherever possible by broadening and strengthening existing non-custodial provisions (Smith 2003: 8–9). He took a 'get tough' rhetorical stance in his statements to the House of Commons (Cavadino and Dignan 2007: 372) and referred to the idea of a 'short, sharp, shock' for young offenders, but did not pursue the idea with any vigour (Windlesham 1993: 158–60). As such, the White Paper included proposals for the reintroduction of a limited number of detention centres with tougher regimes (Newburn 2003: 197), encouraging judges and magistrates to use these for those who would previously have received a prison sentence.

The government believed that shorter sentences in detention centres would reduce the number of juveniles held in custody. Custody should only be used if other alternatives were deemed totally inappropriate (Ball 2004; Newburn 2003: 197). However, the Act also sought to move away from a 'treatment' approach and towards the idea that responsibility was to be borne by individual offenders and their parents. Smith claims that the Act abandoned the rehabilitative ideal in favour of an emphasis on retributive sentencing, deterrence, and 'just deserts' (2003: 8–9). The Act introduced Day Centres which included a provision that allowed courts to add requirements to probation orders (Newburn 2003: 138) and introduced powers such as the Night Restriction Order and the Charge and Control condition under a care order which enabled magistrates to indicate when a child should be removed from his/her home by the local authority (Burney 1985: 4).

Both these orders were seen as 'heightening the punitive aspects of intervention' (Smith 2003: 8). However, the Act reduced the number of juveniles sentenced to custody for indictable offences from 7,700 in 1981 to 4,000 in 1987 (Blackmore 1989: 165–6; Windlesham 1993: 170). This was due, in part, to the introduction of statutory criteria to be met before courts could pass custodial sentences (Blackmore 1989: 165–6). The Act also removed the penalty of imprisonment for begging or soliciting for prostitution (Faulkner 2014: 89), and allowed some groups of prisoners to be released up to six months early (Cavadino and Dignan 2007: 372; Windlesham 1993: 238). Hence this Act gets 'ticks' for both *limiting the use of imprisonment* and for producing *actual decreases in imprisonment*, whilst also receiving a tick for *increases in post-prison release/community controls*.

Table 2.1 contains two sorts of measures—the first lists various non-punitive measures, and the second records punitive measures. The dark vertical line marks Thatcher's departure from office in November 1990. The dark grey shaded cells in the top left-hand side represent those Acts which one might consider to have been open to Thatcherite influence during key stages of their drafting. The 1991 Act is included as it would have been drafted during the late 1980s (Faulkner 2014: 64–6). The cells on the top right-hand side are bordered by a thicker line than the rest of the table; this is

Table 2.1 Charting changes in state-backed punitiveness (1982–98)

Signifiers of Punitiveness	Acts (by year of enactment)											
	82	84	85	86	88	91	93	94	96	97	98	
Decreases in punitiveness												
Limits to the use of imprisonment			✓		✓	✓						T1
Increased rights for suspects		✓										
Limits to police powers		✓										
Diverting cases away from Crown Courts					✓							
Decreases in actual levels of imprisonment	✓					✓						
Increases in punitiveness												
Increased post-prison release/community controls	✓					✓					✓	
Increases in police powers/resources		✓						✓				
Right to silence questioned or amended			✓					✓			✓	T2
Increases in sentence lengths/imprisonment				✓	✓		✓	✓		✓	✓	T3
Mandatory sentences (or similar provisions)				✓			✓			✓		T4
Changes to the burden of proof				✓								
Unduly lenient sentences can be appealed					✓							
'Failure to respond' used in sentencing							✓					
Increases in actual levels of imprisonment							✓					
Increases in youth imprisonment							✓	✓			✓	T5
Changes to case disclosure								✓	✓			T6
Limits to the use of bail								✓				
Limits to the decision-making of parole boards										✓		
Automatic life sentences										✓		
Blurring of civil and criminal law											✓	
	82	84	85	86	88	91	93	94	96	97	98	

intended to highlight the *absence* of decreases in punitiveness after 1991. The dashed line running at about 45° represents the proliferation of ways of being punitive which grew over time. I want here to focus on six trends, marked in Table 2.1 as T1 to T6.

The first trend relates to the desire to limit the use of imprisonment (T1). This is evident in most of the Acts passed before 1993, and harks back to the belief that imprisonment was an undesirable outcome in all but the most severe of cases. This desire was a cornerstone not just of Home Office philosophy, but also of some sections of Conservative Party philosophy, an idea which was firmly rooted in sentencing policies until 1993 (Loader 2006). The Acts passed, especially those in 1982 and 1991, did indeed appear to reduce imprisonment, albeit perhaps not to the degree desired. Nevertheless, these Acts did not reflect the 'get tough' stance often associated with Thatcherite discourse on matters of law and order.[3] The second trend identifiable (T2) relates to the right to silence, which was significantly reduced *after* 1993. Debates about suspects' right to silence had been raised in the 1972 Report of the Criminal Law Revision Committee (Zander 2013: 2). However, the 1972 Report was condemned as a result of its recommendation that adverse inferences could be drawn from a suspect's silence (Zander 2013: 2). Consequently, the Home Office concluded that it was impossible to implement even the uncontroversial recommendations of a report which was so widely regarded as flawed (Zander 2013: 2). In part, then, the questioning of the right to silence was part of a wider pre-Thatcherite debate, but one which came to the fore during the 1980s and the increasingly tough rhetoric around law and order. However, it was also an attempt to undo some of the rights gained from PACE and the curtailing of some police powers associated with that Act. It was not until the 1994 Criminal Justice and Public Order Act that juries were allowed to draw adverse inferences from a suspect's silence (Sanders et al. 2010: 19).

The third and fourth trends (T3 and T4) relate to increases in sentence lengths and the use of mandatory sentences. These had their origins in the 1986 Drug Trafficking Offences Act, and, as an idea about how to tackle crime, were extended in various Acts, most commonly those after 1993. The Crime (Sentences) Act 1997 is considered to have created a more punitive system in that it introduced maxima and minima sentences for certain offences and their subsequent repetition (Robson 2010). In general, the policies introduced by the Conservative government between 1992 and 1997 were characterized as appealing to increasingly populist attitudes to retribution and deterrence (Edwards 2010). Another related trend was increased youth imprisonment after 1993 (T5), an outcome which Whitelaw and others had opposed in the early 1980s. Finally, the sixth trend (T6) relates to changes to the duty of disclosure, which has shifted from the prosecution needing to disclose its case to the defence towards the defence needing to reciprocate (which could be seen as making conviction more likely).

[3] As Matthews notes (2005: 190), as well as sending fewer people to prison the Thatcher governments also improved prison conditions. One might argue that the decrease in those sent to prison was a realpolitik response to the rising costs of the criminal justice system. I would refute this suggestion; political objectives are seldom tempered by economic constraints. In any case, as well as claiming that she would never economize on law and order, Thatcher's government was able to raise the pay of police officers.

The non-punitive measures ceased abruptly in 1991. Allowing for the passage of time between drafting and enactment, one *could*, on the basis of this evidence, read the Thatcher governments as representing the last period of liberal criminal justice policy based firmly on a belief in the rehabilitative ideal. This would be a rose-tinted view, however, since 1982–8 also saw increases in post-prison release and community controls, increases in some sentence lengths, changes to the burden of proof, and other measures which could reasonably be read as deepening punitiveness. Certainly, however, the period from 1993 until 1998 saw a dramatic growth in punitive measures, such as repeated attempts to increase sentence lengths and extend mandatory sentences and changes to the disclosure of a defendant's case which might have tipped the balance in favour of the prosecution. A number of trends can be detected. For example, whilst the 1982 Act did not bring about a wholesale recasting of the criminal justice system along radically more punitive lines, it was part of a wider 'toughening' of the rhetoric around crime, the causes of crime, and how offenders ought to be punished, it nevertheless (via the creation of the Night Restriction Order and Charge and Control conditions) marks the beginning of a more punitive approach. What was key was the developing rhetoric devoted to the notion of 'toughening' the criminal justice system's response to wrongdoing. As such, though 1993 represented a structural break, it was not a completely 'clean' break, as some of what emerged from that point drew heavily on past ideas.

THINKING ABOUT THATCHERITE INFLUENCE ON THE CRIMINAL JUSTICE SYSTEM

The identification of these trends owes much to ideas borrowed from historical institutionalism. One of the key aims of historical institutionalists' analyses is to identify and describe how trends, or 'path dependencies', are produced, shaped, and maintained (Pierson 2004; Thelen and Steinmo 1992). Hall defines an institution as 'the formal rules, compliance procedures, and standard operating practices that structure the relationship between individuals in various units of the polity and economy' (Hall 1986: 19). For Sanders (2006: 42), historical institutionalists are mainly interested in how institutions are constructed, maintained, and adapted over time, whilst Levi defines a path dependency as meaning:

> that once a country has started down a track, the costs of reversal are very high. There will be other choice points, but the entrenchments of certain institutional arrangements obstruct an easy reversal of the initial choice, perhaps the better metaphor is a tree, rather than a path. From the same trunk, there are many different branches and smaller branches. Although it is possible to turn around or to clamber from one to the other... the branch on which a climber begins is the one she tends to follow.
>
> (1997: 28)

Pierson (2004: 20) adds that path dependence refers to a dynamic process which involves a positive feedback and which generates a series of further outcomes depending on the sequence in which these events and processes occur. As such, once a path has been selected and embarked upon, decisions, events, and processes tend to reinforce this path, making the change to an alternative path harder with each step.

More recently another body of institutionalist thinking has emerged out of a critique of historical institutionalism. Going under the name of constructivist institutionalism, this perspective argues that historical institutionalism overlooks the role which *ideas* play in shaping political outcomes (Hay 2011; Ross 2011). The basic observation is that historical institutionalism is too 'sticky' in that it cannot easily allow for individual agency (Bell 2011). Constructivist institutionalism focuses on the ways in which *ideas* can influence institutions and processes. Pierson argues that 'institutional arrangements in politics are typically hard to change' (Pierson 2000: 490) and that 'actors find the dead weight of previous institutional choices seriously limits their room to manoeuvre' (Pierson 2000: 493), suggesting that agency is seriously hampered. Indeed, and as Hay notes, within the auspices of historical institutionalism, change is seen as the outcome of path-dependent processes or from shocks from outwith (Hay 2011: 66). This view overlooks what Hay refers to as 'path-shaping' (as opposed to path-dependent) possibilities (2011: 66). Hay's critique of much current historical institutionalism stresses that whilst it continues to focus on path dependencies, it will remain unable to fully account for institutional changes. By focusing on ideas, constructivist institutionalism forces us to consider *ideational* path-dependence as well as *institutional* path-dependence (2011: 68–9). As Blyth suggests, 'institutional change only makes sense by reference to the ideas that inform agents' responses to moments of uncertainty and change' (2002: 251). Ideas become codified and start to serve as the cognitive filters through which actors are able to conceive of their interests (Hay 2011: 69). Similarly, Blyth argues that 'ideas give substance to interests and determine the form and content of new institutions' (2002: 15). As such, constructivist institutionalism allows one to develop explanations which include novel developments, and counterbalances historical institutionalism's tendency to focus on institutional inertia (Hay 2011: 69).

Such perspectives usefully illuminate criminological analyses. In particular they help us to explain the broad continuation until the early 1990s of older, non-Thatcherite aspirations in criminal justice policy. Whilst the Thatcher governments were ideationally punitive from the outset, between 1979 and at least 1990 that rhetorical radicalism was not wholly reflected in substantive policy commitments. This is not difficult to explain from a constructivist institutionalist perspective. First, ideational radicalism invariably precedes policy and institutional radicalism (Hay 2002, 2015). Second, and more specifically, throughout this period, the Conservatives' punitive electoral advantage went unchallenged. It was only with the 'modernization' of the Labour Party and the toughening of Labour's law-and-order credentials that this lead started to erode. By that time the Conservatives were well on the way to becoming substantively tough on crime to match their rhetoric. Prior to this, the Thatcher governments' priorities were elsewhere. They had, in short, more important priorities in economic policy, housing, and welfare reform which, they perceived, were much more closely bound up with their electoral fortunes. It was only after they had attended to other policy fields that they turned to law and order. By that time, with crime rates rising and a much more concerted challenge from the opposition, they had a greater need to do so.

The Acts I have focused on operated in a number of ways to establish and then promote path-dependent processes in the criminal justice system. Some strengthened earlier provisions (such as those aimed at limiting imprisonment prior to 1993, T1). Others extended a philosophy introduced with regards to one crime type to different crime types such as the introduction of mandatory sentences (T4) in 1986 which was later extended by the 1993 and 1997 Acts. Additionally, some Acts incrementally reinforced an ideal such as the questioning and amendment of the principle of the right to silence (T2). None of the path-dependent processes owe much to *organizational* change, but rather to developments at the *ideational* level.

In other words, it was the recognition that rises in crime were starting to cause anxiety amongst the populace which drove the political interest in crime. As such, it was the ideas which were promoted first by Thatcherism generally and embracing, amongst other things, a punitive attitude towards wrongdoing, then second by the likes of Whitelaw and the Home Office who aimed at diverting people away from imprisonment by making non-custodial sentences sound 'tough', which were adopted by Michael Howard in order to promote his own stance on sentencing and crime control. This reading suggests that the punitive sentences of the recent era are the outcome of several developments: attempts to pander to the wider discourse established by Thatcherism; the real rises in crime caused by Thatcherite social and economic policies (Farrall and Jennings 2012); a growing recognition of popular anxieties about crime; the later arrival of a Thatcherite-minded minister at the Home Office (Howard); and lastly the adoption of this discourse by the Labour Party.

So, in sum, what might account for this state of affairs? There are a range of institutional and political impediments to radicalism in this policy domain which are not well anticipated in the existing institutionalist political science literature. Amongst these I would draw particular attention to the substantial opinion poll lead that the Conservatives enjoyed on this issue when they were elected and the absence of a credible challenge to this before Tony Blair became Shadow Home Secretary in 1992. In addition, one needs to understand the phasing of policy radicalism in other policy domains, which meant that the Thatcher governments could not act radically in all, or even many, policy fields at once and had to phase their radicalism (Hay and Farrall 2014). Furthermore, we must acknowledge the absence, at least in the very early 1980s, of dramatic upward trends in crime rates which might draw attention to the contradiction of the Thatcher administration's tough rhetorical stance on crime and the actual increases in recorded crime and which might have caused her government some embarrassment. Finally, there is the realpolitik consideration that Thatcher needed to place leading figures of the left of the Conservative party ('wets') within her first few Cabinets and give them important portfolios in order to keep her party together in the absence of a more thoroughgoing internal Thatcherite revolution.

Let me conclude by reflecting on why it is that others appear to have missed some of the above. I think that, along with many other branches of the social sciences, there has been a tendency for criminologists to think predominantly in terms of neo-liberalism. This, I think, is especially curious given criminology's focus on wrongdoing and reactions to it. Criminologists are normally very good at acting like magpies—jumping around stealing the shiniest, most exciting ideas and concepts from other social sciences and the humanities. But somehow the recent literature on historical and constructivist institutionalisms has evaded capture thus far. This seriously hinders criminological thinking when it comes to explorations of the state and criminal justice policies. Government policies (A) help to shape social and economic circumstances (B), which impact on crime levels and the perceptions of crime as an important issue (C) which in turn shapes criminal justice policy (D). But getting from (A) to (D) can take a decade or more, hence the need for criminologists to embrace concepts from historical institutionalism. Criminological narratives of change during the post-war era (most notably Garland 2001 or Young 1999) make little reference to specific policies or how these shaped crime and experiences of it. Accordingly, they say little about specific administrations (it all seems to be driven from afar, or to quote Loader and Sparks (2004: 17) on Garland 'rather too top down' and in Feeley's words insufficiently 'anchored in politics' (2003: 117)). Further, they focus on macro-level analyses of the UK and the USA in such a way that important details are often overlooked and the subtle differences between administrations and countries are downplayed. And they push to the background the importance of individuals and their role in influencing events. In the case of Thatcherism this is an especially serious omission, since, if Thatcherism was about anything, it was about an idea.

REFERENCES

Ball, C. (2004), 'Youth Justice? Half a Century of Responses to Youth Offending', *Criminal Law Review*: 28–41.

Bell, S. (2011), 'Do We Really Need a New "Constructivist Institutionalism" to Explain Institutional Change?', *British Journal of Political Science*, 41, 4: 883–906.

Blackmore, J. (1989), *Custodial Control or Community Alternative: An Examination of the Impact of the 1982 Criminal Justice Act in One Local Authority*, Dordrecht: Kluwer.

Blyth, M. (2002), *Great Transformations*, Cambridge: Cambridge University Press.

Burney, E. (1985), *Sentencing Young People: What went Wrong with the Criminal Justice Act 1982?*, Aldershot: Gower.

Cavadino, M. and Dignan, J. (2007), *The Penal System*, 4th edn, London: SAGE.

Crewe, I. (1988), 'Has the Electorate Become Thatcherite?', in R. Skidelsky (ed.), *Thatcherism*, London: Chatto and Windus.

Edwards, I. (2010), 'Essential Resource for Professionals Serving the Criminal Courts since 1837: Penal Policy under the Coalition Government', *Criminal Law & Justice Weekly*, 174: 421–4.

Farrall, S. and Jennings, W. (2012), 'Policy Feedback and the Criminal Justice Agenda', *Contemporary British History*, 26, 4: 467–88.

Farrall, S. and Jennings, W. (2014), 'Thatcherism and Crime: The Beast that Never Roared?', in S. Farrall and C. Hay (eds), *The Legacy of Thatcherism: Exploring and Theorising the Long-Term Consequences of Thatcherite Social and Economic Policies*, Oxford: Oxford University Press: 207–33.

Farrall, S., Burke, N., and Hay, C. (2016), 'Revisiting Margaret Thatcher's Law and Order Agenda: The Slow-Burning Fuse of Punitiveness', *British Politics*, 11, 2: 205–31.

Faulkner, D. (2014), *Servant of the Crown*, Winchester: Waterside Press.

FEELEY, M. (2003), 'Crime, Social Order and the Rise of Neo-Conservative Politics', *Theoretical Criminology*, 7, 1: 111–30.
GAMBLE, A. (1988), *The Free Economy and the Strong State*, Basingstoke: Macmillan.
GARLAND, D. (2001), *The Culture of Control*, Oxford: Oxford University Press.
HALL, P. (1986), *Governing the Economy*, New York: Oxford University Press.
HALL, S. (1980), *Drifting into a Law and Order Society*, London: The Cobden Trust.
HAMILTON, C. (2014), 'Reconceptualising Penality: Towards a Multidimensional Measure of Punitiveness', *British Journal of Criminology*, 54, 2: 321–43.
HAY, C. (1996), *Re-Stating Social and Political Change*, Buckingham: Open University Press.
HAY, C. (2002), *Political Analysis*, Basingstoke: Palgrave Macmillan.
HAY, C. (2011), 'Ideas and the Construction of Interests', in D. Beland and R.H. Cox (eds), *Ideas and Politics in Social Science Research*, Oxford: Oxford University Press: 65–82.
HAY, C. (2015), 'Social Constructivism', in M. Bevir and R.A.W. Rhodes (eds), *The Handbook of Interpretive Political Science*, London: Routledge.
HAY, C. and FARRALL, S. (2014), 'Interrogating and Conceptualising the Legacy of Thatcherism', in S. Farrall and C. Hay (eds), *The Legacy of Thatcherism: Exploring and Theorising the Long-term Consequences of Thatcherite Social and Economic Policies*, Oxford: Oxford University Press: 3–30.
HAYES, M. (1994), *The New Right in Britain*, London: Pluto Press.
HURD, D. (2003), *Memoirs*, London: Abacus.
LEVI, M. (1997), 'A Model, a Method and a Map', in M.I. Lichbach and A.S. Zuckerman (eds), *Comparative Politics*, Cambridge: Cambridge University Press.
LEVITAS, R. (1986), 'Introduction: Ideology and the New Right', in R. Levitas (ed.), *The Ideology of the New Right*, Cambridge: Polity Press.
LOADER, I. (2006), 'Fall of the "Platonic Guardians": Liberalism, Criminology and Political Responses to Crime in England and Wales', *British Journal of Criminology*, 46, 4: 561–86.
LOADER, I. and SPARKS, R. (2004), 'For an Historical Sociology of Crime Policy in England and Wales since 1968', *Critical Review of International Social and Political Philosophy*, 7, 2: 5–32.
MACAULEY, F. (2007), 'Justice-Sector and Human Rights Reform under the Cardoso Government', *Latin American Perspectives*, 34, 5: 26–42.
MARSH, D. and RHODES, R.A.W. (eds) (1992), *Implementing Thatcherite Policies*, Milton Keynes: Open University Press.
MATTHEWS, R. (2005), 'The Myth of Punitiveness', *Theoretical Criminology*, 9, 2: 175–201.
NEWBURN, T. (2003), *Crime & Criminal Justice Policy*, 2nd edn, London: Pearson.
NORRIE, A. and ADELMAN, S. (1989), '"Consensual Authoritarianism" and Criminal Justice in Thatcher's Britain', in A. Gamble and C. Wells (eds), *Thatcher's Law*, Oxford: Blackwell.
O'MALLEY, P. (1999), 'Volatile and Contradictory Punishment', *Theoretical Criminology*, 3, 2: 175–96.
PIERSON, P. (2000), 'The Limits of Design: Explaining Institutional Origins and Change', *Governance: An International Journal of Policy and Administration*, 13, 4: 475–99.
PIERSON, P. (2004), *Politics in Time*, Princeton, NJ: Princeton University Press.
RIDDELL, P. (1985), *The Thatcher Government*, London: Martin Robertson & Co.
RIDDELL, P. (1989), *The Thatcher Decade*, Oxford: Basil Blackwell.
ROBSON, G. (2010), 'Essential Resource for Professionals Serving the Criminal Courts since 1837: Sympathy for Sentencers?', *Criminal Law & Justice Weekly*, 174: 710–12.
ROSS, F. (2011), 'Bringing Political Identity into Discursive Ideational Analysis', *British Politics*, 8, 1: 51–78.
RUSSELL, A.T., JOHNSTON, R.J., and PATTIE, C.J. (1992), 'Thatcher's Children: Exploring the Links between Age and Political Attitudes', *Political Studies*, 40, 4: 742–56.

SANDERS, A., YOUNG, R., and BURTON, M. (2010), *Criminal Justice*, 4th edn, Oxford University Press.

SANDERS, E. (2006), 'Historical Institutionalism', in R.A.W. Rhodes, S.A. Binder, and B.A. Rockman (eds), *The Oxford Handbook of Political Institutions*, Oxford: Oxford University Press.

SAVAGE, S. (1990), 'A War on Crime?', in S. Savage and L. Robins (eds), *Public Policy under Thatcher*, Macmillan, London.

SMITH, R. (2003), *Youth Justice*, Cullompton: Willan Publishing.

TAYLOR, I. (ed.) (1990), *The Social Effects of Free Market Policies*, London: Harvester Wheatsheaf.

TERRILL, R. (1989), 'Margaret Thatcher's Law and Order Agenda', *The American Journal of Comparative Law*, 37, 3: 429–56.

THATCHER, M. (1993), *The Downing Street Years*, London: HarperCollins.

THELEN, K. and STEINMO, S. (1992), 'Historical Institutionalism in Comparative Politics', in S. Steinmo, K. Thelen, and F. Longstreth (eds), *Structuring Politics*, Cambridge: Cambridge University Press.

WALKER, A. and WALKER, C. (eds) (1997), *Britain Divided*, London: CPAG.

WALKER, C. (1993), *Managing Poverty: The Limits of Social Assistance*, London: Routledge.

WILES, P. (1988), 'Law, Order & the State', in C. Graham and T. Prosser (eds), *Waiving the Rules: The Constitution under Thatcherism*, Milton Keynes: Open University Press.

WINDLESHAM, LORD (1993), *Responses to Crime*, vol. 2, Oxford: Clarendon Press.

YOUNG, J. (1999), *The Exclusive Society*, London: SAGE.

ZANDER, M. (2013), *The Police and Criminal Evidence Act 1984*, 6th edn, London: Sweet & Maxwell.

3

THE DOG THAT NEVER QUITE BARKED: SOCIAL IDENTITY AND THE PERSISTENCE OF POLICE LEGITIMACY

Ben Bradford

In many ways the history of British policing over the last half century has been one of constant change. Newburn (2008: 92) provides a list of forty-seven major enquiries and pieces of legislation involving the police over the period 1960–2008. Further legislation like the Police Reform and Social Responsibility Act (2011), and inquiries, such as the 2013 report of the Independent Commission into the future of policing (Brown 2013) have since been added to this list. Structural, policy, and technological developments have been relentless, shaping and reshaping almost every level and aspect of the institution.

On many accounts the legitimacy of the police has also changed significantly over the same period. The fourth edition of Reiner's *The Politics of the Police* (2010) devotes over thirty pages to the development of police legitimacy from 1958 onwards, and he depicts a narrative of decline. From a halcyon period in the 1950s, when the British police had secured a level of public support hard to imagine today, a process of disenchantment and desacralization took hold. By the end of the twentieth century the standing of the police had become contested, tenuous, and fractured. Many factors are thought to have driven this process, from a long series of scandals concerning violence, malpractice, and corruption, via increased social diversity, to the general decline in deference towards authority that occurred over the second half of the twentieth century. Newburn (2008: 111) offers a summary of this process: 'We are now more critical of policing and the police. We ask for more yet, given the greater visibility of the belly of the beast, feel we receive less. We are more demanding and less trusting.' Reiner (2010: 80) is pithier, describing a transformation in the image of the police 'from plod to pig'.

The idea that the police have lost legitimacy, the 'trust and confidence' of the community, and/or 'public support' (terms used more or less interchangeably by many commentators) has become something of an organizing concept, an explicit or tacit understanding that underscores many academic, policy, and organizational debates. From high-level reforms including neighbourhood policing, the last Labour government's PSA23 public confidence target, and the inception of Police and Crime Commissioners, to specific policies such as providing better information on police activities (Wünsch and Hohl 2009) and improving the way officers interact with members of the public (Myhill and Quinton 2011), there have been many attempts to 'enhance public confidence'. Talk of a crisis in legitimacy resurfaces on a regular basis (e.g. Mackenzie and Henry 2009: 10).

Yet there is a danger in overstating the extent to which police legitimacy has declined. An alternative account might emphasize that public attitudes remain stubbornly positive. In 2013/14, for example, the Crime Survey of England and Wales found that 63 per cent of people rated their local police as 'excellent' or 'good', while 76 per cent expressed 'confidence' in local police, an increase of 13 percentage points since 2005/06 (ONS 2015). To be sure, these figures compare unfavourably with those from earlier eras. The 1984 British Crime Survey, for example, recorded that nearly 90 per cent of people rated their local force very or fairly good (Jackson et al. 2013: 35), while the public opinion survey conducted for the 1962 Royal Commission into policing revealed extremely high levels of public support and respect at that time (Loader and Mulcahy 2003; Reiner 2010). Police legitimacy has certainly not remained constant over the last half century, and as we shall see crises have occurred. But consideration of the 'job ratings' awarded to police, characterized as measures of overall trust and confidence (Jackson and Bradford 2010) and strongly associated with legitimacy (Jackson et al. 2013), suggests that public support has remained relatively high, and relatively consistent, over a number of years. Indeed, on most national indicators public opinion has moved in a positive direction over the last decade (ONS 2015). On this basis it might be said that the legitimacy of the police never diminished to quite the extent that has been assumed, and it certainly never collapsed.

Harkin (2014: 43) has recently discussed the apparently puzzling persistence of our support for the police, noting that answers to a question posed over a decade ago by Loader and Mulcahy (2003: 35) remain few and far between: 'why—in the face of corruption scandals, miscarriages of justice, paramilitarization, falling crime detection rates, the decline of visible patrols, the Stephen Lawrence affair, and so on—does confidence in the police remain in certain quarters so *high*?' (emphasis in the original). The currently dominant account of police legitimacy within criminology, Tom Tyler's procedural justice theory (Tyler 2006; Tyler and Huo 2002), asserts that fairness is the most important antecedent of legitimacy. Yet, despite 50 years of scandals, often concerning unfair policing, the collapse in legitimacy remains overstated.

Naturally, there are likely to be many answers to this puzzle. For Harkin (2014) the police fulfil atavistic urges to punish among some sections of the population, and garner legitimacy from the extent to which they are perceived to act against denigrated outgroups. Elsewhere, Sindall et al. (2012) demonstrate that at the aggregate level change in public confidence in the police has tracked change in the crime rate—perhaps the crime decline of the last 20 years served to at first brake, and then reverse, a decline in legitimacy that started in the 1960s and which would have carried on had crime continued to rise.

In this chapter I offer an alternative potential explanation, deriving directly from procedural justice theory. In this view, the police embody a social identity salient to many people's sense of self. When people feel they share an identity (Tajfel 1978) *with* police they are more likely to grant legitimacy *to* police (Hogg 2001). The police thus draw legitimacy from their association with a particular social identity (or set of identities), and from the motivations of individuals to act in ways that support groups to which they feel they belong. Developing this idea provides insight, I argue, into why police legitimacy has not collapsed in the face of the kinds of scandals adumbrated above.

The remainder of the chapter proceeds as follows. After outlining Tyler's procedural justice model and the role of social identity within it, I present empirical evidence from a survey of people living in England and Wales concerning the associations between identity judgements and perceptions of the legitimacy of the police. The chapter closes with some consideration of the dynamic interplay between social identity and police legitimacy.

PROCEDURAL JUSTICE, SOCIAL IDENTITY, AND POLICE LEGITIMACY

Procedural justice theory provides a model for understanding cooperation and compliance in group settings, which is applicable not just in criminal justice contexts but anywhere people are operating in groups marked by internal divisions of labour and power (e.g. workplaces). Scholars in this field are concerned with the ways in which cooperation and compliance is motivated and sustained, with a particular emphasis on the relationship between group authorities and members. The fairness of the procedures through which authorities wield their power is thought to be central to this relationship. When people feel fairly treated by those with power over them they are more inclined to grant legitimacy to that power-holder; legitimacy, in turn, encourages cooperation and compliance.

Social identity provides a key causal mechanism in this process. The way authorities behave towards individuals is 'identity relevant'. Procedural fairness communicates to people interacting with authorities (a) messages of inclusion and status (that the individuals concerned are 'inside' and valued by the group) and (b) that the group itself is worth being a member of (because it treats its members appropriately). When people's sense of identification with a group is activated and made salient, and when they feel more included in it, they are motivated to act in ways that support the group and its authorities (de Cremer and Tyler 2005; Tyler and Blader 2000).

Procedural justice theory has been widely applied within policing contexts over the last two decades, across a range of jurisdictions (Mazerolle et al. 2013). Since questions of social identity lie at the heart of the theory all such research is premised, explicitly or implicitly, on the idea that police represent authority figures within specific social groups. Officer behaviour communicates the value and status the *group as a whole* accords to those with whom they interact. Being treated with dignity and respect by officers who display neutral decision-making and who utilize open, transparent communication processes has effects on people in line with those described above. By contrast, when people find their treatment to be procedurally unfair, they feel excluded from the group, that it does not value them, and that its authorities act in inappropriate ways (Tyler and Wakslak 2004). In turn, police legitimacy is undermined. It is furthermore likely that indirect—vicarious and mediated—experiences of policing have similar effects (Rosenbaum et al. 2005).

These ideas resonate strongly with those aspects of police sociology that have positioned police as important representatives of particular social groups aligned, most importantly, with the idea of the nation state (Loader and Mulcahy 2003; Reiner 2010). The extent to which the 'British bobby' evokes images of an imagined national community of feeling and affect is well known to the point of cliché. As Loader and Mulcahy (2003: 46) note, though, equally pertinent is the association of the 'Mountie' with Canadian national identity (Taylor 1999), or the historical role of the police in forging national identities from diverse regional identities in many European countries (Emsley 1999). This is not to claim that police always represent such identities, nor that all Canadians, for example, associate Mounties with what it is to 'be Canadian', but merely that police in many different contexts have been associated with identities built around ideas of nationhood and nationality.

FROM PROCEDURAL JUSTICE TO (FUTURE) BEHAVIOUR

Procedural justice theory is premised on an inherently relational and discursive notion of social identity. A person's sense of self develops in reflexive reaction to the actions of others, and police officers can provide a mirror (Bradford et al. 2014) in which they imagine, assess, and recreate their social self. To the extent that police represent identities linked with nation and state, their actions provide individuals with a way of imagining their place within these particular groups. It is important to note that this is a notion of social identity recognizant of the multiple forms of self-categorization, group membership, and belonging individuals use to construct their sense of self. All people identify with multiple social groups and draw on multiple social categories when constructing their self-concept. What is at stake in experiences of policing is simply people's relationship with, and tendency to categorize themselves as members of, the group police represent. When this relationship is strengthened by the experience of procedural fairness, other aspects of the social self may become less salient, but this is by no means a necessary outcome (one can feel more 'British' without feeling less of a 'school teacher who supports Manchester United and practices yoga').

Procedural justice theory thus shares much in common with labelling theory. Both assume that the actions of criminal justice actors can influence and shape the identities of the people with whom they interact. As Richard Ericson argued some time ago (1975: 15):

> the criminal justice system ... is perpetually involved in socializing its members, and thereby changing their selves ... aspects of the criminal process (are) radical agents of

identity change, typifying in an accentuated form the secondary socialization process that occurs in many spheres of social life.

An important difference, however, is that while labelling theorists are mostly concerned with the bureaucratic or assigned identities of individuals within the criminal justice system, procedural justice theory takes a much wider view. All those who experience policing are affected, potentially, by the kinds of processes described above.

Procedural justice theory, and identity theory within social psychology more broadly, also share with other criminological theories the idea that identity is closely bound to role-based behaviours (Burke and Stets 2009). When police activity makes salient and strengthens an individual's identification with the group police represent, they are motivated to take on roles linked to this identity, which, given the association of police with the nation state or the community of citizens, may revolve around the idea of the 'law-abiding citizen' (Bradford et al. 2014; Jackson et al. 2012). Enacting roles associated with identities serves to reproduce and solidify the individual's sense of self, and when an identity revolving around citizenship is invoked these roles may include law-abidingness and a willingness to defer to authorities. Policing that denigrates and excludes does not motivate the same role-related behaviours, not least because people's sense that they need to live up to role expectations is diminished when they feel distanced or excluded from related group identities.

Valerie Braithwaite's theory of motivational postures places a similar emphasis on the relationship between identities and roles (Braithwaite 2013). Here, three 'selves' are engaged when an individual experiences legal authority: the moral self, the democratic collective self, and the status-seeking self. Responses to the behaviour of an authority figure will take the form of different postures toward it which, in turn, are conditioned by the way its actions are experienced by the individual in light of their need to maintain a positive self image constructed from the three selves. Braithwaite argues that the experience of fair authority activates or makes salient the moral self, which is law abiding and 'aligned with legitimate authorities' (2013: 95), and the democratic collective self, which sees obeying the law and supporting authority as part of a shared contract with the government and other citizens. Supporting legitimate authority is an important way in which such identities are made 'real' to the individual and expressed by them to others.

COMPLICATING FACTORS

The discussion thus far has focused on the understanding, foundational to procedural justice theory, that police behaviour experienced as fair or unfair affects people's identity judgements, which, in turn, influence the extent to which they grant police legitimacy. There are three important additional points to be made, each of which complicates this understanding. The first is simply that social identity is not the only 'bridge' between fairness and legitimacy. The extent to which people find policing fair or unfair can influence legitimacy in ways that do not involve identity processes.

The second point concerns the relationship between police activity, social identity, and the contexts within which people encounter police. Consider, for example, the kind of interactions envisaged in procedural justice theory. Paradigmatically these comprise dyads formed during an encounter between an individual citizen and a police officer. Some level of shared group membership is assumed, as is the idea that the citizen recognizes the police officer as an important representative of this group. Power within this dyad is also very unevenly distributed—the officer has much more than the citizen—implying that it makes sense to envisage that the police officer can 'do' something to the citizen that alters their sense of self (draws them into or pushes them out of the group).

There are, though, different types of encounters (and relationships) between police and citizens. Notably, Drury, Reicher, Stott, and colleagues have over a number of years considered issues of police activity and legitimacy within crowd settings, such as at football matches or demonstrations (Drury and Reicher 2000; Stott et al. 2011). The relationship is no longer a dyad, and while the police usually retain significantly more power than the crowd the gradient is less steep. It can make more sense to envisage these interactions as *intergroup* encounters, at least in the first instance, not least because the policed have a clearly accessible alternative group identity to hand (e.g. 'Liverpool fans', 'anti-globalization campaigners').

In theorizing such encounters social identity is positioned as more actively relational and dynamic than is usually the case in procedural justice theory. The existence of particular shared identities that precede the encounter between police and citizen are not taken as a given, but identity formation is instead considered to be an active, interactive, and ongoing process. It is argued that in crowd contexts—and surely elsewhere—peoples' identities in relation to the police are defined by their active processes of self-categorization in response to police activity. Consequently the extent to which the police are considered 'proto-typical' group representatives (Sunshine and Tyler 2003) is established by and through the ways crowd members read their behaviour in situ. If police are judged to be behaving fairly a sense of shared identity is promoted and they may be accepted as authority figures empowered to direct group members (i.e. people in the crowd, who now feel a sense of shared group membership with police). If police behaviour is found unfair, however, they are judged to have *excluded themselves*. Unfair policing can 'fuse' crowd members into a group that is 'unified…in opposition to the police' (Drury and Reicher 2000: 582), and police lose the ability to secure willing compliance.

The third point provides a potential, partial, answer to the question posed by Loader and Mulcahy (2003). Simply stated, it is that the kind of 'law-abiding citizen' identity at stake in peoples' experiences of policing must pre-date such experiences and sit somewhat outside their relationship with police. And if they accord the police status as an authority in a group they identify with, even people who have little or no direct experience of policing will be motivated to grant legitimacy (on the basis of a sense of shared group membership).

This claim is important for two reasons. First, a large majority of people associate themselves with identities that can plausibly be linked with the police. The 2009/10 Citizenship Survey, for example, found that 87 per cent of people felt they 'belonged' very or fairly strongly to Britain (DCLG 2011). In a more detailed analysis Heath et al. (2005) also report high levels of identification as 'British'. While these authors note that the increasing salience of English, Scottish, and Welsh identities adds a complicating factor, it is likely many of those who identify with one of the constituent nations of Great Britain simply conceive of 'their' police as Scottish, Welsh, or English rather than British (see e.g. Girling et al. 2000). It almost goes without saying that most people see themselves as law-abiding citizens.

Second, there is an ideological apparatus that surrounds the police, in Great Britain and elsewhere, which is concerned precisely with positioning police as representative of the nation as a community of belonging and affect, and with an identity that can be parsed as the 'law-abiding citizen'. Loader and Mulcahy's (2003) answer to their own question, posed above, revolves around the extent to which people identify with the police as agents of order and stability and cleave to police as authoritative protectors of security and belonging. They apply Bourdieu's concept of symbolic power to explore how the institution of police consistently inserts itself into processes of meaning production and identity formation within particular social contexts. On Loader and Mulcahy's account, these processes frequently coalesce around the identification of and attempts to control the 'dangerous Other' (ibid: 44), defining the boundaries of the group people believe they share with police via the construction of categories denoting 'in' and 'out', 'us' and 'them'.

In sum, it would seem a social identity that the British police can be said to represent is salient to a significant number of people. There is also much to suggest that identification with this group will be associated with the legitimacy people grant to police, so in the next section I turn to some empirical consideration of this issue.

EVIDENCE FROM A SURVEY CONDUCTED IN ENGLAND AND WALES

The data presented in this chapter come from a survey of England and Wales conducted for the European Union FP7 (Seventh Framework Programme)-funded FIDUCIA project.[1] The survey comprised a nationally representative sample of 1,004 people and utilized telephone interviewing. It contained a range of questions regarding police and the criminal justice system, including contact with and trust in the police, police legitimacy, and identity/citizenship (for further details see Bradford et al. 2015).

Three sets of survey items are of interest. The first related to respondents' affiliation with a social identity that can plausibly be linked with the police. Four items probed how important respondents felt 'being British' and 'being a law-abiding citizen' was to how they saw themselves, and how important it was that others saw them in these ways. Affiliation with these identities was common. Some 73 per cent of respondents said bring British was very or fairly important to how they saw themselves, for example, while fully 76 per cent said being a law-abiding citizen was very important to who they were. Confirmatory Factor Analysis (CFA) was used to generate a measure of

[1] http://www.fiduciaproject.eu.

identity based on the four items.[2] All four loaded onto one construct[3] (hence, 'law-abiding British citizen'), and a scale representing the strength of affiliation with this identity was extracted for analysis (mean=0.0; min=−1.5; max=0.9; SD=0.4). Note that we know neither whether an individual identifying strongly was law-abiding, nor whether they were a British citizen. What is important in the current context is merely that they identified themselves as such.

The second set of items related to police legitimacy. The survey instrument utilized a dual component concept of police legitimacy premised on a psychological account of the phenomenon. Here, legitimacy is envisaged to exist, and the police can be said to be empirically legitimate, when people believe (a) that the police wield their power in appropriate ways and (b) that they have a positive moral duty to obey police instructions. Three survey items tapped, first, into respondent's sense of *normative alignment* with police—the extent to which they believed that police act according to their own moral values (see Hough et al. 2013; Jackson et al. 2012 for sample question wordings). Normative alignment thus reflects the justification of power and the extent to which people feel the police share their broader goals and values. Three further items tapped into respondents' sense that they had a *moral duty to obey* the instructions of police officers. This component of legitimacy relates to classic conceptions concerned with the ability of authorities to command obedience. Here, legitimacy is positioned as an unobservable psychological property that is experienced, on a conscious level, as a sense of duty toward the police.

CFA was again used to validate and extract measures of normative alignment (mean=0.0; min=−2.2; max=1.3; SD=0.64) and moral duty to obey (mean=0.0; min=−3.8; max=2.0; SD=1.2). Levels of police legitimacy were, in this sample, high. For example, some 78 per cent of respondents either tended to agree or strongly agreed that police 'shared their own sense of right and wrong', while 79 per cent thought it was to at least some degree their 'moral duty to back the decisions' made by police.

The final set of measures concerned respondents' perceptions of the procedural fairness and effectiveness of the police, and measures of *trust in police procedural justice* (mean=0.0; min=−2.6; max=1.6; SD=0.73) and *trust in police effectiveness* (mean=0.0; min=−2.9; max=2.4; SD=0.96) were created.

SOCIAL IDENTITY AS A PREDICTOR OF POLICE LEGITIMACY

Table 3.1 shows results from three linear regression models predicting the measures of legitimacy. Included as covariates were the trust measures, the identity measure, and a range of control variables: gender, age, ethnicity, contact with the police, and political ideology (on a simple left–right scale). Very few of these controls were significant in any model, and the coefficients are omitted from the table for visual ease.

[2] CFA is a technique that allows responses to a number of survey items to be combined in order to generate a measure of some underlying psychological construct or 'latent variable'—here, a particular aspect of respondents' social selves which revolves around the idea of being a 'law-abiding citizen'.

[3] 'Loaded onto one factor' means responses to all four of the items were, to a significant degree, caused or explained by one and the same underlying construct.

Table 3.1 Linear regression models predicting assessments of police legitimacy

All scales coded such that high=more
Standardized betas

	Normative alignment	Moral duty to obey	
	Model 1	Model 2	Model 3
Trust in effectiveness	0.06*	0.22***	0.24***
Trust in procedural justice	0.73***	0.26***	0.23***
Social identity	0.11***	0.37***	0.35***
PJ * social identity			−0.11***
R^2	0.68	0.47	0.48
N	915	915	915

* p<0.05, ** p<0.01, *** p<0.001

Model 1 predicted respondents' sense of normative alignment with police. This was very strongly correlated with trust in police procedural justice, and only weakly with trust in police effectiveness. Holding constant the trust measures, though, the identity measure had a specific, 'unique', statistical effect on this component of legitimacy. Respondents who identified more strongly as 'law-abiding British citizens' were significantly more likely to feel that police shared and acted on their own moral values.

Model 2 predicted respondents' sense of duty to obey the police. This was strongly associated with trust in procedural justice, but also with trust in effectiveness. Once again, however, the identity measure had a specific, 'unique', statistical effect on this component of legitimacy. Respondents who identified more strongly as 'law-abiding British citizens' were, holding constant the other variables in the model, considerably more likely to feel they had a moral duty to obey the instructions of police officers. This statistical effect was also large—larger, indeed, than the effects associated with the trust measures. The correlation between social identity and duty to obey seems, in this sample, to be stronger than the association between identity and normative alignment.

Finally, Model 3 presents a piece of additional analysis. Including an interaction term,[4] it tests whether the strength of the association between procedural justice and duty to obey varied by strength of identification as a law-abiding citizen. The interaction term is negative and statistically significant, one interpretation being that people who identified more strongly as law-abiding citizens placed less emphasis on procedural justice when making their legitimacy judgements.[5] I return to this point below.

[4] Interaction terms test whether the statistical effect of one explanatory variable on the response variable varies according to the value of another explanatory variable.

[5] A similar interaction effect was tested in the model predicting normative alignment but it was found not to be significant.

CHANGE AND STABILITY IN POLICE LEGITIMACY

The results from the FIDUCIA survey confirm a strong association between social identity and police legitimacy. Those who identified more strongly as 'law-abiding British citizens' granted police more legitimacy *independent of their assessments of police fairness and effectiveness*. There is an association between police legitimacy and social identity that sits apart from experiences of police behaviour; and this relationship was stronger for the duty to obey component of legitimacy, suggesting that social identity is more important when considering people's motivations to defer to the police as group authorities.

It is important to stress the limited nature of the analysis above. It represents merely a 'snap-shot' of opinion. It cannot access any form or process of change, and it cannot disentangle the arrows of causality. Exploratory as they are, though, these findings provide insights into the dynamics of police legitimacy. On the one hand, identification with a group the police can be argued to represent was associated with legitimacy independent of assessments of police behaviour—it seems police are held legitimate not only on the basis of what they do but also on the basis of what they represent. This implies a mechanism of stability in the relationship between police and public. The association of police with a widely shared social identity may provide a reservoir of support (Easton 1965) that can 'top up' legitimacy in the face of behaviour that would otherwise undermine it. Important in this regard is that procedural justice was a weaker predictor of duty to obey when identification was strong (and remember most people identified strongly). 'Strong identifiers' may be inclined to discount reports or even experiences of police unfairness when making legitimacy judgements, because, perhaps, they believe maintaining structures of authority within the group is important.

Positioned thus, the relationship between social identity and legitimacy becomes, potentially, a barrier to reform processes. Despite repeatedly proven acts of malfeasance, it seems police can rely on the goodwill or at least continued commitment of large sections of the population, relieving the pressure to enact fundamental changes to policy and practice. This is an idea that may resonate with campaigners for reform frustrated by the apparent willingness of many people to accept, live with, or simply ignore policing shown to be unfair.

Yet, while I have concentrated here on one particular social identity that seems to be positively correlated with police legitimacy, people have many other identities, some of which will be *negatively* correlated with police legitimacy; for example, those black British identities which formed in direct reaction and opposition to unfair, illegitimate policing (Gilroy 1987). The continued poor relations between police and many black communities and protest groups demonstrate how oppositional identities can become institutionalized and self-reproducing, particularly perhaps when the non-police group is held in low regard by those who continue to identify with and legitimate the police. Group identities (on both sides) can also predispose suspicion, antagonism, and subsequently stabilize *low* levels of legitimacy within particular contexts and relationships.

On the other hand, though, there is a wealth of evidence that procedural justice effects on legitimacy are very widely spread. People's relationships with police can and do change as a result of police unfairness, and police can and do push people out or pull people into the group they represent, with significant downstream implications for legitimacy (Bradford et al. 2014). Here, the interplay between procedural justice, social identity, and legitimacy provides potential mechanisms for change. First, there will be moments in which police activity is identified as so egregiously unfair that the reservoir of support provided by processes of identification runs dry. Events such as the Stephen Lawrence affair may constitute 'crunch-points', during which legitimacy becomes more volatile as it decouples from identity precisely because police behaviour has undermined any claim to represent a social group people can be proud of and will seek to affiliate with. Indeed the right thing for the 'law-abiding citizen' to do in response to such events might well be *opposing* the police, or at least seeking to bring police behaviour back within acceptable bounds, a process that can be seen clearly in the liberal critiques of police that come to the fore in such moments and which seek reform or better regulation.

Second, and building on this, as demonstrated by Reicher, Stott, and colleagues' work on crowd policing, unfairness can have the effect not only of breaking any sense of shared group membership between police and policed but coalescing the latter around oppositional identities. This might happen in particular immediate, local, contexts such as football matches, but it might also happen on a wider scale and over longer time periods. It is notable that many of the genuine crises in police legitimacy over the last half century have occurred in times and places where police activity and/or other factors have combined to sunder any sense of shared identity between police and policed. The 1984–5 miners' strike, the inner city riots of the 1980s (and 2011), and the poll tax riot of 1989 provide well-known examples. These crises, at least in some cases, presented opportunities for change, not least because they brought into sharp relief the social distance between police and (some of) the policed, and the problems this distance created.

In conclusion, it increasingly seems that procedural justice or injustice can have both affective (via identity) and evaluative (direct) effects on legitimacy. Yet identity also seems to shape legitimacy in ways independent from procedural justice. Which of these processes predominates will be context-dependent and vary over time and space, and the prevalence of one over the other may go some way toward explaining why the extent of police legitimacy changes—and equally why it does not. Along no doubt with other factors, the association of the police with a widely shared social identity is likely to be one reason why its legitimacy has not collapsed and, indeed, has remained at a relatively high level despite the history of the last 50 years.

This process relies on a particular ideology that links police with broadly inclusive notions of nation and citizenship, however, and as such it is contingent. Police behaviour—and wider social and political forces—that promote the idea the police do *not* share a community of feeling and affect with the policed will damage legitimacy. If people are made to feel, for example by discriminatory social policies, that they are not 'British citizens' accorded the rights and respect due to them as full members of society, then the extent to which they feel police represent them and are worthy of their support will be diminished. The legitimacy of the police cannot be separated from wider patterns of identity formation shaped by multiple social, cultural, and economic processes, and it is entirely possible that the link between police and a widely shared social identity might in the future be attenuated or broken.

REFERENCES

Bradford, B., Jackson, J., and Hough, M. (2015), *Trust and Attitudes to Justice Abroad. Testing the Legitimacy Model on 'New-crimes' and Addressing Supra-national Trust and Institutional Legitimacy*, Fiducia Project.

Bradford, B., Murphy, K., and Jackson, J. (2014), 'Officers as Mirrors: Policing, Procedural Justice and the (Re)production of Social Identity', *British Journal of Criminology*, 54, 4: 527–50.

Braithwaite, V. (2013), 'Resistant and Dismissive Defiance Toward Tax Authorities', in A. Crawford and A. Hucklesby (eds), *Legitimacy and Compliance in Criminal Justice*, London: Routledge: 91–115.

Brown, J. (ed.) (2013), *The Future of Policing*, London: Routledge.

Burke, P.J. and Stets, J. (2009), *Social Identity Theory*, Oxford: Oxford University Press.

DCLG (2011), *Citizenship Survey 2009/10*, London: Department of Communities and Local Government.

Cremer de, D. and Tyler, T.R. (2005), 'Am I Respected or Not? Inclusion and Reputation as Issues in Group Membership', *Social Justice Research*, 18, 2: 121–53.

Drury, J. and Reicher, S. (2000), 'Collective Action and Psychological Change: The Emergence of New Social Identities', *British Journal of Social Psychology*, 39, 4: 579–604.

Easton, D. (1965), *A Systems Analysis of Political Life*, Chicago: University of Chicago Press.

Emsley, C. (1999), *Gendarmes and the State in Nineteenth Century Europe*, Oxford: Oxford University Press.

Ericson, R. (1975), *Criminal Reactions: The Labelling Perspective*, London: Ashgate.

Gilroy, P. (1987), *There Ain't No Black in the Union Jack*, London: Routledge.

Girling, E., Loader, I., and Sparks, R. (2000), *Crime and Social Control in Middle England: Questions of Order in an English Town*, London: Routledge.

Harkin, D. (2014), 'The Police and Punishment: Understanding the Pains of Policing', *Theoretical Criminology*, 19, 1: 43–58.

Heath, A., Rothon, C., and Anderson, R. (2005), 'Who Feels British', *Sociology Working Paper 2005–05*, Department of Sociology, University of Oxford.

Hogg, M.A. (2001), 'A Social Identity Theory of Leadership', *Personality and Social Psychology Review*, 5, 3: 184–200.

Hough, M., Jackson, J., and Bradford, B. (2013), 'The Governance of Criminal Justice, Legitimacy and Trust', in S. Body-Gendrot, R. Lévy, M. Hough, S. Snacken, and K. Kerezsi (eds), *The Routledge Handbook of European Criminology*, Abingdon: Routledge: 243–65.

Jackson, J. and Bradford, B. (2010), 'Measuring Public Confidence in the Police: Is the PSA23 Target Fit For Purpose?', *Policing: A Journal of Policy and Practice* 4, 3: 241–8.

Jackson, J., Bradford, B., Hough, M., Myhill, A., Quinton, P., and Tyler, T.R. (2012), 'Why Do People Comply with the Law? Legitimacy and the Influence of Legal Institutions', *British Journal of Criminology*, 52, 6: 1051–71.

Jackson, J., Bradford, B., Stanko, E.A., and Hohl, K. (2013), *Just Authority? Trust in the Police in England and Wales*, London: Routledge.

Loader, I. and Mulcahy, A. (2003), *Policing and the Condition of England: Memory, Politics and Culture*, Oxford: Clarendon Press.

Mackenzie, S. and Henry, A. (2009), *Community Policing: A Review of the Evidence*, Edinburgh: Scottish Government.

Mazerolle, L., Bennett, S., Davis, J., Sargeant, E., and Manning, M. (2013), *Legitimacy in Policing*, Washington, DC, USA: Office of Community Oriented Policing Services, US Department of Justice.

MYHILL, A. and QUINTON, P. (2011), *It's a Fair Cop? Police Legitimacy, Public Cooperation, and Crime Reduction. An Interpretive Evidence Commentary*, London: NPIA.

NEWBURN, T. (2008), 'Policing since 1945', in T. Newburn (ed.), *Handbook of Policing*, Abingdon: Routledge: 90–114.

ONS (2015), Crime Statistics, Focus on Public Perceptions of Crime and the Police, and the Personal Well-being of Victims: 2013 to 2014, London: Office for National Statistics.

REINER, R. (2010), *The Politics of the Police*, 4th edn, Oxford: Oxford University Press.

ROSENBAUM, D.P., SCHUCK, A.M., COSTELLO, S.K., HAWKINS, D.F., and RING, M.K. (2005), 'Attitudes toward the Police: The Effects of Direct and Vicarious Experience', *Police Quarterly*, 8, 3: 343–65.

SINDALL, K., STURGIS, P., and JENNINGS, W. (2012), 'Public Confidence in the Police: A Time-Series Analysis', *British Journal of Criminology*, 52, 4: 744–64.

STOTT, C., HOGGETT, J., and PEARSON, G. (2011), '"Keeping the Peace": Social Identity, Procedural Justice and the Policing of Football Crowds', *British Journal of Criminology*, 52, 2: 381–99.

SUNSHINE, J. and TYLER T.R. (2003), 'Moral Solidarity, Identification with the Community, and the Importance of Procedural Justice: The Police as Prototypical Representatives of a Group's Moral Values', *Social Psychology Quarterly*, 66, 2: 153–65.

TAJFEL, H. (1978), 'Inter-individual Behavior and Intergroup Behavior', in H. Tajfel (ed.), *Differentiation Between Groups: Studies in the Social Psychology of Intergroup Relations*, London: Academic Press: 27–60.

TAYLOR, I. (1999), *Crime in Context*, Cambridge: Polity Press.

TYLER, T.R. (2006), *Why People Obey the Law*, Princeton: Princeton University Press.

TYLER, T.R. and BLADER, S. (2000), *Cooperation in Groups: Procedural Justice, Social Identity, and Behavioral Engagement*, Philadelphia, PA: Psychology Press.

TYLER, T.R. and HUO, Y.J. (2002), *Trust in the Law*, New York: Russell Sage Foundation.

TYLER, T.R. and WAKSLAK, C.J. (2004), 'Profiling and Police Legitimacy: Procedural Justice, Attributions of Motive, and Acceptance of Police Authority', *Criminology*, 42, 2: 253–81.

WÜNSCH, D. and HOHL, K. (2009), 'Evidencing a "Good Practice Model" of Police Communication: The Impact of Local Policing Newsletters on Public Confidence', *Policing: A Journal of Policy and Practice*, 3, 4: 331–9.

4

PATROLLING THE BORDERS OF RISK: THE NEW BIFURCATION OF PROBATION SERVICES IN ENGLAND & WALES

Gwen Robinson

INTRODUCTION

To argue that a volume dedicated to analyses of the *Changing Contours of Criminal Justice* would be incomplete without a consideration of the probation field would be a serious understatement. The English and Welsh probation service is among the longest established in Europe (Vanstone 2004), but its recent history has been characterized by significant and rapid changes. Not only has the probation service been exposed to the influences of the kinds of broad social and political developments which have affected the punishment field more generally, but it has also been subject to a number of specific strategies designed to change the way probation is organized and delivered (Mair and Burke 2012; Robinson et al. 2013). Yet in the criminal justice landscape, probation is something of a 'Cinderella' figure, which has often been neglected by scholars of punishment, as well as being relatively invisible to the general public (Robinson 2016). These aspects of probation were recognized by scholars who established a Probation Studies Unit (PSU) at the University of Oxford Centre for Criminological Research in the mid-1990s. In her address to the first colloquium held by the PSU in 1996, Ros Burnett commented on the contradictory position of the probation service being, on the one hand, 'in a pivotal position in the criminal justice system' but, on the other, one of the least frequently visited sites of research, compared with courts, prisons, and the police (Burnett 1997: 116).

Although a number of interrelated factors have influenced the evolution of probation, one of the most significant has been the rise of risk-based reasoning, which has increasingly affected the discourses, practices, and organization of probation work, especially since the 1990s. That risk had, by the end of the first decade of the new century, become an important feature of the culture of probation practice was evidenced in a large study commissioned by the National Offender Management Service as part of its Offender Engagement Programme, launched in 2010 (Rex 2012). In this study, probation practitioners from three Probation Trusts identified *reducing risk*—alongside engaging meaningfully with offenders—as a primary and uncontested element of 'good quality' supervision (Robinson et al. 2014). More recently, however, risk has been shifted from the ethos to the architecture of probation. In the context of a wide-ranging programme of government reforms known as *Transforming Rehabilitation* (TR), probation services in England and Wales have been reconfigured according to a logic of risk, such that old structures have been dissolved and replaced with a National Probation Service responsible for the supervision of high-risk offenders, and twenty-one Community Rehabilitation Companies (CRCs) responsible for the supervision of medium- and low-risk offenders (Ministry of Justice 2013a).

The *Transforming Rehabilitation* (Ministry of Justice 2013b, 2013c) reforms have attracted criticism on a number of grounds—not least because they have transferred a substantial portion of what have for more than a century been public sector probation services to the private sector (e.g. see Allen 2013; Fitzgibbon and Lea 2014).[1] This chapter, however, takes a different stance. It develops a distinct critique of TR, centred upon what I will term the *institutionalization of risk* in the probation context. I will argue that these reforms have created a new 'bordered penality' (Aas 2014) in the probation field that belies the service's knowledge and understanding of risk: that is, a system with new barriers and gaps between services and a potential new battleground between separate organizations in which definitions of risk may well be contested. Ultimately, the chapter questions the legitimacy of the new arrangement for the effective management and rehabilitation of offenders in the community. The chapter begins with an overview of the rise of risk in the probation context, which emphasizes the importance of risk thinking to the re-legitimation of probation services in the last two decades. It then goes on to analyse the impact of the *institutionalization of risk* in the probation field, under a number of thematic headings. These concern, in turn, the creation of new silos of provision; the construction of risk in the new framework; the imbalance of power between the National Probation Service (NPS) and the CRCs; the risk/resources nexus; and possible bifurcation of the purposes of probation services.

THE RISE OF RISK IN THE PROBATION CONTEXT

In the last 20 years, risk has come to dominate probation discourse and practice in England and Wales, with risk-thinking evolving under a number of influences (Robinson 2002, forthcoming). On a macro-level, sociologists have postulated a growing consciousness of risk at the level of society or governance in the latter part of the twentieth century which has impacted many areas of public administration, including criminal justice (e.g. Beck 1992; Giddens 1990). In respect of probation, the 1990s brought legislative changes which placed a new onus on the probation service to

[1] During 2014–15, twenty of the twenty-one contracts to run the CRCs were awarded to private sector companies, the majority in partnership with other organizations.

assess the risks posed to the public by offenders in its pre-sentence reports, and subsequently the service's ability to assess risk, to share information about risk with other agencies, and its acceptance of 'risk management' as a key part of its role became central to its external legitimacy as part of the public protection infrastructure (Kemshall 2003; Nash 2006). Risk was further promoted and embedded under the influence of an international effective practice or 'What Works' movement, which saw the service develop its approach to offender assessment in line with the 'risk principle' at the heart of the Risk-Need-Responsivity (RNR) model of rehabilitation developed by Canadian correctional researchers (Bonta and Andrews 2007). Dictating that offenders posing higher levels of risk of reoffending should be prioritized for resource-intensive rehabilitative interventions because they were most likely to benefit from them, the RNR model emphasized the key role of the assessment of this dimension of risk (alongside risk of harm) and prompted the development of offender assessment instruments capable of assessing dynamic risk factors (Raynor et al. 2000).[2] This culminated in the development of OASys (the Offender Assessment System) by the Home Office,[3] which was introduced for use by probation services and prisons in the early 2000s. By the turn of the century, then, risk had become a key mechanism for operationalizing the twin agendas of public protection and effective rehabilitation, and had come to be accepted as a legitimate means for the service to ration its resources (Robinson 2003).

The idea that resources should follow risk was central to the subsequent introduction and implementation of an Offender Management Model (OMM) in the probation service in the mid-2000s (NOMS 2005). Developed by a senior probation manager seconded to the National Offender Management Service, the OMM introduced a 'tiering framework' to probation services, which sought to structure resource allocation in line with assessments of risk. The framework consisted of four tiers, designed to reflect increasing risk profiles, ranging from low resource intensity (Tier 1) to the highest level (Tier 4) for those offenders assessed as posing high levels of risk of harm and/or reoffending and therefore warranting intensive resources and/or oversight (see Turley et al. 2011: Annex B). Central to the OMM was the idea that those allocated to higher tiers (3 and 4) should be managed by professionally qualified probation officers (POs), whilst lower tier offenders could be managed by probation service officers (PSOs) without the same levels of qualification.

Although the introduction of the Offender Management Model—and indeed the concept of offender management more generally—did not evade criticism (e.g. see Raynor and Maguire 2006; Robinson 2005), and research commissioned by the

[2] Whereas actuarial risk assessment relies upon static factors (such as criminal history, age, gender, previous disposals), risk/need assessment relies on the practitioner's ability to elicit accurate information about dynamic (changeable) variables which have been shown to be predictive of reoffending. Dynamic risk factors are often referred to as 'criminogenic needs'. Academic researchers at Oxford's PSU, in partnership with Warwickshire probation service, developed risk/need assessment instruments for both adult and young offenders (Baker 2005; Roberts et al. 1996).

[3] OASys was designed to meet a comprehensive specification, such that it included both an assessment of reconviction (incorporating both static and dynamic factors) and a structured format for the assessment of risk of harm. It also provided a system for translating the OASys assessment into a supervision or sentence plan.

Ministry of Justice indicated that its implementation was not without problems (Turley et al. 2011), a strength of the model, that has become apparent ten years on, is its systemic design which allowed (in theory at least) for the movement of offenders between the four tiers following their initial allocation. It was thus a dynamic model which had the capacity to be responsive to changes in levels of risk over the course of a community order or licence. The OMM was also predicated on an understanding of risk as a multi-dimensional concept. These are aspects of offender management which have, to a significant extent, been lost in the context of TR reforms, as I will discuss further below.

IN WITH THE NEW: RISK AND PROBATION AFTER *TRANSFORMING REHABILITATION*

Although other ideological and political currents have played important roles in shaping the *Transforming Rehabilitation* reforms,[4] it is indisputable that the rise of risk thinking in probation—and in particular the mantra that 'resources should follow risk'—has played a significant role as one of its key drivers. In the following sections I will examine the consequences of TR from the perspective of risk.

NEW SILOS, NEW BORDERS

A consequence of *Transforming Rehabilitation* has been the construction of a new architecture of probation services. During 2014, the existing thirty-five public sector Probation Trusts were dissolved and replaced with two separate organizational structures: an NPS responsible for the supervision of 'high risk' offenders, and twenty-one CRCs responsible for the supervision of 'medium- and low-risk' offenders (Ministry of Justice 2013a). In this new context, offenders are assigned (at the point of sentencing) to one of two new organizational structures on the basis of their individual risk profile.

The creation of new organizational structures designed to take responsibility for different populations of offenders has ruptured the systemic model of risk management which was at the heart of the OMM. In its place is an essentially static system of separate containers or silos, with new boundaries that appear to be designed to classify and exclude. This new arrangement resembles, at least to some degree, the architecture of the prison estate, with its distinct containers, wherein each accommodates a separate population sorted on the basis of a (security) risk classification. It also appears to bear some of the hallmarks of Aas's (2014) conception of 'bordered penality': that is, a system predicated on ideas about membership and exclusion, and which may produce distinct types of justice. Within the reconfigured field, then, the border

[4] Drivers of the *Transforming Rehabilitation* reforms include the economic imperatives of austerity and neo-liberal thinking regarding the role of the state in service delivery (e.g. see Burke and Collett 2015; Fitzgibbon and Lea 2014).

takes on a new significance and arguably generates new problems for effective risk management.

In any context, the very existence of silos implies gaps, and the existence of a border creates new barriers to the kinds of everyday risk communication and knowledge exchange which had become part of the normal cultural fabric of probation practice. Former colleagues are now employed by separate organizations in different sectors of the criminal justice field, and must communicate through a new border or interface. The risks associated with this arrangement were pointed out by the then Chair of the Probation Chiefs Association, in her evidence to the House of Commons Justice Committee just prior to the implementation of TR:

> Where currently we have one simple model of an offender manager managing the offender's entire journey through their order or licence, we now potentially have a bureaucratic system to put in place that ensures that information moves between two sets of organizations. We all know that points of data and information transfer are potential points of risk.
>
> (Hall quoted in House of Commons Justice Committee 2014: 22–3)

Indeed, it is well known that failures to share or communicate information have emerged from numerous high-profile inquiries into cases of serious offences committed by people under probation or licence supervision, as well as in cases of child deaths in which social services and other agencies have been found wanting (Fitzgibbon 2011). As Fitzgibbon has argued, probation and social work agencies already face a culture of blame when things go wrong: arguably this could be amplified if, in the future, they go wrong in the gap between the new silos between probation services, for example during the transfer of a case across the 'interface' (Fitzgibbon 2011, 2013).

THE (RE)CONSTRUCTION OF RISK

A key question in the reconfigured field of probation concerns the construction of risk and, in particular, the border between 'high' and 'medium' risk, which delimits the separate territories of the new NPS and CRC silos. That 'risk of serious harm' was to become the key dimension of risk in the reconfigured probation field was evident in the Ministry of Justice's January 2013 consultation document *Transforming Rehabilitation: A Revolution in the Way We Manage Offenders*:

> We will not take any risks in protecting the public and the public sector Probation Service will retain ultimate responsibility for public protection and will manage directly those offenders who pose the highest risk of serious harm to the public—this group will include cases subject to Multi-Agency Public Protection Arrangements. They will also continue to carry out assessments of the risk of harm posed by each offender, advise the courts and Parole Board and handle most breach cases. The Probation Service performs a vital role in protecting the public and managing risk—I am determined to preserve that.
>
> (2013b: 6)

The Ministry of Justice's response to the consultation continued in the same vein, explicitly defining 'the high risk cohort' in the planned new structure as 'offenders falling under Multi-Agency Public Protection Arrangements (MAPPA), typically those who have committed a sexual/violent offence, and offenders who do not fall under MAPPA but are assessed as high or very high risk of serious harm (RoSH)' (Ministry of Justice 2013c: 46). Subsequently, guidance on procedures for allocating cases within the new structure confirmed that, post-TR, probation services are relying on a narrow definition of 'high risk': one which is solely concerned with *risk of serious harm* and ignores the dimension of risk that is concerned with probability (NOMS 2014a).

TR then not only privileges risk as the dominant principle for classifying offenders, but it also privileges one dimension of risk. It thus fails to reflect the dynamic and multi-dimensional understanding of the concept which has developed in probation over the last 20 years.[5] To put this another way, the caseload of the new NPS does not correspond to the population of offenders managed at Tier 4 under the framework of the OMM, which included—in theory at least—prolific offenders (posing a very high risk of reoffending) not assessed as posing a high risk of harm. Thus, under the new framework, some types of 'high risk' escape NPS supervision, qualifying instead for supervision by a CRC.

A further observation about the construction of 'high risk' in the post-TR world concerns the particular—and, I would suggest, controversial—ways in which high risk of serious harm has been operationalized. For example, cases allocated automatically to the NPS include all cases meeting MAPPA criteria; yet it is generally accepted that some MAPPA cases (e.g. some registered sex offenders) will not pose a serious risk of harm in the present. Thus, some categories of cases automatically allocated to the NPS appear to defy the 'risk of serious harm' label,[6] whilst (as noted above) other categories of 'high risk' fall within the remit of a CRC. This fact did not go unnoticed in the first report of Her Majesty's Inspectorate of Probation (HMIP) following the implementation of TR:

> In making our judgements about the likely level of risk of serious harm posed by offenders, we noticed that some of the cases automatically allocated to the NPS, for example, because of MAPPA status, were not judged to be likely to commit further sexual or violent harm in the future. Conversely, many of the cases allocated to CRCs, particularly perpetrators of domestic abuse, who were reasonably assessed as medium risk of serious harm, were felt to be more likely to reoffend again in a violent way. While we accept this is a situation which has arisen from a correct interpretation of case allocation [policy], we think that it is worth highlighting that in many medium risk of serious harm cases appropriately allocated to CRCs, there are public protection issues.
>
> (HMIP 2014: 33)

As is clear from this extract, the probation inspectorate was not prepared to be openly critical of the case allocation policy instituted by the TR reforms, pointing instead to

[5] In their joint response to the Coalition government's TR consultation paper, the Probation Chiefs Association and the Probation Association (both now defunct) concurred: '"Risk of harm" is not the right factor on which to divide the work... If a line had to be drawn between the public probation service and contracted services, we think this should be at low risk of harm' (PCA/PA 2013: paras 18 and 22).

[6] Cases qualifying for automatic allocation to the NPS are set out in a Probation Instruction (NOMS 2014a) and include 'exceptional public interest cases'; offenders subject to deferred sentences; and offenders awaiting deportation.

its implications for CRCs: namely, that many complex, demanding cases will continue to fall to CRCs for supervision (see also Clare 2015). A further implication, then, of this case allocation policy—and the constructions of 'high risk' at issue—is that both organizations will need to retain experienced, professionally qualified staff. In support of this argument, it is worth noting that research has demonstrated that when serious further offences are committed by people subject to community supervision, they tend not to be committed by people assessed as 'high risk' on any dimension. This is not because of a deficit in risk assessment technologies or skills, but rather because risk of harm (unlike risk of reoffending) is notoriously difficult to predict.[7] For example, Craissati and Sindall's (2009) analysis of ninety-four serious further offences committed by offenders under supervision in London concluded that this was a heterogeneous group in terms of characteristics and risk profiles, with the majority assessed as posing no more than a 'medium risk' of harm.

AN IMBALANCE OF POWER

The TR consultation document published in January 2013 was clear that the new NPS, to be located in the public sector, would enjoy a strong and valued position in the proposed new framework of probation services. Sure enough, post-implementation, the NPS was given sole responsibility for working in and with the courts and other public bodies within the criminal justice system, such as the Parole Board. It was also given sole responsibility for conducting initial assessments; making decisions about the allocation of cases between the new range of providers; and enabling other providers (including CRCs) to access information about offenders. The TR reforms have therefore created a system in which there is an inherent power imbalance between the two main organizational structures. Not only does the NPS control definitions of (high) risk, but it is also the dominant decision-making body and the point of liaison with other powerful decision-makers. It thus occupies a space between the CRCs and the other (public sector) decision-making bodies in the criminal justice system, creating another new border in the probation field. A correlate of this power imbalance is the creation of a potential battleground at the interface between the two organizations on which definitions of 'high risk' may be contested and fought over.

One such context for potential conflict is the new 'risk escalation' process, which is detailed in a forty-nine-page Probation Instruction (NOMS 2014b). In the event that a CRC wishes to refer a case back to the NPS following an assessment of escalating risk, the NPS retains decision-making power: it can reject such a case if it does not concur with the CRC's assessment of risk. In a practical sense, this is far from ideal because when an offender's risk does escalate, it often requires an immediate response, not a protracted negotiation. But more fundamentally, this means that in the battle over risk the NPS has the high ground.

[7] A new actuarial tool to assess 'Risk of Serious Recidivism' (RSR) has been made available to the NPS. It calculates the likelihood that an individual will commit a serious sexual or violent offence, based on static factors. However, according to the Probation Inspectorate, its early use indicates that it tends not to identify many cases for NPS supervision that would not already be captured on the basis of MAPPA categorization or a longer-standing, clinical assessment of risk of harm derived from the OASys assessment instrument (HMIP 2014: 4).

In light of the above observations, it is perhaps unsurprising that in a case study of the emergence and progress of one CRC, some probation officers reported frustration and status anxiety in light of their exclusion from several areas of work which had become NPS territory: principally, working with 'high risk' offenders, working in the courts, and writing court and parole reports. These are all aspects of probation work which many qualified staff particularly enjoy and which have sometimes motivated people to undertake professional training in probation. In the same study, several interviewees alluded to the idea of the NPS as 'the elite' organization, casting the CRC in the role of 'second class' probation (Robinson et al. 2016). This notion of CRCs as second-class organizations may have something to do with the stigma that many probation staff feel about moving into private sector employment, having qualified and previously practised in a public sector organization. But it belies the fact that, as we have seen, both silos need professionally qualified probation staff. However, the capacity of CRCs to retain such staff in an environment in which the NPS is generally perceived as the superior organization is doubtful. Furthermore, it is far from clear whether and how CRCs will be incentivized to invest in professional training for their staff when this is not a requirement, and when they are likely to be looking for opportunities to cut costs with an eye to maximizing profit (e.g. Leftly 2015; Ministry of Justice 2015a).

THE RISK–RESOURCES NEXUS

I have argued that the formula 'resources follow risk', which has developed and come to be an accepted logic for probation work in the last 20 years, has clearly influenced the decision to split probation services in the way described. However, it is unclear whether much attention has been paid to the potential consequences for this formula of the institutionalization of risk; by which I mean the creation of separate new organizational silos in which 'high' and 'medium/low' risk populations are to be managed.

The idea that resources should follow risk would appear to demand a degree of flexibility in the former, in order to cope with fluctuations in the latter. In other words, decisions about risk (levels, profiles, etc.) should precede decisions about resource allocation, and changes in distributions of risk could demand changes in the distribution of resources. In the context of the tiering framework introduced by the OMM, an increase in the population of Tier 4 offenders, for example, would suggest a need to increase the number of probation staff assigned to work with Tier 4 cases, which (assuming no overall increase in resources) would have consequences for the numbers of staff available to work across Tiers 1–3. Within a single silo, this kind of flexibility would appear to be possible—in theory at least. However, within a system in which resources have been split across more than one silo, as is the case post-TR, this kind of flexibility becomes much more problematic, because the new borders of risk are not permeable. So, for example, an increase in the population of offenders meeting 'high risk' criteria cannot be addressed by transferring staff from one silo (a CRC) to the NPS, so either more suitably qualified workers must be found elsewhere, or the current workforce must manage larger caseloads.

In such a scenario, the most likely solution is a recalibration of risk. Where resources are (relatively) fixed in space, and thus less flexibly deployable, it is definitions and thresholds of risk which must be adaptable. Put another way, now that new organizational structures have been created (in the form of the NPS and CRCs), it seems likely that definitions of (high) risk may well need to shift in the future to fit those relatively inflexible resource silos. Constructions of risk, it seems, may well have to be responsive to particular configurations of resources, rather than the other way round (see Fitzgibbon 2011; Robinson 2002 for examples of this). Given the regional structures of probation resources, it is possible that in the future definitions of risk may become much more localized, reflecting differential resources, as well as differences and changes in offender populations.

We also need to consider the potential consequences of changes in the availability and spread of resources for probation work. As a publically funded organization, the NPS is of course vulnerable to budget cuts in the context of more general pressure on the Ministry of Justice and public spending. Assuming stability in the flow and risk profiles of offenders being sentenced and leaving prison, shrinking NPS resources suggest higher caseloads for its employees, and/or an upward adjustment of the 'high risk' threshold to maintain existing caseloads. Given the decision-making power of the NPS in the new probation landscape, such a scenario is quite feasible. A consequence of this, however, would be an unexpected quantitative bulge in CRC caseloads, as well as a change in the risk profile of CRC cases. For organizations concerned with profit, such a bulge may be a welcome development, although it may also adversely affect the quality of service that can be delivered. In the new framework, therefore, any adjustment in the risk/resources nexus in the public sector NPS will have implications for the rest of the system.

A BIFURCATION OF PURPOSE?

During the 1990s, some commentators claimed that the rise of risk-based reasoning in the probation context was a clear indication that the probation service had become part of the 'new penology' described by Feeley and Simon (1992). For example, Kemshall et al. (1997: 217) argued that the service was 'engaged in a transition from the traditional concerns of the rehabilitative and welfare arm of criminal justice... and the language of "need" to an agency of crime control concerned with the accurate prediction and effective management of offender risk'. However, subsequent research on the implementation of risk in practice by probation services offered evidence that risk-based reasoning did not necessarily dampen probation's rehabilitative efforts (e.g. Robinson 2002; Robinson and McNeill 2004). Meanwhile, other developments in the practice context in the last decade—which have included a growing interest in desistance-focused practice (e.g. Weaver and McNeill 2010)—have further bolstered probation's traditional emphasis on helping offenders change, albeit alongside new priorities to manage risk effectively.

However, the new bifurcation of probation services brings questions of purpose very much back into focus. The rhetoric of *Transforming Rehabilitation* centres on the idea of putting rehabilitation firmly at the heart of what providers of probation services deliver, and it is clear that at least part of the rationale for contracting out rehabilitation services (via the creation of CRCs and a market of providers) has centred on stimulating innovation and creative partnerships in the provision of effective rehabilitation. For example, the consultation paper published in January 2013 stated that 'We will put in place a system which benefits from the innovation and versatility of private and voluntary sector providers...to support the rehabilitation of offenders' (Ministry of Justice 2013b: 9). Although there is tentative evidence that at least some CRCs wish to reclaim rehabilitation and pitch it as their primary business (Robinson et al. 2016), it is too early to evaluate whether (or how) this aspect of TR will be realized across the twenty-one companies. But what of the National Probation Service? The clear message is that its priority is public protection. This is an end that can be achieved via a number of different means, among them rehabilitative ones (Robinson and McNeill 2004). However, at present it is not possible to ascertain the ways in which the NPS is working to achieve public protection, nor the size of the caseloads individual NPS probation workers are managing. It could then be the case that the NPS is performing—or perhaps being pushed toward—a role akin to quarantining, or what Garland (2000) has termed 'penal marking' and 'warehousing': that is, identifying and then containing all those categories of offenders about whom the public is alarmed. Will the NPS simply be performing a role that is akin to patrolling the borders of risk?

It is difficult to predict with any certainty how this lack of clarity about purposes and working methods will affect sentencing practice and, more broadly, the perceived legitimacy of community sentences. How judges and magistrates feel about passing community sentences in the reconfigured probation field is a topic worthy of urgent research attention. Not only do we know little about sentencers' views of private sector provision (Allen 2013), but there is the added issue—referred to above—of CRCs' exclusion from direct work in and with the courts. At best, this will serve to restrict sentencers' direct engagement with CRC staff; at worst it may reduce sentencers' confidence in the delivery of community order requirements. We do know that sentencers' use of community penalties has already been in decline since 2006, and that there was a 7 per cent drop in new community orders commencing in the 12 months to September 2014 (Ministry of Justice 2015b). The TR reforms thus have the potential to deepen a current crisis of legitimacy for community sentencing.

CONCLUSION

Through its developing expertise in the assessment and management of risk since the mid-1990s, the probation service in England and Wales strengthened its legitimacy as a part of the penal system capable of contributing to politically important agendas centred on public protection and reducing reoffending. The organization's approach recognized and developed strategies to work with the dynamic and multidimensional aspects of risk in relation to offending, and it has been at the forefront of developments in multi-agency cooperation around risk management and reduction (e.g. Pycroft and Gough 2010). It is therefore ironic that the probation service should find itself in its current position: fragmented almost beyond recognition and facing new threats to the legitimacy of its newly formed constituent parts.

In this chapter I have developed a distinct critique of TR, centred upon what I have termed the *institutionalization of risk* in the probation context. I have suggested that this institutionalization of risk in the probation context is far from unproblematic, and in fact appears to present a number of potential new risks and challenges to the effective operation of probation services. These largely stem from the creation of a new architecture for probation services: that is, a system with new barriers and gaps between parts of the criminal justice system that need to work cooperatively. Not only have we seen the construction of a new border between the main organizations responsible for delivering probation services (i.e. between the NPS and CRCs), but also between the CRCs and the courts, which are the main commissioners of probation work (Morgan 2003). This new gap between the courts and what are now the main providers of probation services is unlikely to reverse a steady decline in the use of community sentences unless serious and sustained attention is paid to developing lines of communication between these key parts of the criminal justice system. Other new risks and challenges I have identified centre on the enhanced likelihood of communication failures across borders, as well as disputes over risk at the interface between the new main providers of probation services. There will also, I have argued, be ongoing challenges around the distribution of resources across the new, separate silos. These concern both the medium- and longer-term sustainability of a policy of 'resources following risk', and the retention of skilled and experienced staff in separate silos with responsibility for managing differently risky caseloads. Could it be that what we have witnessed in the context of the *Transforming Rehabilitation* reforms constitutes the corruption of risk by the needs of the market for the formal commodification (McCulloch and McNeill 2007) of probation work?

REFERENCES

AAS, K.F. (2014), 'Bordered Penality: Precarious Membership and Abnormal Justice', *Punishment and Society*, 16, 5: 520–41.

ALLEN, R. (2013), 'Paying for Justice: Prison and Probation in an Age of Austerity', *British Journal of Community Justice*, 11, 1: 5–18.

BAKER, K. (2005), 'Assessment in Youth Justice: Professional Discretion and the Use of Asset', *Youth Justice*, 5, 2: 106–22.

BECK, U. (1992), *Risk Society: Towards a New Modernity*, London: SAGE.

BONTA, J. and ANDREWS, D. (2007), *Risk-Need-Responsivity Model of Offender Assessment and Rehabilitation*, Public Safety Canada 2007–06.

BURKE, L. and COLLETT, S. (2015), *Delivering Rehabilitation*, Abingdon: Routledge.

BURNETT, R. (1997), 'An Agenda for Research', in R. Burnett (ed.), *The Probation Service: Responding to Change. Proceedings of the Probation Studies Unit First Colloquium*, Oxford: University of Oxford Centre for Criminological Research.

CLARE, R. (2015), 'Maintaining Professional Practice: The Role of the Probation Officer in Community Rehabilitation Companies', *Probation Journal*, 62, 1: 49–61.

Craissati, J. and Sindall, O. (2009), 'Serious Further Offences: An Exploration of Risk and Typologies', *Probation Journal*, 56, 1: 9–28.

Feeley, M. and Simon, J. (1992), 'The New Penology: Notes on the Emerging Strategy of Corrections and its Implications', *Criminology*, 30, 4: 449–74.

Fitzgibbon, W. (2011), *Probation and Social Work on Trial: Violent Offenders and Child Abusers*, Basingstoke: Palgrave Macmillan.

Fitzgibbon, W. (2013), 'Risk and Privatisation', *British Journal of Community Justice*, 22, 2–3: 87–90.

Fitzgibbon, W. and Lea, J. (2014), 'Defending Probation: Beyond Privatization and Security', *European Journal of Probation*, 6, 1: 6–23.

Garland, D. (2000), 'The Culture of High Crime Societies', *British Journal of Criminology*, 40, 3: 347–75.

Giddens, A. (1990), *The Consequences of Modernity*, Cambridge: Polity Press.

HM Inspectorate of Probation (2014), *Transforming Rehabilitation: Early Implementation*, London: HMIP.

House of Commons Justice Committee (2014), *Crime Reduction Policies: A Co-ordinated Approach? Interim Report of the Government's Transforming Rehabilitation Programme*, London: TSO.

Kemshall, H. (2003), *Understanding Risk in Criminal Justice*, Maidenhead: Open University Press.

Kemshall, H., Parton, N., Walsh, M., and Waterson, J. (1997), 'Concepts of Risk in Relation to Organizational Structure and Functioning within the Personal Social Services and Probation', *Social Policy and Administration*, 31, 3: 213–32.

Leftly, M. (2015), 'Probation Service Faces Job Cuts under Sodexo', *The Independent*, 31 March.

Mair, G. and Burke, L. (2012), *Redemption, Rehabilitation and Risk Management: A History of Probation*, London: Routledge.

McCulloch, P. and McNeill, F. (2007), 'Consumer Society, Commodification and Offender Management', *Criminology and Criminal Justice*, 7, 3: 223–42.

Ministry of Justice (2013a), *Target Operation Model: Rehabilitation Programme*, London: Ministry of Justice.

Ministry of Justice (2013b), *Transforming Rehabilitation: A Revolution in the Way We Manage Offenders*, Consultation Paper CP1/2013, London: Ministry of Justice.

Ministry of Justice (2013c), *Transforming Rehabilitation: A Strategy for Reform*, Cm 8619, London: Ministry of Justice.

Ministry of Justice (2015a), *A Competent Workforce to Transform Rehabilitation*, London: Ministry of Justice.

Ministry of Justice (2015b), *Offender Management Statistics Quarterly Bulletin, England & Wales*, 29 January, London: Ministry of Justice.

Morgan, R. (2003), 'Thinking about the Demand for Probation Services', *Probation Journal*, 50, 1: 7–19.

Nash, M. (2006), *Public Protection and the Criminal Justice Process*, Oxford: Oxford University Press.

NOMS (2005), *The NOMS Offender Management Model*, London: National Offender Management Service.

NOMS (2014a), 'Case Allocation', *Probation Instruction 05/2014*.

NOMS (2014b), 'Risk Escalation', *Probation Instruction 57/2014*.

Probation Chiefs Association and Probation Association (2013), *Transforming Rehabilitation: A Joint Response*, http://www.probationassociation.co.uk/media/730/probation-review-pca-pa-response-final.pdf.

Pycroft, A. and Gough, D. (2010), *Multi-Agency Working in Criminal Justice*, Bristol: Policy Press.

Raynor, P. and Maguire, M. (2006), 'End-to-End or End in Tears? Prospects for the Effectiveness of the National Offender Management Model', in M. Hough, R. Allen, and U. Padel (eds), *Reshaping Probation and Prisons*, Bristol: Policy Press.

Raynor, P., Kynch, J., Roberts, C., and Merrington, S. (2000), *Risk and Need Assessment in Probation Services: an Evaluation*, Home Office Research Study 211, London: Home Office.

Rex, S. (2012), 'The Offender Engagement Programme: Rationale and Objectives', *Eurovista*, 2, 1: 6–9.

Roberts, C., Burnett, R., Kirby, A., and Hamill, H. (1996), *A System for Evaluating Probation Practice*, Probation Studies Unit Report No. 1, Oxford: Centre for Criminological Research, University of Oxford.

Robinson, G. (2002), 'Exploring Risk Management in the Probation Service: Contemporary Developments in England and Wales', *Punishment & Society*, 4, 1: 5–25.

Robinson, G. (2003), 'Risk and Risk Assessment', in W.-H. Chui and M. Nellis (eds), *Moving Probation Forward: Evidence, Arguments and Practice*, Harlow: Pearson Education.

Robinson, G. (2005), 'What Works in Offender Management?', *Howard Journal of Criminal Justice*, 44, 3: 307–18.

Robinson, G. (2016), 'The Cinderella Complex: Punishment, Society and Community Sanctions', *Punishment and Society*, 18, 1: 95–112.

Robinson, G. (forthcoming), 'The Rise of the Risk Paradigm in Criminal Justice', in C. Trotter, G. McIvor, and F. McNeill (eds), *Beyond the Risk Paradigm: Rethinking Practices in Criminal Justice*, Abingdon: Routledge.

Robinson, G. and McNeill, F. (2004), 'Purposes Matter: Examining the "Ends" of Probation Practice', in G. Mair (ed.), *What Matters in Probation*, Cullompton: Willan: 277–304.

Robinson, G., Burke, L., and Millings, M. (2016), 'Criminal Justice Identities in Transition; the Case of Devolved Probation Services in England and Wales', *British Journal of Criminology*, 56, 1: 161–78.

Robinson, G., McNeill, F., and Maruna, S. (2013), 'Punishment in Society: The Improbable Persistence of Probation and other Community Sanctions and Measures', in J. Simon and R. Sparks (eds), *The SAGE Handbook of Punishment and Society*, London: SAGE.

Robinson, G., Priede, C., Farrall, S., Shapland, J., and McNeill, F. (2014), 'Understanding "Quality" in Probation Practice: Frontline Perspectives in England & Wales', *Criminology and Criminal Justice*, 14, 2: 123–42.

Turley, C., Ludford, H., Callana, M., and Barnard, M. (2011), *Delivering the NOMS Offender Management Model: Practitioner Views from the Offender Management Community Cohort Study*, Ministry of Justice Research Series 7/11, London: Ministry of Justice.

Vanstone, M. (2004), *Supervising Offenders in the Community*, Aldershot: Ashgate.

Weaver, B. and McNeill, F. (2010), *Changing Lives? Desistance Research and Offender Management*, Scottish Centre for Crime and Justice Research: Project Report No.03/2010.

5

RACE, ETHNICITY, AND CRIMINAL JUSTICE: REFOCUSING THE CRIMINOLOGICAL GAZE

*Alpa Parmar**

INTRODUCTION

Race is central to understanding the criminal justice system. When we examine policing, sentencing, imprisonment, and victimization through the prism of race, the constancy of disproportionate outcomes and examples of racism is stark. Criminology has an important role to play in reshaping the contours of the race-crime debate. However, in order to do so, it must first refocus the criminological gaze to reveal the centrality of race.

Although race in the criminal justice system, as elsewhere, remains a colour-coded phenomenon, it increasingly intersects with notions of culture, religion, and ethnicity. Racism is pliable and affects groups differently. Current issues of interest to criminologists such as terrorism, child sexual exploitation, policing, and migration reveal how the race-crime debate has shifted significantly over the last 50 years from a focus on skin colour to one concerned with culture, religion, citizenship, and belonging.

Official figures demonstrate that black and minority ethnic groups are over-represented at each stage of the criminal justice process. There are multiple, complex reasons for the over-representation, including individual and institutional racism and structural-contextual norms that prevent change. Gaps in data and research further confound our understanding. So although the disproportionate outcomes are visible, we do not know exactly how or why the patterns persist. While egregious abuses of the criminal justice process have demanded sharper attention towards racism, for the most part, recognition of racism has often been perfunctory. Likewise, although legislation for reform has been implemented, change has often been merely symbolic or artificial. As a result, the criminal justice system remains a key structure that racializes populations.

* Thanks to Mary Bosworth, Roger Hood, Carolyn Hoyle, Sarah Turnbull, Kate West, and Lucia Zedner for their valuable comments in drafting this chapter.

Criminologists have sought to unravel the processes by which crime and criminal justice are racialized by documenting disproportionate outcomes for minority ethnic groups (Bowling and Phillips 2007). Roger Hood's research on race and sentencing in 1992 was one of the first to reveal disturbing evidence of racism in sentencing in Crown Courts in the UK. Since then, the over-representation of minority ethnic groups at the sentencing stage has continued. Unfortunately, criminological attention to race over the last two decades has been sporadic at best and ambivalent at worst, with race often treated as a supplemental rather than constitutive aspect of analysis (Spivakovsky 2012). Typically, scholars observe the numerical incidence of race rather than explore its social construction.

In this chapter, I acknowledge the importance of official statistics while highlighting their limitations for understanding the nature of the relationship between race and crime. I argue that questions about the social construction of race are often absent within academic analyses of crime at a time when race increasingly intersects with criminalization. I draw on my own research with British Asian Muslims to demonstrate the textured nature of these intersections. I discuss the criminological silence about race and contextualize this silence within broader debates across the social sciences following the official charge of institutional racism levelled at the British police in 1999. Criminology is in a pivotal position in being able to influence criminal justice policy and practice. Given this, I suggest that clearer recognition of racialization within criminology is necessary for the future of criminal justice.

RACE MATTERS

Race matters in the criminal justice system. From policing to prisons, black and Asian minority ethnic groups are over-represented when compared to their proportion in the general population. While such figures provide much-needed evidence, they are not static and depend on the changing contextual focus on certain types of crime. Asian people, for instance, were under-represented in stop-and-search figures until 2005, but since then have been gradually more likely to be stopped and searched. At the time of writing, they are almost twice as likely as whites to be stopped and searched by the police. Asians are also now more likely than any other ethnic group to be stopped under suspicion of drug offences (Ministry of Justice 2015). Careful interpretation of broad changes is also needed because wide ethnic categories can mask internal heterogeneity. For example, the increased policing of Asians largely affects Britons of Pakistani or Bangladeshi background (likely to be Muslims) rather than all Asians per se. This variation raises questions about how visible indicators of ethnic and religious background affect the policing of some groups rather than others, and how the racialization of religion and geographical space intersects with policing. They also show that responses to crime are deeply implicated in how race is produced through place and everyday encounters.

Statistics indicate that people of mixed ethnic backgrounds are increasingly likely to be victimized (Ministry of Justice 2015). The same figures show that black people are more likely to be homicide victims than white and Asian people. Looking closely at policing, we can see that black, Asian, and mixed people were more likely to be stopped and searched and that the proportions of these stops resulting in arrest were higher for black and mixed-background people. Whether this is because of higher rates of actual offending among these groups is impossible to know by looking at police activity statistics alone. Rates of prosecution and sentencing were also higher for black and mixed-background people. Average custodial sentences were higher for Asian and black offenders and higher for all black and minority ethnic groups compared to white offenders. White people make up 74 per cent of the British national prison population while 4.1 per cent are mixed ethnic group people, 7.7 per cent are Asian, 12.1 per cent are black, and 2 per cent are those from Chinese or other backgrounds.[1] When compared to the general population[2] we see that black people are particularly over-represented in custody, followed by mixed ethnic group and Asian people.

The reasons for ethnic disproportionalities at various stages of the criminal justice process are not mutually exclusive. Part of the explanation may be attributable to differences in population structures, offending histories, harsher treatment towards specific offences, and the racializing consequences of certain patterns of sentencing. A recent example can be found in the sentencing of 'joint enterprise' cases through which racialized constructions of gangs have acted as a prosecution resource to incarcerate black and mixed-race men for lengthy sentences for violence and murder, despite the fact that those convicted were not directly involved in the commission of the offence or present when the offence took place (see Rozenberg 2016; Williams and Clarke 2016).[3]

The effects of racial disproportionality at the various stages of the criminal justice system are most apparent in the prison population, underscoring the cumulative effects of decisions in the criminal justice process. The numbers are perturbing not only for their disproportionality, but also for their stability over the years. That is to say, despite recognition of the gross over-representation of black and increasingly of Asian people in the criminal justice system, the patterns are becoming more entrenched and incommensurate with proportions in the population.

Official figures provide a picture of the criminal justice process and the workings of practitioners (e.g. police activity) rather than the reality of crime. More precise offending rates could be found in self-report studies, yet these are seldom used in criminological research. The Crime Survey for England and Wales (Office for National Statistics 2016) does include some information on offending levels, however it is not detailed according to the ethnic background of participants and the focus is on victimization. Studies that have utilized self-reporting have not had large enough samples of

[1] Ethnicity data was missing for 1% of prisoners in 2014 (Ministry of Justice 2015).

[2] 2011 Census figures report that the UK population is: 87.1% White; 2% Mixed; 5% Asian/Asian British Indian/Pakistani/Bangladeshi (collectively); 3% Black British/African/Caribbean; 0.9% Other ethnic groups; and 0.1% Gypsy/Irish Traveller/Traveller.

[3] The doctrine of joint enterprise refers to where there is more than one party to the same offence, for example where the accused acts in conjunction with the killer but does not strike the blow that causes death. In 2015 the Commons Justice Select Committee suggested that the threshold for establishing culpability in such cases should be higher. In February 2016 the Supreme Court concluded that the assessment of guilt in such cases had been incorrectly applied for 30 years (Rozenberg 2016).

minority ethnic group participants (see e.g. McAra and McVie 2010; Wikström et al. 2012) and have been overshadowed by methodological concerns about the veracity of disclosure (Bowling 1990; Junger 1989).

The elision of official figures and perceptions of real rates of offending amongst black and Asian people stymie progressive policies and public understanding of the relationship between race and crime. Better attention also needs to be paid to the gaps in the data that obscure meaningful analysis. For instance, although the Ministry of Justice statistics on race and the criminal justice system provide an overview of the breakdown of offence types according to ethnic groups, these data do not provide a comprehensive breakdown according to gender. In other cases, important detail is not given and instead broad offence categories like 'drug offences' are used without information about the distribution of the types of drug offences, which vary greatly in terms of seriousness and ethnic group involvement.

THE SHIFTING CONTOURS OF RACE AND CRIMINAL JUSTICE

Although official figures provide powerful indicators of the over-representation of minority ethnic groups, as I have shown the data does not always disclose the reasons behind these patterns. Structural inequalities are obscured and the ways in which race is recast in contemporary societies are not revealed by numbers alone. In the following section I draw on my own research with British Asian Muslims to demonstrate how a closer analysis of race and its intersections with gender, class, and religion is necessary.

RACIALIZED CRIMINALIZATION OF BRITISH MUSLIMS: FROM VICTIMS TO VILLAINS?

Charting the racialized criminalization of Muslims shows the socio-conceptual agility of race and the pliability of stereotypes when they are attached to notions of criminality. Although British Asian Muslims have become a focus of socio-political attention over the last two decades, they have not always been considered in this fashion. In early studies of crime and deviance, British Asian men, including Asian Muslim men, were perceived as largely law-abiding, subservient, and protected by the close-knit communities to which they were assumed to belong (Mawby and Batta 1980; Wardak 2000). Police stereotypes framed Asian men as deferential and more likely to be victims, whilst also characterizing them as involved in crimes of deceit and deception including fraud and forgery and immigration status violations (Jefferson 1992). Essentialized notions of Asian communities as operating high levels of social control due to their close-knit structures resulted in the perception that Asians were able to sort out problems of crime internally (Mawby and Batta 1980).

The shift in perceptions of British Asians, and the focus on Muslim otherness in particular, ostensibly began at the time of the Rushdie affair in 1989, which represented

Muslims as fanatical, religiously extreme, and violent. Asian Muslim men became the new 'folk devils' in Claire Alexander's (2000) terms, criminalized and racialized an inherent threat. Cultural values once presumed to be protective against crime and deviance were reframed as risky. Asian Muslim men were represented in the media, as members of violent gangs and embroiled in drug use (Alexander 2000; Webster 1997), although they did not feature highly in official crime figures.

Civil disturbances across Northern British towns in 2001 between predominantly British Pakistani and Bangladeshi young men and the police placed British Muslim men more clearly at the centre of the criminalizing process. Media and official accounts focused on cultural rather than structural interpretations of the disorder. The racism and structural disadvantage experienced by those involved in rioting was denied and instead the focus was on the incompatibility between Asian Muslim values and Britishness (Alexander 2004; Kundnani 2001). Closer analysis revealed that the disturbances were more likely to have been sparked by structural factors, including fear of racism about a planned march by the English Defence League, youth disenfranchisement from unemployment, and social inequality in the Northern towns. However, dominant explanations blamed religio-cultural factors and their perceived cultural clash with Western values. An alleged lack of 'community cohesion' between the local white and Asian communities was instead cited as the explanation for the civil disturbances (Home Office 2001).

Since the London terrorist attacks in 2005, Muslim communities in the UK have been regarded as inherently suspect (Pantazis and Pemberton 2009), perceived as 'the enemy within' (Hudson 2007). Concerns over Muslim people's susceptibility towards radicalization and terrorism have been a constant feature in media and public debate. The British Muslim identities of the perpetrators raised questions about citizenship and the strength of belonging felt by minority ethnic groups in Britain. Government counter-terrorist strategies have shaped and responded to these concerns, often with counter-productive consequences. The police's implementation of counter-terrorist legislation, for example, has led to the disenfranchisement of Asian males. Suspicionless searches under section 44 of the Terrorism Act 2000 led to deeper disenfranchisement of British Asian Muslim males (Parmar 2011).

Despite the repeal of section 44 by the Protection of Freedoms Act 2012 and its criticisms (Ashworth and Zedner 2014), use of stop and search under other legislation including the Police and Criminal Evidence Act 1984 has continued to increase for Asians (Ministry of Justice 2015). In a study I conducted, policed Asians questioned their ethnic identities and felt an erosion of their sense of belonging to the UK when they were stopped and searched under terrorist and other legislation. Asian men who were stopped and searched who were not Muslim, felt resentful and aggrieved that they had been misrecognized by the police. As one young Sikh man told me, 'we're all brown in the police's eyes, and to them, that means we're Muslim'. Intra-ethnic tensions were created and accentuated as Asian Sikhs and Hindus felt a need to distance themselves from their Asian Muslim friends. Some deliberately engaged in practices to subvert perceptions that they may be Muslim. For example, one Asian Hindu male recounted that he engaged in performative aspects of masculinity such as excessive drinking to signal markers of 'Britishness' to the outside world (Parmar 2014).

The government's official counter-terrorism strategy 'Prevent' (Home Office 2006, 2015) has been widely criticized for being ill-conceived, pursuing contradictory aims, and using dubious religious criteria as proxies for risk (Kundnani 2009; Spalek and McDonald 2011). The police implementation of Prevent blurs police priorities which, on the one hand, aim to build confidence between the police and Asian communities whilst, on the other, engage in modes of surveillance of the same communities (Ashworth and Zedner 2014).[4] The reach of the Prevent duty has also now been widened to include nurseries, schools, higher education establishments, and landlords all of whom now have a duty to prevent people from being drawn into terrorism and to report anyone they suspect of being radicalized (Home Office Prevent Guidance 2015).

British Asian Muslim identities are racialized and securitized (Hussain and Bagguley 2012). Fears about Muslims tend to go beyond discourses of terrorism and radicalization to spill into fears about migration, sexual predation, and gang culture. Asian Muslims, previously perceived to be victims rather than offenders, are now deemed the 'ultimate other' and the current moral panic extends beyond the nation state (Nayak and Kehily 2013). The fear has become uncontainable and crosses ethnic boundaries as Asian and black Muslims are all implicated; the layers of race and religion intersect in ways that have been previously unaddressed. The boundaries of gender are also transgressed as Muslim women are feared for harbouring terrorists or for travelling to Syria to fight. Perceptions of Muslim women, once framed as oppressed victims of control by Asian Muslim men, are thus disrupting the traditional criminological binary of victim and offender. When we take stock of how racialized criminalization has affected Asian Muslim communities, we see the very pliability of race and why tracing its shifting course is necessary and important.

The complexity of the racialization of crime and its consequences are further revealed in the child sexual exploitation cases reported across the UK over the last five years (Jay Review 2014; Serious Case Review Oxfordshire 2015).[5] Media reports fixed on the Muslim identities of the perpetrators, applying stereotypical tropes of misogyny and religious backwardness to interpret the systematic abuse. At the same time, however, such cases demonstrate the multi-dimensional and intersectional realities of gender, culture, religion, class, and race. For example, Asian Pakistani perpetrators were reported to have told white female victims that their parents were racist towards Asian Muslim men in order to gain their trust. Perpetrators' understanding of police fears about being labelled racist were also thought to have protected the abusers from earlier detection. The offenders' complicity in invoking racialized criminal stereotypes adds a further layer of complexity: for example, one of the perpetrators of sexual abuse in Oxford suggested that his attendance at religious classes (*madrassas*) had left him with little understanding of women.

[4] Also see e.g. Project Champion: http://www.statewatch.org/news/2010/oct/uk-project-champion-police-report.pdf.

[5] In 2013 systematic child exploitation was found and reported in Rotherham, South Yorkshire, and led to the Jay Review published in 2015. Further cases in Rochdale, Greater Manchester, and Oxford were revealed and perpetrators were sentenced in 2013–15. All the perpetrators were reported to be 'Asian' and of Asian-Pakistani background, but this often masked the diversity of ethnic identities and nationalities of the perpetrators who were described as North African and of Pakistani heritage. The victims were predominantly white British females; some were under the care of social services.

Despite the complex realities of race and its connections with crime, mainstream criminology has tended to overlook the subtleties described thus far. In their aim to better reflect the lived experiences of race and crime today, Phillips and Webster (2014), in a recent edited collection, sought to make visible these intersections and to encourage criminological questions that go beyond the dyad of racial disparities in patterns of offending and racial discrimination in criminal justice administration (see also Smith 2014). Contributions to the volume questioned the veracity of static ethnic categories and made clear the utility of theorizing the intersections between race, gender, and citizenship (e.g. Bosworth and Kellezi 2014; Parmar 2014). Criminology has a significant role to play in revealing the racialized realities of the criminal justice system and beyond, in particular through close studies that interrogate the relationships between race, ethnic identities, and crime. However, discussions of race have been muted in broader criminological debates, and it is to this issue I now turn.

CRIMINOLOGY AND THE SILENCE OF RACE

As an interdisciplinary field, criminology is well placed to incorporate ideas from the sociology of race and ethnic and postcolonial studies. However, much of the field appears uninterested and even today relatively little criminological research directly focuses on race. More often, it is one factor to be considered rather than a substantive focus of the research.

The lack of attention to race and ethnicity is neither new, nor peculiar to criminology. With the origins of many of their fundamental assumptions and methodologies based in managing 'race relations', the social sciences have always struggled to address race and racism. Qualitative approaches began with the ethnology of the primitive, while quantitative studies were linked to eugenics and the obsession to categorize and count human beings (Omi and Winant 2015; Marks 1995; Zuberi 2001). In criminology, historical blindness about the legitimation of systemic violence and punishment of innocent populations through colonization (Agozino 2003) provides a context to understanding the current ways in which discussions of race are muted. As Pfohl puts it, 'there is something hauntingly unreal about scholarship that focuses almost exclusively on individual violations of the law while ignoring the systemic terrorism imposed upon innocent people by colonialism' and its continuing legacies (2016: 124).

Together such factors have allowed criminologies of policing, punishment, terrorism, and migration to develop as though race were not central to each. Gulfs have developed between empirical work and theoretical developments. For instance, the complex matrix of issues around citizenship, national identity, religious identity, racialization, ethnic identity, and Islamophobia have been addressed sociologically (Meer and Nayak 2015), but the connections between this empirical work and theoretical developments in criminology have not often been made.

Silences are not simply absences but also need to be understood as a constitutive feature of discourse and practice. As race disappears from public discourse, the naming of racism also becomes difficult and unfashionable. Those who call it out are considered, in the words of critical race feminist theorist Ahmed (2010), 'killjoys'. Such matters are clearly illustrated in the UK, by the public inquiry into the murder of Stephen Lawrence and underscored by charges of institutional racism in the subsequent Macpherson Report of 1999 (Solomos 2003).

Criminologically speaking, the Macpherson Report (1999)[6] seemed to place police racism and racial injustice on the social and political agenda, vindicating criminological research on the over-policing and under-protection of minority ethnic communities (Bowling 1999) and racist police cultures (Smith and Gray 1983; see Loader this volume). Gradually, however, Macpherson's definition of the process of institutional racism was criticized for its inherent contradictions and tautological definition. Institutional racism was described as 'unwitting prejudice, ignorance and thoughtlessness' (Macpherson 1999: s6.34) and thereby almost accidental, while at the same time framed as a 'collective failure'. It was also restricted to a form of inaction rather than an ongoing series of proactive actions that shaped institutional norms (Ahmed 2004a).

The dislocated and ahistorical presentation of the concept of racism (by Macpherson) dissolved links between it, and liberalism and colonialism, obscuring the ties between racism, structure, and governance (Hesse 2004). Consequently, it appears that race operates from an altered, less obvious, and hidden place than it once did and is used ambiguously through policies of policing and securitization (Kapoor 2011). Denial of the meanings and the effects of race obscures the problem of discrimination and the failure to recognize everyday racism (Harries 2014). Against such a backdrop, racism is presented as a remnant of the past and any residual effects of past inequality are reconceived as an individual, personal problem (Gilroy 2012).

Amidst the silence, however, the reality of racism in the criminal justice system is glaring. Minority ethnic groups continue to be over-policed, the numbers of black deaths in police custody continue (and news of them marginalized; see e.g. Greenslade 2016), racism (and its denial) leads to death in prisons (Mubarek Inquiry 2006), and lengthy sentences are imposed on black and Asian people in court (Ministry of Justice 2013, 2015). Racism in the criminal justice system persists despite its official disavowal. Yet, racism is expressed through discourses about citizenship and belonging and recast in commentaries on security and religion, as discussed above. Interpersonal instances of racial hatred have not disappeared, but rather they are also transmitted and mediated by reference to the familiar idea that Britishness and non-whiteness are mutually exclusive (Gilroy 2012).

Notwithstanding criminology's strong ties to criminal justice professions through research partnerships and the increased onus from funding bodies for knowledge to be co-produced, exchanged, and to have impact (HEFCE 2011), there remains considerable distance in how knowledge about race is integrated into the practice of criminal justice. For example, despite the general acceptance of the 16+1 ethnic group classifi-

[6] The Macpherson Report 1999 followed an inquiry into the racist murder of black teenager Stephen Lawrence by a group of five white men in London in 1993. The police investigation into the murder was found to be flawed in numerous ways including the treatment of Lawrence's family, handling of the evidence, and refusal to accept that the attack was racially motivated. In the report the police were labelled as institutionally racist.

cation scheme since 2003 to reflect the census ethnic categories to order the statistics on race and criminal justice (Ministry of Justice 2006), the police, in custody and informally, still adopt the IC (identity code)[7] to describe a person's appearance according to the police officer's perception. IC developed in the 1970s to enable descriptions to be conveyed by the police over the radio and denotes a much less refined ethnic categorization scheme. Notwithstanding the fact that assigning ethnic background according to a visual assessment by the officer risks perpetuating racial stereotypes, the IC ethnic groups lack conceptual coherence and elide nationality, skin colour, and language. The fact that these codes are still used and provide the first form of categorization by the police is problematic for a couple of reasons. In addition to the continued legitimation of ethnic categorization based on a person's appearance, use of the IC devalues the importance of self-ethnic identification that followed from recommendations in the Macpherson Report (1999). This provides a stark example of the distance between the aims of criminal justice reform and actual practice outcomes. Although diversity training, targets for minority ethnic representation, and wider policy changes were introduced alongside ethnic self-identification in Macpherson's recommendations, the resulting changes were cosmetic rather than cultural, diversity training was mocked, and targets for representation were resented for being tokenistic (Foster, Newburn, and Souhami 2005; Loftus 2009).

CONTINUING THE CONVERSATION: WHY CRIMINOLOGY SHOULD TALK ABOUT RACE

Over the past 50 years, some key pieces of scholarship have engaged directly with race. More than ten years ago, Bowling and Phillips (2003) called for a minority research agenda which included the need to move beyond essentialist categorizations of ethnicity within criminology and underscored the role of black and minority group representation in the academy and criminal justice professions. Bowling and Phillips' call was heeded, and notable pieces of scholarship already did address, or have since, the inherently racializing aspects of the criminal justice system (e.g. Bosworth 2004; Tonry 1996; Wacquant 2000). The complexities of 'otherness' when affixed to criminality have been theorized (Hudson 2008) and whiteness interrogated (Hudson 2006; Smith 2014). Criminological spaces where race, citizenship, and punishment overlap have been illuminated (Bosworth 2013; Phillips and Webster 2014) and methodologies that work to reveal how race is produced in everyday criminalized encounters have been written (Goffman 2014; Maher 1997).

Roger Hood's study of sentencing in 1992 was one of the first pieces of work to examine empirically the over-representation of black and Asian people among those convicted in courts in the West Midlands. The study found that 5 per cent of the

[7] Identity Codes, sometimes also called Phoenix Codes or PNC are as follows: IC1 = White North European, IC2 = White South European, IC3 = Black, IC4 = Asian, IC5 = Chinese, Japanese, Nepalese, or Other South East Asian, IC6 = Arabic or North African, IC9 = Unknown. Street wardens, security guards, and bouncers also use IC on a regular basis.

over-representation could be attributed to the 'race of the defendant effect' and the remaining disparity was related to 'legally relevant' criteria such as employment status and the prior record of offenders. Today, a more direct interpretation of racism may have been applied and the racialized aspects of the 'legally relevant' factors of unemployment and prior offending would have been unpacked in explaining the findings. Indeed, there is now greater awareness that what we see in the court setting are the cumulative consequences of the intersection of various forms of disadvantage that disproportionately impact on black and minority ethnic groups. Hood's research was published at a time when racial disparities in criminal justice were discussed within ethnographic or smaller-scale studies and a broader, national picture of such rates was unavailable. In a pre-Macpherson era, where explicit discussions about race were few and far between, Hood's study was important for demonstrating the different perceptions held of black and Asian defendants and for highlighting the enduring salience of race, at the stage of the criminal process where equal treatment and a commitment to just outcomes might be expected the most.

Today, despite the changed socio-political context, many of the same issues persist with regard to sentencing. The 2014 sentencing statistics, for example, show that the number of black people convicted and sentenced by the courts for an indictable offence was three times higher (per 1,000 members of the black population), and the number of mixed-background people sentenced was twice as high (per head of their number in the population), than the number of white people convicted and sentenced (per 1,000 members of the white population) (Ministry of Justice 2015). Although 23 years have passed, not much has changed. Hood's (1992) study thus evinces the stickiness of race (Ahmed 2004b) alongside its viscosity (Saldanha 2007) because although the ethnic categories have been updated (for instance, we now have the mixed group), racial disproportionalities in sentencing towards black, Asian, and mixed-ethnic-group people remain. A contemporary example of the continuities amidst change is clearly demonstrated by the #BlackLivesMatter campaign following the killings of Trayvon Martin in 2012 and Michael Brown and Eric Garner in 2014 by US police. Through the instant global connections made possible via social media, the world could galvanize in seemingly unprecedented ways against racism. The intersections of race, gender, citizenship, civil rights, and humanity were made visible with increased zeal. However, the themes of police brutality towards black people were familiar and embedded within the long-standing, global history of race and policing. These cases and the academic and public responses to them simply made race visible (Potter 2015).

Although the collection and publication of official figures on race and crime as required under section 95 of the Criminal Justice Act 1991 is to be applauded, and represents an important change since the publication of Hood's (1992) research, it is clearly important not only to report disproportionality but also to explain it. Statistics are sometimes treated as a proxy for explaining race and racist practice, and this should be resisted. Furthermore, critical attention towards ethnic categories is needed within criminological research as well as official figures, despite the need for statistics to demonstrate validity. For example, use of broad homogenous ethnic categories such as 'Asian', 'mixed', and the catch-all 'Chinese/other' by official crime statistics remain unrepresentative of the more closely defined ethnic identities that people recognize and live by. Similarly, greater attention is needed to the fact that ethnic group boundaries are fluid rather than concrete. Recognition of race in research refers to more than treating ethnicity as a factor to be considered or added in, alongside gender, once the main theory or analytical approach has been crafted. The complexities and contradictions of racialization should be engaged with, rather than understood in binary terms, which assume a top-down relationship between the oppressor and the oppressed. This would better reflect reality which is often a complex web of social relations where strategies of resistance, contestation, and complicity in racialization coalesce (Bosworth 2003; Gilroy 1993; Knepper 2008).

Scholarship should also pay more theoretical and empirical attention to the significance of whiteness in criminology and the multiple formations of race, an area largely overlooked (with the exception of a few scholars, e.g. Smith 2014; Webster 2008). Deconstruction of the homogeneity of whiteness is key to this approach, as is the understanding of how racial boundaries are formed and mutually constituted. For example, interactions with criminal justice can make people feel non-white and as though their racial identity has changed following incarceration or interactions with the police (Saperstein and Penner 2010). Thus analyses of whiteness can go beyond questions of class and counterclaims that attention to whiteness shifts attention from those who are black, marginalized, or oppressed. Rather, deeper attention to whiteness may reveal how racial inequalities are maintained in the criminal justice system through a lack of ethnic diversity and the ways in which criminal behaviour is explained. Critical attention to the structures that maintain whiteness may also promote reflection within the academy about the under-representation of minority ethnic group scholars within British criminology and the impact this may have on the scope and quality of its inquiry (Alexander 2011; Smith 2014).

This chapter has drawn attention to the ways in which race remains sub-textual within mainstream criminology. Many of the new areas gaining momentum in criminology, including terrorism, borders, and security studies, could incorporate race as a constitutive part of their endeavour by recognizing how racialization is a feature of and underpins these contemporary issues. Closer attention to the concepts employed in criminology provides one approach. Everyday terms, including gangs, migrant, citizenship, and Muslim, are racialized concepts and should be acknowledged as such. Intersectional criminological frameworks are more likely to enable an understanding of how race, gender, class, and other social cleavages converge with crime, and have dynamic effects, beyond analyses that regard such factors are merely cumulative (Collins 2000; Potter 2015). Studies of race and crime could also be deepened through collaborative projects that transgress the qualitative-quantitative academic division of labour that continues to shape criminology. Generative research dialogues across disciplinary and methodological boundaries would also enable ethnographic accounts to get behind the statistics of racial discrimination and racially disproportionate outcomes and help to shift the contours of both criminal justice and criminology.

REFERENCES

AGOZINO, B. (2003), *Counter Colonial Criminology: A Critique of Imperialist Reason*, London: Pluto.

AHMED, S. (2004a), 'Declarations of Whiteness: The Non-Performativity of Anti-Racism', *Borderlands e-journal*, 3, 2.

AHMED, S. (2004b), *The Cultural Politics of Emotion*, Edinburgh: Edinburgh University Press.

AHMED, S. (2010), 'Killing Joy: Feminism and the History of Happiness', *Signs: Journal of Women in Culture and Society*, 35, 3: 571–92.

ALEXANDER, C. (2000), *The Asian Gang: Ethnicity, Identity and Masculinity*, Oxford: Berg.

ALEXANDER, C. (2004), 'Imagining the Asian Gang: Ethnicity, Masculinity and Youth after "the Riots"', *Critical Social Policy*, 24, 4: 526–49.

ALEXANDER, C. (2011), *Sociology's Jurisdiction: Sociology's Identities and Futures for the Discipline*, British Sociological Association Address, 7 April.

ASHWORTH, A. and ZEDNER, L. (2014), *Preventive Justice*, Oxford: Oxford University Press.

BOSWORTH, M. (2003), 'Gender, Race and Sexuality in Prison', in B. Zaitzow and J. Thomas (eds), *Women in Prison: Gender and Social Control*, Boulder: Lynne Rienner.

BOSWORTH, M. (2004), 'Theorizing Race and Punishment: Towards a New Penality', *Critical Criminology*, 12, 2: 221–42.

BOSWORTH, M. (2013), *Immigration Detention*, Oxford: Oxford University Press.

BOSWORTH, M. and KELLEZI, B. (2014), 'Citizenship and Belonging in a Women's Immigration Detention Centre', in C. Phillips and C. Webster, *New Directions in Race, Ethnicity and Crime*, London: Routledge.

BOWLING, B. (1990), 'Conceptual and Methodological Problems in Measuring "Race" Differences in Delinquency: A Reply to Marianne Junger', *British Journal of Criminology*, 30, 3: 483–92.

BOWLING, B. (1999), *Violent Racism: Victimization, Policing and Social Context*, Oxford: Oxford University Press.

BOWLING, B. and PHILLIPS, C. (2003), 'Racism, Ethnicity and Criminology: Developing Minority Perspectives', *British Journal of Criminology*, 43, 2: 269–90.

BOWLING, B. and PHILLIPS, C. (2007), 'Disproportionate and Discriminatory: Reviewing the Evidence on Stop and Search', *Modern Law Review*, 70, 6: 936–61.

COLLINS, P.H. (2000), *Black Feminist Thought: Knowledge, Consciousness and the Politics of Empowerment*, New York: Routledge.

FOSTER, J., NEWBURN, T., and SOUHAMI, A. (2005), *Assessing the Impact of the Stephen Lawrence Inquiry*, Home Office Research Study 294, London: Home Office.

GILROY, P. (1993), *The Black Atlantic: Modernity and Double-Consciousness*, Cambridge, MA: Harvard University Press.

GILROY, P. (2012), '"My Britain Is Fuck All": Zombie Multiculturalism and the Race Politics of Citizenship', *Identities: Global Studies in Culture and Power*, 19, 4: 380–97.

GOFFMAN, A. (2014), *On the Run. Fugitive Life in an American City*, Chicago: University of Chicago Press.

GREENSLADE, R. (2016), 'Why Do UK Media Fail to Cover the Deaths of Black People in Custody?', *The Guardian*, 19 April 2016, available at: http://www.theguardian.com/media/greenslade/2016/apr/19/why-do-uk-media-fail-to-cover-the-deaths-of-black-people-in-custody.

HARRIES, B. (2014), 'We Need to Talk about Race', *Sociology*, 48, 6: 1107–22.

HESSE, B. (2004), 'Discourse on Institutional Racism: The Genealogy of a Concept', in I. Law, D. Phillips, and L. Turney (eds), *Institutional Racism in Higher Education*, London: Trentham.

Higher Education Funding Council for England (HEFCE) (2011), *Higher Education Innovation Funding 2011–12 to 2014–15*, available at: http://www.hefce.ac.uk/Pubs/year/2011/201116.

Home Office (2001), *Community Cohesion*, The Cantle Report, London: HMSO.

Home Office (2006), *Countering International Terrorism: The United Kingdom's Strategy*, London: The Stationery Office.

Home Office (2015), *Revised Prevent Duty Guidance: for England and Wales*, London: Crown Copyright.

HOOD, R. (1992), *Race and Sentencing: A Study in the Crown Court*, Oxford: Clarendon Press.

HUDSON, B. (2006), 'Beyond White Man's Justice: Race, Gender and Justice in Late Modernity', *Theoretical Criminology*, 10, 1: 29–47.

HUDSON, B. (2007), 'Diversity, Crime and Difference', in M. Maguire, R. Morgan, and R. Reiner (eds), *The Oxford Handbook of Criminology*, 4th edn, Oxford: Oxford University Press.

HUDSON, B. (2008), 'Difference, Diversity and Criminology: The Cosmopolitan Vision', *Theoretical Criminology*, 12, 3: 275–92.

HUSSAIN, Y. and BAGGULEY, P. (2012), 'Securitized Citizens: Islamophobia, Racism and the 7/7 London Bombings', *The Sociological Review*, 60, 4: 715–34.

JAY, A. (2014), *Independent Inquiry into Child Sexual Exploitation in Rotherham 1997–2013*, Rotherham Metropolitan Borough Council.

JEFFERSON, T. (1992), 'The Racism of Criminalization: Policing and the Reproduction of the Criminal Other', in L. Gelsthorpe (ed.), *Minority Groups in the Criminal Justice System*, Conference Proceedings of the 21st Cropwood Roundtable Conference, Cambridge: Institute of Criminology.

JUNGER, M. (1989), 'Discrepancies between the Police and Self-Report Data for Dutch Racial Minorities', *British Journal of Criminology*, 30, 3: 273–84.

KAPOOR, N. (2011), 'The Advancement of Racial Neoliberalism in Britain', *Ethnic and Racial Studies*, 36, 6: 1–19.

KNEPPER, P. (2008), 'Rethinking the Racialization of Crime: The Significance of Black Firsts', *Ethnic and Racial Studies*, 31, 3: 503–23.

KUNDNANI, A. (2001), 'From Oldham to Bradford: The Violence of the Violated', *Race & Class*, 43, 2: 41–60.

KUNDNANI, A. (2009), *Spooked: How Not to Prevent Violent Terrorism*, London: Institute of Race Relations.

LOFTUS, B. (2009) *Police Culture in a Changing World*, Oxford: Oxford University Press.

MCARA, L. and MCVIE, S. (2010), 'Youth Crime and Justice: Key Messages from the Edinburgh Study of Youth Transitions and Crime', *Criminology & Criminal Justice*, 10, 2: 179–209.

MACPHERSON, LORD (1999), *The Stephen Lawrence Inquiry*, Cm 4262-I, London: The Stationery Office.

MAHER, L. (1997), *Sexed Work*, Oxford: Oxford University Press.

MARKS, J. (1995), *Human Biodiversity: Genes, Race and History*, Herndon, VA: Aldine/Transaction.

MAWBY, R. and BATTA, I. (1980), *Asians and Crime: The Bradford Experience*, Middlesex: Scope Communication.

MEER, N. and NAYAK, A. (2015), 'Race Ends Where? Race, Racism and Contemporary Sociology', *Sociology*, 39, 6: 3–20.

Ministry of Justice (2003), *Race and the Criminal Justice System: An Overview to the Complete Statistics 2004–2005*, London: Crown Copyright.

Ministry of Justice (2013), *Race and the Criminal Justice System 2012*, London: Crown Copyright.

Ministry of Justice (2015), *Race and the Criminal Justice System 2013–2014*, London: Crown Copyright.

Mubarek Inquiry (2006), *Report of the Zahid Mubarek Inquiry*, London: The Stationery Office.

Nayak, A. and Kehily, M.J. (2013), *Gender, Youth and Culture: Global Masculinities and Femininities*, 2nd edn, Basingstoke: Palgrave Macmillan.

Office for National Statistics (2016), *Crime Survey for England and Wales: Year Ending December 2015*, http://www.ons.gov.uk/peoplepopulationandcommunity/crimeandjustice/bulletins/crimeinenglandandwales/yearendingdecember2015.

Omi, M. and Winant, H. (2015), *Racial Formation in the United States*, 3rd edn, New York: Routledge.

Pantazis, C. and Pemberton, S. (2009), 'From the "Old" to the "New" Suspect Community: Examining the Impacts of Recent UK Counter-Terrorist Legislation', *British Journal of Criminology*, 49, 5: 646–66.

Parmar, A. (2011), 'Stop and Search in London: Counter-Terrorist or Counter-Productive?', *Policing and Society*, 21, 4: 369–82.

Parmar, A. (2014), 'Configuring Ethnic Identities: Resistance as a Response to Counter-Terrorist Policy', in C. Phillips and C. Webster (eds), *New Directions in Race, Ethnicity and Crime*, London: Routledge.

Pfohl, S. (2016), 'The Criminological Imagination in an Age of Global Cybernetic Power', in J. Frauley (ed.), *C Wright Mills and the Criminological Imagination: Prospects for Creative Inquiry*, Abingdon: Routledge.

Phillips, C. and Webster, C. (eds) (2014), *New Directions in Race, Ethnicity and Crime*, London: Routledge.

Potter, H. (2015), *Intersectionality and Criminology: Disrupting and Revolutionizing Studies of Crime*, Abingdon: Routledge.

Rozenberg, J. (2016), 'Correcting the Joint Enterprise Law Won't Lead to Mass Prison Releases', *The Guardian*, available at: http://www.theguardian.com/commentisfree/2016/feb/18/joint-entrerprise-law-corrected-prison-releases-uk-supreme-court

Saldanha, A. (2007), *Psychedelic White: Goa Trance and the Viscosity of Race*, Minneapolis, MN: University of Minnesota Press.

Saperstein, A. and Penner, A. (2010), 'The Race of a Criminal Record: How Incarceration Colors Racial Perceptions', *Social Problems*, 57, 1: 92–113.

Serious Case Review into Child Sexual Exploitation in Oxfordshire (2015), Oxfordshire Safeguarding Board.

Smith, D. and Gray, J. (1983), *Police and People in London*, vol. 4, London: Policy Studies Institute.

Smith, J. (2014), 'Interrogating Whiteness Within Criminology', *Sociology Compass*, 8, 2: 107–18.

Solomos, J. (2003), *Race and Racism in Britain*, 3rd edn, Basingstoke: Palgrave Macmillan.

Spalek, B. and McDonald, L.Z. (2011), *Preventing Religio-Political Extremism amongst Muslim Youth: A Study Exploring Police-Community Partnership*, Birmingham: University of Birmingham.

Spivakovsky, C. (2012), *Racialized Correctional Governance*, Farnham: Ashgate.

TONRY, M. (1996), *Malign Neglect: Race, Crime and Punishment in America*, Oxford: Oxford University Press.

WACQUANT, L. (2000), 'The New "Peculiar Institution": On the Prison as Surrogate Ghetto', *Theoretical Criminology*, 4, 3: 377–89.

WARDAK, A. (2000), *Social Control and Deviance: A South Asian Community in Scotland*, Aldershot: Ashgate.

WEBSTER, C. (1997), 'The Construction of "Asian" Criminality', *International Journal of the Sociology of Law*, 25, 1: 65–86.

WEBSTER, C. (2008), 'Marginalized White Ethnicity, Race and Crime', *Theoretical Criminology*, 12, 3: 293–312.

WIKSTROM, P.-O., OBERWITTLER, D., TREIBER, K., and HARDIE, B. (2012), *Breaking Rules: The Social and Situational Dynamics of Young People's Urban Crime*, Oxford: Oxford University Press.

WILLIAMS, P. and CLARKE, B. (2016), *Dangerous Associations: Joint Enterprise, Gangs and Racism*, London: Centre for Crime and Justice Studies.

ZUBERI, T. (2001), *Thicker than Blood: How Racial Statistics Lie*, Minneapolis, MN: University of Minnesota Press.

PART II

JUSTICE, COURTS, AND SECURITY

6

RESEARCHING THE GLOBAL CRIMINAL COURT

*Ana Aliverti**

INTRODUCTION

The criminal courts are peculiar settings where suspiciousness, mistrust, and an obsession to make the everyday flow of strangers intelligible abound. Preliminary sorting devices are followed by highly formal, ritualistic, staged courtroom ceremonies, in what Pat Carlen described as 'dramaturgical discipline' (1976a: 32). Paul Rock referred to Crown Court proceedings as 'ceremonial, disciplined, and staged' where spatial segregation 'reinforced the symbolic boundaries between groups' (Rock 1993: 27, 208), most notably the insiders (professional and court staff) and the outsiders (the 'civilians', the 'strangers'). Criminal courts can appear hermetically sealed by the various material and symbolic devices that set them aside from the messiness of the social world outside. Seemingly 'blind to variations of condition and climate in the wider world', he (ibid: 263) observed, the parties often seek to prevent that messiness from leaking into the courtroom. The archaic rituals, attires, and formality of language, particularly in the Crown Court, are singular reminders not only of the endurance and importance of tradition for the court system, but also of its resistance to change (Jacobson et al. 2015: 70).

Yet, the criminal court is also an open system 'whose actions are shaped to a considerable extent by its relationship to the larger environment' (Feeley 1979: 281). The courts are not only influenced by the outside world but may also replicate and contribute to reproduce the power relationships within the communities they serve and wider social inequalities (Hood 1962: 74). As socio-legal and criminological scholars have documented, the criminal law and its institutions have played a key role in perpetuating class, gender, and racial inequalities (Bowling and Phillips 2002; Eaton 1986; Hood 1992; McBarnet 1981; McConville et al. 1994). Less criminological attention, however, has been devoted to study how globalization and mass mobility has shaped the criminal justice system.

* I am grateful to the editors of this volume for their helpful comments on earlier drafts. This chapter draws on material from the project entitled: 'Foreigners before the criminal courts: immigration status, deportability and punishment', generously funded by the British Academy. I am also indebted to interviewees and court staff for supporting this project, and to Rachel Seoighe for research assistance.

Criminal justice research in Britain has largely neglected citizenship—and the attendant social hierarchies that stem from it—in contemporary criminal justice practices. In the same way that some ethnographers have conceived of courts as discrete, closed social systems detached from the surrounding social world, criminal justice scholars have worked within a paradigm of national closure. By adopting this bounded, territorialized conception of the criminal justice system and of the state, criminologists have, until recently, failed to place contemporary penal practices in the context of past and present global inequalities—and the role of the state in forging and perpetuating them (see though Aas 2012, 2014; Aliverti 2015a; Bosworth 2012, 2013, 2014; Carrington et al. 2016; Kaufman 2015). In a deeply stratified and globalized world, it is suggested (Aas 2013b), the exercise of the state's penal power can no longer be assumed to be circumscribed by the state's frontiers nor can it be disconnected from geopolitical hierarchies on the global scale.

As Aas puts it, we need to 'locate the state and the exercise of "internal punishment" within the broader sphere of global geopolitical relations' (ibid: 21). Such a project not only entails examining the increased enmeshing of criminal and migration law powers, in what Aas calls 'bordered penality' (2014). It also directs our attention to the mundane enactment and recreation of global hierarchies, or 'globalized stratifications', in the domestic sphere (Bosworth 2014: 135; Bosworth et al. 2008: 270; Phillips 2008: 324). Citizenship and migration status, woven with race and gender, are crucial for understanding the importance of identity in contemporary criminal justice practices and the hierarchies that transpire from them (Hudson and Bramhall 2005; Phillips 2003; Volpp 2000).

Drawing on eighteen interviews with criminal justice operators and the observation of hearings and review of court files in seventy cases from the Birmingham criminal courts during a six-month period from March to August 2015, this chapter delves into the importance of citizenship, and its material and symbolic effects in contemporary criminal justice practices. It starts by drawing attention to the scholarly neglect of questions about diversity, migration, and justice, suggesting that such inattention has deep epistemological roots. It then discusses the 'inner life' of two criminal courts pointing to how the makeup and everyday practices of these courthouses are deeply shaped by globalization, mass mobility, and its control. In sum, this chapter raises broader questions for criminologists and criminal justice scholars researching 'national' criminal justice institutions on the need to rethink these institutions—their role, routines, culture, and challenges—under conditions of mass mobility.

CRIMINAL JUSTICE AND GLOBALIZATION: THE CONTOURS OF A GLOBAL COURT

As Zedner (2004: 167) has observed, the criminal court is 'an emblematic legal institution' and 'a key institution in the relationship between citizen and state'. The courtroom is the civic forum par excellence where citizens are called to account and apprised of their rights and duties (Duff 2011; Duff et al. 2007). The criminal process is, at least in part, shaped by the imperative of imparting civic education to those who appear before the courts and to broader society, and ultimately strengthening social cohesion. Both symbolically and materially, punishment is a paradigmatic form of public and civic dishonour (Wacquant 2014: 287) that purports to repair the ties linking offenders to their fellow citizens that have been severed by crime. Historical and normative accounts of the criminal courts portray them as bounded, territorialized in their jurisdiction, circumscribed by the 'citizenry of a bounded political community' (Fraser 2008: 400). Strongly moulded by this Westphalian model, it is not surprising that ethnographic accounts of the criminal courts have taken for granted the 'frame' of justice. Fraser (2010: 12) explains that justice is assumed 'to concern relations among fellow citizens, to be subject to debate within national publics, and to contemplate redress by national state'. As a consequence, profound social changes in the courts studied by ethnographers and the social world outside have gone unnoticed.

Few, scattered references remind us of those changes, however. In their study of Sheffield's magistrates' court, Bottoms and McClean (1976: 149) identified non-English-speaking defendants as one of the groups most likely to be represented in court because of language barriers. In her work on a London magistrates' court, Carlen (1976a: 36) referred to the police's typology of defendants before it. 'Immigrants and foreigners' were a particularly difficult category to grasp for the police. Eliding race, nationality, and migration status, the 'coloured people' stood out as 'exotic', different, and for that matter hard to decipher, defying the simple moral types within which the police often operate. Even more recent studies continue to gloss over the diversity of the court population brought about by migration, hinting at it by vague allusions to language barriers, the presence of interpreters, and the defendant's prospective deportation (Jacobson et al. 2015: 127, 154, 158, 175). Yet, the daily business of the criminal courts is loaded with traces of the 'border' and its operation, brought home by the court's clientele.

Birmingham, the research site, has witnessed extensive immigration since the 1950s and 1960s during decolonization, and subsequently in the 2000s onwards following the opening of European internal borders to Eastern European countries. Pakistan, India, Ireland, Jamaica, Bangladesh, and Poland feature as the main countries of birth outside Britain of Birmingham residents (Birmingham City Council 2013b: 11). It currently stands as one of the most diverse cities in the country, second only to London, and home to a population more likely to have been born outside the UK and less likely to be white British than the national average.[1] Almost half of its foreign-born population have resided in the UK for less than ten years (ibid).

The staff and clientele of Birmingham courts—particularly in the magistrates' court—mirror the demographic makeup of the city's population. Many of the practitioners and magistrates[2] were born abroad or have parents or grandparents who were,

[1] According to the last census in 2011, 22.2 per cent of its population was born abroad, above the national average of 13.8 per cent (Birmingham City Council 2013b: table 4).

[2] While information on country of birth of magistrates is not available, Birmingham magistracy is on average slightly more ethnically diverse than the national average (Courts and Tribunals Judiciary 2015b). The percentage of judges in the Midlands who identify themselves as black and minority ethnic (BME) is higher than in London, and one of the highest in the country, second only to the South East region (Courts and Tribunals Judiciary 2015a: 9).

and they master several languages. In some cases, solicitors communicate with their clients in Bengali, Urdu, Punjabi, or Polish, and are often able to pick up inaccuracies by court translators. In the Crown Court, the demographic contrast between 'the town and the gown' is starker (Feeley 1979: 122; Rock 1993: 61). It is comparatively a more homogeneous environment where judges[3] are predominantly male, monolingual,[4] and white British. Their style, as Rock (1993: 61) put it, is 'invariably patrician'. It is also more unusual to hear local accents among judges and barristers, than within the solicitors-magistrates circle.

In both sites, it is common to overhear people speaking in languages other than English in corridors and public spaces. Inside the courtrooms, interpreters have become familiar figures. Their frequent appearance to assist witnesses and defendants, or to translate documents, have resulted in the adaptation of the architectural and acoustic setting of the courtroom, and the pace and progress of proceedings, to accommodate them. Interpreters are needed on an everyday basis to assist witnesses and defendants through court proceedings (Aliverti and Seoighe 2017). Daily, court clerks are required to translate official documents, like driving licences and insurance certificates, and gauge their validity to ascertain the defendant's criminal liability. Parties frequently defer to experts or interpreters, or conduct a simple internet search on customs and traditions of other countries to scrutinize the credibility of witnesses.

In one case, involving a Vietnamese man who claimed to be a minor, his barrister confessed to me he had difficulties in persuading the judge that his mother conceived him in her late fifties: 'He has no family in the UK so I need to rely on the interpreter [to find out] if in Vietnam women conceive at 58. Determination of age is very difficult because I can't find proof.' The police found the defendant inside an apartment together with one hundred marihuana plants. He pleaded guilty to the charge of cultivation of cannabis. He had no identity documents to produce. Although the circumstances in which he left Vietnam and arrived into Britain were unclear, he told the court that he left his Vietnamese passport with co-workers in Russia where he had temporarily resided. Upon arriving in the UK in the back of a lorry, he was detained by the police and subsequently released, only to be picked up on the streets by three men, and taken to the flat.[5] Mistrustful of the defendant's vague and erratic version of events, the judge passed a custodial sentence, reducing it only by 20 per cent for his guilty plea and noting: 'I have no idea whether you will be released to the community or be held in [immigration] detention [upon serving your sentence]. Whatever the way you need to comply with the licence order.'

This example illustrates some of the logistical and legal challenges posed by mass migration to the everyday work of the criminal courts. In Birmingham, cases involving people whose identities are not 'fixed', on whom there is little or no reliable 'official' information, and whose final fate depends on decisions made elsewhere are common.

[3] There are fifteen permanent circuit judges at Birmingham Crown Court. I interviewed seven of them, all of whom were male and white. This group is less likely than magistrates to be drawn from the local area; many reside elsewhere.

[4] A number of judges I interviewed mentioned that they speak some French.

[5] The judge suggested that the defendant was trafficked into the UK, however there was no further examination as to whether he was a trafficking victim.

Mass migration and its control have made significant inroads into the courthouse, shaping not only who reaches the courts and why, but also criminal justice routines, especially concerning how and when to liaise with immigration authorities.

Criminal courts are now obliged to inform the Home Office about the sentences passed against foreign nationals and their systems have been adapted accordingly to ensure the smooth routing of this information (National Audit Office 2014: 12).[6] Since the entry into force of the UK Borders Act 2007,[7] non-EEA foreign nationals sentenced to a period of more than 12 months' imprisonment are automatically liable to deportation. Judges have been virtually exonerated from making deportation orders,[8] and Crown Court judges said that they barely make them. One judge put it bluntly:

> I haven't made a deportation order in respect of anybody. I may say 'I hope the Home Office will consider the fact that I regard you as a dangerous individual and your status in this country should be looked at' but I don't make deportation orders and I don't think any judge does really.

A prosecutor at the Complex Crime Unit agreed: 'What the immigration department does [with the defendant] afterwards is a matter for them and really doesn't form part of our considerations [for prosecuting a case].' Judges, prosecutors, probation officers, and defence lawyers are keen to emphasize the strict division of labour between criminal adjudication and immigration enforcement. 'Immigration' is largely perceived by court operators as an unavoidable tactical partner and a source of information in court proceedings. Probation staff, at both courts, routinely run immigration checks on people whom they suspect are in the country illegally. A chief probation officer at the magistrates' court asserted:

> We are fully focused on making sure that they are not treated any differently irrespective of immigration status . . . Regardless of the immigration status, as long as we do the basic preliminary checks with the enforcement unit, we will still make a proposal to the court based on seriousness, risk and need.

Yet, court staff insist, the institutional channels are far from aligned. Belying the appearance of a perfectly synchronized system that emerges from policy documents and instructions,[9] a chief probation officer at the Crown Court admitted: 'There is no follow up of cases [involving foreign nationals eligible for deportation] through the system.'

The obstinate division of criminal and immigration workload by criminal justice operators can be read as an attempt to isolate criminal justice adjudication from the highly politicized field of migration controls. At the same time, as Kaufman (2015: 110) observed in relation to the prison, it works to deny how the criminal court has changed

[6] Logistically, when judges pass sentences which trigger 'automatic deportation' the court certifies it in the 'order of imprisonment' in the case file and communicates it to the Home Office through an automated system. Such information is also fed into the 'EXHIBIT' system used by the Crown Courts.

[7] s. 32(1), (2).

[8] Judges can still recommend a deportation order against a foreign national offender, s. 3(6) of the Immigration Act 1971.

[9] See e.g. Ministry of Justice 2014.

under conditions of mass migration and its control. Even if the court's business continues apparently undisturbed, mass migration poses significant challenges to its everyday work.

BRINGING THE BORDER WITHIN: MIGRATION STATUS, DEPORTABILITY, AND PUNISHMENT

Migration status and deportability loom large in criminal justice adjudications. If the person is 'removable' and she is charged with a minor offence, for example a minor driving offence, a prosecutor stated, it might not be in the public interest to prosecute her. Irregular migration status exacerbates the costs of the pre-trial process since irregularity is almost always translated in legal terms as a flight risk, vanquishing any attempt to obtain bail (Wolfe et al. 2011: 356). Defence counsel often brings up the migration status and potential deportability of their clients to persuade judges to pass lenient sentences.[10] 'He will be whisked off by the immigration authorities', a lawyer reminded the district judge, 'This is not to say that he will get off scot free, but he will be out of a country quite soon.' His client, a man who had pleaded guilty to a charge of theft, had apparently overstayed his visa. Migration status and deportability can limit sentencing options, since deportable convicted defendants are sometimes judged as unsuitable for non-custodial sentences. Pre-sentence reports are simply not prepared for them. In these cases, judges are confronted with two stark choices: to release them without a penalty or to keep them behind bars.

The defendant's migration status may also surface during proceedings, a fact that was exploited by some couples in domestic disputes. In one of them, the defendant, a Pakistani man who had entered an arranged marriage with a British woman, adduced in his defence for assault and stalking of his wife that she had threatened to report him to the Home Office. His solicitor argued: 'He knows she will inform the Home Office. She has done it before.' So too, an independent domestic violence court advisor noticed that the dependent status of women is sometimes used by male partners accused of domestic abuse to discredit their claim: 'Often [her immigration status] will be used as an excuse by him to say the reason why [she accused him] is because he hasn't sent the immigration papers off so she's made this allegation up.'[11] An example of how migration control intrudes into the private sphere, shaping intimate relationships (Erez et al. 2009; Menjívar and Salcido 2002), these instances also reveal the strategic use of migration status as a bargaining power within domestic disputes and depict the criminal process as its battleground.

[10] However, according to the Court of Appeal, the sentencing judge should not substitute an unduly lenient sentence in light of the prospective deportation of a convicted foreign national defendant: *R v Rahimi* [2011] EWCA Crim 2268 [at 10].

[11] The Crown Prosecution Service in its policy for prosecuting cases of domestic violence considers migration status as a specific source of vulnerability of victims of domestic abuse: http://www.cps.gov.uk/legal/d_to_g/domestic_abuse_guidelines_for_prosecutors/#a80.

Despite the salience of migration status and nationality in criminal litigation, such information is not systematically conveyed to the courts. In Britain, criminal justice statistics do not include nationality data. Although the police are supposed to verify the identity of every person they arrest, in practice this check is not systematically done. Neither the police[12] nor the criminal courts are required to collect data on the nationality of arrestees and defendants. Even where this information is recorded by the prison service such data may be inaccurate. Ascertaining national status is fraught with difficulty. For one, there are plenty of definitional issues. The question of 'who is a foreign national?' elicited different answers from interviewees: people born abroad, non-UK residents, EU nationals, illegal migrants, non-EU migrants, second or third generations, Old Commonwealth migrants, etc. Tracking proof of formal citizenship poses other sets of challenges. Some defendants are adamant to hide it. Others are stripped of it. Yet other people are simply unable to produce a passport for bureaucratic reasons beyond their control (Engbersen and Broeders 2009: 880).

To navigate the 'sea of undifferentiated strangers' (Rock 1993: 219), court staff rely on clues or hints, like name, accent, language, police antecedents, features of the charge, and so on. While none of them are entirely trustworthy, they lay bare deep-rooted, racialized conceptions and images of the 'citizen' (Kaufman 2015: 155; Weber 2011: 461). One judge confessed to me: 'You might go without ever being aware that you have a foreign national in front of you', while the probation officer at the magistrates' court complained: 'I think the frustrating aspect... is that identity—we often don't know who we're dealing with, which is the basic core of our system'. Yet another probation official in charge of foreign nationals admitted that they simply do not have a reliable system to identify foreigners among offenders. In a recent report, the National Audit Office (2014: 22) decried the poor and piecemeal approach of various criminal justice and immigration agencies to collect, share, and make use of information on 'foreign national offenders' to ensure their prompt removal. It protested that cross-border criminal background checks were only pursued on 30 per cent of foreign national arrestees and that timely identity checks were not systematically performed.

These instances make apparent that 'nationality' is a vague and poor sorting mechanism within the criminal justice system. They also cast doubts about the state's ability to render its population intelligible and thus governable (Torpey 1998). Since data on the defendant's nationality and background is not routinely gathered, criminal decision-making is often based on inaccurate and incomplete information, and risks leading to unjust outcomes.

NEGOTIATING BELONGING: CRIMINAL ADJUDICATION AND CIVIC STRATIFICATION

Attempts to differentiate people on citizenship grounds are not just undermined by practical difficulties of identification. Conceptually, 'citizenship' is elusive and the

[12] In the West Midlands, the police are only required to state the country of birth of arrestees.

distinction between citizens and non-citizens is not 'a dichotomous one, but rests on a continuous and reversible gradation often connected with ethnoracial and ethnonational hierarchies' (Chauvin and Garcés-Mascareñas 2012: 242). Citizenship is, in other words, both a legal category and a question of degree.

Just as immigration detainees contest the grounds of their detention by laying claim to alternative membership categories (Bosworth 2012: 131, 2014: 88), in the courtroom, lawyers often appeal to that idea of gradation, or 'shades of grey', of citizenship. These 'practices of citizenship' capture the emotional and normative dimensions of citizenship (Bosniak 2000: 479). Length of residence, employment, and marital status are moulded to enhance the defence's plea in mitigation. Pleas in mitigation reveal the ideological structure within which the courts operate, the value system held by judges, and their expectations about individuals' roles in society (Eaton 1986: 43). Underscoring their clients' 'civic capital', defence lawyers often appeal to markers of belonging and deservingness hoping to persuade judges to keep custody to a minimum, to pass a non-custodial sentence, or better still to discharge the defendant: 'He has been in the country for a number of years without getting into trouble', 'He has come to the UK to improve his life', 'He works, he doesn't rely on benefits', 'He is the breadwinner of the family', 'He has children and works long hours to support his family', 'He is a man of responsibility.' In so doing, lawyers put their litigation skills to work to shape 'facts', while taking stock of and strategically utilizing expectations about 'good' migrants, which are deeply gendered. This 'identity talk' does more than seeking to reduce guilt; it realigns the defendant's actions to those expectations and in doing so it reinforces them (Gathings and Parrotta 2013).

Much in the same way that court ethnographers have described the courtroom as a stage where the parties perform roles and dramatize facts (Carlen 1976b, 1976a; Feeley 1979), the court can also be characterized as a civic forum where claims about national identity and belonging are laid bare, contested, and negotiated. Some litigants use them to voice their loyalty to Britain's liberal values presenting competing notions of Britishness. In one of the cases observed, a man claimed he was treated disrespectfully by a police officer who rudely told him to remove his car from the pavement, adding: 'This is not Iraq, you cannot park like this.' This exchange spiralled out in his arrest for a charge of racially aggravated assault against the police officer and two of his colleagues. During examination-in-chief, he expressed his rage and disappointment at the treatment he received from the officers, who he perceived to have acted to protect themselves. At the same time, he emphasized his respect for the law: 'I was in love with the law... I grew up in this country.' In turn, the officers who had arrested and interviewed him maintained that the defendant accused them of being part of an Indian conspiracy[13] against Iraqi Muslims charging two of the officers of acting as 'puppets of the British government'.

This case staged two competing notions of Britishness: on the one hand, that representing the rule of law, fairness, and equal treatment; and on the other, that of the Empire, reasserting racial stereotypes and subordination. It also vividly illustrates

[13] The police officers were of Asian background. Apparently the police officer who arrested the defendant was able to understand Kurdish as the defendant was speaking on the phone.

what Mezzadra and Neilson (2013: 157) calls 'temporal borders': 'the working of time through different generations and successive migratory movements—they explain—divides and stratifies migrants within wider vistas of citizenship and also divides them from each other'. Indeed, while common past migratory experience or shared religious, linguistic, or cultural backgrounds could unite and elicit empathy, the working of the border temporally can in turn be a source of social division, resentment, and fragmentation (Aliverti 2015b: 218; Bosworth 2014: 207; Millings 2013: 1084). In this case, these tensions are exacerbated by power relations. In the eyes of the defendant, the ethnic background of the officers casts doubts on their authority and the power they wield.

Such tensions are also apparent in the testimonies of some practitioners. One of the solicitors, himself a child of migrants, explained: 'EU people get in trouble because they have different standards of childrearing and are short-sighted. They don't care about sending kids to school.' 'This might sound racist', he immediately cautioned, conjecturing that his parents' community when they arrived in the UK probably acted in the same way. Another solicitor of Asian background explained that some 'foreign nationals' reach the courts because of differing cultural standards: 'Some people when they come to the United Kingdom, foreign nationals, they bring with them their state of mind or the way of thinking they were back in their own country, what seems normal to them is very different here.' 'Culture' is often highlighted to account for the criminality of foreigners, entrenched with gendered and racialized stereotypes. 'With the Romanians—the solicitor continued—you often have the women who commit shoplifting offences . . . But they are not really the beneficiaries because they seem to do it and the profits or the funds of whatever they generate goes to the males . . . It seems to be almost a way of life for them.' A similar 'orientalization' of culture and criminal behaviour surfaces in relation to Eastern Europeans and alcohol. In one case the district judge asked the defence lawyer why his client was driving while drunk to which the solicitor speculated: 'Perhaps it is a cultural thing. We see this in certain communities. Binge drinking.' Similarly, a Crown Court judge confessed that sometimes he needed to remind himself and warn the jury not to resort to stereotypes in judging the cases before them, particularly at a time when 'race and immigration are such a big problem'.[14]

While ignorance of the law is not a defence in English criminal law, advocates representing racialized immigrant clients sometimes resort to 'cultural defences' and ignorance of the vernacular rules in a bid to contextualize offending and excuse or mitigate their client's liability (Chiu 1994; Volpp 2000: 105). To demonstrate multicultural sensitivity and avoid unfair outcomes, courts in Western jurisdictions sometimes take into consideration the defendants' cultural and religious background and traditions when assessing their liability and blameworthiness (Poulter 1989). In US courts, anthropologists often appear as expert witnesses to testify about cultural practices in communities from which the defendant is drawn (Rosen 1977).[15]

[14] Stereotypes based on alienage and national traits may influence judicial decision-making. Wolfe et al. (2011) concluded that cultural stereotypes of non-citizens as dangerous and crime-prone can explain enhanced sentencing outcomes for non-citizens vis-à-vis citizens (see also Hartley and Armendariz 2011; Wu and D'Angelo 2014; Light et al. 2014).

[15] Expert evidence appears to be less common in English criminal courts (Woodman 2009: 32).

Although appeals to culture stem from the laudable goal of accommodating difference in culturally pluralist societies, legal scholars have averted to the potential pitfalls of this litigation strategy. Phillips (2003) argued that the use of cultural evidence in a criminal defence risks perpetuating patriarchal practices to the disadvantage of women and reinforcing stereotypical representations of the non-Western 'other'. She observed that lawyers often pick up certain characteristics of these defendants and attribute them to a particular culture, such as the heightened sense of sexual outrage for men, and the submissiveness and passivity for women (Phillips 2007: 85). Volpp (2000) noticed the selective appeal to culture in the courtroom. Similar behaviours are frequently interpreted according to different lenses based on the defendant's identity. Culture, she pointed out, is only raised in relation to parties from a non-white background resulting in racialized immigrant defendants more likely to be perceived as passive, lacking agency, and determined by their culture of origin (Volpp 2000: 112). In contrast, bad or aberrant behaviour by white defendants is generally conceived as a product of individual deviancy or dysfunctionality.

Beyond the legal outcome of the case, some scholars pointed to the damaging effects of playing the 'culture card'. This 'vulgar use of culture' (Fournier 2002: 8) is linked to colonial thinking which caricatures non-Anglo Saxon cultures as backward, misogynist, and inferior, perpetuates long-standing racialized hierarchies, and legitimizes controls and exclusions (Bosworth 2014: 181; Chiu 1994; Cunneen 2011: 261). At the same time, it depicts mainstream culture as progressive and civilized while '[e]xtraterritorializing... problematic behaviour by projecting it beyond the borders' of Western culture (Volpp 2000: 115). Further, by implying that mainstream culture is monolithic, fixed, and bounded, such appeals also obscure the multicultural nature of contemporary Britain. The recurrent attempts to depict Britain as a mono-cultural society clash with the empirical reality of a hyper-diverse society that has been historically forged by successive flows of international migration. Whilst failing to unmask the prejudices underpinning the 'cultural rhetoric' in criminal justice, criminal practitioners and criminologists risk reproducing and entrenching broader social patterns of discrimination and inequalities.

CONCLUSION

This chapter depicted some of the distinctive features of the criminal courts in an age of mass migration. These features, which have been largely neglected in academic scholarship, embody an aspect of the new contours of criminal justice that demands more careful academic consideration. Globalization is an 'in here' phenomenon (Aas 2013a: 3): it takes place inside the local and the national profoundly shaping its institutions. These criminal courts are globalized sites where the boundaries of the national are continuously eroded and at the same time reasserted (Brown 2010).

The examination of the everyday work of the criminal courts vividly reveals the tensions involved in adjudicating justice under conditions of mass mobility. The presence of the 'foreign national' as part of the stable clientele of the criminal justice system brings home the importance of national identity for criminal justice decision-making and exposes how this is constructed by officials. Criminal proceedings are not only about adjudicating criminal liability and apportioning guilt. They are also civic forums where claims, ideas, and images about who counts as a citizen and who does not are ventilated, asserted, and contested.

Ultimately, this study suggests that civic status matters in criminal justice. Enmeshed with race, gender, and class, migration status influences people's trajectories in and out of the criminal justice system (Eagly 2013). Despite attempts to accommodate difference in the courtroom, the criminal courts remain entangled in a frame of reference that assumes a bounded and culturally homogeneous national space populated by fellow citizens. The moulding of institutional practices and academic research around the 'citizen', blind to the impact migration status makes in shaping people's lives, is out of sync with the social world in which the criminal justice system operates and risks perpetuating social and global inequalities.

REFERENCES

Aas, K.F. (2012), '"The Earth is One but the World Is Not": Criminological Theory and its Geopolitical Divisions', *Theoretical Criminology*, 16, 1: 5–20.

Aas, K.F. (2013a), *Globalization and Crime*, London: SAGE.

Aas, K.F. (2013b), 'The Ordered and the Bordered Society: Migration Control, Citizenship and the Northern Penal State', in K.F. Aas and M. Bosworth (eds), *The Borders of Punishment: Criminal Justice, Citizenship and Social Exclusion*, Oxford: Oxford University Press: 21–39.

Aas, K.F. (2014), 'Bordered Penality: Abnormal Justice and the Precarious Membership', *Punishment & Society*, 16, 5: 520–41.

Aliverti, A. (2015a), 'Doing Away with Decency? Foreigners, Punishment and the Liberal State', in A. Ericksson (ed.), *Punishing the Other: The Social Production of Immorality Revisited*, Abingdon: Routledge.

Aliverti, A. (2015b), 'Enlisting the Public in the Policing of Immigration', *British Journal of Criminology*, 55, 2: 215–30.

Aliverti, A. and Seoighe, R. (2017), 'Lost in Translation? Examining the Role of Court Interpreters in Cases Involving Foreign National Defendants in England and Wales', *New Criminal Law Review*, 20 (forthcoming).

Birmingham City Council (2013a), *2011 Census: Key Statistics for Birmingham and its Constituent Areas*, Birmingham: Birmingham City Council, available at: http://www.birmingham.gov.uk/cs/Satellite?c=Page&childpagename=Planning-and-Regeneration%2FPageLayout&cid=1223408087932&pagename=BCC%2FCommon%2FWrapper%2FWrapper.

Birmingham City Council (2013b), *Population and Migration Topic Report, 2011 Census in Birmingham*, Birmingham: Birmingham City Council.

Bosniak, L. (2000), 'Citizenship Denationalized', *Indiana Journal of Global Legal Studies*, 7, 2: 447–509.

Bosworth, M. (2012), 'Subjectivity and Identity in Detention: Punishment and Society in a Global Age', *Theoretical Criminology*, 16, 2: 123–40.

BOSWORTH, M. (2013), 'Can Immigration Detention Centres Be Legitimate? Understanding Confinement in a Global World', in K.F. Aas and M. Bosworth (eds), *The Borders of Punishment: Migration, Citizenship, and Social Exclusion*, Oxford: Oxford University Press: 149–65.

BOSWORTH, M. (2014), *Inside Immigration Detention*, Oxford: Oxford University Press.

BOSWORTH, M., BOWLING, B., and LEE, M. (2008), 'Globalization, Ethnicity and Racism: An Introduction', *Theoretical Criminology*, 12, 3: 263–73.

BOTTOMS, A. and MCCLEAN, J. (1976), *Defendants in the Criminal Process*, London: Routledge & Kegan Paul.

BOWLING, B. and PHILLIPS, C. (2002), *Racism, Crime and Justice*, Harlow: Pearson Education.

BROWN, W. (2010), *Walled States, Waning Sovereignty*, New York: Zone Books.

CARLEN, P. (1976a), *Magistrates' Justice*, London: Wiley-Blackwell.

CARLEN, P. (1976b), 'The Staging of Magistrates' Justice', *British Journal of Criminology*, 16, 1: 48–55.

CARRINGTON, K., HOGG, R., and SOZZO, M. (2016), 'Southern Criminology', *British Journal of Criminology*, 56: 1–20.

CHAUVIN, S. and GARCÉS-MASCAREÑAS, B. (2012), 'Beyond Informal Citizenship: The New Moral Economy of Migrant Illegality', *International Political Sociology*, 6, 3: 241–59.

CHIU, D. (1994), 'The Cultural Defense: Beyond Exclusion, Assimilation, and Guilty Liberalism', *California Law Review*, 82, 4: 1053–125.

Courts and Tribunals Judiciary (2015a), *Judicial Diversity Statistics 2015*, London: Judicial Office.

Courts and Tribunals Judiciary (2015b), *Serving Magistrates Statistics 2015*, London: Judicial Office, available at: https://www.judiciary.gov.uk/publications/judicial-statistics-2015/.

CUNNEEN, C. (2011), 'Postcolonial Perspectives for Criminology', in M. Bosworth and C. Hoyle (eds), *What Is Criminology?*, Oxford: Oxford University Press: 249–66.

DUFF, R. (2011), 'Responsibility, Citizenship, and Criminal Law', in R. Duff and S. Green (eds), *Philosophical Foundations of Criminal Law*, Oxford: Oxford University Press: 125–48.

DUFF, R., FARMER, L., MARSHALL, S., and TADROS, V. (2007), *The Trial on Trial: Towards a Normative Theory of the Criminal Trial*, Oxford: Hart.

EAGLY, I. (2013), 'Criminal Justice for Noncitizens: An Analysis of Variation in Local Enforcement', *New York University Law Review*, 88, 4: 101–91.

EATON, M. (1986), *Justice for Women?*, Milton Keynes: Open University Press.

ENGBERSEN, G. and BROEDERS, D. (2009), 'The State versus the Alien: Immigration Control and Strategies of Irregular Immigrants', *West European Politics*, 32, 5: 867–85.

EREZ, E., ADELMAN, M., and GREGORY, C. (2009), 'Intersections of Immigration and Domestic Violence: Voices of Battered Immigrant Women', *Feminist Criminology*, 4, 1: 32–56.

FEELEY, M. (1979), *The Process Is the Punishment: Handling Cases in a Lower Criminal Court*, New York: Russell Sage Foundation.

FOURNIER, P. (2002), 'The Ghettoisation of Difference in Canada: "Rape by Culture" and the Danger of a "Cultural Defence" in Criminal Law Trials', *Manitoba Law Journal*, 29, 1: 1–39.

FRASER, N. (2008), 'Abnormal Justice', *Critical Inquiry*, 34: 393–422.

FRASER, N. (2010), *Scales of Justice: Reimagining Political Space in a Globalizing World*, New York: Columbia University Press.

GATHINGS, M.J. and PARROTTA, K. (2013), 'The Use of Gendered Narratives in the Courtroom: Constructing an Identity Worthy of Leniency', *Journal of Contemporary Ethnography*, 42, 6: 668–89.

HARTLEY, R. and ARMENDARIZ, L. (2011), 'Border Justice? Sentencing Federal Narcotics Offenders in Southwest Border Districts: A Focus on Citizenship Status', *Journal of Contemporary Criminal Justice*, 27, 1: 43–62.

HOOD, R. (1962), *Sentencing in Magistrates Courts: A Study in Variations of Policy*, London: Stevens & Sons Limited.

HOOD, R. (1992), *Race and Sentencing*, Oxford: Oxford University Press.

HUDSON, B. and BRAMHALL, G. (2005), 'Assessing the "Other": Constructions of "Asianness" in Risk Assessments by Probation Officers', *British Journal of Criminology*, 45, 5: 721–40.

JACOBSON, J., HUNTER, G., and KIRBY, A. (2015), *Inside Crown Court: Personal Experiences and Questions of Legitimacy*, Bristol: Policy Press.

KAUFMAN, E. (2015), *Punish and Expel: Border Control, Nationalism, and the New Purpose of the Prison*, Oxford: Oxford University Press.

LIGHT, M., MASSOGLIA, M., and KING, R. (2014), 'Citizenship and Punishment: The Salience of National Membership in U.S. Criminal Courts', *American Sociological Review*, 79, 5: 825–47.

MCBARNET, D. (1981), *Conviction: Law, the State and the Construction of Justice*, London: Macmillan Press.

MCCONVILLE, M., HODGSON, J., BRIDGES, L., and PAVLOVIC, A. (1994), *Standing Accused: The Organisation and Practices of Criminal Defence Lawyers in Britain*, Oxford: Oxford University Press.

MENJÍVAR, C. and SALCIDO, O. (2002), 'Immigrant Women and Domestic Violence: Common Experiences in Different Countries', *Gender & Society*, 16, 6: 898–920.

MEZZADRA, S. and NEILSON, B. (2013), *Border as Method, or, the Multiplication of Labor*, Durham, NC: Duke University Press.

MILLINGS, M. (2013), 'Policing British Asian Identities: The Enduring Role of the Police in Young British Asian Men's Situated Negotiation of Identity and Belonging', *British Journal of Criminology*, 53, 6: 1075–92.

National Audit Office (2014), *Managing and Removing Foreign National Offenders*, London: National Audit Office HC 441, available at: http://www.nao.org.uk/report/managing-and-removing-foreign-national-offenders/.

PHILLIPS, A. (2003), 'When Culture Means Gender: Issues of Cultural Defence in the English Courts', *The Modern Law Review*, 66, 4: 510–31.

PHILLIPS, A. (2007), *Multiculturalism without Culture*, Princeton, NJ: Princeton University Press.

PHILLIPS, C. (2008), 'Negotiating Identities: Ethnicity and Social Relations in a Young Offenders' Institution', *Theoretical Criminology*, 12, 3: 313–31.

POULTER, S. (1989), 'The Significance of Ethnic Minority Customs and Traditions in English Criminal Law', *Journal of Ethnic and Migration Studies*, 16, 1: 121–8.

ROCK, P. (1993), *The Social World of an English Crown Court: Witnesses and Professionals in the Crown Court Centre at Wood Green*, Oxford: Oxford University Press.

ROSEN, L. (1977), 'The Anthropologist as Expert Witness', *American Anthropologist*, 79, 3: 555–78.

TORPEY, J. (1998), 'Coming and Going: On the State Monopolization of the Legitimate "Means of Movement"', *Sociological Theory*, 16, 3: 239–59.

VOLPP, L. (2000), 'Blaming Culture for Bad Behavior', *Yale Journal of Law & the Humanities*, 12: 89–116.

WACQUANT, L. (2014), 'Marginality, Ethnicity, and Penality: A Bourdieusian Perspective on Criminalization', in R. Duff, L. Farmer, S. Marshall, M. Renzo, and V. Tadros (eds), *Criminalization: The Political Morality of the Criminal Law*, Oxford: Oxford University Press: 270–306.

WEBER, L. (2011), '"It Sounds Like They Shouldn't Be Here": Immigration Checks on the Streets of Sydney', *Policing and Society*, 21, 4: 456–67.

WOLFE, S., PYROOZ, D., and SPOHN, C. (2011), 'Unraveling the Effect of Offender Citizenship Status on Federal Sentencing Outcomes', *Social Science Research*, 40, 1: 349–62.

WOODMAN, G. (2009), 'The Culture Defence in English Common Law: The Potential for Development', in M. Foblets and R. Dundes Renteln (eds), *Multicultural Jurisprudence*, Oxford: Hart: 7–34.

WU, J. and D'ANGELO, J. (2014), 'Unwarranted Disparity in Federal Sentencing: Noncitizen Crime as a Social/Group Threat', *Criminal Justice Review*, 39, 1: 58–80.

ZEDNER, L. (2004), *Criminal Justice*, Oxford: Oxford University Press.

7

ACCESS TO CRIMINAL JUSTICE: CHANGING LEGAL AID DECISION-MAKING IN THE LOWER COURTS

*Richard Young**

INTRODUCTION

This chapter examines the changing contours of legal aid decision-making in the lower criminal courts of England and Wales over the past 50 years. The story emphasizes the value of repeated engagement with a particular issue in charting and attempting to bring about change, and illustrates the shifting sands of the research enterprise. The processes of securing funding and obtaining research access to the institutions of criminal justice have undergone significant reshaping in recent times. A further key development is the sharpening imperative to demonstrate the impact of research on the world beyond the academy. Legal aid research exemplifies the difficulties and contingencies involved in achieving this.

This, then, is a story not just about the evolving dynamics of how defendants gain access to legal aid funding, but also of how academics gain access to, and struggle to influence, a criminal justice system itself in constant flux. Its focus is not on macro-level societal changes and their effect on the criminal process, variously described in terms such as neo-liberalism (e.g. Sommerlad 2008) or marketization (e.g. Brown with Carasso 2013), but at the meso- and micro-levels. To adopt the theoretical language of Hawkins (2002: 48–59), the analysis centres not so much on 'the surround' (the socio-political environment) but rather on 'the field' (the legal and administrative setting in which legal aid decisions take place), and on decision-making 'frames' (the interpretive behaviour of decision-makers).

Legal aid may be defined as funding provided by the state to enable defendants of limited means to access the services of lawyers in meritorious cases. This chapter concentrates on the merits test for granting criminal legal aid. Whereas the legal merits

* Thanks are due to Ed Cape, Vicky Kemp, and Dave Wall for sharing their research recollections with me, and also to the editors of this collection for their constructive feedback on an earlier draft of this chapter. Responsibility for any defects remains mine alone.

test has remained virtually unchanged during the period under discussion, its interpretation and surrounding governance have altered substantially.

THE COLONIZATION OF THE MAGISTRATES' COURTS BY DEFENCE LAWYERS: 1966–1992

Following a gradual relaxation of the conditions for granting legal aid over the first half of the twentieth century, by 1963 this funding was available for summary proceedings whenever this was deemed by the magistrates' courts to be 'in the interests of justice' (Goriely 1996: 34–44). In practice, however, only 1.2 per cent of those dealt with summarily were legally aided in 1964 (Departmental Committee 1966: para. 32). Some defendants paid for legal representation privately, but most of those appearing in the magistrates' courts were unrepresented (Zander and Glasser 1967).

In 1966 the Departmental Committee on Legal Aid in Criminal Proceedings, chaired by Mr Justice Widgery, argued against the automatic grant of legal aid for summary proceedings, favouring instead the retention of a discretionary approach. The Committee noted evidence of apparent inconsistency in applying the interests of justice test but concluded that a more precise formula was impracticable (Departmental Committee 1966: paras. 161–2). Its one gesture towards consistency was to provide guidance—the Widgery criteria—to which it proposed regard should be had in deciding whether the interests of justice required a grant of legal aid. These criteria centred on whether the defendant was likely to lose liberty or livelihood; suffer serious damage to reputation; whether the case might require the tracing, interviewing, or expert cross-examination of witnesses; involve a substantial question of law; the defendant might not be able to understand the proceedings or to state their own case; or it was in the interests of someone else (e.g. a child complainant) that the individual be represented. These criteria were not exhaustive; other matters could be taken into account in determining the interests of justice.

The Widgery criteria duly formed the basis of guidance issued to court decision-makers, and were also taken into account by the High Court when exercising judicial review over the discretionary power to grant legal aid.[1] The problem of apparent inconsistency persisted, however (see Borrie and Varcoe 1970: 30–5; Paterson with Birch and Green 1971); ten years later, the Royal Commission on Legal Services (1979: para. 14.7) reported compelling evidence that those criteria were not working well. They were said to be both complex and imprecise, and open to a wide range of interpretation in cases of the same type. Research by Burney (1979), Hansen (1982), Bridges (1982), and Darbyshire (1984) confirmed that magistrates' courts, individual justices' clerks, and court clerks operating under their authority, pursued radically different policies on the grant of legal aid, and interpreted the interests of justice test and the Widgery criteria in markedly different ways. The High Court did little to rein in this inconsistency during the 1970s and 1980s, emphasizing instead that those taking

[1] See e.g. *R v Havering Juvenile Court, ex parte Buckley* (Lexis CO/554/83, 12 July 1983) (CO/554/83).

decisions on criminal legal aid had wide discretion when applying the interests of justice test.[2]

A more striking 'problem', however, was the huge growth in applications and grants for legal aid in the years following the Widgery Report (Goriely 1996: 44). During this period, lawyers successfully colonized the magistrates' courts, such that by 1983 the bulk of those facing either way charges[3] in that setting were legally aided (ibid). Their achievement is largely attributable to the recognition by magistrates' courts that lawyers *generally* facilitated the efficient running of the courts (McConville et al. 1994: 6–7; Parker et al. 1981: 50).[4] In particular, justices' clerks were said to favour granting legal aid as it facilitated informal negotiation and the avoidance of trials, and because it relieved them of the burden of helping unrepresented defendants, leaving them free to concentrate on providing legal advice to the magistrates. Legal aid grants and costs continued to spiral during the 1980s (even though the number of defendants proceeded against was now falling) and in 1989, for the first time, more grants of legal aid were made than the number of proceedings for either way offences in magistrates' courts, with 15 per cent of grants being for summary offences[5] (McConville et al. 1994: 300). This phenomenon of less serious matters increasingly attracting legal aid was labelled 'Widgery drift'.

The rise in legal aid expenditure became a matter of growing concern to government in the 1980s which led to reform to limit costs and monitor service (e.g. through quality and cost audits). This reform agenda focused on reducing the number of suppliers of legal aid by limiting payments to those holding 'contracts', and reducing the number of contracts on offer. Further rationing involved freezing and cutting the rates of legal aid pay, and making most payments on the basis of standard fees rather than paying for work actually done. Reductions in the scope of the scheme included restricting some categories of suspect to telephone advice when detained in police stations. A substantial body of research has examined the implications of these changes for the legal profession, legal services, and access to justice.[6] Of most interest here is the attempt to regulate more closely grants of legal aid. Notably, the Legal Aid Act 1988 created the Legal Aid Board (a quasi-autonomous agency) to take over administration of the legal aid fund from the Law Society (the representative body for solicitors), and provided the Lord Chancellor with the power to transfer legal aid

[2] See, in particular, *R v Macclesfield Justices, ex parte Greenhalgh* (1979) 144 JP 142; *R v Cambridge Crown Court, ex parte Hagi* (1979) 144 JP 145; *R v Havering Juvenile Court, ex parte Buckley* (Lexis CO/554/83, 12 July 1983), and *R v Stratford Magistrates Court, ex parte Gorman* (Lexis CO/687/89, 12 June 1990).

[3] 'Either way charges', such as for theft and burglary, are those which can be heard either in the lower criminal courts (the magistrates' courts), or in the higher tier of criminal court (the Crown Court).

[4] Not all court clerks accept this however, with some taking the view that unrepresented defendants can be processed more quickly than those who have a lawyer speaking for them: Young (1996: 158–9). A stream of initiatives over the last 20 years designed to 'speed up' summary justice is likely to have led an increasing number of magistrates' courts to regard lawyers as more of a hindrance than a help in many cases: see further Kemp (2010: 74–8).

[5] Less serious offences, such as most motoring offences, are classified as 'summary' and can only be prosecuted in the magistrates' courts.

[6] See e.g. Bevan (1996), Wall (1996a), Smith (1996), Moorhead (1998, 2004), Sommerlad (1999, 2001, 2004), Cape (2004), Bridges and Cape (2008), and Smith and Cape (forthcoming).

decision-making from the magistrates' courts to the Board.[7] In its Report to the Lord Chancellor in 1989, however, the Board stated that transfer would not be justified: legal aid applications were dealt with speedily; the existing system combined expertise and flexibility, and there was no pressure for change from the courts (Legal Aid Board 1989: 17–18).

The Board was nonetheless concerned about the continuing variation in grant rates, and invited bids to undertake research into this phenomenon. It is worth exploring how a team from Birmingham University came to secure this commission as it illuminates certain features of the research enterprise at that time.

THE BIRMINGHAM RESEARCH: 1992

FUNDING CONTEXT

The tension between academic freedom and the requirements of the funders of universities was intensifying in the 1980s as the higher education budget was squeezed under the Thatcher government. A rudimentary assessment of research (based on just five outputs per department) by the University Grants Committee (UGC), a body consisting largely of academics, was undertaken in 1986 with a view to reassuring universities that shrinking allocations were being determined fairly (Jump 2013). Academics lost a significant degree of control over the distribution of funding when the UGC was abolished in 1988 under the Education Reform Act. The second 'research selectivity exercise' was implemented the following year by its replacement, the Universities Funding Council (UFC). By 1992 the UFC had itself been replaced by the Higher Education Funding Council for England (HEFCE), and a rebranded and more rigorous 'research assessment exercise' (RAE) was about to take place. Pressure was mounting on individual academics to produce more original work and to compete for alternative sources of funding in the shape of research grants. It was against this backdrop that we made our bid to the Legal Aid Board.[8]

SCOPE AND TIMING

At that time, individual government departments and the agencies they sponsored were under increasing pressure from the Treasury to use their funds efficiently, a trend that has continued to this day. Thus when these bodies commission or fund research it is likely that they will (a) institute a process of competitive tendering, and (b) seek to define the scope of the research narrowly to ensure that it produces policy-relevant results. The overall aim is to secure a tightly circumscribed outcome at the cheapest price possible. The danger is that academics accept whatever research money is on

[7] s. 22 of the 1988 Act put the Widgery criteria on a statutory footing.

[8] This account of the 1992 research draws on an unpublished paper, 'The Politics of Criminal Legal Aid Research' which I gave at the SLSA conference held in Exeter on 31 March 1993.

offer, regardless of any accompanying conditions as to the subject to be tackled and approach to be taken, thus compromising their ability to conduct independent research focused on more fundamental issues.

We were, accordingly, somewhat wary of entering into this particular tendering process. On the positive side, research into criminal legal aid fitted well with our existing interests. Moreover, the Board's anxiety about disparity of grant rates could be viewed 'within a broader theoretical frame of reference' (Morgan 2000: 77) as a concern about the justice of the existing system for determining legal aid applications.[9] More troubling was the Board's proposed timescale. The Board wanted the findings of the study to be taken into account by the Justices' Clerks Society (JCS) who were in the process of preparing fresh guidance on how the interests of justice test should be interpreted by administrative staff based within the magistrates' courts. Accordingly, the expectation was that the research was to involve small samples of applications for legal aid and to be completed in a matter of weeks. The chance to use research to influence policy was attractive, but academic integrity required that the study was designed such that it was capable of producing reliable, valid, and generalizable findings. In the event, we were able to persuade the Board to fund a more ambitious study, which reflects the fact that there is usually more room for negotiation than tender documents would suggest.

ACCESS

Access to the courts proved simple to arrange. At that time magistrates' courts operated on a decentralized model so we wrote to the relevant justices' clerk in each of our six target courts explaining the project; all agreed to participate without further ado. No objections were raised to our accessing paper-based court filing systems with a view to extracting information from a weighted but otherwise random sample of 1,201 legal aid application forms.[10] We also conducted interviews with court clerks and solicitors in each of the courts studied.

SHIFTING POLITICAL CONTEXT

In January 1992, before the research got properly underway, the Lord Chancellor invited the Legal Aid Board to draw up proposals regarding how it might take over responsibility for determining legal aid applications from the magistrates' courts.[11] Our planned research was not designed to evaluate the strengths and weaknesses of the existing system, let alone the pros and cons of the Board taking over the decision-making function. We realized, however, that during the course of the research much material would be uncovered relevant to the question of how well the existing system

[9] There is an important difference between policy-led research, and policy-relevant research, as discussed in Sanders (1987).

[10] Applications that were refused were over-sampled in order to illuminate variation in grant rates.

[11] This followed an internal confidential audit (which we were given sight of) which concluded that many legal aid decisions could not have been properly considered by court personnel given the sketchy information provided by applicants.

worked. In addition, a question was added to the interview schedules seeking the views of defence solicitors and court clerks on the proposed transfer of responsibility to the Board.

Accordingly, the draft research report delivered to the Board went well beyond a simple explanation of differing grant rates by including discussion of how the different elements of the system inter-related. A final section was included in which the views of court clerks and solicitors on the issue of transferring responsibility for criminal legal aid to the Board were discussed. These views were almost uniformly hostile. It was felt that transfer would lead to unacceptable delays for defendants and for court proceedings and entail an inappropriate inflexibility in decision-making.

The Board responded by asking us to delete this final section. The objections to it were, first, that it fell outside our terms of reference and would detract from our explanation of varying grant rates; second, that it was based merely on the views of courtroom actors; and, third, that we had assumed that the Board would take over the system as it stood whereas in fact the Board was planning to propose changes to the system prior to accepting responsibility for decision-making, so as to address some of the very problems the report identified.[12] While there was some force in the first two objections, it was the third point that ultimately we found convincing.

There was nothing that could reasonably be considered as political censorship or undue sensitivity on the part of the Board in all this. We were not asked to alter any points of substance which did fall within the terms of reference, and that includes the criticisms made of the handling of legal aid appeals by the Board's own area offices and area committees (Young et al. 1992: 96–9). Nor did our research contract prevent us from publishing our views on transfer elsewhere. It was simply that the Board regarded these views on transferring legal aid decision-making away from the courts as out of place in the report that it wished to publish as the product of the research that it had commissioned. It is fair to conclude that the Board's request that one section of the report be deleted was not borne of a desire to suppress inconvenient findings.

RESEARCH IMPACT

At this time there was nothing in the research assessment exercise to encourage academics to strive to ensure that their research made a mark beyond the academy. Many, though, sought to bring about practical reform through their work, long before the term 'public criminology' became popular (Rock 2014). In the final version of our report to the Legal Aid Board (Young et al. 1992) we did not make any explicit policy recommendations. Nonetheless, the findings were detailed enough to influence the policy debate about the transfer of decision-making away from the courts, and we did conclude by questioning whether 'a decision making process as open-ended and opaque as that now operated by the magistrates' courts is in the best interests of justice'

[12] In brief, the Legal Aid Board recommended that a system of 'early cover' be introduced, which would allow solicitors to self-authorize a limited grant of legal aid encompassing representation at a first hearing. This would enable the Board to determine an application for a full grant of legal aid without holding up court proceedings (Legal Aid Board 1993). Following opposition to these proposals from the courts and the legal profession, the Lord Chancellor declined to adopt them on the ground that they might lead to delays.

(ibid: para. 21.34). We also published a short article in a practitioner journal commenting on the idea of transferring decision-making responsibility to the Legal Aid Board (Young and Sanders 1992). Primarily, however, we envisaged that our findings would be taken up in new guidance to be issued to those applying the interests of justice test, and I accepted a small follow-up commission from the Legal Aid Board to summarize our report's findings with exactly this end-result in mind.[13]

At that time, however, most academics did not seek to bring about policy change in a particularly structured or planned way, and rarely built into their initial plans any 'pathways to impact', as they have become known subsequently. Most attempts at influencing policy were in practice rather ad hoc and undocumented.[14] This left the field fairly wide open for others to dominate the process of translating research findings within the policy process. The findings of our own project were presented by the then Lord Chancellor, Lord Mackay, in a particularly biased fashion when he addressed the Law Society national conference in October 1992. The Lord Chancellor's starting point was 'the need to control public expenditure' and it was against that background that he explained his policy plans:

> The recent research conducted for the Legal Aid Board into the application of the interests of justice test revealed alarming inconsistencies in practice between courts . . . Action must and will be taken to see that effective procedures are in place and are properly adhered to, and that legal aid is only granted where it is demonstrably justified under the terms of the present legislation. In the interests of justice field, we are working on revised guidance to the courts on the proper interpretation of the interest of justice criteria.

The implication of the speech was that too much criminal legal aid was being granted because the magistrates' court clerks had adopted a too generous interpretation of the merits test. That stark conclusion could not reasonably be based on the results of our study, at least not without considerable qualification. What we had in fact found was that magistrates' court clerks paid little attention to the Widgery criteria, or to the guidance on their interpretation, but instead generally determined applications using offence-based rules of thumb. Variation in grant rates between courts was largely attributable to differences of approach in relation to what those rules of thumb should be. At the margins, however, the Widgery criteria sometimes played a greater role, although there were significant differences in interpretation (and some misinterpretation) of those criteria amongst the decision-makers. Whilst the structured application form directed the attention of court clerks to each of the Widgery criteria in turn, some of its wording was misleading, effectively making the test more restrictive (Young et al. 1992). Certainly, many of the Widgery criteria were being interpreted far too restrictively by court clerks. For example, in relation to the 'serious damage to reputation criterion', the Lord Chancellor's Guidance from 1984 noted that 'reputation for these purposes is a question of good character, including honesty and trustworthiness, and is not related to social class'. In practice low-granting courts placed little or no weight on this criterion in the case of the unemployed, with some

[13] The guidance eventually appeared in 1994 (see note 19 below).

[14] See further note 18 below, and accompanying text.

decision-makers taking the view that only those of high social class had a reputation worth preserving.

Moreover, as emphasized in our conclusion, we had deliberately picked courts with consistently high or low grant rates in order to be able to examine and explain variation. The problem of disparity was thus presented, the report stressed, in accentuated form (ibid: para. 21.32). It also stressed that the interests of justice test was highly discretionary and that therefore court clerks were generally acting within the law in pursuing their differing legal aid policies. None of these caveats were referred to by the Lord Chancellor in addressing the Law Society.

I sought to put the record straight by writing an article for the *Criminal Law Review* which argued that the interests of justice test needed to be interpreted *more* generously in a number of important respects (Young 1993). It would be naive to think that ministers are swayed from their chosen course by academic articles. But it was nonetheless important to respond to the misuse of our research findings.[15]

These findings tallied with those produced at the same time by a research team at the University of Leeds (Wall and Wood 1994). David Wall and Adrian Wood examined 5,500 applications for legal aid across 1992–3 and collected data from decision-makers using some of the same instruments developed for the Birmingham research. They found evidence of further 'Widgery drift' with 22 per cent of these applications made in respect of summary offences (Wall 1996b: 119). More importantly, they demonstrated convincingly that court clerks were committed to, and succeeded in, maintaining a particular level of legal representation in the magistrates' courts notwithstanding a particular (and short-lived) legislative change which made it significantly less likely that defendants would receive a custodial sentence (ibid: 122–7). The researchers concluded that attempts to change existing procedures would have to be carefully engineered to take account of the working practices of legal advisers and the courts, and also the needs of defendants (ibid: 136), points that were woven into their submissions to the Home Affairs Select Committee,[16] and the Lord Chancellor's Department in early 1993, and in their response to draft legal aid guidance the following year (Wall and Wood 1994: 79). There was thus no shortage of attempts by academics to influence the policy debate at this juncture, although their effectiveness remains uncertain.[17]

[15] One can see this as an attempt to under-state the impact of research, whereas the temptation under the Research Excellence Framework (discussed below) is now to overstate it (and perhaps to remain silent when one's findings are unjustifiably invoked to legitimate policy change), a point taken up in the conclusion below.

[16] This submission can be found within Appendix 3 to the Centre for Criminal Justice Studies, University of Leeds, Fifth Annual Report 1992–3.

[17] In Wall and Wood (1994: para. 6.2) it is stated that: 'The research has already informed the development and administration of policy by the Lord Chancellor's Department in a number of ways.' No details are given, however—in the 1990s there was no pressing need to document evidence of 'impact' (i.e. for REF purposes). Looking back, Dave Wall thinks that the study contributed to the weight of research evidence 'supporting the need to retain a robust legal aid system [which] ultimately prevented the budget from being slashed as much as the government of the day originally intended. More specifically, one of our findings was that there were some very practical reasons for keeping the existing system intact as it simply "oiled the wheels of the court" and kept them running smoothly... It was a point that seemed to be well accepted [by] all parties' (personal email communication, 25 February 2016).

THE CONTINUING DEBATE ON 'ALTERNATIVE ARRANGEMENTS': 1993–2005

Draft guidance issued by the Lord Chancellor's Department in the wake of Lord Mackay's 1992 speech signalled to court clerks that when none of the Widgery criteria applied, legal aid should be refused unless the case was 'sufficiently serious' and that cases of that kind were 'likely to be exceptional' (cited in Young 1993: 5). More balanced guidance was issued to the courts in 1994 which attempted to reassert the need for individualized judgement and to structure decision-making in terms of the Widgery criteria.[18] The Lord Chancellor's interest in transferring that decision-making away from the courts altogether and in finding ways to reduce the level of grants of legal aid was intensifying, however. A factor at this time was the reports of the National Audit Office which expressed formal reservations as to whether magistrates' courts were discharging their duties properly when deciding whether or not to grant legal aid.[19] This led the Lord Chancellor to issue an ultimatum in a Green Paper: 'Unless there is a marked improvement, very soon, in the way in which the courts carry out their functions, alternative arrangements will have to be implemented' (Lord Chancellor's Department 1995: para. 10.11).

The options considered in the Green Paper included a transfer of responsibility for making decisions about legal aid either to the Legal Aid Board or to solicitors. At the same time, the government indicated that it favoured replacing the Widgery criteria with a new set of interests of justice criteria that would be more straightforward to apply and to audit (ibid: para. 10.16). The magistrates' courts remained opposed to losing their power over legal aid[20] and, in the event, the government did not pursue these proposals. The interests of justice test and the Widgery criteria continued to govern decision-making, at least in theory.

An important change to the surrounding legal framework was then ushered in by the Human Rights Act 1998, which allowed defendants to invoke in domestic courts Article 6 (the right to a fair trial) of the European Convention on Human Rights. This includes the right to be afforded legal assistance free of charge (subject to a means test) where the interests of justice so require. As part of the growing recognition of the importance of rights, the High Court exhibited a greater willingness in the 1990s to quash refusals of legal aid.[21]

In a further attempt to limit the growth in legal aid expenditure, the Access to Justice Act 1999 saw the replacement of the Legal Aid Board with the Legal Services Commission (LSC)—a non-departmental public body at arm's length from its

[18] *Guidance on the Interests of Justice Test for the Grant of Criminal Legal Aid*, London: Lord Chancellor's Department, Justices' Clerks Society, Legal Aid Board, May 1994.

[19] National Audit Office Report by the Comptroller and Auditor-General, *The Administration of Legal Aid in England and Wales*, London: HMSO, 1992 and subsequent reports from 1993–5.

[20] See *The Lawyer*, 9 May 1995.

[21] See *R v Gravesham Magistrates Court, ex parte Baker*, Times Law Reports, 30 April 1997; *R v Scunthorpe Justices, ex parte S*, Times Law Reports, 5 March 1998; and *R v Chester Magistrates' Court, ex parte Ball and another* (1999) 163 JP 757. This was even more evident in the mid-2000s: *R (on the application of Matara) v Brent Magistrates Court* [2005] EWHC 1829.

sponsoring body, the Lord Chancellor's Department. The latter was then renamed the Department for Constitutional Affairs (DCA) in 2003. In the following year the DCA issued a consultation paper on its proposal to transfer authority to grant legal aid from the courts to the LSC. It reasoned that this change was necessary to gain better control over grant decisions, alleging that magistrates' courts, in particular, had been too 'favourable to defendants, and certainly inconsistent, in applying the interests of justice test... there is also some evidence that the test has not been applied rigorously in all courts' (DCA 2004: paras. 40, 45).

The House of Commons Constitutional Affairs Committee (HCCAC) took evidence on this proposal and both the Magistrates' Association and JCS argued that the DCA critique was unsubstantiated (HCCAC 2004: paras. 67, 74). The Committee itself questioned what evidence existed to bear out the DCA's claims (ibid: paras. 67, 87), and, in the event, the government decided to adopt a different approach to reform. It proposed that decisions on granting legal aid should remain with the magistrates' court but under a 'service-level agreement' with the LSC, which would become accountable for the application of the merits test.[22] It was envisaged that this accountability would require the LSC to exercise more robust control over the grant process.

The LSC accordingly commissioned further research on the operation of the interests of justice test, with a view to providing an evidence base on such issues as whether there was a need to revise existing procedures and guidance, the content of training for decision-makers, and the matters to be covered by the service-level agreement. It took the view that it would be sensible to engage the same research team as before. I was now based at the Centre for Criminology at the University of Oxford and by chance had the capacity to take another look at legal aid, working this time with Aidan Wilcox.

THE OXFORD RESEARCH: 2005

By the mid-2000s the research landscape looked very different to that of the early 1990s. The research assessment exercise (now rebranded as the 'Research Excellence Framework' (REF)) was now a prominent feature of everyday life. Moreover, the 2008 REF was to see a shift away from the system of awarding a single grade to each department in favour of 'quality profiles' which indicated the proportion of each school's published work in each quality category. The pressure on each and every research-active academic to produce four internationally excellent publications was thus ramping up. The 2008 REF also placed significant weight on the 'research environment' including the level of research grants obtained from external sources. Oxford University was perhaps less troubled by such pressures than many less prestigious institutions but the Centre for Criminology relied on short-term research grants to maintain much of its activities, with many staff reliant on this 'soft money' for their

[22] A change effected by the Criminal Defence Service Act 2006.

future employment. At this time it was, however, becoming much harder to obtain research grants from governmental bodies on reasonable terms. Rock (2014: 423) has written how policy makers were now looking for:

> argument that was focused on the small in scale and succinct in its presentation (no more than two sides of A4); timely—that is available for use precisely when the administrators and politicians wanted it for practical purposes; unburdened by what would be considered irrelevant preamble and context... unequivocal, clear and simple;... and, where possible, supportive of proposals that were being taken forward at the time.

We were told during a Home Office visit to the Oxford Centre in the mid-2000s that what policy makers really wanted was everything 'boiled down to two bullet points'. My own frustrations at the time were expressed as follows:

> First, the deadlines for bidding for Home Office contracts have become increasingly tight, to the point of absurdity. Sometimes as little as two weeks is provided for potential research teams to be identified, designs to be drawn up, literature reviews completed, and tender documents submitted. Secondly, the typical specification of how quickly the Home Office wishes the research to begin and be completed, how many interim reports it will need, how many data it demands be collected and analysed, and how little money it is prepared to pay, is designed to depress the most indefatigable researcher.
>
> (Young and Sanders 2003: 374)

In truth, the government had 'largely turned its back on public criminology and looked to business consultants, market researchers and special advisers instead' (Rock 2014: 423). Tendering processes were structured and operated accordingly, and the attraction of seeking such funding reached vanishing point. So when the LSC directly commissioned us to conduct academic research on legal aid *and* proved receptive to reasonable discussions about how it might be carried out, it was certainly a refreshing change. Unfortunately the LSC was not the only governmental body with a finger in this particular research pie.

ACCESS

Unlike in 1992, before beginning fieldwork we had to secure a 'privileged access agreement' from the DCA, which had taken on the role of powerful gatekeeper for anyone wishing to conduct research in the courts. Despite the fact that it was the DCA itself that had tasked the LSC with taking on accountability for legal aid decision-making by the courts, it proved remarkably unhelpful when it came to the practical arrangements for setting up the research commissioned by the LSC to this end.[23] The nub of the problem was that the DCA claimed that (unspecified) 'data processing legislation' meant that it could not provide us with access to the court filing systems but only to a sample of a set number of files. The difficulty here is that without the chance to examine the filing systems there was no way of telling whether particular courts filed legal aid application forms in specific ways. Relying on court staff to present us with a

[23] Ed Cape (who conducted research on legal aid at roughly the same time) similarly found that the DCA 'around 2005 was really difficult to work with' (personal email communication, 7 March 2015).

selection of files would virtually preclude the possibility of constructing a representative sample.

Moreover, on learning that we were making preliminary visits to the courts to explain the research and discuss how it might be conducted, the DCA instructed court staff not to talk to us, thus making it even more unlikely that we could arrange for a sensible sample to be drawn. This led to a somewhat frosty email exchange and a tense meeting at the DCA in an attempt to cut the Gordian knot. Although we were supported by the LSC we were unable to persuade the DCA that its interpretation of the requirements of data protection legislation was overly restrictive and harmful to valid research. In order to allow the research to go ahead at all we therefore had to accept that court staff would be responsible for making a set number of legal aid application forms available for analysis. The effect of all this was that the sample was unrepresentative in certain ways (see Young and Wilcox 2005: 23). The chances of research affecting policy are obviously somewhat reduced when the findings have to be subjected to caveats deriving from the problematic nature of the access afforded and the resultant limits on the data sampled.

FINDINGS

The main findings were that little had changed since the 1992 study in the sense that decision-makers continued to pay little attention to the Widgery criteria, and that when they were used they were often misinterpreted. For example, whereas the High Court had by this time made it clear that 'serious damage to reputation' was a criterion applicable to anyone of 'good character',[24] in practice many court clerks (and applicant solicitors) regarded it as restricted to those of high social class or repute such as vicars (ibid: 57). Similarly the need for 'expert cross-examination' was often wrongly interpreted as restricted to cases where experts needed to be cross-examined (ibid: 69), again in ignorance of a High Court decision to the contrary.[25] Judicial authority and administrative guidance relating to the Widgery criteria rarely influenced front-line decision-making. As before, the wording of the standard application form, and the guidance, was found to be defective in a number of respects.

On the positive side, decision-making overall seemed more defensible both because it was less idiosyncratic, and because a much greater proportion of legally aided cases now carried serious consequences or involved greater legal complexity. Thus, whereas in 1992 just under 7 per cent of the researched cases resulted in a custodial sentence, in 2005 the corresponding figure was 22 per cent (Young and Wilcox 2007: 118). This reflected the fact that the rate of custodial sentencing had increased sharply since the early 1990s (Cape and Moorhead 2005: 45). Similarly, procedural and evidential innovations such as abolition of the right to silence by the Criminal Justice and Public Order Act 1994, the 'plea before venue' procedure introduced by the Criminal Procedure and Investigations Act 1996, and the bad character provisions of the

[24] *R v Scunthorpe Justices, ex parte S*, Times Law Reports, 5 March 1998; *R v Chester Magistrates Court, ex parte Ball and another* (1999) 163 JP 757.

[25] *R v Liverpool City Magistrates, ex parte McGhee* [1993] Crim LR 609.

Criminal Justice Act 2003 had greatly added to the complexity of summary justice (Young and Wilcox 2005: 167). To the extent that there had been a genuine increase in the number and proportion of grants of legal aid over the preceding decade, this was largely attributable to an increase in the number, complexity, and severity of magistrates' court cases, rather than to lawyers generating demand for their own services (Cape and Moorhead 2005: 38–45). As we observed: 'It is not that court clerks have become more generous over time. They have simply adapted to the changed world they find themselves operating in' (Young and Wilcox 2007: 119).[26]

We also argued that, given this greatly altered context: 'Legally-informed, court-based, flexible, rapid, legal aid decision-making is now essential to the functioning of summary justice' (Young and Wilcox 2005: 167). In other words, we took the view that it would be a serious mistake to transfer decision-making away from the court and into a centralized bureaucracy.[27] Instead, we intimated that the LSC should use the device of the Service Level Agreement to improve the accountability, accuracy, and consistency of decision-making in ways which did not heap disproportionate bureaucratic demands on already busy court staff. How then to square this circle?

IMPACT

The report of this research was much more explicit about how to achieve change in decision-making than the equivalent 1992 document. Existing decision-making norms were so entrenched and decision-making itself so focused on the standard application form that there seemed little point in simply issuing new guidance. Our main proposal was therefore that the standard application form should be redesigned so that it incorporated certain key legal norms—particularly those that ran counter to erroneous understandings of the Widgery criteria. Included within the Report was a redesigned version of the standard application form, so there could be no doubt about what we were suggesting (ibid: 154–6). Thus, for example, the 'expert cross-examination criterion' prompt was rendered as follows: 'The proceedings may require the skilful cross-examination of a prosecution witness (whether an expert or not).' We also included 'guidance boxes' alongside each Widgery criterion prompt. This was, in other words, an attempt to weave accurate interpretations of the law into the everyday routines of solicitors' application practices and clerks' decision-making.[28] The very simplicity of this rather modest-looking proposal was designed to promote its rapid assimilation.

Just as in 1992, our sense was that the body which had funded us took our research findings seriously, and shared our concern that the Widgery criteria should be

[26] There was, in other words, little evidence in this setting over this period to support the thesis (Bevan 1996) that suppliers (lawyers) were inducing demand for legal services and thus driving the costs of legal aid upwards.

[27] For a contrary view, see Darbyshire (1999: 383–4).

[28] We were influenced here by work on the importance of 'communication formats' in shaping the practices of front-line decision-makers: Ericson and Haggerty (1997: 33). See also Ericson (2007: 380).

interpreted correctly, even if this meant a higher level of grants in some respects. Thus the LSC adopted our key recommendation by bringing into use (with minor modifications) the application form we had designed. It was, however, almost immediately withdrawn and replaced by one that omitted all of the embedded guidance. On enquiry, we discovered that the reintroduction of means testing in the magistrates' court in October 2006[29] had necessitated changes to the legal aid application form and that, in making these changes, all the elements we had proposed had been removed, most likely through an oversight. When criminal justice consists of so many constantly moving parts and new policy initiatives there is obviously a risk that the impact of research will be short-term, as here. Could we have done more to publicize this turn of events and thus brought some pressure to bear on those with the power to (re)implement our key recommendation? On reflection I think we could have done, but we were busy on other fronts and, in any case, by the mid-2000s I had virtually ceased writing short pieces for practitioner journals aimed at influencing the worlds of practice and policy. As I noted at the time:

> academics are currently under enormous pressure to do more with less. As staff–student ratios worsen, as library budgets and research grants are cut, as responsibility (but rarely power) is devolved to academic departments (now 'budget centres'), so increases the pressure to run several research projects simultaneously (to generate income for one's department...), publish scholarly books and articles (so as to generate more income through the Research Assessment Exercise), to teach better (to satisfy external funding bodies), to teach more students (to bring in more income), and to carry ever greater administrative burdens. In this new research context it becomes difficult to justify writing short articles for practitioner journals (since these count for nothing in the Research Assessment Exercise) and to engage in other forms of activity designed to influence policy (but with no measurable outputs or gain to the university).
>
> (Young and Sanders 2003: 374)[30]

That last sentence now sounds rather quaint in light of the fact that only a few years later academics were incentivized by the rules announced in 2009 (governing the REF held in 2014) to demonstrate the impact of their research on the world beyond the academy. Such impact counted for 20 per cent of each department's overall rating in that exercise, and is almost certain to count for even more in REF 2020. Shortly before the 'impact agenda' hoved into view, however, a further chance had arisen to translate some of our research findings into policy change.

[29] The means test had been abolished in 2001 on the basis that the cost of administering it outweighed the revenue saved, but ministers had failed to take into account that solicitors had been filtering out potential applications. Abolition thus resulted in a sharp increase in the number of legally aided defendants and high-profile cases of very rich defendants securing public funding to defend relatively minor charges: Sanders, Young, and Burton (2010: 504).

[30] Ed Cape has similar recollections in relation to his legal aid research conducted at the same time (Cape and Moorhead 2005): '[We] didn't do as much "impact" work as we might have done... one of the problems is that once a piece of work has been done it is on to the next thing, and impact and policy work was not built in to research contracts' (personal email communication, 7 March 2016).

THE EXPERT PANEL AND ITS AFTERMATH: 2008–2016

In 2008, I was invited to take part in a joint project run by Her Majesty's Courts Service (HMCtS) and the LSC 'to analyse decision-making on the grant of legal aid'.[31] This involved participating in an 'expert panel' made up primarily of members of the JCS. The idea was to meet to discuss each criterion for grant with a view to distilling the 'correct approach' which could then underpin training and guidance for decision-makers. This presented an opportunity to try to ensure at least that the gap between the judicial review cases and the guidance (and associated training) was closed. The difficulty was that the panel was likely to be dominated by the 'expertise' of practitioners who research had repeatedly shown to share ingrained, legally inaccurate, norms.

In the event, the 'expert panel' met just once, in September 2008. The main point I pressed on that occasion was that any new guidance should reflect and cite the relevant judicial review case-law. The draft guidance produced and circulated to members of the panel in November 2008 included some but not all of the case-law, with predictable consequences. For example, under the section on 'Other reasons' for granting legal aid (i.e. beyond the Widgery criteria), the draft guidance stated 'Examples in this category could include the likelihood of a demanding community order, and the need for expert examination of a defence witness' but did not provide citations to the case-law which had established that precisely these matters were relevant to the interests of justice test.[32] One justices' clerk responded by email: 'Not convinced! I see the difficulty of giving examples, but if you can't think of a good one, leave it out?' The justices' clerk's inference that someone had dreamed up implausible examples would (I trust) not have been drawn had it been made explicit that these norms had been laid down by the High Court of England and Wales.

In my own response to the draft guidance I pressed again the point that decision-makers would discount any examples or norms that did not accord with their own entrenched views unless the case-law citation was included. The second iteration of the draft guidance in December 2008 noted:

> The comments made by [justices' clerk quoted above] and Richard demonstrate the tension which exists throughout this document between attempting to produce working guidance which can be applied in a simple, practical manner, whilst at the same time not short-changing the known law as it stands. The guidance cannot ride roughshod over the law, but nor can it be an academic textbook.

[31] This section draws on my unpublished paper entitled 'Bridging the gaps between judicial review, administrative guidance, and low visibility decision-making in the courts: a case-study of academic impact', given at a University of Leeds symposium on 'Justice in the Criminal Courts in the 21st Century' held on 6 and 7 June 2013.

[32] On the significance of a demanding community order, see *R v Liverpool City Magistrates, ex parte McGhee* (CO/0289/927, 3 March 1993). The relevance of expert examination of a defence witness was established in *R v Gravesham Magistrates Court, ex parte Baker*, Times Law Reports, 30 April 1997.

The compromise reached was to incorporate the judicial review norms into the guidance but to relegate the citations of the relevant cases to footnotes.[33]

There was then a very long silence, and enquiries revealed that other concerns had elbowed their way up the policy agenda. Indeed, it was not until late August 2012 that the final version of the guidance was published by the LSC on its website. A requirement to use this guidance was presumably part of the 'service level agreement' between the LSC and the courts, but as matters turned out there was no chance to assess whether it made any difference to the behaviour of court clerks. The government's continuing frustration at the level of control exerted by the LSC over decision-making (in both civil and criminal legal aid) resulted in it securing the abolition of the Commission as of 1 April 2013. The Legal Aid, Sentencing and Punishment of Offenders Act 2012 (LASPO) transferred the Commission's powers and functions to the Lord Chancellor working through a new executive body (the Legal Aid Agency) established within the Ministry of Justice (which itself had replaced the DCA in 2007). This reflected a commitment to tighten 'stewardship' of the legal aid fund, establish stronger ministerial accountability, and enable the Ministry of Justice to put strict controls in place to manage the costs of the scheme (Lord Chancellor's Department 2010: para. 10.10).

During 2014–15, the Legal Aid Agency in stages duly took over decisions on the grant of legal aid, so that court staff were no longer involved in this process. Instead, Agency administrative staff now handle applications on an electronic basis at a 'small number of centralised sites'.[34] They are still applying the same interests of justice test, according to the same Widgery criteria—both test and criteria were re-enacted by s. 17 of LASPO 2012. Quite how they are applying these criteria must remain a matter of speculation. Legal Aid Agency statistics indicate an overall grant rate of 95 per cent, in line with historic trends, but do not include a breakdown by courts, Agency decision-making teams, or individuals.[35] Hence variation in application rates (by solicitors) and grant rates (by decision-makers) are no longer discernible. The fact that the body administering legal aid is now so closely tied to government gives rise to a concern that decision-making will be moulded by a mission of cost-cutting (Cape 2013: 5; Smith and Cape forthcoming). More restrictive decision-making norms will not necessarily be reflected in a lower grant rate however as solicitors may adjust their practices so as to avoid wasting time making applications likely to be refused. Further in-depth research is accordingly needed before any assessment can be made of the implications of the new centralized system of legal aid decision-making.

Whether any such research will take place may be doubted. The abolition of the LSC led to the disappearance of its independently managed research arm, the Legal Services Research Centre. This Centre had carried out and commissioned important research into legal aid, including the critique by Cape and Moorhead (2005) of the

[33] The influence of the 'impact agenda' can be seen in my subsequent (successful) request that my contribution to the process of drawing up the new guidance be acknowledged somewhere in the guidance document itself.

[34] Legal Aid Agency, *Changes to Criminal Legal Aid Processing* (issued 4 February 2015), p3, https://www.gov.uk/guidance/legal-aid-reforms.

[35] Ministry of Justice, *Legal Aid Statistics in England and Wales: October to December* 2015, p13, https://www.gov.uk/government/statistics/legal-aid-statistics-october-to-december-2015.

supplier-induced demand thesis noted above.[36] According to one of the Centre's researchers, it enjoyed a productive relationship with the LSC 'with research helping to inform policy and practice—but it seemed that [the Ministry of Justice] finally caught on to this and wanted to take back power'.[37] By contrast the Legal Aid Agency appears to have no remit for funding or facilitating research (Smith and Cape forthcoming).[38]

It is worth adding that the closure of the LSC website resulted in the disappearance of the interests of justice guidance that the Expert Panel had produced. Thus while the process of drawing up the guidance and bringing it into use had taken four years, its web lifetime was just seven months. Further pressure by myself and my HMCtS contact eventually resulted in its reappearance on the Legal Aid Agency website, although locating it remains a challenge unless one knows the URL.[39] The key recommendation of the Oxford research relating to the redesign of the legal aid application form has also unexpectedly enjoyed a new lease of life. Thus Form CRM14, version 10, issued in 2013, incorporated a few of our suggestions concerning how to present the Widgery criteria.[40] As of April 2016 both the guidance and the standard application form continue to be shaped to some extent by the findings of research.

CONCLUSION

We have seen that the architecture surrounding the interests of justice test has been subject to much change over the past 50 years: the back-office administration of legal aid passed from the Law Society to the Legal Aid Board, a body which was then replaced by the LSC that in turn was replaced by the Legal Aid Agency. As for the front-line, the key decision-makers were once quasi-judicial court clerks working in a decentralized court structure, whereas they are now centralized bureaucrats working within an agency of the Ministry of Justice. Those who most obviously stood to gain from extensive grants of legal aid (the courts and the representative body of solicitors) have had their powers stripped as part of the attempt to gain control of the criminal legal aid budget. Throughout all this upheaval the interests of justice test and the Widgery criteria have been retained. Yet this one constant factor has itself enabled a massive expansion of state-funded representation in the magistrates' courts, and is open to new interpretation in light of changes in sentencing patterns and the

36 One of the researchers in the Legal Services Research Centre at the time recollects that the Cape and Moorhead (2005) research was commissioned because of a sense 'that the "supplier-induced demand" thesis was one that was in danger of severely undermining the legal profession and so we obtained funding from the LSC to examine this important topic and use[d] this as a vehicle to bring the issue out into the open in a considered way' (Vicky Kemp, personal email communication, 1 March 2016).

37 Vicky Kemp (personal email communication, 1 March 2016).

38 Not one of the 187 documents published by the Legal Aid Agency and hosted on its website as of 1 April 2016 could be categorized as research.

39 The key document is now entitled *LAA Guidance on the Consideration of Defence Representation Order Applications*, and can be found at: https://www.gov.uk/guidance/work-out-who-qualifies-for-criminal-legal-aid.

40 The related 'guidance boxes' we had advocated have not resurfaced, however.

complexity of court proceedings. Indeed, there can be few better illustrations of the point that discretion is a dynamic and adaptable phenomenon (Hawkins 1992: 45).

Seeking to influence a world in such constant flux is not easy, especially when the policy agendas of those involved have rarely meshed with broader academic concerns centring on fundamental issues of justice and the rule of law. What the above clearly shows, however, is that policy-making is dispersed across networks, and policy makers have different interests, viewpoints, and agendas to one another. The concern of the Lord Chancellor's Department/DCA/Ministry of Justice has been excessive generosity in the grant of legal aid, whereas the Legal Aid Board/LSC have been more troubled by inconsistency and inaccuracy in the application of law, while practitioner and parliamentary bodies have questioned whether there is evidence to support policy change. This created opportunities for independent research to bring about some measure of progressive reform, even in unpromising political circumstances. Thus Cape and Moorhead (2005: 66–70) so effectively publicized the way that broader changes to the criminal process were fuelling demand for legal aid that the government may[41] have felt compelled to introduce a legal aid impact test as part of its criminal justice policy reviews. 'This was never more than a half-hearted, back of the envelope, exercise but there was, at least, some recognition that legal aid costs should not be seen in isolation' (Cape 2013). Research may also have fuelled the case for *not* reforming policy at certain times. Thus a quarter of a century elapsed before the initial governmental plan to transfer legal aid decision-making from local courts to national bureaucrats (first mooted in the late 1980s) came to fruition. Quite what the role of research was in impeding that development is impossible to assess, but that it had some part to play seems plausible.[42] If researchers had roundly declared that court clerks were 'too generous' in their grants of legal aid one can imagine these findings being acted upon with alacrity.

In my own case (building on work carried out with colleagues), the strategy of using High Court decisions as 'trumps' in the effort to close the gap between legal norms and everyday decision-making proved reasonably productive, at least in terms of changing the 'communication formats'[43] around the interests of justice test. But the above account reveals that precisely because the tectonic plates of policy-making are constantly shifting, any academic impact may be 'lost through the cracks' (but may also reappear unexpectedly). Achieving lasting academic impact in such a setting may necessitate a willingness to exploit whatever opportunities present themselves, dogged monitoring of policy documents, persistent nagging of officials in order to drive research-related matters up their agenda, and a certain amount of dumb luck. That said, the overall trend throughout this period has been towards greater centralization, tighter ideological control of policy and practice, and a concomitant reduction in the role that research and researchers are able to play. To return to Hawkins' theoretical

[41] No public acknowledgement was made of the link between the research and the introduction of the impact test, and subsequent policy development within the Ministry of Justice focused on cutting legal aid eligibility rather than moderating the actions of government departments which produced the demand for legally aided services (private communication from Ed Cape, 25 February 2016).

[42] See note 18 above.

[43] See note 29 above.

triptych (Hawkins 2002), the decisive shift in the surround in favour of dismantling the welfare state has led to a reconfiguration of the field designed to ensure that decision-making frames are focused much more on efficiency and economy than on ensuring that citizens are properly represented when charged with a criminal offence (Smith and Cape forthcoming; Sommerlad 2008).

Finally, we have also seen that the nature of the academic endeavour itself has been subject to much change. To simplify, prior to the research selectivity exercises, academics often sought to influence the world of policy in quite pragmatic ways simply out of a sense of wanting to improve the world around them or even more basically out of the urge to 'speak truth to power'. For a time, research selectivity had the effect of undercutting this activity in favour of major works of scholarship assigned high value by fellow academics (although such works often have the greatest impact on the world in the long run of course).[44] Now the changing rules around research selectivity have refocused attention on 'impact' beyond the academy by attaching a substantial monetary value to it. The result is that universities are placing significant pressure on academics to 'make important things happen', and to collect evidence of the causal link between their research and this impact. Decisions on recruitment, pay, probation, progression, and promotion are increasingly being shaped by this agenda.

All of this has undoubtedly led to a greater willingness, even enthusiasm, to engage with the inner workings of the world of policy in the attempt to see research translated into practice. Yet some obvious worries remain, including that academics will be tempted into working on projects that have the greatest chance of impact precisely because the findings are likely to be palatable to policy makers, or that they will focus more on impact than quality in the way they conduct and write up the research,[45] or that universities will construct 'impact case-studies' in ways which overstate the likely contribution of academic work, which is usually just one of a myriad of influences on the ever-shifting terrain of policy (Young and Sanders 2003: 333). Moreover, we saw above that tighter control both over research funding and research access have made more difficult the production of valid findings on which to base policy. All of this raises issues of academic freedom, integrity, and independence. In charting and influencing the changing contours of criminal justice we need to cling to these values. Ultimately what profit would follow from changing the world whilst losing our soul?

REFERENCES

BEVAN, G. (1996), 'Has There Been Supplier-Induced Demand for Legal Aid?', *Civil Justice Quarterly*, 15: 98–114.

BORRIE, G. and VARCOE, J. (1970), *Legal Aid in Criminal Proceedings: A Regional Survey*, Birmingham: Institute of Judicial Administration, University of Birmingham.

BRIDGES, L. (1982), 'Legal Aid League Tables—New Data, Wider Discrepancies', *LAG Bulletin*, June: 8.

[44] See e.g. Zedner (2003), Oswald (2009), Fernandez-Armesto (2009).

[45] See further Gorard (2008).

Bridges, L. and Cape, E. (2008), *CDS Direct: Flying in the Face of the Evidence*, London: Centre for Crime and Justice Studies.

Brown, R. with Carasso, H. (2013), *Everything for Sale? The Marketisation of UK Higher Education*, Abingdon: Routledge.

Burney, E. (1979), *JP: Magistrate, Court and Community*, London: Hutchinson.

Cape, E. (2004), 'The Rise (and Fall?) of a Criminal Defence Profession', *Criminal Law Review*: 401–16.

Cape, E. (2013), *Criminal Defence: The Value and the Price*, Keynote Speech to the Conference of the Criminal Law Committee of the Law Society, London, 17 May.

Cape, E. and Moorhead, R. (2005), *Demand Induced Supply? Identifying Cost Drivers in Criminal Defence Work*, London: Legal Services Research Centre, Legal Services Commission.

Darbyshire, P. (1984), *The Magistrates' Clerk*, Chichester: Barry Rose.

Darbyshire, P. (1999), 'A Comment on the Powers of Magistrates' Clerks', *Criminal Law Review*: 377–86.

Department for Constitutional Affairs (DCA) (2004), *Criminal Defence Service Bill*, Consultation Number CP 17/04, Cm 6194.

Departmental Committee on Legal Aid in Criminal Proceedings (1966), *Report of the Departmental Committee on Legal Aid in Criminal Proceedings*, Cm 2934, London: HMSO.

Ericson, R. (2007), 'Rules in Policing: Five Perspectives', *Theoretical Criminology*, 11, 3: 367–401.

Ericson, R. and Haggerty, R. (1997), *Policing the Risk Society*, Oxford: Clarendon Press.

Fernandez-Armesto, F. (2009), 'Poisonous Impact', *Times Higher Education*, 3 December.

Gorard, S. (2008), 'A Reconsideration of Rates of "Social Mobility" in Britain: Or Why Research Impact Is Not Always a Good Thing', *British Journal of Sociology of Education*, 29, 3: 317–24.

Goriely, T. (1996), 'The Development of Criminal Legal Aid in England and Wales', in R. Young and D. Wall (eds), *Access to Criminal Justice*, London: Blackstone.

Hansen, O. (1982), 'What a Difference a Clerk Makes', *LAG Bulletin*, March: 11.

Hawkins, K. (1992), 'The Use of Legal Discretion: Perspectives from Law and Social Science', in K. Hawkins (ed.), *The Uses of Discretion*, Oxford: Clarendon Press.

Hawkins, K. (2002), *Law as Last Resort: Prosecution Decision-Making in a Regulatory Agency*, Oxford: Oxford University Press.

House of Commons Constitutional Affairs Committee (HCCAC) (2004), *Draft Criminal Defence Service Bill*, Fifth Report of Session 2003–04, HC 746-1.

Jump, P. (2013), 'Evolution of the REF', *Times Higher Education*, 17 October.

Kemp, V. (2010), *Transforming Legal Aid: Access to Criminal Defence Services*, London: Legal Services Research Centre, Legal Services Commission.

Legal Aid Board (1989), *Report to the Lord Chancellor*, Cm 688, London: HMSO.

Legal Aid Board (1993), *The Legal Aid Board's Advice to the Lord Chancellor's Department on the Implications of its Taking over Responsibility for Criminal Legal Aid in the Magistrates' Courts*, London: Legal Aid Board.

Lord Chancellor's Department (1995), *Legal Aid—Targeting Need: The Future of Publicly Funded Help in Solving Legal Problems and Disputes in England and Wales*, Cm 2854, London: HMSO.

Lord Chancellor's Department (2010), *Proposals for the Reform of Legal Aid in England and Wales*, CP 12/10; Cm 7967.

McConville, M., Hodgson, J., Bridges, L., and Pavlovic, A. (1994), *Standing Accused*, Oxford: Clarendon.

Moorhead, R. (1998), 'Legal Aid in the Eye of a Storm: Rationing, Contracting, and a New Institutionalism', *Journal of Law and Society*, 25, 3: 365–87.

Moorhead, R. (2004), 'Legal Aid and the Decline of Private Practice: Blue Murder or Toxic Job?', *International Journal of the Legal Profession*, 11, 3: 159–90.

Morgan, R. (2000), 'The Politics of Criminological Research', in R. King and E. Wincup (eds), *Doing Research on Crime and Justice*, Oxford: Oxford University Press.

Oswald, A. (2009), 'REF Should Stay Out of the Game', *The Independent*, 26 November.

Parker, H., Casburn, M., and Turnbull, D. (1981), *Receiving Juvenile Justice*, Oxford: Basil Blackwell.

Paterson, A. with Birch, C. and Green, S. (1971), *Legal Aid as a Social Service*, London: Cobden Trust.

Rock, P. (2014), 'The Public Faces of Public Criminology', *Criminology and Criminal Justice*, 14, 4: 412–33.

Royal Commission on Legal Services (1979), *Final Report*, Cm 7648, London: HMSO.

Sanders, A. (1987), 'Some Dangers of Policy-Oriented Research—the Case of Prosecutions', in I. Dennis (ed.), *Criminal Law and Justice*, London: Sweet & Maxwell.

Sanders, A., Young, R., and Burton, M. (2010), *Criminal Justice*, 4th edn, Oxford: Oxford University Press.

Smith, R. (1996), 'Legal Aid on an Ebbing Tide', *Journal of Law and Society*, 23, 4: 570–9.

Smith, T. and Cape, E. (forthcoming), 'The Rise and Decline of Criminal Legal Aid in England and Wales', in A. Flynn and J. Hodgson (eds), *Access to Justice and Legal Aid: Comparative Perspectives on Unmet Legal Need*, Oxford: Hart Publishing.

Sommerlad, H. (1999), 'The Implementation of Quality Initiatives and the New Public Management in the Legal Aid Sector in England and Wales: Bureaucratisation, Stratification and Surveillance', *International Journal of the Legal Profession*, 6, 3: 311–43.

Sommerlad, H. (2001), '"I've Lost the Plot": An Everyday Story of the "Political" Legal Aid Lawyer', *Journal of Law and Society*, 28, 3: 335–60.

Sommerlad, H. (2004), 'Some Reflections on the Relationship between Citizenship, Access to Justice, and the Reform of Legal Aid', *Journal of Law and Society*, 31, 3: 345–68.

Sommerlad, H. (2008), 'Reflections on the Reconfiguration of Access to Justice', *International Journal of the Legal Profession*, 15, 3: 179–93.

Wall, D. (1996a), 'Legal Aid, Social Policy and the Architecture of Criminal Justice: The Supplier Induced Inflation Thesis and Legal Aid Policy', *Journal of Law and Society*, 23, 4: 549–69.

Wall, D. (1996b), 'Keyholders to Criminal Justice?: Solicitors and Applications for Criminal Legal Aid', in R. Young and D. Wall (eds), *Access to Criminal Justice*, London: Blackstone.

Wall, D. and Wood, A. (1994), *The Administration of Criminal Legal Aid in the Magistrates' Courts of England and Wales: Final Report to the ESRC*, Leeds: Centre for Criminal Justice Studies.

Young, R. (1993), 'The Merits of Legal Aid in the Magistrates' Courts', *Criminal Law Review*: 336.

Young, R. (1996), 'Will Widgery Do?: Court Clerks, Discretion, and the Determination of Criminal Legal Aid Applications', in R. Young and D. Wall (eds), *Access to Criminal Justice*, London: Blackstone.

Young, R. and Sanders, A. (1992), 'A Wise and Sensible Move?', *New Law Journal*, 142, 6572: 1409–17.

Young, R. and Sanders, A. (2003), 'The Forester's Dilemma: The Influence of Police Research on Police Practice', in L. Zedner and A. Ashworth (eds), *The Criminological Foundations of Penal Policy*, Oxford: Oxford University Press: 333–75.

Young, R. and Wilcox, A. (2005), *Understanding the Interests of Justice: A Study of Discretion in the Determination of Applications for Representation Orders in Magistrates' Courts*, Oxford: Centre for Criminology, University of Oxford.

Young, R. and Wilcox, A. (2007), 'The Merits of Legal Aid in the Magistrates' Courts Revisited', *Criminal Law Review*: 109–28.

Young, R., Moloney, T., and Sanders, A. (1992), *In the Interests of Justice? The Determination of Criminal Legal Aid Applications by Magistrates' Courts in England and Wales: Report to the Legal Aid Board*, Birmingham: University of Birmingham.

Zander, M. and Glasser, C. (1967), 'A Study in Representation', *New Law Journal*, 117: 815.

Zedner, L. (2003), 'Useful Knowledge? Debating the Role of Criminology in Post-War Britain', in L. Zedner and A. Ashworth (eds), *The Criminological Foundations of Penal Policy*, Oxford: Oxford University Press.

8

RATIONALES FOR SENTENCING IN ENGLAND AND WALES OVER FIVE DECADES—RATATOUILLE WITHOUT A RECIPE?

Andrew Ashworth

Sentencing is probably the criminal justice system's highest point of visibility. Sentences are reported in newspapers, on the television, radio, and social media; they are discussed in the pubs and cafés. The unfailing human interest in crime and punishment also means that sentencing is a political issue: the government is expected to 'do something about' crimes in general, or crimes of a particular type, often by increasing sentence levels. The proper role of the state in matters of sentencing has been the subject of controversy for centuries. If we go back only so far as the eighteenth century, we find the seminal texts written by Beccaria and Bentham (Beccaria 1764; Bentham 1789). What is evident from these writings and the mass of subsequent literature is that almost all 'theories of punishment' have both a philosophical and an empirical dimension. That duality is more obvious with consequentialist rationales for sentencing such as deterrence and incapacitation, but it is also evident in many prominent forms of desert rationale. Thus, while Andreas von Hirsch maintains that deserved punishment is 'an integral part of everyday judgments of praise and blame', that the essence of sentencing is to impose deserved censure on wrongdoers, and that sentence levels should reflect the principle of penal restraint or parsimony (on which see von Hirsch 1993: 40–6; Duff 2001: 86–8), he also accepts that there must be an element of hard treatment in sentencing because otherwise there would be insufficient deterrence and lawlessness would prevail (von Hirsch 1986: 52, 48). Thus the desert rationale for sentencing has empirical underpinnings in terms of the relationship between the overall level of sanctions and levels of offending (but cf. Moore 1987 for 'pure' retributivism).

While most rationales for sentencing have an empirical element, the volume of empirical research relevant to sentencing rationales has not been high in the last 50 years. And, when such empirical research has been carried out, its implications have not always been translated into policy. Indeed, as this chapter will discuss, there are occasions on which relevant research has been either ignored or misinterpreted. The aim of the chapter is thus to examine the interplay between sentencing rationales, research, and policy in the last five decades. Starting in the 1960s, the chapter will trace the influence of the various rationales on sentencing policies developed by governments, the judiciary, and sentencing councils in England and Wales. It will consider whether there is a dominant sentencing rationale or a more complex and nuanced interaction between various rationales, and what the role of criminological research is in this field.

FIVE DECADES OF DIVERGENT POLICIES

This section traces the influence of various sentencing rationales, and it discusses rehabilitation, incapacitation, deterrence, and desert in turn. The historical sketch will necessarily be selective, but an attempt will be made to identify the most significant policy shifts and to consider their links to developments in sentencing theory and relevant research.

REHABILITATION

In the mid-1960s the rehabilitative rationale was still in full vigour. There was strong support for the view that the state's main role in dealing with offenders was to train and to treat them so as to change or remove the traits that led them to commit offences. This was still the era of what David Garland described as 'penal welfarism' (Garland 1985), and the use of terms such as treatment, resocialization, and reintegration gives some indication of the range of techniques employed (see further von Hirsch et al. 2009: ch. 1). Perhaps the high-water mark of this approach was the justification offered by the British government for introducing discretionary release on parole: the 1965 White Paper claimed that prisoners reached a 'peak in their training', at which point their release under supervision would maximize their chances of law-abidance (Home Office 1965a: para. 5). On this basis, provisions for the early supervised release of prisoners were introduced for the first time in the Criminal Justice Act 1967. The rehabilitative rationale also underpinned the welfare-oriented provisions of the Children and Young Persons Act 1969, which sought to 'de-criminalize' the response to juvenile offending and even to raise the age of criminal responsibility to 14, provisions that remained unimplemented following a change of government in 1970 (Bottoms 1974; Home Office 1965b).

The rehabilitative rationale depends to a large extent on the effectiveness of the methods it uses, and doubts began to be raised in the late 1960s and early 1970s. Research into the effectiveness of Intensive Matched Probation (IMPACT) found that overall reconviction rates were the same as for ordinary probation, although it did identify one small sub-group that consistently fared better on IMPACT (Folkard 1976). Disappointment at these results was compounded by the findings of the meta-survey of research into rehabilitative techniques by the American criminologist Robert Martinson in 1974, which were encapsulated in the phrase 'nothing works'. Although

Martinson himself tried to emphasize that this was too reductive a generalization, the stark phrase heralded what has been called 'the decline of the rehabilitative ideal' in the United States (Martinson 1974, 1979; cf. Garland 2001; Zedner 2002). Martinson's work was known in England and Wales, but it did not have the same negative impact because of the more nuanced findings of a similar meta-survey of rehabilitative measures by Stephen Brody (Brody 1976), which was sufficient to ensure that efforts to find successful rehabilitative approaches continued (as, indeed, they did in the United States: Cullen and Gendreau 2001).

Thus in the 1980s considerable effort was put into rehabilitative initiatives for young offenders. The use of police cautions was encouraged and rose significantly during the decade; and for those young people who were prosecuted, a rehabilitative non-custodial measure called 'intermediate treatment' was developed. The overall result was that the use of custody for juveniles declined from 7,900 in 1981 to 2,400 in 1989, a spectacular example of rehabilitative and decarcerative (Scull 1977) principles in action. While such policies might not have been expected of a Conservative government elected partly on a 'law and order' ticket, tougher measures for adults were signalled in the late 1980s. Not only did the Criminal Justice Act 1988 contain a number of repressive measures, including increases in some maximum penalties (Faulkner 2014: 89), but also Home Office ministers began to emphasize the punitive elements of the probation order rather than its rehabilitative elements (Faulkner 2014: 90). Thus when the Criminal Justice Act 1991 was passed, it stated that a probation order should be imposed where desirable 'in the interests of a) securing the rehabilitation of the offender or b) protecting the public from harm from him'. In this way the rehabilitative purpose was reaffirmed, but risk management was introduced as an alternative rationale. However, the 1990s saw increasing interest in the 'what works' movement, a movement structured around the belief that rehabilitative techniques can be effective if they are properly monitored and carefully evaluated (McGuire 1999).

In 2001 the Halliday Report went so far as to claim that investment in cognitive-behavioural programmes could reduce reoffending 'by 5–15 percentage points' (Halliday 2001: para. 1.49), but Tony Bottoms denounced this claim as 'reckless' (Bottoms 2004; see further Bottoms and von Hirsch 2010: part IIIA), and a careful examination of cognitive behavioural programmes in prisons and probation by Colin Roberts emphasized the complexities of establishing and evaluating them and concluded that the programmes alone were 'unlikely to deliver the outcomes in reducing offending that have been expected of them' (Roberts 2004: 156). Nevertheless, even in the heyday of repressive policies, there was a place for rehabilitative measures 'so that the offender can learn new skills and attitudes which make him or her less likely to offend' (Home Office 2002: para. 5.8; see also paras. 0.17, 5.4, 6.1). In the same vein, there has been much interest in ways of encouraging offenders to desist from offending, particularly by identifying factors or 'hooks' that may assist offenders. The desistance movement is a well-established off-shoot of the rehabilitative rationale, with growing empirical support (e.g. Burnett 2004; Farrall et al. 2011).

The Oxford Centre played a significant part in the development of assessment tools for probation officers. Colin Roberts and Ros Burnett developed a tool called ACE, which was a forerunner of OASys (Offender Assessment System), still used in the preparation of pre-sentence reports (Merrington 2004). That also gave rise to the development of a specific assessment tool for youths, called Asset (Baker 2004). The Centre also evaluated intensive supervision and surveillance programmes for young offenders, introduced by the Youth Justice Board and targeted on high-risk offenders but, as with the IMPACT experiment a couple of decades earlier, the results were on a rather modest scale (Moore 2004). Rehabilitation continues to figure in government policy: the coalition government of 2010–15 proclaimed a 'rehabilitation revolution', and the Offender Rehabilitation Act 2014 provides for more released prisoners to be supervised and introduces a system of paying providers of supervision by results. To what extent these initiatives will employ techniques that are truly rehabilitative remains to be seen, as does their comparative effectiveness.

INCAPACITATION

The incapacitative rationale extends to various disqualifications (from driving, from acting as a company director, and so on), but our interest here is its use as a justification for extended loss of liberty for offenders deemed to present a danger to the public. This rationale, sometimes termed 'public protection', has had its place in penal policy for many years. At the start of the 1960s the relevant sentence was 'preventive detention', introduced by the Criminal Justice Act 1948 for recidivists over the age of 30 who could be sentenced to between 5 and 14 years' imprisonment. The sentence was designed to deal with 'professional criminals' but came to be applied to persistent non-serious offenders, leading to overly severe sentences which the Lord Chief Justice sought to eliminate by a 1962 Practice Direction (Ashworth 2015: 205–7). As a result of this initiative and of empirical research which confirmed that most offenders subjected to this sentence posed no serious threat (Hammond and Chayen 1963; West 1963), preventive detention fell into disuse in the 1960s. The Criminal Justice Act 1967 introduced the extended sentence, allowing courts to extend a sentence beyond its normal length in order to protect the public against persistent offenders who were 'a real menace to society' (Home Office 1965a). Again, the measure quickly fell into disuse: serious offenders already received long sentences (sometimes life imprisonment), and extending the sentences of non-serious offenders was largely regarded as inappropriate by the judiciary.

Incapacitative theory re-emerged in the Criminal Justice Act 1991. As we will see below, the main rationale in that Act was proportionality; but a large exception to this was the power to pass longer than proportionate sentences on violent or sexual offenders for public protection. The power was not often used by the courts, largely for the same reasons as before, although the discretionary sentence of life imprisonment came to be used more frequently and the Crime (Sentences) Act 1997 introduced an automatic life sentence for the second serious sexual or violent offence. This was based on flawed claims (Hood and Shute 1996), and the Court of Appeal used its power under the Human Rights Act 1998 to extend the 'exceptional circumstances' proviso so as, in effect, to reintroduce a proportionality constraint (*Offen (No. 2)* [2001] 1 Cr App R 372). However, the Criminal Justice Act 2003 replaced this sentence and, in addition to raising the level of minimum terms in respect of life imprisonment for murder (Mitchell and Roberts 2012), introduced a new sentence of Imprisonment for

Public Protection (IPP), which was mandatory for many offenders convicted of a second sexual or violent offence and which led to indefinite detention. Harry Annison (2015) has charted the political and judicial footprints on the scandal that IPP became, particularly between 2005 and its relaxation in 2008—indeterminate imprisonment for relatively non-serious offences, the unpreparedness of the prisons for the influx of prisoners on indeterminate sentences, and the government's failure to provide courses to enable prisoners to demonstrate their suitability for release (Ashworth and Zedner 2014: ch. 7). Moreover, the scandal continues despite the abolition of IPP by the Legal Aid, Sentencing and Punishment of Offenders Act 2012, and some 4,614 IPP prisoners were still in prison in June 2015.[1]

Have these incapacitative sentences been based on empirical research? The Floud Report reviewed the research up to 1980 and was pessimistic about the possibility of predicting at a higher level than 50 per cent whether offenders would be dangerous to release (Floud and Young 1981: Appendix C). A Home Office research report in 1981 was even more pessimistic, although it emphasized that the calculation contains several unknowns (Brody and Tarling 1981). Extensive research in the United States has not improved upon these prediction rates (Ashworth and Zedner 2014: ch. 6; Skeem and Monahan 2011). Yet these criminological findings have been persistently ignored by governments in their desire to bring forward politically attractive measures for 'public protection' against 'dangerous offenders', and until 2010 they continued to do this despite the evident malfunction of all previous measures. Then, in 2010, came a short sentence in a Green Paper issued by the Coalition government: 'The limitations of our ability to predict future serious offending... [call] into question the whole basis on which many offenders are sentenced to IPPs' (Ministry of Justice 2010: para. 186).

This sudden and unexpected recognition of the accumulated empirical research featured in a confluence of liberal political forces in 2010 that signalled the end of IPP (Annison 2015: 74–6), and the injustice of detaining thousands of repeat offenders whose offences were not of high seriousness was recognized in 2012 by the substantial narrowing of the criteria for imposing indeterminate protective sentences (Ashworth 2015: 238–48). However, the sentence of life imprisonment (mandatory for murder, discretionary for several other offences) remains in frequent use and, as Catherine Appleton (2010) demonstrated, decisions on release and recall have a substantial predictive element. In general the Parole Board is considerably risk-averse in its decisions, as research by Roger Hood and Stephen Shute (2000) has shown, and the release of indeterminate sentence prisoners is a slow process. There remains the enormous practical problem that some 19 per cent of the prison population of England and Wales are serving life imprisonment or another indeterminate sentence. More attention now needs to be given to release, preparation for release, and a fair policy for recall for breach of licence (Appleton 2010; Padfield and Maruna 2006).

DETERRENCE

There is a well-known distinction between individual deterrence (sentences designed to deter the particular offender) and general deterrence (sentences aimed at deterring

[1] http://www.parliament.uk/briefing-papers/Sn06086.pdf.

potential imitators from committing future offences). Both forms of the deterrent rationale employ the same method—fear of the consequences. Individual deterrence as a sentencing rationale is largely confined to repeat offenders, and has returned to prominence in recent years. In earlier decades the leading principle in sentencing persistent offenders was said to be 'progressive loss of mitigation': a first offender received mitigation for a good record, but with subsequent convictions that claim to mitigation was lost, but even if the offender had several previous convictions he should not receive a sentence above the 'ceiling' proportionate to the offence (Thomas 1979: 41). Whether the judges always applied this principle in practice is doubtful, but it was entrenched in Court of Appeal judgments, and in the Criminal Justice Act 1991 Parliament attempted to express it in statute. Unfortunately some judges took the new provisions to mean that they were required to disregard previous convictions—which was not what the legislation said—and judicial clamour led to the repeal of section 29 of the 1991 Act and its replacement with a provision that explicitly enabled courts to take account of previous convictions (Ashworth 1995: 160–2; see generally Roberts 2008). Individual deterrence clearly lay behind the enactment of section 143(2) of the Criminal Justice Act 2003, which (in brief) requires courts to 'treat each previous conviction as an aggravating factor'. This form of words harks back to the 'cumulative principle' adopted by some nineteenth-century judges, adding more to the sentence on each conviction with little regard to the seriousness of the offences (Radzinowicz and Hood 1986: 237–8); it espouses the method of individual deterrence ('increase punishment' for repeat offenders: Home Office 2002: para. 5.10), probably combined with an element of incapacitation. This same combination also underlies the growing number of mandatory minimum sentences. Thus the White Paper, that led to the introduction of mandatory minima for repeat domestic burglars and drug dealers in the Crime (Sentences) Act 1997, made assertions about the preventive effectiveness of this type of sentence, completely unsupported by empirical evidence (Home Office 1996: paras. 11.2, 12.8, 12.9). Since then, Parliament has added several more mandatory minimum sentences (Ashworth 2015: 105–7, 233–7).

However, the rationale for introducing these mandatory minima is probably based as much, if not more, on general deterrence. There is a lengthy history of judicial confidence in the general deterrent effect of high sentences, and this has sometimes been used as a justification for passing 'exemplary' sentences on some offenders in order to deter others. This judicial confidence has been manifested in several cases of riot, from the Notting Hill race riots of 1958 (on which see Ashworth 1983: 344–6) to the widespread riots of August 2011 and the judgment in *Blackshaw* emphasizing deterrence (see [2012] 1 Cr App R (S) 679: at paras 4, 75, 85–6, 91, 125) and also in cases of football hooliganism and 'mugging', among others (Cross 1981: 136–40). In these cases the argument was for marginal general deterrence, that is, implying that raising the sentence level by a certain amount would dissuade more people from offending. So confident are the judiciary in this belief that when the 1991 Criminal Justice Act required custodial sentences to be 'commensurate with the seriousness of the offence', Lord Taylor CJ held that this should be interpreted as 'commensurate with the punishment and deterrence which the seriousness of the offence requires' (*Cunningham* (1993) 14 Cr App R (S) 444, at 447). Not only was this a flagrant misreading of the statute, which was intended to place a proportionality limit on custodial sentences (Ashworth 2015: 107–9), but it went against Lord Taylor's own reasoning on another occasion. When in 1996 Michael Howard as Home Secretary proposed mandatory sentences for deterrent reasons (mentioned above), Lord Taylor responded by stating that general deterrence might work through increasing the probability of being caught but that the evidence of its effectiveness by raising sentence levels was 'flimsy and dubious' (Taylor 1996).

Reviews of the evidence on general deterrent strategies emphasize the many conditions that must be satisfied if they are to have a chance of working. For example, deterrence operates through fear, and the threat must be brought to the attention of potential offenders and must not be discounted by reference to other factors such as a perceived low risk of detection. When the Labour government was elected in 1997 a review of the evidence on deterrence was commissioned from Cambridge University (von Hirsch et al. 1999). Its somewhat negative findings on marginal general deterrence by raising sentence levels (as distinct from increasing the speed and frequency of detection) were studiously ignored in subsequent policy initiatives by a government wary of appearing 'soft on crime'. International reviews of deterrence research since then have not yielded more encouraging outcomes for the supporters of the deterrent rationale (e.g. Doob and Webster 2003; Webster and Doob 2012). Moreover, there is little empirical support for the suggestion that more austere prison conditions will exert a deterrent effect (Burnett and Maruna 2004). However, both governments and the judiciary continue to act on the assumption that marginal general deterrence works, adopting a simplistic model that makes unfounded assumptions about the rationality of decision-making by offenders. The 1990 White Paper drew attention to these factors and to the untenability of the 'rational choice' perspective here (Home Office 1990: para. 2.8), but we have seen that Michael Howard in his tenure as Home Secretary denied or ignored these findings, and they seem not to have influenced policy since then. Despite the evidence, there seems to be an enduring political and judicial attraction to the belief that marginal general deterrence works.

DESERT AND PROPORTIONALITY

We have seen how both governments and the judiciary have placed emphasis, at different times, on incapacitative, deterrent, or rehabilitative rationales for sentencing. However, it was not until 1990 that there was a government-led discussion of rival theories. The White Paper of 1990, in one of the last manifestations of the 'Platonic guardians' (Loader 2006), put forward a bifurcated structure for sentencing. The primary principle was to be that 'the severity of the sentence of the court should be directly related to the seriousness of the offence', with an exception for serious sexual and violent offenders for whom longer incapacitative sentences were to be available (Home Office 1990: paras. 1.6, 1.8). The institutionalization of proportionality or desert as the leading rationale for sentencing was, however, poorly accomplished. The Criminal Justice Act 1991 was drafted in an allusive manner, not articulating the proportionality principle clearly and stating only that decisions to impose a custodial sentence and then decisions as to the length of the custodial sentence should be based on 'the seriousness of the offence'. The Act was immediately under attack from the judiciary, and we have already noted under subheading 'Deterrence' how Lord Taylor managed to reintroduce the deterrent rationale which it had been the government's intention to suppress. When Michael Howard was appointed Home Secretary in 1993 he proclaimed that 'prison works', and the general atmosphere of resentment against offenders in the mid-1990s was so powerful that even judges who were not punitive by inclination found themselves imposing higher sentences (e.g. Lord Bingham CJ in *Brewster* [1998] 1 Cr App R (S) 181, 184). The driving force behind this movement was not desert or proportionality so much as deterrence and incapacitation, as became abundantly clear in the 1996 White Paper on mandatory sentencing, which led to the Crime (Sentence) Act 1997 (Home Office 1996, discussed earlier under subheading 'Incapacitation'). Neither the legislature nor the judiciary applied the intention of the 1991 Act so as to place emphasis on proportionality: the provisions of sections 1 and 2 of the Act withered on the vine, and it was no surprise when the Halliday Report summarized the drift of sentencing policy in the 1990s by recording 'the gradual erosion of the approach set out in the Criminal Justice Act, with its emphasis on linking punishment to the seriousness of the offences under sentence' (Halliday 2001: para. 0.2; also para. 1.34).

Halliday sought to reconfigure the proportionality principle by incorporating a recidivist premium, so that 'the severity of the punishment should reflect the seriousness of the offence and the offender's criminal history' (Halliday 2001: para. 2.8). This approach diverges significantly from that of prominent desert theorists, who argue in favour of limiting the recidivist premium so as to preserve proportionality to the seriousness of the offence (e.g. Duff 2001; von Hirsch 1993). The Halliday approach to previous convictions was adopted in the Criminal Justice Act 2003, a statute that muddied the waters considerably by requiring courts to have regard to five purposes when passing sentence—punishment, deterrence, rehabilitation, public protection, and reparation. To give courts a choice from five 'purposes' is hardly compatible with the idea of sentencing guidelines, for which the 2003 Act also provided, and the early guidance issued by the Sentencing Guidelines Council stated that 'the sentencer must start by considering the seriousness of the offence', which includes culpability and any harm which the offence caused, was intended to cause, or might foreseeably cause (Sentencing Guidelines Council 2004: para. 1.3). However, this guideline has rarely been referred to by the courts, and it is unclear to what extent the proportionality element in Halliday's modified scheme still exerts an influence on sentencers.

It is certainly true that the definitive sentencing guidelines laid down by the Sentencing Guidelines Council (until 2010) and now the Sentencing Council are influenced by a kind of proportionality. However, their approach fails to recognize the principle of penal restraint that leading writers on proportionality insist upon, as noted in the opening paragraph above. This is bound up with the rationale of desert theory: 'if penal hard treatment is to supplement rather than replace censure, it must not be so harsh that it effectively drowns out the law's moral voice' (Duff 2001: 87). This element of desert theory is sometimes overlooked in a more populist version of 'just deserts'. Thus Garland has argued that the rise of 'just deserts': 'has also re-established the legitimacy of an explicitly retributive discourse, which in turn has made it easier for politicians and legislatures to openly express punitive sentencing and to enact more draconian laws' (Garland 2001: 9).

However, the rise of penal populism is surely as much connected with deterrent and incapacitative policies as with proportionality (Pratt 2007). Certainly there is no necessary connection between proportionality and increased severity, as can be seen from experiences in Finland, Sweden, and Minnesota (von Hirsch and Ashworth 2005: ch. 6). In practice much depends on the nature of a state's political system, culture, and institutions (Lappi-Seppala 2013), leading Nicola Lacey to argue that attention should be given to the 'broad socio-economic, cultural and political conditions [that] structure the waxing and waning of popular conceptions of desert', and also to the 'different institutional structures [that] affect the way in which such popular conceptions feed into the development and implementation of policy' (Lacey 2008: 19). Thus there is no consensus about the level at which cardinal proportionality should be set, since it is culturally and politically determined (Ashworth 1989: 344–5; Lacey and Pickard 2015: 227–8).

Is there an empirical component in the desert rationale? There is a separate theory of 'empirical desert' that seeks to ascertain a community's intuitions about justice and desert and to base sentencing on the findings, aiming to maximize the criminal law's effect on behaviour (for fuller details see Robinson 2008: chs. 7 and 8; Robinson et al. 2014; Slobogin and Brinkley-Rubenstein 2013). Returning to the von Hirsch-Duff account of desert, however, it contains a preventive element in its justification of hard treatment (punishment): if it can be shown that a reduction in penalty levels would not have the effect of increasing crime, then that reduction should be made on the principle of penal restraint or parsimony that forms part of modern desert theory (e.g. von Hirsch 1993: 40–2). This raises the question of the connection between crime rates and punishment levels, and we may refer back to the recent work of Lacey (2008) and Lappi-Seppala (2013) in demonstrating the importance of political institutions and socio-economic conditions rather than focusing solely on the sentencing system.

FROM 'NOTHING WORKS' TO 'PRISON WORKS'?

How should the influence of the various sentencing rationales in England and Wales over the last 50 years be characterized? The crude headlines might be the decline of the rehabilitative ideal ('nothing works') followed by the rise of just deserts, swiftly overlaid by waves of deterrent and incapacitative sentences ('prison works'). Those headlines mask other significant movements, which must be incorporated in a more nuanced account.

The rise of just deserts proved to be a false dawn in England and Wales. While the aim of the 1991 Criminal Justice Act was to give priority to proportionality, the Act soon came to be side-lined and ignored, so that within ten years the Halliday Report was referring to its 'erosion' (Halliday 2001: para. 0.2). Proportionality exerts some effect on the structure of sentencing guidelines, but without the element of penal restraint on which modern desert theorists insist. Instead, both the government and the judiciary have placed increased emphasis on deterrence and on incapacitation. In particular, the enactment of more mandatory and mandatory minimum sentences has been driven by deterrent reasoning rather than proportionality, and the burgeoning of indeterminate sentences for 'public protection' stems from incapacitative reasoning. The slogan 'prison works', introduced by Michael Howard as Home Secretary in 1993, proved to be a significant step in the escalation of penal severity. Feeding on heightened public concern about crime, it foreshadowed a period of penal populism in which politicians and the mass media 'talked up' sentence levels, tapping into deep concerns about risk, uncertainty, and vulnerability (see further Loader 2006; Pratt 2007; Ramsay 2012).

Yet rehabilitative measures have continued to be tried and evaluated throughout the five decades, albeit sometimes within the punitive envelope of a strictly enforced court order. Effectiveness, in terms of the reduction of reoffending, remains the touchstone of success in this sphere, whether the rationale is rehabilitation or desistance (as is evident from the Offender Rehabilitation Act 2014 and the privatization of supervision). There have also been developments in restorative justice: the government's action plan commits it to increasing the use of restorative justice across the criminal justice system, with equal access by victims irrespective of the location or the type of crime committed against them (Ministry of Justice 2014). If the language of this action plan is translated into reality, it promises to bring restorative justice in from the margins to more widespread involvement in criminal justice. Yet these 'green shoots' in rehabilitation and restorative justice must be viewed in the context of a sentencing system characterized by the use of imprisonment at a significantly higher rate than that of our European neighbours, mostly sustained by deterrent and incapacitative rhetoric (for a different view, identifying proportionality as the main driver of severity, see Lacey and Pickard 2015). There appears not to be any sentencing rationale that is dominant, and a major task for the academy is not only to continue developing criminological research into the effects of particular policies and to devise convincing rationales for particular responses to crime, but also to attempt to bridge the undoubted gap between theory and research on the one hand and penal policy and politics on the other (Loader and Sparks 2010: ch. 5).

REFERENCES

ANNISON, H. (2015), *Dangerous Politics: Risk, Political Vulnerability and Penal Policy*, Oxford: Oxford University Press.

APPLETON, C. (2010), *Life after Life Imprisonment*, Oxford: Oxford University Press.

ASHWORTH, A. (1983), *Sentencing and Penal Policy*, London: Weidenfeld and Nicolson.

ASHWORTH, A. (1989), 'Criminal Justice and Deserved Sentences', *Criminal Law Review*, 340–55.

ASHWORTH, A. (1995), *Sentencing and Criminal Justice*, 2nd edn, London: Butterworths.

ASHWORTH, A. (2015), *Sentencing and Criminal Justice*, 6th edn, Cambridge: Cambridge University Press.

ASHWORTH, A. and ZEDNER, L. (2014), *Preventive Justice*, Oxford: Oxford University Press.

BAKER, K. (2004), 'Is Asset Really an Asset?', in R. Burnett and C. Roberts (eds), *What Works in Probation and Youth Justice*, Cullompton: Willan.

BECCARIA, C. (1764, [1963]), *On Crimes and Punishments*, Indianapolis, IN: Bobbs-Merrill.

Bentham, J. (1789, [1948]), *An Introduction to the Principles of Morals and Legislation*, Oxford: Blackwell.

Bottoms, A.E. (1974), 'On the Decriminalisation of the Juvenile Court', in R. Hood (ed), *Crime, Criminology and Public Policy*, London: Heinemann.

Bottoms, A.E. (2004), 'Empirical Research Relevant to Sentencing Frameworks', in A.E. Bottoms, S. Rex and G. Robinson (eds), *Alternatives to Prison*, Cullompton: Willan.

Bottoms, A.E. and Hirsch, A. von (2010), 'The Crime-Preventive Impact of Penal Sanctions', in P.F. Cane and H.M. Kritzer (eds), *Oxford Handbook of Empirical Legal Research*, Oxford: Oxford University Press.

Brody, S.R. (1976), *The Effectiveness of Sentencing*, Home Office Research Study 35, London: HMSO.

Brody, S.R. and Tarling, R. (1981), *Taking Offenders Out of Circulation*, Home Office Research Study 64, London: HMSO.

Burnett, R. (2004), 'One-to-One Ways of Promoting Desistance', in R. Burnett and C. Roberts (eds), *What Works in Probation and Youth Justice*, Cullompton: Willan.

Burnett, R. and Maruna, S. (2004), 'So Prison Works, Does it?', *Howard Journal of Criminal Justice*, 43, 4: 390–404.

Cross, R. (1981), *The English Sentencing System*, 3rd edn, London: Butterworths.

Cullen, F.T. and Gendreau, P. (2001), 'From Nothing Works to What Works: Changing Professional Ideology in the 21st Century', *Prison Journal*, 81, 3: 313–38.

Doob, A. and Webster, C. (2003), 'Sentence Severity and Crime: Accepting the Null Hypothesis', *Crime and Justice*, 30: 143–95.

Duff, R.A. (2001), *Punishment, Communication and Community*, New York: Oxford University Press.

Farrall, S., Hough, M., Maruna, S., and Sparks, R. (eds) (2011), *Escape Routes: Contemporary Perspectives on Life after Punishment*, Abingdon: Routledge.

Faulkner, D. (2014), *Servant of the Crown: A Civil Servant's Story of Criminal Justice and Public Service Reform*, Hook: Waterside Press.

Floud, J., and Young, W. (1981), *Dangerousness and Criminal Justice*, London: Heinemann.

Folkard, S. (1976), *IMPACT volume 2*, Home Office Research Study 36, London: HMSO.

Garland, D. (1985), *Punishment and Welfare*, Aldershot: Gower.

Garland, D. (2001), *The Culture of Control*, Chicago, IL: University of Chicago Press.

Halliday, J. (2001), *Making Punishments Work*, London: Home Office.

Hammond, W.H., and Chayen, E. (1963), *Persistent Offenders*, London: H.M.S.O.

Hirsch, von, A. (1986), *Past or Future Crimes*, New Brunswick, NJ: Rutgers University Press.

Hirsch, von, A. (1993), *Censure and Sanctions*, Oxford: Oxford University Press.

Hirsch, von, A. and Ashworth, A. (2005), *Proportionate Sentencing*, Oxford: Oxford University Press

Hirsch, von, A., Ashworth, A., and Roberts, J. (2009), *Principled Sentencing: Readings on Theory and Policy*, 3rd edn, Oxford: Hart Publishing.

Hirsch, von, A., Bottoms, A.E., Burney, E., and Wikstrom, P.-O. (1999), *Criminal Deterrence: An Analysis of Recent Research*, Oxford: Hart Publishing.

Home Office (1965a), *The Adult Offender*, London: HMSO.

Home Office (1965b), *The Child, the Family and the Young Offender*, London: HMSO.

Home Office (1990), *Crime, Justice and Protecting the Public*, London: HMSO.

Home Office (1996), *Protecting the Public: The Government's Strategy on Crime in England and Wales*, London: HMSO.

Home Office (2002), *Justice for All*, London: HMSO.

Hood, R. and Shute, S. (1996), 'Protecting the Public: Automatic Life Sentences, Parole and High Risk Offenders', *Criminal Law Review*, 11: 788–800.

Hood, R. and Shute, S. (2000), *The Parole System at Work*, Home Office Research Study 202, London: Home Office.

Lacey, N. (2008), *The Prisoners' Dilemma: Political Economy and Punishment in Contemporary Democracies*, Oxford: Oxford University Press.

Lacey, N. and Pickard, H. (2015), 'The Chimera of Proportionality', *Modern Law Review*, 78, 2: 216–40.

Lappi-Seppala, T. (2013), 'Imprisonment and Penal Demands', in S. Body-Gendrot, M. Hough, R. Levy, K. Kerezsi, and S. Snacken (eds), *European Handbook of Criminology*, Abingdon: Routledge.

Loader, I. (2006), 'Fall of the "Platonic Guardians": Liberalism, Criminology and Political Responses to Crime in England and Wales', *British Journal of Criminology*, 46, 4: 561–86.

Loader, I. and Sparks, R. (2010), *Public Criminology*, London: Routledge.

McGuire, J. (1999), *Reducing Reoffending: Guidelines from Research and Practice*, London: Wiley.

Martinson, R. (1974), 'What Works? Questions and Answers about Prison Reform', *Public Interest*, 35: 22–54.

Martinson, R. (1979), 'New Findings, New Views: A Note of Caution regarding Sentencing Reform', *Hofstra Law Review*, 7, 2: 243–58.

Merrington, S. (2004), 'Assessment Tools in Probation', in R. Burnett and C. Roberts (eds), *What Works in Probation and Youth Justice*, Cullompton: Willan.

Ministry of Justice (2014), *Restorative Justice Action Plan for the Criminal Justice System for the Period to March 2018*, London: Ministry of Justice.

Mitchell, B. and Roberts, J. (2012), *Exploring the Mandatory Life Sentence for Murder*, Oxford: Hart Publishing.

Moore, M. (1987), 'The Moral Worth of Retribution', in F. Schoeman (ed.), *Responsibility, Character and the Emotions*, Cambridge: Cambridge University Press.

Moore, R. (2004), 'Intensive Supervision and Surveillance Programmes for Young Offenders', in R. Burnett and C. Roberts (eds), *What Works in Probation and Youth Justice*, Cullompton: Willan.

Padfield, N. and Maruna, S. (2006), 'The Revolving Door at the Prison Gate: Exploring the Dramatic Increase in Recalls to Prison', *Criminology and Criminal Justice*, 6, 3: 329–52.

Pratt, J. (2007), *Penal Populism*, London: Routledge.

Radzinowicz, L. and Hood, R. (1986), *The Emergence of Penal Policy in Victorian and Edwardian England*, London: Stevens.

Ramsay, P. (2012), 'Imprisonment under the Precautionary Principle', in G.R. Sullivan and I. Dennis (eds), *Seeking Security*, Oxford: Hart Publishing.

Roberts, C. (2004), 'Offending Behaviour Programmes: Emerging Evidence and Implications for Practice', in R. Burnett and C. Roberts (eds), *What Works in Probation and Youth Justice*, Cullompton: Willan.

Roberts, J. (2008), *Punishing Persistent Offenders*, Oxford: Oxford University Press.

Robinson, P. (2008), *Distributive Principles of Criminal Law: Who Should be Punished and How Much?*, New York: Oxford University Press.

Robinson, P., Barton, J., and Lister, M. (2014), 'Empirical Desert, Individual Prevention and Limiting Retributivism: A Reply', *New Criminal Law Review*, 17, 2: 312–75.

Scull, A. (1977), *Decarceration: Community Treatment and the Deviant—A Radical View*, Englewood Cliffs, NJ: Prentice-Hall.

Sentencing Guidelines Council (2004), *Overarching Principles: Seriousness*, London: Sentencing Guidelines Council.

Skeem, J., and Monahan, J. (2011), 'Current Directions in Violence Risk Assessment', *Current Directions in Psychological Science*, 21(1), 38–42.

Slobogin, C. and Brinkley-Rubinstein, L. (2013), 'Putting Desert in its Place', *Stanford Law Review*, 65, 1: 77–136.

Taylor, Lord (1996), 'Continuity and Change in the Criminal Law', *King's College Law Journal*, 7: 1–11.

Thomas, D.A. (1979), *Principles of Sentencing*, 2nd edn, London: Heinemann.

Webster, C. and Doob, A. (2012), 'Searching for Sasquatch: Deterrence of Crime through Sentence Severity', in J. Petersilia and K. Reitz (eds), *Oxford Handbook of Sentencing and Corrections*, New York: Oxford University Press.

West, D. J. (1963), *The Habitual Prisoner*, London: Heinemann.

Zedner, L. (2002), 'Dangers of Dystopia in Penal Theory', *Oxford Journal of Legal Studies*, 22, 2: 341–66.

9

THE USE OF IMPRISONMENT AS A SANCTION: LESSONS FROM THE ACADEMY

*Julian V. Roberts and Lyndon Harris**

Which offenders should be sent to prison rather than punished in the community? How can a legislature ensure that only the most serious crimes are punished by imprisonment? These basic questions of sentencing policy are relevant to all jurisdictions. In England and Wales, sentencing policy and practice has evolved in response to a myriad of influences, including political and populist pressures. Much of the recent penal reform debate has focused on the use of imprisonment, which has risen steadily in recent years and has attracted a great deal of academic research and critical commentary. Over the past decade, a number of organizations and individuals have advanced reform proposals in this area, often guided by input from academics. For example, a review commissioned by Lord Carter recommended measures to reduce the use of custody (Carter 2007) although this part of his report was not adopted. The independent inquiry into 'English Prisons Today' sponsored by the Howard League also advocated greater 'justice reinvestment' and more sparing use of custody (Howard League 2010). The most recent (and to date most significant) independent inquiry was commissioned by the British Academy. The Inquiry's final report sets out the theoretical, moral, and political arguments why courts should reduce their reliance on custody as a sanction and hence the number of people in prison (see British Academy 2014: 52–85). The report was written by academics, and contains reform proposals ranging from the modest (i.e. dealing with more offenders by way of financial penalties and community-based sanctions), to the more radical (removing imprisonment as the maximum penalty for certain offences)[1] (see British Academy 2014: 86–102).

Members of the Oxford Centre for Criminology, the fiftieth anniversary of which is celebrated in this volume, have played an important role in the evolving debate about the use of imprisonment. Indeed, research on the use of imprisonment has long been a focus of scholarship at Oxford. Max Grünhut, an early pioneer of Oxford penology, published an important volume exploring the use of imprisonment (Grünhut 1948).[2]

* Our thanks to the editors of this volume and Mike Hough for helpful comments on a previous draft.

[1] The proposal to remove custody as an available sentencing disposal for certain offences has also been made by individual academics, most notably Ashworth (2013).

[2] Grünhut (1948) explored several issues of concern to current debates over the use of custody, including ordinal proportionality and the imprisonment of female offenders.

Centre scholars have been publishing on the use of imprisonment ever since (e.g. Ashworth 1989; Walker 1965[3]). Many studies have explored empirical aspects of sentencing, going back to pioneering work by Roger Hood (e.g. Hood 1962, 1972, 1995).[4] Their presence has been significant with regard to independent reports: Ian Loader and Carolyn Hoyle were members of the Howard League's Commission while other members of the Centre, including Andrew Ashworth, have been members of the Sentencing Advisory Panel, the Sentencing Commission Working Group, the Sentencing Guidelines Council, and the Sentencing Council of England and Wales.[5]

Central to the academic critique of contemporary sentencing has been the claim that prison is over-used as a sanction. As will be seen later in this chapter, the courts have actually been moving in the opposite direction to that advocated by the academy over the past decade, the use of custody has increased while the use of community orders has declined. Despite the steady accretion of scholarship over the years by academics throughout the United Kingdom, the impact on the policy and practice of the courts has been modest.[6] Successive governments have legislated in a way that reflects little awareness of, or alternatively an indifference to, the lessons from the academy.

This chapter draws upon the recent scholarly literature to highlight some lessons for sentencing policy that policy makers should have learned from the academy. Scholars have addressed a range of subjects relating to sentencing policy. This chapter examines the scholarship relating to the use of custody as a sanction. We begin by noting recent sentencing trends regarding the use of imprisonment, before turning to the academic literature in three areas: (i) the misuse of new or amended sanctions (referred to as 'net-widening'); (ii) the 'custody threshold'; and (iii) public attitudes to the use of custody. In each area we highlight the policy lessons to be drawn from the academic contributions.

RECENT TRENDS IN THE USE OF CUSTODY

Table 9.1 summarizes trends for indictable offences (all courts) over the period 2003–14 and reveals that the proportionate use of immediate custody rose slightly over this period, from 24 per cent to 27 per cent of all cases. The proportion of cases resolved by a fine declined from 23 per cent to 19 per cent, while community orders dropped significantly, from one-third of all cases in 2003 to 21 per cent in 2014 (Table 9.1). Sentence lengths have increased, particularly for certain crimes. For example, the average minimum term for murder increased by approximately one-third between 2005

[3] Nigel Walker was Reader in Criminology at Oxford during the 1960s and published several important works on sentencing prior to moving to Cambridge (e.g. Walker 1965, 1969).

[4] Hood's landmark study of 1962 contained lessons that remain unheeded today. For example, Hood noted that there was 'no evidence to show that short-term imprisonment meets with more success (i.e. non-reconviction) than does fining or probation for the majority of offenders' (p. 121).

[5] Other members of the Centre such as David Faulkner joined after having made a distinguished contribution to the evolution of sentencing policy (see Faulkner 2014).

[6] It is beyond the scope of this chapter to explain why academic writing has had only a limited impact on the nature and direction of sentencing policy, although one explanation involves the rise of populist punitiveness (see Pratt 2007) and the concomitant decline in policy makers' interest in 'expert' or 'elite' opinion.

Table 9.1 Volumes and rates (percentages of all disposals), indictable offences, all courts, England and Wales, 2003–14

	2003	2004	2005	2006	2007	2008	2009	2010	2011	2012	2013	2014
Immediate custody	80,794	79,938	76,291	73,532	74,037	79,058	80,265	82,939	87,558	81,082	77,843	75,770
Rate	24	25	25	24	24	25	25	24	26	26	27	27
Suspended sentence	2,055	2,143	5,610	20,799	27,254	28,455	31,131	34,176	34,422	31,883	35,429	38,928
Rate	1	1	2	7	9	9	10	10	10	10	12	14
Community sentence	109,549	111,013	111,724	102,971	105,142	102,782	107,924	108,495	100,286	82,815	66,487	58,879
Rate	33	35	37	34	34	33	33	31	29	27	23	21
Fine	77,097	63,999	57,382	50,665	48,452	48,736	55,351	59,437	58,288	53,667	53,159	53,571
Rate	23	20	19	17	16	15	17	17	17	18	18	19
Other Disposals	62,971	58,713	54,495	53,521	56,306	55,910	51,921	62,375	61,304	56,669	57,981	53,661
Rate	19	19	18	18	18	18	16	18	18	19	20	19
Total offenders	332,466	315,806	305,502	301,488	311,191	314,941	326,592	347,422	341,858	306,116	290,899	280,809

Source: Ministry of Justice (2015) Criminal Justice System Statistics Quarterly: Crown Court Data Tool

Table 9.2 Prison population totals and rates per 100,000, EU Countries, 2015

Ranking	Jurisdiction	Prison population total	Prisoners per 100,000 population
1	England & Wales	85,982	148
2	Poland	72,609	191
3	France	66,864	100
4	Spain	63,025	136
5	Germany	61,906	76
6	Italy	52,434	86
7	Romania	28,355	143
8	Czech Republic	20,628	195
9	Hungary	18,424	187
10	Portugal	14,238	138
11	Greece	11,798	109
12	Belgium	11,769	105
13	Netherlands	11,603	69
14	Slovakia	9,991	184
15	Bulgaria	9,028	125

Source: Institute for Criminal Policy Research (2015) World Prison Brief: Prison Population Totals

and 2013, as did the average sentence length for other homicide offences such as manslaughter.[7]

Table 9.2 places the United Kingdom within a comparative context and shows that at the time of writing, the UK has one of the highest rates of imprisonment. The English rate of 148 per 100,000 population is significantly higher than other Western European countries such as Germany and Italy. In addition, while the prison population has been relatively stable over the period 2010–15, at almost 86,000 prisoners, it remains approximately double the size of 20 years ago (Ministry of Justice 2015). This is the statistical context in which to consider the academic contribution to the policy debate about the use of custody as a sanction.

[7] When Parliament enacted schedule 21 to the Criminal Justice Act 2003, giving statutory 'guidance' for determining the length of the minimum term for offences of murder, its effect was to significantly increase sentencing levels. This increase in the sentencing for murder had an impact upon other homicide offences. The Court of Appeal (Criminal Division) stated: 'Parliament's intention it seems is clear: crimes which result in death should be treated more seriously and dealt with more severely than before' (see *R v Wood (Clive)* [2009] EWCA Crim 651; [2010] 1 Cr App R (S) 2 (p. 6)). The impact was also felt more widely, as the perceived need to retain a proximate relationship between sentencing for murder and manslaughter was applied to other offences of violence. As such, sentencing levels have also increased for violent offences against the person: for example between 2009 and 2013, the length of sentence for grievous bodily harm with intent (Offences against the Person Act 1861 s.18) for males aged 21+ rose from 50 months to 71.7 months (guilty plea) and from 72 months to 93.5 months (not guilty plea) (see Banks 2015). There has been an increase in the average custodial sentence length from 12.6 months at the beginning of the decade to 15.6 months in the most recent year (2014), an increase of approximately one-quarter (Roberts and Ashworth 2016).

'WIDENING OF THE NET'

One frequent approach to reducing the use of custody involves the introduction of alternative measures such as home detention curfew and conditional and suspended sentences of imprisonment. An important academic lesson concerns the dangers of creating alternatives to custody and simply assuming this increased range of disposals will reduce the volume of admissions to prison (Stanley and Baginsky 1984). The creation of alternative sanctions was prolific in the Criminal Justice Act 2003. However, approximately a decade after the Act received Royal Assent, a number of the provisions were repealed, some never having been commenced.[8] Their misapplication results in the new (alternative) sanction being applied to the non-custodial caseload rather than reducing the number of cases of immediate custody, a phenomenon referred to as 'net-widening' (Cohen 1971). The most recent manifestation of this phenomenon in England and Wales concerns the amended suspended sentence order (SSO).

A legislative change in 2005[9] removed an important restriction on the imposition of a suspended sentence and the result was a dramatic rise in the number of SSOs. As can be seen in Table 9.1, these orders accounted for only 1 per cent of cases in 2003 but 14 per cent in 2014. Across all courts, SSOs rose from 2,855 in 2004 to 52,979 in 2014 (Roberts and Ashworth 2016: Table 1). Another way of understanding the use of custody is to represent terms of imprisonment as a percentage of all sentences imposed. Since a court should not impose a SSO unless the custodial threshold has been passed and a custodial sentence is unavoidable,[10] this measure combines terms of immediate custody with SSOs. In 2003, these forms of custody together accounted for 25 per cent of all indictable cases; by 2014 this had risen to 40 per cent.

The 2005 reforms to the suspended sentence were intended to reduce the use of imprisonment. They did not; as noted above, the courts continued to impose custody with the same frequency (see Table 9.1). The fact that the proportion of community orders fell to the same degree that the SSOs increased strongly suggests courts have misapplied the suspended sentence and used it to replace community orders rather than terms of custody. This was directly contrary to Parliamentary intention. In 2008, a House of Commons Committee report acknowledged that the legislative changes brought about by the 2003 Act had failed to have the desired effect, noting that 'there has been no evidence of a shift to community penalties for those who might previously have been imprisoned for short periods' (House of Commons Justice Committee

[8] Custody plus (a short custodial sentence followed by an extended licence period) was never commenced and repealed in 2012. Intermittent custody (involving e.g. the custodial sentence being served at weekends) was piloted in 2004, and despite high compliance rates (see Penfold et al. 2006) was abandoned in 2006 and repealed in 2012.

[9] Prior to the Criminal Justice Act 2003, a court imposed a suspended sentence of custody where the circumstances were 'exceptional' (see Powers of Criminal Courts (Sentencing) Act 2000 s. 118). The result of such a high threshold test was to limit the use of the suspended sentence. In 2005, Parliament repealed s. 118 of the 2000 Act and commenced s. 189 of the 2003 Act, removing the requirement for 'exceptional circumstances' and granting courts the power to impose a SSO where the court considered it was 'appropriate'. Additionally, the new form of suspended sentence under the 2003 Act included the requirement to impose one (or more) of a list of community 'requirements' also available under the new form of community order commenced at the same time.

[10] See s. 189 Criminal Justice Act 2003 and Sentencing Guidelines Council (2004: 20–6).

2008: para. 86). Notwithstanding this recognition, the only action Parliament took was to extend the scope of the SSO in 2012 to enable sentences of 24 months and below to be suspended.[11] Numerous academics (e.g. Ashworth 2015: 318–22; Ashworth and Player 2005; Hedderman and Barnes 2015; Wasik 2014) have drawn attention to this example of 'up tariffing' which occurs when a sentence designed to replace immediate custody is applied to less serious cases. Sparks (1971) and Bottoms (1981) first documented the misapplication of the suspended sentence following its introduction by the Criminal Justice Act 1967.

ACADEMIC CONTRIBUTIONS TO THE USE OF SENTENCING DISPOSALS

The most recent academic contribution to the debate about imprisonment has been a collective response to the Sentencing Council's proposed guideline regarding the use of various disposals, including immediate custody and the SSO (see Harris et al. 2016). In that joint submission, scholars advocated a more robust and principled approach to the use of custody. The proposed guideline draws attention to the statutory provisions enabling sentencers to impose an SSO *only* once they have determined that the custody threshold is crossed and a custodial sentence is unavoidable, and thereby may go some way to reducing the 'net-widening' effect. However, the academic response notes that this is an insufficient remedy, citing similar guidance contained within the existing guideline which has been ineffective (ibid). As such, the response encourages the Sentencing Council to provide further, more tangible guidance in an attempt to give effect to Parliamentary intent as to how the various sentencing disposals contained within the 2003 Act should operate.[12]

Further, the Harris et al. (2016) response notes the paucity of the existing guidance contained within the Sentencing Guidelines Council's New Sentences: Criminal Justice Act 2003 and the lack of guidance from the Court of Appeal as to the meaning of the provision governing the use of the SSO and the circumstances in which it is appropriate to impose such a sentence. The authors argue that this has led to an unprincipled and inconsistent application of the SSO. The academic response calls for clearer, more tangible guidance in the form of principles and examples to illustrate the appropriate use of the SSO. However, in doing so, the submission recognizes that the responsibility does not solely (or predominantly) sit with the Sentencing Council (or its predecessor); the current situation is the creation of Parliament and exists in part due to an absence of guidance from the Court of Appeal. The message from the academy has been clear and evidence-based, yet policy makers have ignored this important academic research, and the consequence is evident from the trends seen in Table 9.1.

[11] Previously, the order was available only where the custodial sentence was between 14 days and 12 months, inclusive. The Legal Aid, Sentencing and Punishment of Offenders Act 2012 s.68(1) extended this to 24 months on 3 December 2012, see SI 2012/2906.

[12] At the time of writing (April 2016), the Council is considering a new guideline which would help prevent courts from misusing the sanction in the way that has been identified by the academic community.

New (or reformed) sanctions designed to replace some cases of custody should be constructed in such a way that courts cannot impose it in cases which formerly attracted a community order. This means crafting a clearer set of statutory provisions, accompanied by an equally clear sentencing guideline. This may include a clear statutory requirement to first impose a term of custody before considering whether it may be suspended.

THE 'CUSTODY THRESHOLD'

Another area to which academics have contributed concerns the so-called custody threshold which must be crossed before a term of imprisonment is imposed. Section 152(2) of the Criminal Justice Act 2003 entitled 'General restrictions on imposing discretionary custodial sentences' states that:

> The court must not pass a custodial sentence unless it is of the opinion that the offence, or the combination of the offence and one or more offences associated with it, was so serious that neither a fine alone nor a community sentence can be justified for the offence.[13]

Academic critiques of the current custodial threshold fall under one of two main objections. The first objection concerns the clarity of language and the way in which the test has been interpreted and applied by the courts. It is said that the provision is vague and allows a subjective interpretation; as a result, it is inconsistently applied. Padfield (2011) advocated rejecting a 'threshold', suggesting that a 'custody zone' may be preferable. The threshold concept was premised upon the false sense of security created by the term which, Padfield argued, suggested clarity where there was none.

The second critique is that although the provision purports to focus upon *offence* seriousness, by virtue of section 143 of the Criminal Justice Act 2003 the test in fact expands to encompass *case* seriousness, opening the door to consideration of the offender's previous convictions and other non-offence related matters. Thus when determining whether the custody threshold has been crossed, a court considers the seriousness of the case, but in so doing must consider each prior conviction to enhance crime seriousness, unless it would be unreasonable to do so. Yet prior convictions are generally regarded as unrelated to the seriousness of the crime. Accordingly, the test is theoretically inconsistent.

Taken together, these critiques help explain why the custodial threshold has not restrained the use of custody as was intended by Parliament. Despite the 'tight' language of s. 152, it has proved ineffective in restricting custody to the most serious cases. This can be demonstrated by noting the custody rate for an offence of comparatively low seriousness such as shop theft. In 2012, approximately one-third (31 per cent) of offenders (8,096 individuals) convicted of theft from a shop were sentenced to imprisonment, either immediate or suspended (Sentencing Council 2014: Figure 2.2).

[13] Similar threshold provisions regarding the use of custody exist in other common law jurisdictions such as New Zealand and Canada (see Roberts and Baker 2008 for examples).

An alternative approach could follow a Canadian sentencing provision in relation to youths. This provision prohibits the use of custody unless one of a number of conditions is met.[14] In 2013, the House of Commons Justice Committee recommended to the government that a similar approach be adopted in England and Wales (2013: paras 64, 73). However, the government rejected the proposal, stating that such a measure 'would be too prescriptive and may place the public at significant risk' (2013: 11). If the view that the language is 'tight', and that 'tightness' is a positive feature of the provision as currently formulated, it is the vagueness of the concept that requires attention. This was the focus of the academic response to the Sentencing Council's draft guideline which suggested that such clarity could be achieved through a Sentencing Council guideline in the form of vignettes and/or an exposition of principles to apply when considering the custody threshold (Harris et al. 2016).

To ameliorate the problem of people entering custody as a result of their prior convictions, we advocate a modification of the current provision, to eliminate the power of prior convictions to justify imposition of an immediate sentence of imprisonment. In so doing, the role of prior convictions would be limited to increasing sentence severity and would not have an impact upon sentence type. While this would not directly address the problems surrounding the clarity of the custodial threshold, it would limit the number of low-seriousness offences resulting in immediate custody as it would no longer be possible for an offender to be pushed across the custody threshold by virtue of his or her prior convictions—the decision to imprison would *actually* be based solely on the seriousness of the offence, a far more theoretically sound approach.

The Standing Committee for Youth Justice advocated the exploration of penal equivalents to custodial sentences for youth offenders (2010: 16 et seq.). In doing so, it reviewed non-custodial disposals used in other jurisdictions and concluded that the UK should develop intensive therapeutic models to be used as alternatives to custodial sentences. This view was shared by the Howard League who, in its report echoed the conclusions of the United Nations Committee on the Rights of the Child that alternatives to youth detention should be developed (Allen 2011: 9). In the context of adult offenders, more targeted use of community sanctions has been advocated, in addition to the reduction in the use of custody (Heard 2015).

A further reform would be to enact a presumption against imprisonment for certain categories of offence. Few jurisdictions operate such a system[15] and consequently support for such a measure in England and Wales has been limited. Most notably, the British Academy advocated the removal of imprisonment as the maximum sentence for some offences, or alternatively a restriction against imprisonment unless 'exceptional circumstances' were present (2014: 95 et seq.). The example

[14] s. 39(1) of the Youth Criminal Justice Act 2003 establishes four 'gateways' to custody. A court 'shall not' commit a young person to custody unless (i) the offender has committed a violent offence, or (ii) has failed to comply with a non-custodial sentence, or (iii) has committed an offence for which an adult would be liable to imprisonment for more than two years and has a history that indicates a pattern of findings of guilt, or (iv) in exceptional cases where the young person has committed an indictable offence, the aggravating circumstances of which are such that the imposition of a non-custodial sentence would be inconsistent with the purposes and principles of sentencing in the youth court (see Bala et al. 2009).

[15] See e.g. Keagle (2015: 38 et seq.).

given in the paper was for 'pure property offences', a proposal previously made by Ashworth (2013).

Parliament could review the current statutory formulation, and revise the statutory wording. The general view—from academics and the courts—appears to be that although the statutory language is 'tight', the definition of a custody threshold remains elusive and vague and as such, inconsistency occurs.[16] That said, an improved form of words appears difficult to formulate, with little by way of academic proposals in this regard. The custody threshold provision could be reformed, possibly by noting specific criteria which must be met before a court may impose a term of custody. The use of prior convictions to justify a custodial sentence could be more actively discouraged. An offender could only be imprisoned on his prior record when the previous offending is so extensive that he/she constitutes a real threat to the community. Penal equivalents could be developed which would permit a court to more easily impose a community sanction in place of a term of immediate imprisonment (see Morris and Tonry 1998). Parliament could introduce a rebuttable statutory presumption in favour of suspending all terms of immediate custody beneath some threshold, possibly three or six months.

PUBLIC ATTITUDES TO THE USE OF CUSTODY

Academic research into the use of custody has sustained several important conclusions.[17] The academic contribution in this domain has been to demonstrate that given sufficient information, and time in which to consider specific cases, public support for imprisonment as a sanction is not as high as many politicians appear to believe. Research by Hough and others has repeatedly illustrated this more parsimonious public attitude toward the use of custody (e.g. Hough and Moxon 1988; Hough and Roberts 1998; Kirby and Jacobson 2014; Mitchell 1998; Mitchell and Roberts 2012; see Roberts and Hough (2005) for a review). As noted, section 152(2) of the Criminal Justice Act 2003 establishes a seriousness threshold for the imposition of a term of custody. Courts have also been criticized for being influenced by populist punitiveness. The argument has been made that a more punitive social response to crime has led to a lowering of the custodial threshold, with a result that ever-larger numbers of offenders become 'eligible' for imprisonment. This alleged receptiveness to public punitiveness has been cited as an explanation for the rising prison population since 1995 (Millie et al. 2005: 102).

A poll-based reading of public opinion would suggest strong support for imprisonment as a sanction and little tolerance for mitigation which would bring a case bound for custody back in the realm of a community-based penalty. Public opinion surveys routinely demonstrate widespread criticism of the courts and disenchantment with sentencing practices (Hough and Roberts 2016). But how strongly attached are

[16] See e.g. Padfield (2011) and *R v Howells* [1999] 1 WLR 307, CA (Crim Div).

[17] There is of course a significant international academic literature relating to public opinion and sentencing policy; space limitations restrict us to focusing on contributions from the United Kingdom.

members of the public to the use of custody? We offer several empirical demonstrations of public support for a nuanced approach to sentencing, one which considers alternatives and takes mitigation seriously.

ATTITUDES TO CUSTODY FOR SERIOUS CRIMES

In one study (Roberts and Hough 2011), respondents were assigned (at random) to read one of three offence descriptions. The crimes described would, under current sentencing practice, normally be considered sufficiently serious as to justify a term of custody. For example, one was described as 'an assault where the victim suffered many cuts and severe bruising after being punched in the face several times by the offender'. Under the definitive assault guideline such an offence would likely result in a custodial sentence between six and 18 months. People were then asked whether all, almost all, most, only some, or no offenders convicted of this type of crime should be sent to prison. Across the three offences, approximately one-third of the respondents stated that all offenders convicted of these offences should be imprisoned, while around one in five held the view that only some or no offenders convicted of these crimes should be sent to prison. In view of the seriousness of these crimes it is surprising that such a small proportion (around a third) took the position that *all* such cases should be imprisoned. This finding suggests that the public do not always view custody as the primary response to offending. Additional evidence comes from public attitudes to mitigating factors at sentencing.

SUPPORT FOR ALTERNATIVES TO CUSTODY

Imprisonment is the most familiar sentencing option for many people. Yet, research has demonstrated that the public are often satisfied with alternative sanctions if they are made salient. For example, in one study respondents who initially supported imprisonment were asked whether a non-custodial alternative would be acceptable; a majority of participants changed their minds and supported the community-based alternative (Hough et al. 2009). Finally, when respondents have been asked to choose between the greater use of alternative sanctions or building more prisons, studies in many jurisdictions have found much higher levels of public support for the former (see Gelb 2011 for a review).

SUPPORT FOR MITIGATING FACTORS

There has been little research into public perceptions of mitigating factors. If the view of the public as punitive and inflexible sentencers is correct, it would be reasonable to expect little sympathy for pleas in mitigation. Indeed, this is the finding emerging from opinion polls. In order to explore the public's approach to mitigation in case scenarios, the Sentencing Advisory Panel commissioned some original empirical research. Respondents were asked to review a list of thirteen potential mitigating factors or circumstances and asked them to state whether each factor should result in a more lenient sentence in all, most, some, or no cases. The specific factors were selected to represent a range of forms of personal mitigation. The responses revealed considerable public support for most sources of personal mitigation. In fact, only a single circumstance—the fact that the offender was only 18 at the time of the offence—failed to be endorsed by a majority of the public as a mitigating circumstance in all, most, or some cases (Hough et al. 2009). This finding is consistent with earlier research by Russell and Morgan (2001).

SENSITIVITY TO COST-EFFECTIVE SENTENCING

Finally, we turn to the question of whether the costs of sentencing options should play a role in the determination of sentence—a recurring issue in the international sentencing literature. One of the principal arguments against the use of custody as a sanction is that it is expensive, relative to community-based alternatives. For this reason, sentencers in some jurisdictions are encouraged to consider the costs of custody when determining sentence. This is not the case in England and Wales, and this may contribute to the comparatively high use of imprisonment (see Table 9.2).

The link between the costs of sanctions and their use has been explored to only a limited extent by researchers. Hough et al. (2009) provided participants with specific cost estimates for custody and non-custodial sanctions and then asked them to consider whether this information should affect the determination of sentence. Respondents were assigned at random to consider either an assault where the victim sustained cuts and bruising for which medical treatment was required, or a social security fraud, valued at around £20,000. Respondents were more likely to support than oppose taking account of costs at sentencing. Across the two offences, 40 per cent of respondents believed that costs should be considered in all or most cases; 35 per cent of respondents stated that courts should never consider costs. This demonstrates public sensitivity to the relative costs of different disposals. A sentencing system which discourages courts from considering the costs of different disposals would therefore appear to be inconsistent with public opinion.

These findings support a growing international literature that suggests the public are aware of the costs of custody, and are interested in sanctions that are more cost effective. Support for alternative sanctions under these conditions was considerable. In Canada, Doob (2000) found that respondents provided with information about the costs of imprisonment were less likely to support incarcerating the offender. The most recent test of the hypothesis comes from a survey of US respondents which found that over two-thirds of the sample believed that the costs of imprisonment justified greater use of community penalties (Hartney and Marchionna 2009). The increased public interest in the costs of imprisonment may well have been further stimulated by the deep cuts to public services resulting from the financial crisis of 2008–10.

The general conclusion from this line of research (and work by other academics) is that public views are more flexible than policy makers believe, and that there is greater support for alternatives to imprisonment. People are likely to be receptive to increasing the use of alternative sanctions—if these disposals are cost-effective. Taken together, this suggests there is an opportunity to reduce the use of custody, and the costs of sentencing, without generating active public opposition.[18] Moreover, the Ministry of Justice and other bodies should make a greater effort to educate the public about the costs of imprisonment as well as the lower reoffending rates associated with community-based penalties. This initiative should also include distributing data on the costs of different disposals, and the reoffending rates of disposals to all sentencers.

CONCLUSIONS

Several conclusions may be drawn from the academic contribution to the ongoing debate over the use of imprisonment. First, it is clear that introducing new or amending existing sanctions carries important dangers in terms of widening the net of punishment. The latest example of this tendency is the SSO in England and Wales, and it is to be hoped that the government, the Court of Appeal, or the Sentencing Council will take steps to correct the problem which has arisen.

Second, the principal mechanism to restrict the use of custody as a sanction (the custody threshold provision) has proven inadequate. Academic commentary and scholarship has highlighted different ways in which the existing provision could be amended or strengthened to more effectively ensure that custody is restricted to the most serious cases (Harris et al. 2016). Here the options include introducing presumptions against the use of short prison terms, the creation of 'non-imprisonable' offences, and the revision of sentencing ranges in the definitive sentencing guidelines.

Third, there is clear evidence that expanding the use of alternatives to imprisonment, and considering the costs of disposals is consistent with public opinion. The era of austerity provides a unique opportunity in this regard, as the public are likely to see much appeal in punishing offenders in more cost-effective ways. Again, there are lessons both for Parliament and the Sentencing Council. The former could consider statutory reforms consistent with this perspective, while the latter could more actively discharge one of its statutory duties, namely to 'have regard to ... the costs of different sentences and their relative effectiveness in preventing re-offending'.[19]

If successive governments over the past 20 years had implemented some of the policy recommendations made by academics, the contours of sentencing would be very different. There would be greater use of community punishments than at present and by consequence fewer admissions to custody. Whether Parliament, the Ministry of Justice, or other bodies engaged in law reform will take the necessary steps to reduce the use of custody is unclear; should the political will arise, the academy has clearly provided some important lessons.

[18] A considerable body of research has documented public misperceptions in the area of sentencing and sentencing policy. Improving public knowledge is therefore a necessary step in any move towards more liberal sentencing policies, but the accumulated research suggests that improving public knowledge is far from easy (e.g. Feilzer 2007; Maruna and King 2004).

[19] Coroners and Justice Act 2009 s. 120(11)(e). One possibility would entail providing courts with 'penal equivalents'.

REFERENCES

ALLEN, R. (2011), *Last Resort? Exploring the Reduction in Child Imprisonment 2008–11*, London: Prison Reform Trust.

ASHWORTH, A. (1989), *Custody Reconsidered: Clarity and Consistency in Sentencing*, London: Centre for Policy Studies.

ASHWORTH, A. (2013), *What if Imprisonment Were Abolished for Property Offences?*, London: The Howard League.

ASHWORTH, A. (2015), *Sentencing and Criminal Justice*, 6th edn, Cambridge: Cambridge University Press.

ASHWORTH, A. and PLAYER, E. (2005), 'Criminal Justice Act 2003: The Sentencing Provisions', *Modern Law Review*, 68, 5: 822–38.

BALA, N., CARRINGTON, P., and ROBERTS, J.V. (2009), 'The Youth Criminal Justice Act: A Qualified Success', *Canadian Journal of Criminology and Criminal Justice*, 51, 2: 131–68.

BANKS, R. (2015), *Banks on Sentence*, 10th edn, Etchingham: Robert Banks.

BOTTOMS, A. (1981), 'The Suspended Sentence in England, 1967–1978', *British Journal of Criminology*, 21, 1: 1–26.

British Academy (2014), *A Presumption against Imprisonment: Social Order and Social Values*, London: British Academy.

CARTER, LORD (2007), *Securing the Future: Proposals for the Efficient and Sustainable Use of Custody in England and Wales*, London: Ministry of Justice.

COHEN, S. (1971), 'The Punitive City: Notes on the Dispersal of Social Control', *Contemporary Crises*, 3, 4: 341–63.

DOOB, A. (2000), 'Transforming the Punishment Environment: Understanding Public Views of What Should Be Accomplished at Sentencing', *Canadian Journal of Criminology*, 42, 3: 323–40.

FAULKNER, D. (2014), *Servant of the Crown*, Hook: The Waterside Press.

FEILZER, M. (2007), 'The Magic Bullet', *Prison Service Journal*, 170: 39–44.

GELB, K. (2011), *Alternatives to Imprisonment: Community Views*, Victoria: Sentencing Advisory Council.

GRÜNHUT, M. (1948), *Penal Reform: A Comparative Study*, Oxford: The Clarendon Press.

HARRIS, L., ASHWORTH, A., BOIS-PEDAIN, A. DU, HOUGH, M., JACOBSON, J., LIGHTOWLERS, C., MANSON, A., PADFIELD, N., PLAYER, E., QUIRK, H., and STARK, F. (2016 in press), 'Academic Response to the Sentencing Council's Consultation Paper on the Draft Guideline for the Imposition of Community and Custodial Sentences', *Sentencing News*, 2016 Issue 1, London: Sweet and Maxwell.

HARTNEY, C. and MARCHIONNA, S. (2009), 'Attitudes of US Voters toward Nonserious Offenders and Alternatives to Incarceration', *Focus: Views from the National Council on Crime and Delinquency*, June 2009, Oakland, CA: National Council on Crime and Delinquency.

HEARD, C. (2015), *Community Sentences since 2000: How They Work—and Why They Have Not Cut Prisoner Numbers*, London: Centre for Crime and Justice Studies.

HEDDERMAN, C. and BARNES, R. (2015), 'Sentencing Women: An Analysis of Recent Trends', in J.V. Roberts (ed.), *Exploring Sentencing Practice in England and Wales*, London: Palgrave Macmillan.

HOOD, R. (1962), *Sentencing in Magistrates' Courts*, London: Stevens and Sons.

HOOD, R. (1972), *Sentencing the Motoring Offender*, London: Heinemann.

HOOD, R. (1995), *Race and Sentencing*, Oxford: The Clarendon Press.

HOUGH, M. and MOXON, D. (1988), 'Dealing with Offenders: Popular Opinion and the Views of Victims in England and Wales', in N. Walker and M. Hough (eds), *Public Attitudes to Sentencing*, Aldershot: Gower.

HOUGH, M. and ROBERTS, J.V. (1998), 'Attitudes to Punishment: Findings from the 1996 British Crime Survey', *Research Findings*, No. 64, London: Home Office.

HOUGH, A. and Roberts, J.V. (2016), 'Public Opinion, Crime, and Criminal Justice', in S. Maruna, A. Liebling, and L. McAra (eds), *Oxford Handbook of Criminology*, 6th edn, Oxford: Oxford University Press.

HOUGH, M., ROBERTS, J.V., JACOBSON, J., MOON, N., and STEEL, N. (2009), *Public Attitudes to the Principles of Sentencing*, Sentencing Advisory Panel Research Report No. 6, London: Sentencing Advisory Panel.

House of Commons Justice Committee (2008), *Fifth Report: Towards Effective Sentencing*, HC 2007–08, 184-I.

House of Commons Justice Committee (2013), *Youth Justice*, Seventh Report of Session 2012–13, London: House of Commons.

Howard League (2010), *Do Better, Do Less: Report of the Commission on English Prisons Today*, London: Howard League for Penal Reform.

KEAGLE, H. (2015), *Manual on New Jersey Sentencing Law*, New Jersey: New Jersey Superior Court (Appellate Division).

KIRBY, A. and JACOBSON, J. (2014), 'Public Attitudes to the Sentencing of Drug Offences', *Criminology and Criminal Justice*, 14, 3: 334–50.

MARUNA, S. and KING, A. (2004), 'Public Opinion and Community Penalties', in A. Bottoms, S. Rex, and G. Robinson (eds), *Alternatives to Prison*, Cullompton: Willan.

MILLIE, A., JACOBSON, J., and HOUGH, M. (2005), 'Understanding the Growth in the Prison Population in England and Wales', in C. Emsley (ed.), *The Persistent Prison*, London: Francis Boutle.

Ministry of Justice (2015), *Prison Population Figures 2015: Population Bulletin: Weekly 27 November 2015*, London: Ministry of Justice.

MITCHELL, B. (1998), 'Public Perceptions of Homicide and Criminal Justice', *British Journal of Criminology*, 38, 3: 453–72.

MITCHELL, B. and ROBERTS, J.V. (2012), 'Sentencing for Murder: Exploring Public Knowledge and Public Opinion in England and Wales', *British Journal of Criminology*, 52, 1: 141–58.

MORRIS, N. and TONRY, M. (1998), *Between Prison and Probation*, Chicago, IL: University of Chicago Press.

PADFIELD, N. (2011), 'Time to Bury the Custody Threshold?', *Criminal Law Review*, 8: 593–612.

PENFOLD, C., HUNTER, G., and HOUGH, M. (2006), *The Intermittent Custody Pilot: A Descriptive Study*, London: Home Office.

PRATT (2007), *Penal Populism*, London: Routledge.

ROBERTS, J.V. (2006), 'Reducing the Use of Incarceration: A Review of Recent International Experiences', *Judicial Studies Institute Journal*, 5: 41–53.

ROBERTS, J.V. and ASHWORTH, A. (2016), 'The Evolution of Sentencing Policy and Practice in England and Wales, 1996-2015', in M. Tonry (ed.), *Crime and Justice*, New York: Oxford University Press.

ROBERTS, J.V. and BAKER, E. (2008), 'Sentencing Structure and Reform in Common Law Jurisdictions', in S. Shoham, O. Beck, and M. Kett (eds), *International Handbook of Penology and Criminal Justice*, New York: Taylor and Francis.

ROBERTS, J.V. and HOUGH, M. (2005), *Understanding Public Attitudes to Criminal Justice*, Maidenhead: Open University Press.

ROBERTS, J.V. and HOUGH, M. (2011), 'Custody or Community? Exploring the Boundaries of Public Punitiveness in England and Wales', *Criminology and Criminal Justice*, 11, 2: 185–202.

RUSSELL, N. and MORGAN, R. (2001), *Sentencing of Domestic Burglary*, London: Sentencing Advisory Panel.

Sentencing Council (2014), *Theft Offences Sentencing Data*, London: Sentencing Council of England and Wales.

Sentencing Guidelines Council (2004), *New Sentences*, London: Sentencing Guidelines Council.

SPARKS, R.F. (1971), 'The Use of Suspended Sentences', *Criminal Law Review*: 384–96.

STANLEY, S. and BAGINSKY, M. (1984), *Alternatives to Prison*, London: Peter Owen Publishers.

WALKER, N. (1965), *Crime and Justice in Britain*, Edinburgh: Edinburgh University Press.

WALKER, N. (1969), *Sentencing in a Rational Society*, London: Heinemann.

WASIK, M. (2014), 'Sentencing—The Last Ten Years', *Criminal Law Review*, 7: 477–91.

10

AN AWKWARD FIT: OFFENDERS WITH MENTAL DISABILITIES IN A SYSTEM OF CRIMINAL JUSTICE

Jill Peay

In 1976 John Monahan asked how we reconciled the principle of minimizing erroneous convictions with the confinement of many people predicted to be violent to save ourselves from the few who would cause harm (1976: 21). Tony Bottoms responded that two different conceptions of the same offender applied at different stages in the criminal justice system (1977: 92). Drawing on the work of Duster (1970) he illustrated how classicism, with its conception of rational actors, dominated the determination of guilt, but the later stages of the system drew on positivism to emphasize pathology and psychic disturbance in the offender. Whether this is morally justified, or as Roger Hood (1974) had previously questioned in his *Tolerance and the Tariff* lecture, empirically justified, are separate matters. But both Hood and Bottoms agreed that if long sentences must be imposed, they should be justified on retributive grounds. Pathologizing offenders, even with the purported beneficent aim of reforming them, was problematic.

This shifting portrayal of offenders—from rational actors behaving in strategic ways to avoid conviction or minimize punishment, to individuals at the mercy of an array of deterministic factors—bedevils the attainment of a principled approach to criminal justice. Having two different conceptions of the same offender within one system is problematic enough, but introducing offenders with mental disabilities into that mix complicates matters further. On the one hand, the promise is enticing that medical treatment for mental disorder in the context of offending might reduce, as a side effect, subsequent offending. Such treatment could both heal offenders and protect us from future harm. On the other hand, where such offenders are perceived as non-rational or non-autonomous actors their presence challenges the prevailing values in the earlier process of establishing guilt. Without a finding of guilt, the system is confined to a health intervention. With a finding of guilt either incapacitative punishment or an indefinite health intervention can result. Offenders with mental health difficulties grate against the delivery of the system's core values of fairness and justice.

Indeed, in the subsequent delivery of deserved punishment, deterrence, or rehabilitation such offenders sit awkwardly. Are these offenders to be coerced or individuals in need of treatment? How can periods of imprisonment or psychiatric detention be justified in the context of a complex interaction between disorder and criminality where neither dominates?

Treating as an exceptional group individuals in whom offending and disorder co-occur, as if the disorder is *the* underlying cause of offending, has also been challenged. Recognizing that these offenders may not be exceptional, or may not even be a 'group' in any meaningful sense, casts an important light on how the criminal justice system responds to offenders overall (Peay 2011). This chapter seeks to examine the impact their presence has had on both our understanding and operation of that system. First, it is important to state the obvious. If one in four of us will experience a mental disorder at some point in our lives and offending is commonplace then there will be an overlap in time between the occurrence of crime and the existence of a mental disorder in some of those caught up in the criminal justice system (ibid). Second, studies of custodial sentenced populations (in all jurisdictions) reveal high levels of mental disorder; in our own prison population only one in ten offenders do not have some diagnosable mental disorder (Fazel and Danesh 2002; Singleton et al. 1998). Whether this reflects a crystallization effect whereby it is predominantly only those offenders with mental disabilities who are unsuccessful, and are thereafter prosecuted, convicted, and sentenced to custody; or whether the process of prosecution and subsequent punishment produces disorder in vulnerable offenders; or whether what we define as disorder is systematically biased towards those who deviate from societal norms, whether by choice or necessity, is not the primary focus here. Rather, it is what effect or effects the presence of offenders with mental disabilities has had on the criminal justice system. In short, have the dilemmas such offenders pose acted like grit in an oyster, producing remarkable reforms across the system? Or have the challenges thrown up by mental disability to a system which presupposes a necessary degree of rationality in offenders in order to make conviction and punishment intellectually tenable largely been an ignored inconvenience or an ignorable sub-specialty?

The chapter looks at three areas. First, the fairness of methods of release from incarceration; second, the impact of therapeutic and rehabilitative endeavours; and finally, issues arising out of what constitutes a fair trial. The counterintuitive order reflects in part the historic role of scholars at the Oxford Centre and in part a shift towards the scope for making a substantive difference, rather than a formal legal difference. I argue that the key reason why offenders with mental disorder are so awkward for the system to manage, and to reconcile with its own values, is because the intersection of disability with offending makes a formidably malleable combination. An attributed lack of rationality or lack of volitional control enhances perceived dangerousness; but offenders' disorders may make them both less culpable and more amenable to therapeutic or rehabilitative endeavours, drawing on our humanitarian instincts. These two contrasting images—of threat and illness—constantly shift the shape of the disordered offender, evoking changing emotional responses in us, and making 'them' ungraspable or unknowable to a system that aspires to work with presumed certainties.

The chapter touches on a period from the mid-1970s until early 2016. Throughout that time mentally disordered offenders (and their curious counterpart, ordered offenders) have artificially structured how we conceptualize the place of an offender's mental life in crime and the system's response to the dilemmas such offenders pose. Yet if the causes of crime in any one individual are complex and multi-factorial, including poverty, relative deprivation, age, gender, class, employment, family setting, drink and drugs, personal associations, and opportunities (Reiner 2016), then adding an element of mental disability is likely neither to be the determining factor nor the ultimate explanation. As such, empirical and socio-legal scholarship in this area should have as much to contribute to an understanding of ordered offending as it does to disordered offending; indeed, arguably more.

RELEASE FROM INCARCERATION: A 20-YEAR SAGA

One of the best examples of the 'grit in the oyster' theme arises from the work of Larry Gostin (1975, 1977) and in particular the publication of *A Human Condition*. Gostin's work was highly influential in the reform of the Mental Health Act 1959 (MHA 1959): the subsequent Mental Health Act 1983 (MHA 1983) embodied a new paradigm of rights for those with mental disorder. Gostin published an analysis of this in 1983 when he was a visiting fellow at the Oxford Centre for Criminological Research (Gostin 1983). The relevant saga associated with this new paradigm relates to a progressive chipping away at the Home Secretary's executive discretion to determine periods of incarceration without effective judicial control. Ultimately, many of those executive powers have been removed from the Home Secretary's domain; a removal consistent with Hood's early cautionary assertion that administrative review should only be used 'where it can genuinely be claimed that the offender's behaviour is unpredictably dangerous' (1974: 13).

The story starts with the case of *X v the United Kingdom*.[1] X was a restricted patient who had been conditionally discharged from Broadmoor Hospital in 1971. He was recalled in 1974 following a matrimonial dispute not involving physical violence. There was no medical recommendation for recall and no suggestion that he had breached the terms of his discharge. Deprivation of liberty of convicted offender-patients raises issues under both Article 5(1)(a) and (e), and Article 5(4) of the European Convention on Human Rights (ECHR). And whilst the fact of the conviction under Article 5(1)(a) is highly unlikely to change, unsoundness of mind under Article 5(1)(e) is subject to change (indeed, ameliorating or curing the condition is the underlying objective for the psychiatric confinement). Thus, periodic review under Article 5(4) becomes critical as a method of ensuring that the deprivation of liberty remains lawful. But as Article 5(4) requires that review be conducted 'by a court' and that release

[1] *X v the United Kingdom*, Series A No 46 (judgment given 5 November 1981). Gostin notably acted as an advocate in this case.

be ordered if detention is not lawful, the question arose as to whether the arrangements for review under the 1959 Act were compliant. In *X v UK*, the European Court of Human Rights (ECtHR) held that they were not. Curiously, it was not the egregious recall with its dubious evidential basis that concerned the ECtHR: recall did not breach the *Winterwerp*[2] criteria of the need for objective medical evidence of unsoundness of mind of the kind or degree warranting compulsory confinement since *Winterwerp* did not apply to recall decisions which fell under the guise of an emergency. Rather, the ECtHR's focus was on the concept of a court—the essential characteristics of which were independence of the executive and of the parties to the case. Under the MHA 1959 the Home Secretary had the power to discharge restricted patients but the Mental Health Review Tribunal (now the First-tier Tribunal (Mental Health)—MHT) could only advise the Home Secretary so to do. Yet, the Home Secretary was clearly not a court exercising a judicial function because he was a member of the executive and a party to the case (as the detaining authority). In practice, the Home Secretary had rejected up to 56 per cent of all positive recommendations from the independent MHT (see Gostin 1977; Peay 1981). The government's solution to the ECtHR's ruling of a breach in *X v UK* was swift: the Mental Health (Amendment) Act 1982 included provisions giving MHTs the power to discharge restricted patients, and henceforth these were to be chaired by lawyers 'with substantial judicial experience in the criminal courts' (Peay 1989: 1). Such lawyers could presumably be relied upon not to make wayward decisions with their new powers.

But why was a case concerning an offender with a mental disorder the first to chip away at the Home Secretary's powers? Why was it not a case involving the indefinite detention of children or other prisoners? Three immediate possibilities present themselves. First, psychiatric patients subject to compulsory detention had regular access to lawyers during their confinement as a result of the ABWOR (assistance by way of representation) scheme which applied to MHTs. This equivalent of legally aided assistance (later extended to representation) may well have generated challenges that would otherwise not have been forthcoming. Second, the prolonged periods of incarceration for offenders with mental disorders, offenders who in many cases retained capacity despite their placement in a psychiatric hospital, and for whom little seemingly active treatment was being offered (see Peay 1989), was problematic. For those for whom justice was a prevailing value, periods of incarceration that went well beyond what might have been considered a proportionate sentence for the crime committed would have caused significant discomfort if rehabilitative objectives were not being pursued and offenders remained effectively in limbo. As with *X v UK*, this was least defensible when such an offender-patient was recalled from conditional discharge in the community. Third, offender-patients subject to the MHA are exposed to interventions that are much more intrusive—compulsory medical treatment for mental disorder—than those permitted under a sentence of imprisonment. Yet whether an offender became an offender-patient seemed to many an arbitrary decision: many prisoners languished in prison with disorders that could have gained them access to a hospital bed; whilst some patients occupying those hospital beds were

[2] *Winterwerp v the Netherlands* (1979–1980) 2 EHRR 387.

seemingly in receipt of little active treatment. Perhaps the unfairness of it all was simply overwhelming.

After the drama of *X v UK*, there were a series of challenges to the relationship between the Parole Board and the Home Secretary, who took the final decision in cases of discretionary life-sentenced prisoners. The issue was not then thought to arise in long determinate sentences because the purpose following conviction was punishment: the detention could not become arbitrary because it remained justified under the Article 5(1)(a) 'after conviction by a competent court' exception.[3] Discretionary life sentences arose in cases of serious offending in the context of mental instability which presented a risk of future similar offending. The human rights argument was made with a new twist. If public protection were to be the grounds for indefinite detention then such detention needed to be subject to periodic review by a body which had the power to determine release if the underpinning mental instability (or other factor justifying the need for public protection) abated. After all, once the punitive period had expired, further detention could only be justified if the grounds for detention persisted. Not only did a 'court-like' body need to be involved, but the causal link needed to be established between the objectives of the original sentencing court and the detention. Again, the government was forced to act: the powers of the Parole Board were extended under the Criminal Justice Act 1991 giving them the power to take the final decision about release in discretionary life-sentence cases.[4]

Then came the challenge to the indefinite detention of children during Her Majesty's pleasure (Children and Young Persons Act 1933 s. 53(1)) in the case of Jon Venables and Robert Thompson.[5] In practice, Her Majesty's pleasure meant for so long as the Home Secretary considered appropriate. The murder of James Bulger by Thompson and Venables, two 10-year-old boys, brought this to a head. The Home Secretary set the tariff at 15 years in the context of overwhelming 'public interest' in the case. The trial judge, perhaps best placed to assess the boys' needs for retribution and deterrence, had put it at eight years; the Lord Chief Justice raised it to ten. The Home Secretary's ultimate tariff was challenged by judicial review, and resulted in the House of Lords quashing the 15-year period.[6] By a majority the House of Lords held:

> the Secretary of State in fixing a tariff in respect of the period of detention to be served by an offender by way of punishment and deterrence was exercising a function comparable to that of a sentencing judge; that, while a sentencing judge might take into account general considerations of public confidence in the administration of justice, natural justice would require him to ignore as irrelevant public petitions or public opinion as expressed in the media; and that in giving weight to public protests about the level of the tariff to be fixed to the detriment of the applicants the Secretary of State had misdirected himself and his exercise of discretion had been unlawful . . .

[3] See *R (on the application of Black) v Secretary of State for Justice* [2009] UKHL 1 para. 74. Notably, Article 5(4) does bear on decisions made by the Parole Board with respect to the re-release of recalled prisoners, and here the Parole Board does now make final binding decisions, see *R (on the application of Smith) v Parole Board* [2005] UKHL 1.

[4] *Weeks v UK* (1988) 10 EHRR 293; *Thynne, Wilson and Gunnell v UK* (1991) 13 EHRR 666.

[5] *R v Home Secretary, ex parte Venables and Thompson* (1998) AC 407.

[6] *R v Home Secretary, ex parte Venables and Thompson* (1998) AC 407.

In the course of the judgment their Lordships made a number of trenchant observations, and explained by a majority why the Home Secretary had not behaved as a court-like body.[7] Moreover, his decision was unlawful since section 44(1) of the 1933 Act required the welfare of the child to be considered. Fixing an unreviewable period of detention, even for the purposes of punishment, which could not take account of changes in the child subsequent to the commission of the offence, was inconsistent with the duty to keep a child's detention under continuous review.

Given that the House of Lords ruling made clear that a tariff must be capable of review where relevant events occurred after the commission of an offence and sentence, it was inevitable that further challenges would be brought. Mandatory life-sentence prisoners came into view.[8] Here the sentence was divided into a tariff period for punishment and a subsequent indefinite period subject to Parole Board review based on the continuing dangerousness of the offender. Again, it was the setting of the tariff that was problematic. Moreover, following the ECtHR's ruling on the Home Secretary's lack of independence in *V v UK*[9] and the passage of the Human Rights Act 1998 (HRA 1998), incorporating the ECHR into domestic law, the House of Lords cut straight to the quick.

Anderson[10] had committed a double murder of vulnerable victims. The sentencing judge and the Lord Chief Justice set the tariff at 15 years. The Home Secretary increased it to 20 years under section 29 of the Crime Sentences Act 1997. The House of Lords issued a section 4 declaration under the HRA 1998 arguing that the Home Secretary was carrying out a sentencing function thus breaching Article 6(1). He was not independent from the executive or the legislature. Moreover, the House of Lords refused to solve the problem by rewording the Home Secretary's power as a duty to follow the recommendations of the trial judge.

The upshot of this judgment was the Criminal Justice Act 2003, which established a statutory framework for the sentencing of mandatory lifers.[11] This, in turn, has resulted in some very lengthy periods of detention under the tariff before mandatory lifers become eligible for consideration for release on life-licence. Paradoxically, as research has amply demonstrated, such periods are often longer than the public would tolerate given the nature of the murder involved (Mitchell and Roberts 2012).

Finally in this sequence there was a challenge to the independence of the Parole Board itself.[12] The government responded by moving the Board from working with NOMS (the National Offender Management Service) to the Access to Justice Group, which played no direct part in the early release of prisoners, within the Ministry of Justice.

Thus, what started with a relatively narrow point in *X v UK* has expanded. It is, of course, possible that many of the changes would have occurred without the impetus from *X v UK*. Moreover, these largely procedural changes may have made little

[7] A view given further weight in *V v UK* (1999) Application no. 24888/94 where the ECtHR held that permitting the Home Secretary to set the tariff breached Article 6(1) which required an independent and impartial tribunal.

[8] *R (Anderson) v Home Secretary* (2002) UKHL 46.

[9] *V v UK* (1999) Application no. 24888/94.

[10] *R (Anderson) v Home Secretary* (2002) UKHL 46.

[11] See s. 269(5) and s. 270 and schedule 21.

[12] *R (on the application of Brooke and others) v the Parole Board and another* [2008] EWCA Civ 29.

difference to the periods of detention that offenders serve: indeed, the introduction of the statutory framework under the Criminal Justice Act 2003 has hardly promoted the cause of punitive restraint. Yet clearly there has been a shift to greater indeterminacy in periods of incarceration;[13] emerging judicial interest in and control over deprivation of liberty can only be a valuable counterweight. And it is certainly arguable that the mixed experiences of those subject to psychiatric detention, and the mixed motives of those justifying such detention, have provided fertile grounds for legal challenge.

TAKING HORSES TO WATER: FACILITATING EFFECTIVE TREATMENT

The issue of preventive detention is one that has rightly preoccupied criminological scholars. Ashworth and Zedner (2014) have explored in-depth both the fundamental issues it raises and the associated use of criminal law to prevent or reduce the risk of anticipated future harms. Pifferi (2016) has also documented its historical roots in the contrasting American and European approaches, with America adopting a reformist correctional agenda, and Europe favouring an initial punitively proportionate sentence followed by an indeterminate period based on social defence grounds. Both approaches are rife with problems.

These problems are magnified when one considers the UK and its long-standing policy with respect to offenders with mental disorder. Here, the humanitarian approach is one of diverting offenders whose disorders are of a nature and degree to justify admission to hospital from a penal disposal to a psychiatric one. Thereafter, detention is justified on the basis of the continuation of the disorder to the requisite degree; and even then only where further detention is warranted in the interests of the offender-patient's health or safety or for the protection of other persons.[14] These fused objectives create a context in which both beneficent aims and a justice-based social protection agenda vie with one another in any individual case.

When introduced in 1959 the notion that the courts could, at the point of sentence, forgo any further involvement in an offender's trajectory by sending him or her irrevocably into the hospital system was revolutionary. On its face, and regardless of the offender's potential for reoffending or its gravity (excluding convictions for murder), the courts could choose a therapeutic disposal over a penal one. Where there was not thought to be a risk of further offending that would cause serious harm to the public, decisions about subsequent release would lie in the hands of the clinicians and the MHT. Where such a risk was predicted, a restriction order was imposed and release would be determined by the Home Secretary, taking (but not necessarily following) advice from the clinical team.[15]

[13] Including, notably, the abolition of fixed time periods for restriction orders under the Mental Health Act 2007.

[14] s. 72(1)(a)(ii) MHA 1983.

[15] As documented above, under the MHA 1983 the MHT also gained the power to discharge restricted patients.

Since the statutory framework required the continuing presence of mental disorder to the requisite degree to make detention lawful, the offender-patient's response to treatment for mental disorder is critical. But even this seemingly straightforward issue can be contested. What was meant by treatment? What was treatment trying to achieve? How could clinicians know when it had been successful given that treatment necessarily took place in a secure setting? Treatment for mental disorder, and particularly mental disorder in the context of serious offending, was not like mending a broken leg or removing an inflamed appendix. The uncertainties involved, and the differing thresholds for being certain, made the process subject to many vagaries.[16]

In practice, continued detention of offender-patients appeared mainly to reflect not their responsiveness to treatment (which was understandably hard to demonstrate with the degree of confidence that discharging bodies would have wished) but the seriousness of their index offences and predictions about their likely future offending (Peay 1981, 1989). Pinning down this covert justification was, of course, problematic: devotees of McBarnet's (1981) work would argue that the MHT was keeping strictly within its legal remit when it did this, by failing to find the disorder sufficiently absent. This was known as the double-negative dilemma. Since the MHT could not be satisfied that the disorder was not-present, they refuse to discharge on this basis and then consider whether there were grounds for detention on the basis of a prediction of future harm.[17] Notwithstanding, most socio-legal scholars would recognize that there is a frustrating difference between making something subject to legal regulation, as the MHA 1959 had done, and ensuring that regulation occurs in practice (Jones 1980: 11).

Thus, the anxieties expressed in the 1970s that a reformative or therapeutic approach to offenders could lead to lengthy periods of detention were powerfully illustrated in the disordered offender-patient population. Over the passing decades there has been a blurring of objectives for disordered and ordered offenders across the therapeutic and penal populations, so that techniques practised in the former have come increasingly to be applied in penal regimes. This has been most marked in the Dangerous and Severe Personality Disorder (DSPD) programme (O'Loughlin 2014). The anxiety in the 1970s was that detention without effective treatment became detention grounded in the passage of time, first on retributive grounds and then on predictive grounds. Therapy with offender-patients could disclose more reasons to be anxious about reoffending. More recently, the failure of offenders to take advantage of the opportunities to rehabilitate, or to be perceived to fail to take responsibility for change, has been detrimental to their prospects of release. The intersection between risk and release is one that has favoured a cautionary strategy.

The other dynamic, between treatment and discharge, has been more intriguing. As therapeutic approaches have been applied more extensively to offender populations, there has been recognition that to be successful such endeavours needed offenders to be engaged and motivated; and not simply coerced into treatment. Most recently, the

[16] The contestation about what constitutes successful treatment persists even with respect to more modern therapeutic endeavours like cognitive behaviour therapy; see Johnsen and Friborg (2015).

[17] The burden was reversed following the case of *R (on the application of H) v Mental Health Review Tribunal* [2001] 3 WLR 512 so that the MHT had positively to be satisfied by the detaining authority that the disorder was present to the requisite degree.

concern has been that that the therapeutic process may pose direct risks to offenders beyond the risk of prolonged detention. And that the rehabilitative agenda, where applied to manifestly needy or vulnerable offenders whose choices are limited, poses questions for those who deliver such rehabilitative programmes. As Elaine Player has pointed out, uncertainties about the legal and ethical framework in which their duty of care arises shifts the focus towards those who do the detaining.[18] Moreover, if service delivery is inadequate or, more worryingly, damaging, what implications are there for those who are detained pursuant to such an agenda? Painful lessons learned by mental health professionals from the Inquiries after Homicide era should be a cautionary warning for criminal justice personnel who become involved in assessing change prior to release of risky offenders (Crichton 2011; Peay 1996).

The blurring of objectives within the offender-patient and offender populations, with a growing reliance in the latter on indeterminacy, has been variously documented (Rutherford 2010; and Annison 2015 on indeterminate sentences for public protection). That trend has also manifested itself in the judgment from the Court of Appeal in *Vowles*, which deals with the use of section 45A of the MHA 1983, by explicitly reversing an albeit dubious therapeutic initiative with one that achieves a more protective agenda (see Eastman and Peay 1998; Peay 2016).

Greater convergence between the therapeutic and penal regimes has also been reflected in therapeutic endeavours in both contexts. Here, the role of Grendon Prison, opened in 1962, has been important in the burgeoning of therapeutic community approaches within the prison system, and arguably critical to an understanding of the role of coercion and consent to successful treatment. The work of Genders and Player (1995, 2010), and their development of a chronology of treatment success, was notably based on work with offenders who had volunteered for therapy in Grendon; and who had done so at the cost of any early parole consideration. These were offenders who were as close as one could come to a volunteer consenting group within an inherently coercive system. Working with offenders with a personality disorder (offenders who would now potentially fall under the broader MHA 1983 definition of mental disorder) who retain the capacity to make treatment decisions has highlighted how consent can be critical to the success of such endeavours with some offenders (Zlodre et al. 2015). Involuntary treatments can have no effect at all, or indeed, be detrimental (Martin et al. 2012). Both the earlier MacArthur and Nordic studies, which had established the complex relationships between perceived coercion, due process, and patient satisfaction, had highlighted such questions about the potential relationships between perceived coercion and treatment success (see Peay 2003: 126) so it is encouraging to see these questions empirically examined. Regrettably, the government failed to learn the Grendon lesson with the subsequent DSPD initiative (O'Loughlin 2014) so that the pilot treatment programmes were dogged by the need to motivate offenders (some of whom had been compelled into the programme) before any 'treatment'—largely developing skills in managing their own criminogenic risks—could commence (Pickersgill 2013). The extension of the DSPD programme to more 'conventional' offenders through the Offender Personality Disorder Pathway

[18] Personal communication.

(OPDP) represents another optimistic investment in the goal of offender rehabilitation, but it may ultimately simply establish a basis for widespread, rather than contained, failure.

If most offenders are dealt with, not within the hospital system, but within the penal system, and most offenders there have some form of mental disorder (broadly defined) (Singleton et al. 1998) then the issue of consent to treatment becomes not only critical to success but essential to lawful treatment. Offenders cannot lawfully be given medical treatment without their consent, where they have the capacity to give that consent. In contrast, within the hospital system, an offender subject to detention under the MHA 1983 can be subject to compulsory treatment regardless of that offender-patient's capacity to give consent. Although many within the hospital system will not have that inherent capacity, genuinely engaging motivated offenders and patients in consensual treatment or rehabilitation is most likely to bring whatever success is possible (Zlodre et al. 2015). Ironically, both regimes have conflicted agendas which may disrupt their principal objectives.

Two issues arise. First, coerced consent can obviously be engineered within the prison system—in all sorts of ways prisoners will cooperate if they believe that it will enhance their prospects of release. But is coerced consent—superficial consent—enough to facilitate a process of real change? And can it bring risks of causing preventable harm by inmate on inmate in the context of poorly managed group therapy (Genders and Player 2010)? Second, where treatment is compelled on unwilling recipients is that likely to undermine effective treatment?

UNFAIR TRIALS AND EFFECTIVE PARTICIPATION

Ensuring that defendants with mental disabilities receive fair trials has been an issue of prominent recent concern. However, prior to the changes effected by the Criminal Procedure (Insanity and Unfitness to Plead) Act 1991 it could be argued that the law and the criminal justice system were uninterested in the fate of those who were found unfit to plead under the 1836 *Pritchard* criteria.[19] Such individuals went from court (where the allegations against them were not heard, let alone resolved) into indefinite psychiatric care: a curious disposal for those, for example, whose deficits were primarily communicative rather than cognitive. Individuals in respect of whom the prosecution would not have been able to substantiate criminal allegations found themselves in psychiatric detention on the basis that they lacked the requisite skills to do one of the following: plead to the indictment, understand the course of proceedings, instruct a lawyer, challenge a juror, or understand the evidence. This was, to modern eyes, problematic: in 1836 it was probably regarded as an appropriate paternalistic response, saving the individual from the rigours that would ensue in and from a criminal trial. Attempting to solve this dilemma has led to a five-year period of research and reflection by the Law Commission (2010, 2016a, 2016b).

[19] *Pritchard* (1836) 7 C & P 303.

The 1991 Act did not change the substantive test for unfitness, but it did introduce two important procedural changes. First, that there would be a 'trial of the facts' following any determination that the accused was unfit to plead; in essence, establishing the *actus reus* of an offence. For those individuals in respect of whom, despite their disability (and disability is being used here to mean a lack of ability to plead to the indictment etc.), the prosecution could not make out to the satisfaction of a jury that the defendant had 'done the act or made the omission charged' then the accused would receive an acquittal. Second, the judge's disposal options where a positive finding was made were increased from indefinite psychiatric detention to a hospital disposal with or without restrictions, a supervision order in the community, or an absolute discharge. These changes have, in turn, contributed to the rise in the number of findings that defendants were unfit to plead, from approximately sixteen a year (Grubin 1991) to around one hundred a year (Mackay 2016).

However, this rebalancing of the rights of vulnerable individuals who cannot fairly be tried, with the need to protect the public from the serious harms that such individuals might do if there were no state intervention, was far from complete. Since 2010, the Law Commission has been involved in a programme of work on unfitness, and they have recently produced their final Report, together with draft legislation, the Criminal Procedure (Lack of Capacity) Bill.[20] The Report has largely been well-received, albeit the government's response is awaited (Loughnan 2016).[21] Interestingly, there is now also an emphasis, at least within the Report, on the rights of victims and those affected by the alleged offence or offences.[22] This element was brought most prominently to the fore over the prosecution for historic child sexual offences of Lord Janner, who suffered from severe dementia. The prosecution was controversial and procedurally complex.[23] In the event, Lord Janner died before the 'trial of the facts' could take place. Perhaps never before had the public interest in taking a case to 'trial' been weighed so prominently against an understandable squeamishness about pursuing a demented man for whom no state intervention could have been justified.[24]

The Commission has recommended a series of nuanced but clever changes which will, on the one hand, make it more likely that unfit defendants will be diverted away from conventional trials: these include a broader and clearer test of unfitness covering both those whose decision-making skills are impaired and those whose cognitive and emotional disorders may jeopardize their ability to participate effectively in the trial (Law Commission 2016a). On the other hand, there is an emphasis on ensuring that the trials of those defendants, who can fairly be tried, will take place. These include an enhanced procedure for remanding defendants to hospital and delaying their trial;[25]

[20] See http://www.lawcom.gov.uk/project/unfitness-to-plead/ and Law Commission 2016b.

[21] For a critical response see Padfield (2016).

[22] See Law Commission 2016a Report: para. 1.1.

[23] See for comment on the process http://www.theguardian.com/commentisfree/2015/jun/29/lord-janner-cps-child-sex-offences.

[24] Interestingly, the Report recommends an additional procedure for diverting accused individuals away from the 'alternative finding hearing' where such diversion from court adjudication would be in the interests of justice. Law Commission (2016a): 1.67–8.

[25] See Law Commission Report (2016a): para. 1.58.

giving additional support to defendants;[26] and facilitating a global assessment of capacity which will not exclude a defendant, as before, simply because there was one element from a list of five or six capacities they could not fulfil.[27] As the threshold for fitness will be tightened—it currently permits defendants to be tried with only 'rudimentary' capacities (Brookbanks and Mackay 2010)—diversion from conventional trial will be more likely; but the enhanced safeguards for fair trials may in turn facilitate more trials. The Commission has notably recommended greater assistance for vulnerable defendants by way of an intermediary to secure effective participation. Shamefully, a provision to this effect has sat unimplemented in statutory form for a number of years.[28] If implemented, the trial process will become more fairly accessible to many more defendants, which is to be welcomed.

Finally, the Commission has recommended introducing a mechanism for enabling guilty pleas even if the accused's capacity to participate effectively in a trial is impaired. Facilitating guilty pleas is expedient and in keeping with the normal approach to defendants where a sentence discount can be a powerful inducement to an early guilty plea. But it is a tactic that should give pause for thought. The number of offenders in prison with profound mental disorders is troubling. Since the bulk of those in prison plead guilty, it is arguably likely that many of those with mental disorder have also pleaded guilty. Thus, the Commission is to be commended for proposing a separate assessment, once a defendant has been found unfit for trial, to consider whether or not the defendant might nonetheless have the capacity to plead guilty. This will protect those who are identified as unfit (albeit presenting a difficult choice for those whose capacities have been established as impaired), but it will not protect those who are not identified as being unable to participate effectively. Here the Commission proposes screening for all those under 18; and if resources do not permit that, to make screening mandatory for those under 14. In that context some of the most egregious examples may be avoided. The solution is comprehensive screening (see Brown et al. 2016); but, in a context where the Commission has been acutely aware of limited resources, this is not going to happen. Justice comes with a price tag.

If implemented, the Commission's proposals would affect both those categorized as mentally unfit and those currently mentally fit. Whilst the Report discusses the advantages of having a diagnostic threshold, and it details the kinds of disability that can affect fitness[29] its test of unfitness is one grounded in capacities.[30] In adopting this approach the test will apply to *all* defendants, and not just those most closely associated with mental disorder or disability. This is potentially revolutionary. If criminal

[26] Draft Bill s. 3(3).

[27] See Draft Bill s. 3(2). A defendant is to be regarded as lacking the capacity to participate effectively in a trial if the defendant's relevant abilities are not, taken together, sufficient to enable the defendant to participate effectively in the proceedings on the offence or offences charged.

[28] Youth Justice and Criminal Evidence Act 1999 s. 33BA, which makes provisions for defendants similar to those already in existence for vulnerable witnesses, has not been brought into force. The amendment dates from s. 104 of the Coroners and Justice Act 2009.

[29] 'Defendants may be unfit to plead for a variety of reasons, including difficulties resulting from mental illness (longstanding or temporary), learning disability, developmental disorder or delay, a communication impairment or some other cause or combination of causes' (2016: para. 1.1).

[30] See Draft Bill s. 3(4) and (5).

justice personnel had been operating with a conception of unfitness as applying only to the manifestly ill and disabled, then the Commission's proposals could open up many more prosecutions to a rigorous examination of whether defendants have the capacity to participate effectively in their own trials. Indeed, the Commission's focus on ensuring that the new test will apply in both the youth and magistrates' courts (where unfitness does not currently apply) will rightly reinforce this. It should also be remembered that in other jurisdictions defendants are much more frequently judged incompetent to stand trial (Poythress et al. 2002).

The Commission's Report is lengthy and nuanced, as is the Draft Bill.[31] If implemented in total it would achieve a real shift toward fairness for vulnerable defendants. The shift from thinking of such defendants as 'mentally unfit' to having vulnerabilities is itself noteworthy since it places such defendants on a continuum with all defendants. Moreover, in keeping with an approach that respects equal treatment, the Commission is recommending that the 'trial of the facts'[32] no longer be confined to issues of *actus reus*[33] but will include *mens rea*, rightly giving the benefit of the defences of mistake, self-defence, and accident to those found unable to participate effectively in their trials.

CONCLUSIONS

The important contribution that consideration of offenders with mental disabilities in the criminal justice system can make to understanding that system has been illustrated with reference to three areas: release, treatment, and trial. In each, the tale is of complexity. For some offenders there is a clear justification for treatment: those with psychotic disorders being perhaps the prime example. For others, their capacities and culpabilities locate their offending more easily within the penal system. But this crude division does not reflect the bulk of offenders, both within the hospital and the penal system, who have a variety of needs and who pose a series of challenges to mental health and criminal justice agencies. Moving away from perceiving such offenders as within clear categorical groups, while insisting that the multiple attractions of a rehabilitative agenda should not undermine the right to a determinate period of punishment, would enhance a system based on justice rather than aspiration. Moreover, understanding that consensual engagement facilitates the prospects of effective therapeutic endeavour, even where 'treatment' can easily be coerced, is an important lesson. It is one applicable across the spectrum of offenders within the criminal justice system.

[31] It should be recognized that whilst enhancing the position of vulnerable defendants in a number of important ways detailed above, the Report also enhances social protection measures, including e.g. introducing electronic monitoring where a defendant breached a supervision order, with the potential for custody for a breach of these further restrictions (see para. 1.87).

[32] They would rename this as the alternative finding hearing.

[33] Itself an impossible distinction to sustain, see *B(M)* [2012] EWCA Crim 770—a case on voyeurism.

REFERENCES

ANNISON, H. (2015), *Dangerous Politics: Risk, Political Vulnerability and Penal Policy*, Oxford: Clarendon Press.

ASHWORTH, A. and ZEDNER, L. (2014), *Preventive Justice*, Oxford: Oxford University Press.

BROOKBANKS, W. and MACKAY, R. (2010), 'Decisional Competence and "Best Interests": Establishing the Threshold for Fitness to Stand Trial', *Otago Law Review*, 12, 2: 265–84.

BROWN, P., STAHL, D., APPIAH-KUSI, E., BREWER, R., WATTS, M., PEAY, J., and BLACKWOOD, N. (2016 in submission), 'The Fitness to Plead Assessment Tool: Development and Validation of a Standardised Instrument to Assess the Psycholegal Capacities Required to Stand Trial in England and Wales', *British Journal of Psychiatry*.

CRICHTON, J. (2011), 'A Review of Published Independent Inquiries in England into Psychiatric Patient Homicide 1995–2010', *Journal of Forensic Psychiatry and Psychology*, 22, 6: 761–89.

DUSTER, T. (1970), *The Legislation of Morality*, Glencoe: Free Press.

EASTMAN, N. and PEAY, J. (1998), 'Sentencing Psychopaths: Is the "Hospital and Limitation Direction" an Ill-Considered Hybrid?', *Criminal Law Review*, 93–108.

FAZEL, S. and DANESH, J. (2002), 'Serious Mental Disorder in 23,000 Prisoners: A Systematic Review of 62 Surveys', *Lancet*, 359: 545–50.

GENDERS, E. and PLAYER, E. (1995), *Grendon: A Study of a Therapeutic Prison*, Oxford: Clarendon Press.

GENDERS, E. and PLAYER, E. (2010), 'Therapy in Prison: Revisiting Grendon 20 Years On', *Howard Journal of Criminal Justice*, 49, 5: 431–50.

GOSTIN, L. (1975), *A Human Condition*, vol. 1: *The Mental Health Act from 1959 to 1975. Observations, Analysis and Proposals for Reform*, London: MIND (National Association for Mental Health).

GOSTIN, L. (1977), *A Human Condition*, vol. 2: *The Law Relating to Mentally Abnormal Offenders: Observation, Analysis, and Proposals for Reform*, London: MIND (National Association for Mental Health).

GOSTIN, L. (1983), 'Contemporary Social Historical Perspectives on Mental Health Reform', *Journal of Law and Society*, 10, 1: 47–70.

GRUBIN, D. (1991), 'Unfit to Plead in England and Wales, 1976–88: A Survey', *British Journal of Psychiatry*, 158, 4: 540–8.

HOOD, R. (1974), *Tolerance and the Tariff: Some Reflections on Fixing the Time Prisoners Serve in Custody*, presented to NACRO in the House of Lords, 22 July 1974.

JOHNSEN, T. and FRIBORG, O. (2015), 'The Effects of Cognitive Behavioral Therapy as an Anti-Depressive Treatment Is Falling: A Meta-Analysis', *Psychological Bulletin*, 141, 4: 747–68.

JONES, K. (1980), 'The Limitations of the Legal Approach to Mental Health', *International Journal of Law and Psychiatry* 3, 1: 1–15.

Law Commission (2010), *Unfitness to Plead*, Consultation Paper No. 197.

Law Commission (2016A), *Unfitness to Plead Report*, vol. 1: *Report*.

Law Commission (2016B), *Unfitness to Plead Report*, vol. 2: *Draft Legislation*.

LOUGHNAN, A. (2016), 'Between Fairness and "Dangerousness": Reforming the Law on Unfitness to Plead', *Criminal Law Review*, 7: 449–64.

MCBARNET, D. (1981), *Law, the State and the Construction of Justice*, London: Palgrave Macmillan.

MACKAY, R. (2016), 'Unfitness to Plead: Appendix A Unfitness to Plead—Data on Formal Findings from 2002 to 2014', *Law Commission: Unfitness to Plead Report*, 13 January 2016, available at: http://www.lawcom.gov.uk/wp-content/uploads/2016/01/apa.pdf.

Martin, M., Dorken, S., Wamboldt, A., and Wootten, S. (2012), 'Stopping the Revolving Door: A Meta-Analysis on the Effectiveness of Interventions for Criminally Involved Individuals with Major Mental Disorders', *Law and Human Behavior*, 36, 1: 1–12.

Mitchell, B. and Roberts, J. (2012), 'Sentencing for Murder: Exploring Public Knowledge and Public Opinion in England and Wales', *British Journal of Criminology*, 52, 1: 141–58.

Monahan, J. (1976), 'The Prevention of Violence', in J. Monahan (ed.), *Community Mental Health and the Criminal Justice System*, New York: Pergamon.

O'Loughlin, A. (2014), 'The Offender Personality Disorder Pathway: Expansion in the Face of Failure?', *Howard Journal*, 53, 2: 173–92.

Padfield, N. (2016), 'Editorial: "Prosecuting" Those Who Are Unfit to Be Prosecuted?', *Criminal Law Review*: 227–8.

Peay, J. (1981), 'Mental Health Review Tribunals: Just or Efficacious Safeguards?', *Journal of Law and Human Behavior*, 5, 2: 161–86.

Peay, J. (1989), *Tribunals on Trial: A Study of Decision-Making under the Mental Health Act 1983*, Oxford: Clarendon Press.

Peay, J. (ed.) (1996), *Inquiries after Homicide*, London: Duckworth.

Peay, J. (2003), *Decisions and Dilemmas: Working with Mental Health Law*, Oxford: Hart Publishing.

Peay, J. (2011), *Mental Health and Crime*, Abingdon: Routledge.

Peay, J. (2016), 'Responsibility, Culpability and the Sentencing of Mentally Disordered Offenders: Objectives in Conflict', *Criminal Law Review*, 3: 152–64.

Pickersgill, M. (2013), 'How Personality Became Treatable: The Mutual Constitution of Clinical Knowledge and Mental Health Law', *Social Studies of Science*, 43, 1: 30–53.

Pifferi, M. (2016), *Reinventing Punishment: A Comparative History of Criminology and Penology in the 19th and 20th Century*, Oxford: Clarendon Press.

Poythress, N., Bonnie, R., Monahan, J., Otto, R., and Hoge, S. (2002), *Adjudicative Competence: The MacArthur Studies*, Kluwer Academic/Plenum Publishers.

Reiner, R. (2016), *Crime: The Mystery of a Common Sense Concept*, Cambridge: Polity Press.

Rutherford, M. (2010), *Blurring the Boundaries: The Convergence of Mental Health and Criminal Justice Policy, Legislation, Systems and Practice*, London: Sainsbury Centre for Mental Health, available at: http://www.rcpsych.ac.uk/pdf/Blurring_the_boundariesreportSCMH2010.pdf.

Singleton, N., Meltzer, H., and Gatward, R. (1998), *Psychiatric Morbidity among Prisoners in England and Wales*, London: Stationery Office.

Zlodre, J., Yiend, J., Burns, T., and Fazel, S. (2015), 'Coercion, Competence and Consent in Offenders with Personality Disorder', *Psychology, Crime and Law*, 22, 4: 1–16.

11

CRIMINAL JUSTICE IN THE SERVICE OF SECURITY

*Lucia Zedner**

INTRODUCTION—BACK TO THE FUTURE?

If the criminological equivalent of a De Lorean time machine were to whisk us back to the 1960s, we would find ourselves in a very different criminological world. No one could then have predicted the ending of the Cold War or the effect on high-level policing as the intelligence agencies and secret services emerged from the dark shadows they once occupied. New technologies such as actuarial risk assessment instruments, surveillance, and data mining were then unknown. Globalization, mass migration, the lifting of border controls and their consequences for the exercise of sovereign state control were not foreseeable. And while the Troubles in Northern Ireland were to accustom the UK to terrorist atrocities long before 9/11, the scale of threat posed by contemporary terrorism was far in the future.

Not only has the world and the challenges posed for policing and criminal justice changed dramatically, so too has criminal justice scholarship. Those few engaged in criminological teaching and research in the 1960s[1] would likely have doubted that many topics now firmly on the criminological agenda had anything to do with their discipline (Martin 1988). Subjects like actuarial justice, surveillance, situational crime prevention, private security, insurance, border control, detention and deportation, counter-terrorism and security, data retention, and cybersecurity were outside the scope of criminology as then conceived. Just as the territory of criminal justice has grown so too have the interdisciplinary resources upon which criminologists draw. These now include (but are not limited to) economics, migration, security and war studies, transitional justice, politics, and international relations. In short, the scope and ambitions of criminal justice scholarship, the objects of its attentions, and the disciplinary and theoretical resources upon which it draws have transformed the subject almost beyond recognition (Zedner 2007a). Nonetheless, or so this chapter will

* I am grateful to Carolyn Hoyle, Mary Bosworth, and David Rose for their incisive comments on an earlier draft.

[1] And there were very few—as David Downes observed, 'In 1960, perhaps a few dozen academics, including post-graduate students and Home Office researchers, could be defined as criminologists' (1988: 45).

argue, the seeds of these changes were always inherent in the pursuit of criminal justice, both as practice and academic discipline.

Long before the advent of the 'security state' (Ericson 2007; Ramsay 2012), security was an integral facet of criminal justice. The authority of the state to criminalize and punish derives from its duty to provide for public safety and good order. Security grounds and justifies the coercive powers of the police and the pains of punishment. It forms the normative bedrock of criminal justice. To fulfil this state security obligation, agents of criminal justice are armed with coercive powers to stop, search, detain, arrest, interrogate, prosecute, and sanction. Individuals subject to the state's penal power endure incursions on their freedom of movement and association; loss of reputation, employment, family, and home; even life-long deprivation of liberty. Precisely because these are among the most coercive powers the state can exert over its citizens, the criminal justice system fulfils a second, no less important, security obligation. As well as affording citizens security *collectively*, criminal justice provides for their security *individually* by protecting against excessive or arbitrary exercise of state power. Criminal justice requires that justice is done not only to those who have been wrongfully harmed, but also to individuals who find themselves subject to the coercive powers of policing, process, and punishment.

This chapter explores how the tension between these two conceptions of security—collective and individual—has played out in the policies, practices, and institutions of criminal justice, as well as in criminal justice scholarship. It asks for whom criminal justice provides security by considering moments of crisis that have brought to light the failings of the criminal process. It goes on to chart the countervailing and recurrent demands for public protection, to suggest that the role of criminal justice as safeguard of individual liberties has been increasingly overshadowed by the growing salience of public safety and national security. Finally, it analyses the expansion of security laws, measures, and practices at the close of the last century and examines the rapid acceleration of this trend post 9/11. The advent of the 'security state' has not only furnished criminal justice scholars with novel objects of enquiry and provoked new seams of scholarship that grapple with changes in the scope, rationale, and aims of criminal justice, it has also gravely threatened the protections once deemed a constituent part of what it means to talk about criminal *justice*. The chapter concludes by exploring a recent case, involving a trial held largely in secret, that exemplifies the hazards of a criminal justice process subjugated to the service of security and considers its implications for criminological scholarship.

CRIMINAL JUSTICE AS SAFEGUARD—FOR WHOM?

The idea of criminal justice as safeguard of individual rights has long been a central object of criminological enquiry. At least since the 1968 publication of Herbert Packer's *The Limits of the Criminal Sanction*, researchers have been alert to the irresolvable tension between seeking to protect the public by bringing suspected offenders to trial and the need to safeguard suspects against the unwarranted exercise of state power.

Packer's models of Crime Control and Due Process provide an enduring framework for exploring this tension and, more importantly, their interdependence (McBarnett 1981: 156; Packer 1968), of which we will say more below. Partly inspired by Packer, in the 1970s a new genre of theoretically informed critical enquiry turned its attention to decisions to arrest, charge, prosecute, bail, and plea bargain. Researchers sought to understand the workings of the criminal process and to explain the yawning gap between law and practice (see e.g. Baldwin and McConville 1977, 1979; Bottoms and McClean 1976). They exposed a hitherto largely invisible domain of decision-making by criminal justice officials, informed more by professional or 'canteen' culture, preconceptions, and prejudice than by legal rules. Evidence of discriminatory police practice, forced confessions, and pressure to plead guilty (Bottoms and McClean 1976: 6) revealed 'the murky world of exchange and barter beneath' (Ashworth 1988: 113) and disclosed that procedural safeguards were routinely bypassed in order to secure convictions.

If the central role of the criminal process is to bring defendants to justice according to procedures that guard against the arbitrary exercise of state power (Zedner forthcoming), then to say that it has struggled to fulfil this is surely an understatement (Rose 1996). At least since the 1970s, research showed the realities of policing and prosecution to be distant from the due process requirements of certainty, accountability, and fair treatment (McConville et al. 1991). And the decades since have been punctuated by periodic public revelations of misconduct, miscarriage of justice, and racial discrimination. To name only the most prominent, these included the 1977 Royal Commission on Criminal Procedure (Philips 1981); the 1981 Scarman Inquiry following the Brixton riots (Scarman 1982); serious miscarriage of justice cases (notably the Guildford Four, the Maguire Seven, and Birmingham Six) in the late 1980s that prompted the 1991 Royal Commission on Criminal Justice (Runciman 1993); and the Stephen Lawrence case that led to the Macpherson Inquiry (Macpherson 1999).

Each one furnished disturbing evidence of excessive use of police discretion and subversion of procedural safeguards. Like the revolving beam of a lighthouse, these inquiries briefly cast their bright light on the shadowy waters of misconduct, only to plunge it back into darkness until the next scandal inevitably erupted. Although important reforms sometimes ensued,[2] most of these inquiries attracted critical academic attention for their failure to address ingrained pathologies or to propose root-and-branch reform. Young and Sanders dismissed the 1993 Royal Commission report as a 'confidence trick' (1994), while others accused it of 'minimalising miscarriages' in favour of 'safeguarding convictions' (Bridges and McConville 1994).

Perhaps this should not surprise. The history of criminal justice has been similarly punctuated by demands that the state's larger duty to protect the public should trump individual due process rights. The drive to 'Law and Order' politics in the 1970s (Hall et al. 1978), media-inspired mass 'moral panics' (Cohen 1980) about new types of offender or offending (mugging, raves, joy-riding, illegal immigration etc.), and the upsurge of 'popular punitivism' in the 1980s have each informed public debate and

[2] Not least the Police and Criminal Evidence Act 1984.

penal policy (Pratt 2000, 2007). And in the 1990s, as Garland so acutely observed, the 'culture of control' became a powerful driver of criminal justice policy (1996, 2001). Often targeted at recent migrants, racial minorities, and other marginalized groups (Bowling and Phillips 2002; Young 1999), the demand for public protection operates not only at the level of political rhetoric or populist mandate but also propels policy formation. Larger shifts in the construction of crime as a 'normal social fact', innovations in situational crime prevention and community safety (Crawford 1998; Hope and Sparks 2000), and the rise of mass surveillance (Goold 2004) were also rapidly changing the penal landscape in the 1990s.

By the close of the twentieth century, security of a more coercive kind gained increasing salience as new preventive criminal offences, extended police powers, preventive civil measures (notably the ASBO),[3] and indefinite preventive punishments proliferated (Ashworth and Zedner 2014; Ericson 2007). These not only provided academics with new objects of enquiry but, by challenging conventional conceptions of criminal justice, also prompted new seams of scholarship that sought to analyse and explain the political and sociological drivers of change. 'New penology', 'actuarial justice', 'prudentialism', 'precaution', 'risk', and 'security' became the *lingua franca* of criminology (Feeley and Simon 1992, 1994; Hope and Sparks 2000; O'Malley 1998: Zedner 2000, 2004: ch. 8). Well before the terrorist atrocities of the twenty-first century, therefore, the role of criminal justice in the service of public safety and security was an established object of academic enquiry and concern.

Of course the British state was no stranger to sustained existential threats to its security. Thirty years of sectarian 'Troubles' in Northern Ireland and the IRA bombing campaign in mainland Britain (Hillyard 1994) had long securitized (to use an ugly but apposite term) criminal justice. In Northern Ireland, successive 'Special Powers', 'Emergency Provisions', and 'Temporary Provisions' Acts had extended police powers of stop and search, abolished juries in terrorist trials, limited the right to silence, lowered the burden of proof, and diluted rules of evidence (Walker 2004). Some of these counter-terrorism powers were incorporated into the mainstream policing of ordinary criminal conduct and were later extended to mainland Britain as special powers were normalized into everyday criminal justice practice (Hillyard 2005). Curiously, outside Northern Ireland, this securitization of criminal justice remained largely beyond criminological notice at the time and, even in the 1990s, few criminologists considered counter-terrorism to be their concern. Given the sizeable criminological interest in terrorism and counter-terrorism today, it is a moot question why earlier generations were not similarly engaged in the policing of the IRA, the resort to emergency powers, and erosions of due process that resulted, not least given their longstanding interest in breaches of procedure within the mainstream criminal process.

Nor indeed did criminologists then appreciate the profound implications of the growing convergence between the once-distant police and security services. The

[3] Anti-Social Behaviour Orders, introduced under the Crime and Disorder Act 1998, could be imposed on those deemed to have behaved 'in a manner that caused or was likely to cause harassment, alarm or distress' to the public and prohibited the defendant 'from doing anything described in the order' for at least two years. Breach was a criminal offence and could result in up to five years' imprisonment.

ending of the Cold War had deprived the security services of their primary purpose, causing them to cast around for new fields of endeavour that included high-level policing of serious, organized, and transnational crime (Lustgarten and Leigh 1994). 9/11 was something of a gift, albeit a tragic one, for the security services because it provided them with a new *raison d'être* and assured funding. Criminologists who suddenly became interested in questions of security after 9/11 commonly write as if terrorism were unknown in the UK before the London bombings in 2005. Yet major bomb attacks by the IRA on Canary Wharf and at Aldwych in London in 1996 and 'the biggest peacetime explosion England has ever seen' in Manchester, which injured 200 and caused £700 million damage (Anderson 2013: 233), had happened only years before. Policing in the 1990s already relied upon intelligence-focused operations (not least by the Anti-Terrorist Branch and Special Branch) that drew heavily upon working in close partnership with MI5.[4] The effect of this increased coordination was partially to blur the historic divide between the security services and the police, though it raised significant issues about the problems of using intelligence as evidence in the criminal process (Justice 2009: Part 3). In a bid to rationalize and consolidate existing powers, a major review of terrorism laws by Lord Lloyd of Berwick in 1996 led to the omnibus Terrorism Act 2000 that made permanent many long-standing 'temporary' provisions and very significantly extended the scope of counter-terrorism laws even before the events of 9/11.

CRIMINAL JUSTICE IN THE SERVICE OF SECURITY OF A DIFFERENT KIND

While 9/11 and the subsequent bombings in Madrid, Bali, and London undoubtedly had a cataclysmic impact on criminal justice worldwide (see e.g. Stuntz 2002), as we have shown, the UK had a much longer history of counter-terrorism policing. Given this historical context, it is unclear why the demand for security in the UK post 9/11 was allowed to override the rights of individuals suspected or accused of involvement in terrorism-related activity in ways that far outstripped powers earlier invoked against IRA suspects. Although Lord Lloyd's 1996 review had recommended that counter-terrorism laws 'should approximate as closely as possible to the ordinary criminal law and procedure' and that new powers must 'strike the right balance between the needs of security and the rights and liberties of the individual' (Lloyd 1996: para. 3.1), the welter of counter-terrorism legislation that followed in the years after 9/11 undermined ordinary due process protections to an unprecedented degree (Walker 2004; Zedner 2005, 2012).[5]

Part of the explanation is political. Following the 7/7 bombings in 2005, then UK Prime Minister Tony Blair shifted the parameters of the possible by declaring, 'Let no

[4] RUSI Monitor (2009), *The Changing Nature of Counter-Terrorism Policing*, https://rusi.org/publication/changing-nature-counter-terrorism-policing.

[5] These included the Anti-Terrorism, Crime and Security Act 2001; the Prevention of Terrorism Act 2005; the Terrorism Act 2006; and the Counter-Terrorism Act 2008.

one be in any doubt that the rules of the game have changed.'[6] Use of police power increased radically: for example, suspicionless searches under section 44 of the Terrorism Act 2000 rose from 10,200 in 2001–2 to 210,000 in 2009.[7] Under the breathtakingly wide powers of schedule 7 of the Terrorism Act 2000, thousands were stopped and searched at ports, airports, and international rail stations without any requirement of suspicion.[8] In 2011–12 alone 69,109 people were stopped and examined under schedule 7 powers.[9] New laws also undermined procedural protections by side-stepping the criminal process (Zedner 2007b), for example by permitting the indefinite detention of foreign national terror suspects in Belmarsh prison, until the practice was declared unlawful in 2004.[10] Those consequently released from Belmarsh did not get beyond the prison gate before they were subject to new civil preventive measures called Control Orders, now Terrorism Prevention and Investigation Measures or TPIMs (Ashworth and Zedner 2014: ch. 8; Zedner 2007c). These orders imposed tight surveillance and very substantial restrictions on the abode, freedom of movement, association, and communication of those suspected of involvement in terrorism but for whom prosecution was said to be impossible, whether on security grounds or because incriminating intelligence was not admissible as evidence—and no trial was ever held.

Academics were quick to react to these disturbing developments. In the early 2000s, for example, a small reading group of scholars with a pre-existing interest in security (e.g. Loader 2002; Zedner 2000) began meeting in Oxford to consider the implications of the new security agenda for the practices and institutions of criminal justice and to discuss the growing corpus of security scholarship. At their best, reading groups create a space to explore and test early intuitions and ideas, to develop the conceptual tools and theoretical frameworks needed to understand new objects of enquiry. This small Oxford group enabled its members to tackle some dauntingly complex questions about the implications of security for their field. A spate of publications ensued,[11] and, many exploratory articles later, monographs followed (see e.g. Ashworth and Zedner 2014; Lazarus forthcoming; Loader and Walker 2007; Zedner 2009). The flourishing of Oxford security scholarship chimed with the interests and attracted the attention of academics elsewhere (e.g. Hudson 2012; Hudson and Ugelvik 2012; Ramsay 2012; Sullivan and Dennis 2012).[12] Security scholarship burgeoned as criminologists sought to respond to rapid, dramatic, often unprecedented changes in the police power of the state and to reassert human rights protections (Ashworth 2002, 2007; Goold and Lazarus 2007). Younger scholars, alert to the need to inform public debate and policy formation were quickest to engage with government and seek to influence reform (see e.g. Lazarus et al. 2007). What sustained this scholarship

[6] I. Cobain, 'London Bombings: The Day the Anti-Terrorism Rules Changed', *The Guardian*, 7 July 2005, http://www.theguardian.com/uk/2010/jul/07/london-bombings-anti-terrorism.

[7] s. 44 was repealed and replaced in 2010 (Bowling and Marks forthcoming).

[8] https://www.liberty-human-rights.org.uk/human-rights/countering-terrorism/schedule-7.

[9] Ibid.

[10] Following the 'Belmarsh case', *A and others v Secretary of State for the Home Department* [2004] UKHL 56.

[11] See e.g. the publications by Ashworth, Goold, Lazarus, Loader, and Zedner in the chapter references.

[12] As well as special issues of *San Diego Law Review* (2011) 48(4) Symposium on 'The Morality of Preventive Restriction of Liberty' and *Criminal Law and Philosophy* (2015) 9(3) 'Symposium on Preventive Justice'.

in the longer term was a powerful sense that criminal justice as a safeguard of individual rights was under threat (Ashworth 2006; Ashworth and Zedner 2014; Loader 2002; Zedner 2012).

Whereas previous generations of scholars upheld criminal justice as due process, today they are driven as much by the stark recognition that many serious cases never get as far as the criminal trial (Zedner 2007b). Police powers that permit suspicionless stops, police public order containment or 'kettling' (Ashworth and Zedner 2014: 59–64), extended powers of police custody, and resort to civil and administrative measures substantially weaken the protections once available to those subject to prosecution and trial. Recourse to these powers suggests a political will to use any available legal means to fight the gravest threats, even at the expense of due process. It may well be, as Simon suggests, that 'counter-terrorism offences are being used as an investigative tool rather than as a means to convict culpable wrongdoing' (Simon 2015: 88; see also Anderson 2013). So, while there were 315 terror-related arrests in 2015, only thirty-five were subsequently convicted.[13] Moreover, neither closer cooperation between security services and the police, nor the 'eroding difference' between intelligence and evidence (Roach 2010: 48–54), can overcome the fact that intelligence is often unverifiable, fragmentary, based upon suspicion rather than fact, and gathered by dubious means. As such, it is often not admissible as evidence subject to the rules of disclosure, challenge, and testing that apply in the open forum of a criminal court.

Whereas criminologists could once observe the operations of policing and process first hand, engage in action research, and formulate evidence-based recommendations for reform,[14] the increasing securitization of criminal justice has led much of the action to happen elsewhere, away from public view and academic scrutiny. Resort to secret evidence and closed proceedings are now commonplace in immigration and counter-terrorism cases outside the criminal process, for example in the operation of the Special Immigration Appeals Commission (SIAC) and in Control Order/TPIMs hearings (Kavanagh 2010; Tomkins 2011). The claim is that these are necessary to keep information out of the public domain to protect intelligence agencies and national security interests. 'Closed material proceedings' (CMPs) prohibit public attendance and the security-cleared Special Advocates, appointed in security-sensitive cases, are not permitted to communicate with clients without special permission once they have seen the evidence. These hearings are problematic because they radically undermine the defence capacity of those subject to them, inhibit public accountability, and place proceedings beyond the view of researchers. Furthermore, in the name of risk management, new 'forms of institutional protectionism' restrict access and deny researchers the cooperation they once enjoyed (Hannah-Moffat 2011: 445).

[13] Home Office, *Operation of Police Powers under the Terrorism Act* 2000 *and Subsequent Legislation: Arrests, Outcomes, and Stop and Search, Great Britain, Quarterly Update to September* 2015, section 3, https://www.gov.uk/government/publications/operation-of-police-powers-under-the-terrorism-act-2000-quarterly-update-to-september-2015/operation-of-police-powers-under-the-terrorism-act-2000-and-subsequent-legislation-arrests-outcomes-and-stop-and-search-great-britain-quarterly-u#arrests-and-outcomes-1.

[14] For all its faults, noted above, the Runciman Royal Commission commissioned twenty-two separate research studies that sought to document the underlying problems behind miscarriages of justice and suggest means of their resolution. The resulting reports are listed in the Runciman Report 1993, 254–5.

SECURITY AS THREAT TO CRIMINAL JUSTICE: A CASE STUDY

To document the many ways in which, post 9/11, security has expanded, distorted, and undermined the workings of criminal justice and, in so doing, substantially shut its doors to academic scrutiny would take a whole book. In the hope that one powerful illustrative example will make the point rather more concisely, what follows documents a single case: a case that lays bare what happens when criminal justice protections are compromised in the interests of national security.

In 2014 an unprecedented legal and political storm arose over the attempt to hold a criminal trial entirely in secret. In a case against two men suspected of terrorism-related activity prosecutors successfully applied for the identities of the defendants to be anonymized and the trial to be held in camera on grounds of national security. Lawyers for the Crown Prosecution Service claimed that the circumstances of the case were so 'exceptional' that if the case were to be heard in public it would have 'disastrous consequences' that might render prosecution impossible.[15] Even the fact that the trial was to be heard in secret was subject to a media blackout. When news that there was to be a secret trial was eventually made public, it was met by a barrage of criticism from lawyers, politicians, journalists, and academics who condemned it as a totally unprecedented departure from the principle of open justice, inconsistent with the rule of law and democratic accountability.[16] Although partial resort to closed proceedings is not uncommon in criminal trials involving serious sexual offences, vulnerable witnesses, or the very young, to hold an entire criminal trial in secret was exceptional and widely deemed to set a dangerous precedent. Open justice is a central tenet of the criminal trial: it serves the ends of transparency, accountability, and the public confidence essential to the delivery of justice in a modern democratic society.

Legal action brought by a number of news media organizations challenging the ban was swiftly heard by the Court of Appeal, which overturned the order, limited how much of the trial could be heard in secret, and required that the names of the defendants be made public.[17] In its judgment, the Court of Appeal expressed 'grave concern' as to the effects of holding a trial in private on the grounds that:

> The Rule of Law is a priceless asset of our country and a foundation of our Constitution. One aspect of the Rule of Law—a hallmark and a safeguard—is open justice, which includes criminal trials being held in public and the publication of the names of defend-

[15] T. Whitehead and D. Barrett, 'Secret Terror Trial Is "Assault" on British Justice', *The Telegraph*, 4 June 2014, http://www.telegraph.co.uk/news/uknews/terrorism-in-the-uk/10876499/Secret-terror-trial-is-assault-on-British-justice.html.

[16] Not only by the liberal press, see T. Whitehead and D. Barrett, 'Secret Terror Trial Is "Assault" on British Justice', *The Telegraph*, 4 June 2014, http://www.telegraph.co.uk/news/uknews/terrorism-in-the-uk/10876499/Secret-terror-trial-is-assault-on-British-justice.html. P. Johnston, 'Secret Trials: "Democracies Die behind Closed Doors"', *The Telegraph*, 5 June 2014, http://blogs.telegraph.co.uk/news/philipjohnston/100274921/secret-trials-democracies-die-behind-closed-doors/. For further discussion see Zedner forthcoming.

[17] *Guardian News and Media Ltd v AB and CD* [2014] EWCA Crim 1861.

ants. Open justice is both a fundamental principle of the common law and a means of ensuring public confidence in our legal system.[18]

Although the Court accepted that there were compelling grounds for the core of the trial to be held in camera, it ordered that the remainder—the swearing in and reading of charges to the jury, parts of the judge's introductory remarks, the prosecution opening, the verdicts, and, if convictions were to result, the sentences—should be heard in open court. In the interests of accountability and to allow for some measure of public scrutiny, it further acceded that the identity of the defendants be revealed and ten accredited journalists could hear most of the trial. Although some acclaimed the Court of Appeal judgment as a victory for open justice, others criticized the Court's deference to national security concerns: the human rights organization Liberty lamented, 'Shutting the door on the core of a criminal trial is a dangerous departure from our democratic tradition.'[19] Against this view, the former Independent Reviewer of Terrorism Legislation, Lord Carlile, sought to defend the decision on the grounds that, 'Most right-thinking members of the public would agree that if national security, particularly people's safety, is affected, then there may well have to be some parts of a trial held in secret.'[20]

In the event, although the names of the defendants and limited details of the case were subsequently published, well over two-thirds of the trial was heard in closed proceedings. The ten selected journalists permitted to attend were subject to stringent restrictions as to confidentiality and all were required to give up their notes to the court at the close of proceedings. Even today little is known other than that one defendant, named as Mounir Rarmoul-Bouhadjar, pleaded guilty to a terrorism-related possession offence, and the other, Erol Incedal, was acquitted of the more serious preparatory act of terrorism charge and found guilty only of the lesser charge of possessing 'a bomb-making document on a memory card likely to be useful to a terrorist'.[21] These bare facts aside, nothing is known, even today, as to why it was deemed necessary to hold the core of the trial in secret and there is every prospect that we will never be permitted to know what prompted this gross departure from open justice.

We are left with the two questions. First, how is it that a criminal justice system renowned throughout the world for its adherence to the rule of law (Albrecht 2011; Allan 1998), fair, and open justice (Ashworth and Redmayne 2010: ch. 2; Sanders et al. 2010) has come to condone a set of arrangements that reduced a criminal trial on very serious charges to such a sorry state? And second, how might academics who seek to examine such a case in detail, in order to understand why the protections of open

[18] *Guardian News and Media Ltd v AB and CD* [2014] EWCA Crim 1861 s.10. The judgment continued, 'It is readily apparent that, from time to time, tensions between the principle of open justice and the needs of national security will be inevitable. All the more so, given the emergence of the Agencies from the shadows, their close cooperation with the Police in the CJS and the extension of the law's reach over the past decades.' Ibid. s. 15.

[19] D. Casciani, 'Fully Secret Terror Trial Blocked by Court of Appeal', *BBC News*, 12 June 2014, http://www.bbc.co.uk/news/uk-27806814.

[20] Ibid.

[21] 'Erol Incedal Secret Terror Trial: Suspect Convicted of Possessing Terrorist Information', *The Telegraph*, 7 November 2014, http://www.telegraph.co.uk/news/uknews/terrorism-in-the-uk/11235297/Erol-Incedal-secret-terror-trial-Suspect-convicted-of-possessing-terrorist-information.html.

justice were so violently overridden in the name of security, go about doing so when so little is in the public domain? The ethnographic studies and action research of previous generations that painted such rich, fine-detailed portraits of policing are rendered impossible when doors are closed and institutions are unwilling to admit researchers. Lawyers and criminologists once enjoyed what now seems the luxury of criticizing procedural values for providing a rhetorical legitimating cover for practices devoted to securing convictions (McBarnet 1981: 156). The Incedal case might make modern-day academics rather charier of dismissing due process protections than their predecessors.

CONCLUDING THOUGHTS

At a time when, at least in Britain, academic *impact* is understood primarily as the influence that scholars must try to bring to bear in the 'real' world,[22] this chapter has suggested that the causal relationship between subject and scholarship is rarely uni-directional. Rather the changing face of criminal justice scholarship results from the complex interplay between shifts in the scope, aims, and workings of criminal justice and in academic attempts to understand, inform, and shape those changes. Impact may now be a vaunted kitemark of the academic game but it tends to obscure how far the substantive concerns, intellectual puzzles, and core questions of criminal justice scholarship are themselves shaped and informed by the changing world outside the academy. It is no small irony that as the expectation that academics should have impact has grown so their capacity to conduct empirical research into criminal justice institutions, even one as constitutively open and public as the criminal trial, has been diminished.

Criminal justice has historically been presented as a servant of two masters. On the one hand, it labours to protect the public against depredation by offenders and, in so doing, serves the security obligation of the state. On the other hand, the criminal process is supposed to protect the rights of individuals who find themselves caught up in it. In this second role, decades of criminal justice scholarship have revealed the criminal process to be a very imperfect set of structures, mechanisms, and practices by which to protect the individual against arbitrary and unwarranted state coercion. And yet, as this chapter has made clear, time and again collective claims of public protection have proven to be the more powerful master. Calls for a 'rebalancing of the criminal justice system in favour of the law-abiding majority' (most recently Home Office 2006), driven by diverse moral panics, signal crimes or crises, arise with predictable frequency. Claims to rebalance criminal justice are problematic because they rely on the dubious claim that the good of public safety can be assured only by sacrificing the liberties of the individual defendant (Ashworth and Redmayne 2010: 432). Nonetheless, the demand for public protection and security has repeatedly proven a powerful lever

[22] See e.g. http://www.esrc.ac.uk/research/evaluation-and-impact/what-is-impact/ and http://www.rcuk.ac.uk/innovation/impacts/.

with which to demand increased resources, new police powers, more extensive criminal laws, and, not least, radical curtailments to the criminal process and trial with little regard for the fact that such overly extensive powers threaten individual security and compromise human rights.

Criminal justice scholars need to contest much more vigorously the conventional wisdom that the security of the individual suspect or defendant stands in conflict with collective security. This claim rests on a false, though enduring dichotomy drawn between individual and collective interests. Viscount Runciman in his 1993 Royal Commission Report expressed the underlying flaw in this dubious premise more eloquently than perhaps he realized: 'there is a potential conflict of the interests of justice on the one hand and the requirement of fair and reasonable treatment for everyone involved, suspects and defendants, on the other' (Runciman 1993: 8).[23]

When justice is placed on one side of the scales and the requirements of fair and reasonable treatment for defendants on the other something is seriously rotten in the state of criminal justice. The architects of a criminal justice system worth the name ought surely not to find it so difficult to recognize that securing the rights of the individual in the criminal process is inherent in, and indivisible from, securing justice for us all. For so long as they struggle to grasp the basic truth that justice is not to be balanced against the rights of defendants and that we all have a vested security interest in a criminal justice system that it is fair and reasonable, it remains the task of academics to point the way.

REFERENCES

Albrecht, P.-A. (2011), *Securitized Societies. The Rule of Law: History of a Free Fall*, Cambridge: Intersentia.

Allan, T.R.S. (1998), 'Procedural Fairness and the Duty of Respect', *Oxford Journal of Legal Studies*, 18, 3: 497–515.

Anderson, D. (2013), 'Shielding the Compass: How to Fight Terrorism without Defeating the Law', *European Human Rights Law Review*, 3: 233–46.

Ashworth, A. (1988), 'Criminal Justice and the Criminal Process', *British Journal of Criminology*, 28, 2: 111–23.

Ashworth, A. (2002), *Human Rights, Serious Crime and Criminal Procedure*, The Hamlyn Lectures, London: Sweet & Maxwell.

Ashworth, A. (2006), 'Four Threats to the Presumption of Innocence', *South African Law Journal*, 123: 62–96.

Ashworth, A. (2007), 'Security, Terrorism and the Value of Human Rights', in B. Goold and L. Lazarus (eds), *Security and Human Rights*, Oxford: Hart Publishing: 203–26.

Ashworth, A. and Redmayne, M. (2010), *The Criminal Process*, 4th edn, Oxford: Oxford University Press.

Ashworth, A. and Zedner, L. (2012), 'Prevention and Criminalization: Justifications and Limits', *New Criminal Law Review*, 15, 4: 542–71.

Ashworth, A. and Zedner, L. (2014), *Preventive Justice*, Oxford: Oxford University Press.

[23] For insightful discussion see Young and Sanders 1994: 154.

BALDWIN, J. and MCCONVILLE, M. (1977), *Negotiated Justice: Pressures on Defendants to Plead Guilty*, London: Martin Robertson.

BALDWIN, J. and MCCONVILLE, M. (1979), *Jury Trials*, Oxford: Oxford University Press.

BOTTOMS, A.E. and MCCLEAN, J.D. (1976), *Defendants in the Criminal Process*, London: Routledge.

BOWLING, B. and MARKS, E. (forthcoming), *The Rise and Fall of Suspicionless Searches*.

BOWLING, B. and PHILLIPS, C. (2002), *Racism, Crime and Justice*, London: Longman.

BRIDGES, L. and MCCONVILLE, M. (1994), 'Keeping Faith with Their Own Convictions: The Royal Commission on Criminal Justice', *Modern Law Review*, 57, 1: 75–90.

COHEN, S. (1980 [1972]), *Folk Devils and Moral Panics*, Oxford: Martin Robertson.

CRAWFORD, A. (1998), *Crime Prevention and Community Safety: Politics, Policies, and Practices*, London: Longman.

DOWNES, D. (1988), 'The Sociology of Crime and Social Control in Britain, 1960–1987', *British Journal of Criminology*, 28, 2: 45–57.

ERICSON, R. (2007), *Crime in an Insecure World*, Cambridge: Polity.

FEELEY, M. and SIMON, J. (1992), 'The New Penology: Notes on the Emerging Strategy of Corrections and its Implications', *Criminology*, 30, 4: 449–74.

FEELEY, M. and SIMON, J. (1994), 'Actuarial Justice: The Emerging New Criminal Law', in D. Nelken (ed.), *The Futures of Criminology*, London: Sage: 173–201.

GARLAND, D. (1996), 'The Limits of the Sovereign State: Strategies of Crime Control in Contemporary Society', *British Journal of Criminology*, 36, 4: 445–71.

GARLAND, D. (2001), *The Culture of Control: Crime and Social Order in Contemporary Society*, Oxford: Oxford University Press.

GOOLD, B.J. (2004), *CCTV and Policing: Public Area Surveillance and Police Practices in Britain*, Oxford: Oxford University Press.

GOOLD, B. and LAZARUS, L. (eds) (2007), *Security and Human Rights*, Oxford: Hart Publishing.

HALL, S., CRITCHER, C., JEFFERSON, T., CLARKE, J., and ROBERTS, B. (1978), *Policing the Crisis: Mugging, the State, and Law and Order*, London: Macmillan.

HANNAH-MOFFAT, K. (2011), 'Criminological Cliques: Narrowing Dialogues, Institutional Protectionism, and the Next Generation', in M. Bosworth and C. Hoyle (eds), *What is Criminology?*, Oxford: Oxford University Press: 440–55.

HILLYARD, P. (1994), 'The Normalization of Special Powers from Northern Ireland to Britain', in N. Lacey (ed.), *A Reader on Criminal Justice*, Oxford: Oxford University Press: 63–102.

HILLYARD, P. (2005), 'The "War on Terror"—Lessons from Ireland', *European Civil Liberties Network*: 1–4, available at: http://www.ecln.org/essays/essay-1.pdf.

Home Office (2006), *Criminal Justice System Review: Rebalancing the Criminal Justice System in Favour of the Law-Abiding Majority*, London: Home Office.

Home Office (2015), *Operation of Police Powers under the Terrorism Act 2000 and Subsequent Legislation: Arrests, Outcomes, and Stop and Search, Great Britain, Quarterly Update to September 2015*, London: Home Office.

HOPE, T. and SPARKS, R. (eds) (2000), *Crime, Risk and Insecurity: Law and Order in Everyday Life and Political Discourse*, London: Routledge.

HUDSON, B. (2012), 'Who Needs Justice? Who Needs Security?', in B. Hudson and S. Ugelvik (eds), *Justice and Security in the 21st Century*, Oxford: Routledge: 6–23.

HUDSON, B. and UGELVIK, S. (eds) (2012), *Justice and Security in the 21st Century: Risks, Rights and the Rule of Law*, London: Routledge.

Justice (2009), *Secret Evidence*, London: Justice.

KAVANAGH, A. (2010), 'Special Advocates, Control Orders and the Right to a Fair Trial', *Modern Law Review*, 63, 5: 836–57.

Lazarus, L. (2007), 'Mapping the Right to Security', in B. Goold and L. Lazarus (eds), *Security and Human Rights*, Oxford: Hart Publishing: 325–46.
Lazarus, L. (forthcoming), *Securing Legality*, Oxford: Hart Publishing.
Lazarus, L., Goold, B.J., and Swiney, G. (2007), *Public Protection, Proportionality and the Search for Balance*, Ministry of Justice Research Series 10/07.
Lloyd, L.J. (1996), *Inquiry into Legislation on Terrorism*, Cm 3420, London: HMSO.
Loader, I. (2002), 'Policing, Securitization and Democracy in Europe', *Criminal Justice*, 2, 2: 125–53.
Loader, I. and Walker, N. (2007), *Civilizing Security*, Cambridge: Cambridge University Press.
Lustgarten, L. and Leigh, I. (1994), *In from the Cold: National Security and Parliamentary Democracy*, Oxford: Clarendon Press.
McBarnet, B. (1981), *Conviction: Law, the State and the Construction of Justice*, London: Macmillan.
McConville, M., Sanders, A., and Leng, R. (1991), *The Case for the Prosecution*, London: Routledge.
Macpherson, W. (1999), *Report of the Stephen Lawrence Inquiry*, Cmnd 4262, London: HMSO.
Martin, J.P. (1988), 'The Development of Criminology in Britain 1948–60', *British Journal of Criminology*, 28, 2: 35–44.
O'Malley, P. (ed.) (1998), *Crime and the Risk Society*, Aldershot: Ashgate.
Packer, H. (1968), *The Limits of the Criminal Sanction*, Stanford, CA: Stanford University Press.
Philips, C.H. (1981), *Report of the Royal Commission on Criminal Procedure*, Cmnd 8092, London: HMSO.
Pratt, J. (2000), 'Dangerousness and Modern Society', in M. Brown and J. Pratt (eds), *Dangerous Offenders: Punishment and Social Order*, London: Routledge: 35–48.
Pratt, J. (2007), *Penal Populism*, London: Routledge.
Ramsay, P. (2012), *The Insecurity State: Vulnerable Autonomy and the Right to Security in the Criminal Law*, Oxford: Oxford University Press.
Roach, K. (2010), 'The Eroding Distinction between Intelligence and Evidence in Terrorism Investigations', in N. McGarrity, A. Lynch, and G. Williams (eds), *Counter-Terrorism and Beyond: The Culture of Law and Justice after 9/11*, Abingdon: Routledge.
Rose, D. (1996) *In the Name Of The Law: The Collapse of Criminal Justice*, London: Vintage.
Runciman, G. (1993), *Report of the Royal Commission on Criminal Justice*, Cm 2263, London: HMSO.
Sanders, A. and Young, R. (1994), 'The Rule of Law, Due Process and Pre-Trial Criminal Justice', *Current Legal Problems*, 47, 2: 125–56.
Sanders, A., Young, R., and Burton, M. (2010), *Criminal Justice*, 4th edn, Oxford: Oxford University Press.
Scarman, L. (1982), *The Scarman Report: The Brixton Disorders*, London: Pelican.
Simon, J. (2015), *Preventive Terrorism Offences*, DPhil, University of Oxford.
Stuntz, W. (2002), 'Local Policing after the Terror', *Yale Law Journal*, 111, 8: 2137–94.
Sullivan, G.R. and Dennis, I. (eds) (2012), *Seeking Security: Pre-Empting the Commission of Criminal Harms*, Oxford: Hart Publishing.
Tomkins, A. (2011), 'National Security and the Due Process of Law', *Current Legal Problems*, 64, 1: 215–53.
Walker, C. (2004), 'Terrorism and Criminal Justice: Past, Present and Future', *Criminal Law Review*: 311–27.

YOUNG, J. (1999), *The Exclusive Society*, London: Sage.

YOUNG, R. and SANDERS, A. (1994), 'The Royal Commission on Criminal Justice: A Confidence Trick?', *Oxford Journal of Legal Studies*, 14, 3: 435–48.

ZEDNER, L. (2000), 'The Pursuit of Security', in T. Hope and R. Sparks (eds), *Crime, Risk and Insecurity*, Abingdon: Routledge: 200–14.

ZEDNER, L. (2004), *Criminal Justice*, Oxford: Oxford University Press.

ZEDNER, L. (2005), 'Securing Liberty in the Face of Terror: Reflections from Criminal Justice', *Journal of Law and Society*, 32, 4: 507–33.

ZEDNER, L. (2007a), 'Pre-Crime and Post-Criminology?', *Theoretical Criminology, Special Issue, Criminology: Public Intellectuals and Public Policy*, 11, 2: 261–81.

ZEDNER, L. (2007b), 'Seeking Security by Eroding Rights: The Side-Stepping of Due Process', in B. Goold and L. Lazarus (eds), *Security and Human Rights*, Oxford: Hart Publishing.

ZEDNER, L. (2007c), 'Preventive Justice or Pre-Punishment? The Case of Control Orders', *Current Legal Problems*, 60, 1: 174–203.

ZEDNER, L. (2008), 'Fixing the Future: The Pre-Emptive Turn in Criminal Justice', in B. McSherry, A. Norrie, and S. Bronitt (eds), *Regulating Deviance: The Redirection of Criminalization and the Futures of Criminal Law*, Oxford: Hart Publishing.

ZEDNER, L. (2009), *Security*, Abingdon: Routledge.

ZEDNER, L. (2012), 'Terrorizing Criminal Law', *Criminal Law and Philosophy*, 6, 3: 99–121.

ZEDNER, L. (forthcoming), 'Security against Arbitrary Government in Criminal Justice', in P. Asp, A. du Bois Pedain, and M. Ulväng (eds), *Criminal Law and the Authority of the State*, Oxford: Hart Publishing.

PART III

PUNISHMENT, POLICY, AND PRACTICE

12

PRISONER COPING AND ADAPTATION

Ian O'Donnell

The contours of imprisonment have been reshaped over the past 50 years. This chapter explores continuity and change in the pains of confinement, highlighting a variety of ways that prisoners cope with an environment characterized by conflict, disconnection, and tedium. Sentence lengths have increased in many countries and some US prisons now have a hospice in addition to a death row. In the former, death is certain and comes soon after arrival. In the latter, execution is far from inevitable and the wait for it is long and fraught. The aim in both places is bleak: to prevent premature death. Another recent phenomenon in the US, which leads the world in the incarceration stakes, is the use of prolonged solitary confinement as an administrative measure. Adverse mental health consequences routinely follow involuntary isolation, but some prisoners display remarkable resilience and there is much to be learned from their accounts of psychological survival.

As the numbers in custody have surged, the prisoner society has come under strain. Whatever bonds of solidarity may have existed in the past have frayed and what brings prisoners together today is not their shared status as 'outlaws' but their allegiance to a faith tradition, a political ideology, or a street gang; rather than uniting in their opposition to staff, they are pitted against each other. These divisions are deepened by the drugs culture that permeates many prisons, and the associated problems of distribution, consumption, and debt collection. They are reinforced by the introduction of differentiated regimes which enhance prisoner compliance through small, but by no means insignificant, rewards. In short, prisons have become more variegated places since the Penal Research Unit, forerunner of the Centre for Criminology, was established at Oxford University in 1966.

Thinking about 'coercive confinement' in general rather than imprisonment in particular yields a more nuanced perspective on incarceration trends. The implications of such a conceptual shift will be teased out below alongside some (highly tentative) musings about possible futures of imprisonment. I will argue that scientific advances—in combination with humankind's genius for devising new ways of inflicting pain—create a context for the decentring of the prison, the customization of punishment, and the tightening of the penal screw. Understanding these processes will be the key to mapping the contours of imprisonment over the next 50 years.

CHANGING PAINS

According to Ben Crewe (2011: 522), the metaphor of 'tightness' captures the contemporary experience of imprisonment better than the ideas of 'depth' and 'weight' as conceptualized by Roy King and Kathleen McDermott (1995), who adapted the idea of depth from David Downes's (1988) comparative study of Dutch and English penal policy. For King and McDermott (1995: 90), depth is defined by 'the extent to which a prisoner is embedded into the security and control systems of imprisonment', while weight relates to, 'the degree to which relationships, rights and privileges, standards and conditions serve to bear down on them'. These variables do not necessarily go hand in hand; life in a high-security prison can be tolerably light.

Tightness, on the other hand, describes a carceral experience where power is exercised softly, but grips the prisoner in so many ways that wriggling free of it becomes all but impossible. This concept adds sophistication to our understanding of the experience of imprisonment. It allows for situations where the depth is moderate (security measures are not too oppressive), and the weight is bearable (good relationships and conditions exist), but the prisoner feels enmeshed. A reduced dependence on coercion is accompanied by a sustained effort to connect prisoners to the administration of their own sentences. They become caught up in the protocols that dictate how far, and at what pace, they will progress towards an amelioration of conditions or an enhanced prospect of release.

Prison life has improved in many material respects, at least in the economically developed world: hygiene is better; the diet is more balanced and nutritious; visitation is more frequent; health care, while perhaps not equivalent to that available outside, is routinely available; corporal punishment is a thing of the past; capital punishment is almost extinct; there is a growing awareness of the human rights standards which prison treatment should satisfy; there is a renewed emphasis on inspection and monitoring by local, national, and supra-national bodies. Notable among the latter are the Council of Europe Committee for the Prevention of Torture and Inhuman or Degrading Treatment or Punishment (CPT) and the United Nations Subcommittee on the Prevention of Torture and other Cruel, Inhuman or Degrading Treatment or Punishment (SPT).

But when prisoners are recruited as agents in their own transformation they become vulnerable to insidious and invidious new pressures. Encouraged to believe that they can play a role in directing their own futures, they become responsible, in part, for decisions about the privileges they are granted and the timing of their release. This can have a stifling effect as they attempt to negotiate the layers of regulations according to which they must conduct their lives. It also divides the prison population according to whether its members wish to comply, win privileges, and ease the passage through their sentence, or remain defiant and accept the associated costs. Even among the former group there may be differentiation, with several levels of regime enhancement available. This creates a context where prisoners are incentivized to make decisions that have adverse implications for social cohesion; individual advancement occurs at the expense of the peer group. Cleaner, more humane living conditions are undoubtedly important, but spending longer in them struggling with labyrinthine rules and procedures (and aware that personal progress contributes to the disintegration of prisoner solidarity) adds an unwelcome twist to the experience.

There has been a contraction in the breadth of ambition associated with the expressed aims of imprisonment, a shift from lofty aspirations about creating productive members of society to performance measures that lend themselves to easy quantification. To some degree this constriction of purpose was brought about by the disappointing results of penal practice: the outcomes of rehabilitative programmes were unimpressive and recidivism rates remained stubbornly high. In addition, it reflects the encroachment of new public management ideas and a belief that prisons should not be immune from the three Es of economy, efficiency, and effectiveness (O'Donnell 2016). It could be said that today's aims reflect imperatives that relate to the smooth running of the institution rather than the transformation of the prisoner (and, as a corollary, the improvement of society). The emergence in recent decades of cognitive behavioural interventions, in tandem with more elaborate approaches to programme design and better measurement of effects, have renewed confidence in the potential for imprisonment to catalyse meaningful personal change and to promote community safety. This is an area where criminal justice research has played an important role.

TIME WORK

Prison life is characterized by stultifying repetition. Successful adaptation involves devising routines to cope with boredom and finding ways to insert meaningful activities into a timetable that is not of the prisoners' design. Once the tumult of the initial period is past, and before the trepidation that accompanies release emerges, coping with imprisonment means devising effective ways to fritter away large amounts of time. For prisoners serving short terms, there can be weight and depth, and even tightness, but because the temporal dimension does not come to exercise an oppressive independent presence, it can be handled once the turbulent early phase is over. For the long-termer, identifying ways to deal with time's potentially overwhelming burden is essential for the preservation of mental integrity. Only when the prisoner has found an effective way of working with time can he or she breathe freely.

How prisoners deal with the passage of time has attracted scant scholarly attention, despite its critical relevance to successful adaptation. Elsewhere I have offered the concept of the 'pain quotient' (PQ) as a way of thinking about the interplay between time and imprisonment:

> The two key variables involved in estimating the PQ are time to be served (this takes account of sentence length and point in sentence) and life to be lived (this takes account of chronological age and life expectancy). The sentence itself, or the amount of time served, or the prisoner's age tell us little when considered independently. They are merely numbers in the penal lottery. It is only when they are viewed dynamically, and interactively, that these factors can be used to sketch out the temporal parameters of pain.
>
> (O'Donnell 2014: 201–2)

For a prisoner with a lot of life to live and a short time to serve, the PQ is small and time orientation is relatively unimportant. For a prisoner whose remaining prison term exceeds his life expectancy it is large, and significant adjustments are required in the interests of psychological survival. Devising ways to cope with time has always been a challenge for prisoners and will always remain so. It is of more pressing importance today given the rise, across many countries, in sentence lengths. Truncating perceived duration is the key to successful adaptation. If prisoners do not find ways to lighten time's burden it can become crushing.

MAINTAINING BODILY INTEGRITY

Some challenges are constant over time and across space. One of these is how to reduce violence without creating prison regimes that are so deep they breach acceptable minimum standards. When aggressive and non-conforming young men are gathered together against their wills, the potential for conflict is obvious. When they place a disproportionate emphasis on respect and fighting prowess the scene is set for this potential to be realized. Hard drug use plays a role here also. Prisoners have long been surreptitious brewers and distillers but heroin has made its presence felt in recent decades (Crewe 2005). In addition to being accompanied by a risk of lethal infection if the drug is taken intravenously and unsterilized injecting equipment is shared, the associated trade further divides prisoners and creates a range of new problems associated with the protection of those who become vulnerable on account of undischarged debts.

Despite the ubiquitous threat of force and a history of hostile relations between captives and captors, collective violence is uncommon in the prison systems of developed countries. There is nothing in recent years to parallel the carnage of the riots at Attica Correctional Facility, New York, in 1971 (forty-three fatalities) and at New Mexico State Penitentiary, Santa Fe, in 1980 (thirty-three fatalities). The trend in interpersonal violence appears to be in the same direction and, as far as homicide is concerned, prisoners in the US and UK are at least as safe as comparable groups in the community (Mumola 2005; Sattar 2001). When it comes to sexual violence they may not be, especially in the US (O'Donnell 2004). There is no doubt that assault, theft, and robbery are common in prisons (Edgar et al. 2012), but whether they are significantly more hazardous places in these respects than the areas of urban deprivation from which many prisoners are drawn, and the domestic environments in which they dwell when at liberty, is less clear.

What we know about prison violence in Africa, Asia, or Central and South America leaves no room for complacency. Extremes include the 111 prisoners at Carandiru Penitentiary, São Paulo, Brazil, killed by military police who stormed the prison after a riot in 1992 (Cavallaro 1997), and the horror of what is known in South Africa as the 'slow puncture' of deliberate HIV infection of one prisoner by another (Luyt 2013). The prison systems of many poor countries are overcrowded, under-resourced, and controlled by their inmate populations. We know little about the experience of imprisonment under such conditions, how it has changed, or its prospects. As in so many areas our understanding leans heavily towards Anglo-American perspectives where the scholarship is abundant. A criminology without borders—which the Oxford Centre for Criminology is well-positioned to foster—has an important role to play in redressing this imbalance.

AN ABSENCE OF CONNECTIVITY

Advances in information and communications technology mean that prisons have become increasingly porous places. Access to telephones is widespread (calls are sometimes made using devices that have been smuggled into the prison). In-cell radios and televisions are an option for many. Temporary release and furloughs are sometimes possible. Financial support may be available for prison visits. Letters are permitted and censorship is less intrusive than in the past when the permitted volume of correspondence was small and its contents were read before being passed on. Prisoners often receive small amounts of money from the authorities and a mechanism usually exists to allow family and friends to transfer funds to their prison accounts so that they can purchase foodstuffs, tobacco, magazines, and perhaps even art and craft materials. All of the foregoing relieves much of the monotonous misery that characterized earlier times.

But prisoners may *feel* more marooned from loved ones today given the plethora of ways of keeping in touch, many of which require only rudimentary literacy skills (e.g. text messaging, emailing, tweeting, sharing photographs and video clips, updating social networking sites). Compared to the pen and paper that were the only options until the end of the twentieth century—and that many prisoners lacked the capacity to use to any great effect—this is a far greater degree of relative deprivation; the digital divide is wide, and prison systems have been slow to narrow it.

In a world where communication is defined by instantaneity, prisoners are more cut off than ever; when company of one's choosing is only a click or a swipe away, the separation that prison entails is all the more debilitating. The acceleration of time which technological innovation has allowed—and the accompanying intensification of experiences—hardly penetrated the penal realm. Timetables and daily routines recall the mid-nineteenth century and prisoners exist as 'cavemen in an era of speed-of-light technology' (Johnson 2005: 263). In his classic account of prison life, Gresham Sykes (1958) wrote about the losses of liberty, goods and services, sexual relationships, autonomy, and security. To this list it might be appropriate to add another, namely the denial of connectivity.

The feeling of disconnection is exacerbated when prisoners are a long way from home. Often this involves urban men held in remote rural prisons whose visitors must undertake arduous journeys to prevent relationships from foundering. Occasionally national borders must be crossed. In 2015 the authorities in Norway began transferring prisoners to penal institutions in the Netherlands in an attempt to cope with overcrowding and lengthy waiting lists for prison admission. This followed a similar deal being struck between Belgium and the Netherlands (Pakes and Holt 2015). Videoconferencing offers a partial solution to the problem of distance but it lacks the psychological engagement of a direct encounter and the spontaneity allowed by internet access.

COPING *IN EXTREMIS*

Prisoners find ways to adapt to even the grimmest surroundings and their resilience should not be underestimated. In an exploration of how men and women cope with the rigours of solitary confinement, including in the supermax facilities that blight the US, I have offered what I call the seven Rs of survival. While of particular relevance to the long-term isolate who is segregated for reasons of discipline, protection, or perceived administrative necessity, these stratagems can be adopted by prisoners serving sentences of any length in conditions of any kind (O'Donnell 2014: 222–55). They are listed next in descending order of popularity and ascending order of importance. *Rescheduling* involves using different intervals to gauge the passage of time. *Removal* is routine work and exercise, busyness as an end in itself. *Reduction* comprises ways of lightening the burden of prison time by ensuring that there is less of it to deal with, such as by sleeping for longer. *Reorientation* involves resetting temporal horizons so that the focus is emphatically on the present. *Resistance* entails holding fast against the system through, for example, fighting or litigating. *Raptness* is absorption in an activity like creative writing, craftwork, or painting. *Reinterpretation* is when prisoners reimagine and recast their predicament by finding a framework of meaning and a sense of common purpose; while rare the potential rewards are substantial.

There may be some who feel that any recognition of successful coping in extreme custody is a dangerous distraction; that it offers a source of consolation to a state that is complacent about the harms it causes. But this kind of academic self-censorship must be guarded against. The harms of custody are nuanced and anyone who takes prisons and prisoners seriously can hardly fail to become aware of this. There is no gainsaying that prisons further diminish the life chances of those who already bear the weight of multiple layers of disadvantage or that protracted isolation constitutes a significant, and sometimes overwhelming, psychological burden. However, it is also true that the period of confinement brings stability, removes a range of threats to life, and can unlock a potential that may have remained hidden in the hurly burly of life on the street.

One standpoint that remains insufficiently developed is that of the men and women who are the subjects of attention. While ex-prisoners have contributed to the literature on confinement, sometimes with penetrating insight, and a few among them have acquired graduate degrees, the emergence of an organizational structure to promote the work of ex-convicts within the academy is at an early stage (Ross et al. 2014). The criminological enterprise could do more to facilitate contributions from the men and women whose lives are grist to its intellectual mill. Of particular importance are the views of the growing number of older prisoners, for whom incarceration poses specific social and medical challenges (American Civil Liberties Union 2012), as well as those who find themselves at the bottom of the prison hierarchy because the offences they have committed attract the opprobrium of their peers. Neither must sight be lost of the minority of prisoners for whom any prospect of release has been removed. These largely invisible groups will have much to say about the changing pains of confinement.

PUTTING PRISON IN ITS PLACE

There is a general acknowledgement—more honoured in the breach than the observance—that to make sense of trajectories of social control requires the adoption of a framework of analysis that is historically informed, interdisciplinary, and not exclusively focused on the criminal justice system. It is necessary to recall that in the mid-twentieth century the deviant and difficult were held in an array of institutions of which the prison was a minor player. Accordingly, any attempt to use the rate of imprisonment as a proxy for a country's level of punitiveness is fraught with difficulty. To chart the contours of confinement requires a widening of the analytical lens.

Taking Ireland as a case study, consider that in the late 1950s the country held around 400 prisoners, but more than 30,000 of its citizens were involuntarily detained in psychiatric hospitals, reformatory and industrial schools, mother and baby homes, and Magdalen asylums. This resulted in an aggregate rate, of what Eoin O'Sullivan and Ian O'Donnell (2007) term 'coercive confinement', that exceeded 1,000 per 100,000 population (all the more remarkable given the high level of emigration at the time). The conditions in these institutions were austere and, while some of them may ostensibly have been orientated towards the welfare of their inmates, they were experienced as degrading, stigmatizing, and punitive places (O'Sullivan and O'Donnell 2012). Adopting this broader frame of reference reveals that increasing prisoner numbers in the latter half of the twentieth century do not necessarily imply a punitive turn and must be viewed against a background of deinstitutionalization—particularly of women and children—that has gone largely unremarked. The pattern is of the carceral reach narrowing but its grip intensifying.

Reformatory and industrial schools, or their functional equivalents, were common across Europe, Australia, and the United States. So too were Magdalen asylums and mother and baby homes. The detention of the mentally ill was widespread. Given the international relevance of these institutional forms, the rubric offered by O'Sullivan and O'Donnell might prove useful to researchers outside Ireland in terms of remembering the past, understanding the present, and imagining the future. At the very least it highlights the limitations of any analysis of penal change that is restricted to short-term trends and equates punitiveness with imprisonment.

DECENTRING

In *Punishment and Welfare*, David Garland described how the penal-welfare complex that emerged at the end of the nineteenth century and the beginning of the twentieth caused the partial displacement of the prison. The creation of specialist institutions to deal with habitual inebriates, juveniles, and the mentally deficient, together with the establishment of a professional probation service meant that: 'the prison was *decentred*—shifted from its position as the central and predominant sanction to become one institution among many in an extended grid of penal sanctions' (Garland 1985: 23; italics in original). This is the history of the prison when we think in terms of coercive confinement (see above) and it may be the future of the prison when we think in terms of incarceration delivered in community settings (see below).

When Garland wrote of decentring what was at issue was the place of the prison within the overall apparatus of social control; it was but one of many sites of coercive confinement, its scale and significance varying over time. When I write of decentring what is at issue is the consolidation of imprisonment accompanied by the dispersal of penal discipline, a blurring of boundaries between the prison and the domestic environment. Technological change plays a vital role and electronic monitoring will accelerate the decentring process by allowing the individual's usual place of residence to be reconstituted as his or her place of confinement. This heralds a return to widespread coercive confinement but without the massive physical infrastructure that was formerly required. Under these new arrangements the buildings become less important, the relationships between keeper and kept evaporate, and control is maintained dispassionately—and continuously—through electronic surveillance and swift application of penalties for any detected violation. Certainty, celerity, and severity join forces as never before.

My argument is that the wheel of penal change may be about to begin another revolution. Having been decentred, the prison moved centre-stage in the closing decades of the twentieth century and now it appears that another phase of decentring may lie ahead. As happened during the first phase, it is likely that the waning of the prison will be accompanied by a rise in the numbers under some form of control. The institution will become less dominant as people are incarcerated in their own homes and monitored from afar, rather than gathered together behind fortified perimeters under the gaze of professional gaolers. A dwindling need for humans to carry out the surveillance function may be accompanied by the further erosion of discretion, of advising, assisting, and befriending; a stripping away, in other words, of the humanity that can soften the impact of harsh punishment. Modern technology allows a studied indifference to offenders; they command less personal attention and this reinforces their status as socially redundant as well as morally repugnant.

The rationale underpinning Bentham's panopticon was that prisoners would comply with the regime's requirements because they could not be sure at any given moment whether they were being directly observed by an attentive watchman. Today there is no ambivalence in this regard—the technology has evolved to such a degree that all prisoners can be tracked at all times. The offender wearing a tag around his or her ankle (or, in future years perhaps, carrying a subcutaneous implant) cannot escape being monitored; any attempt to tamper with the device will trigger an immediate alarm. When surveillance is total the panopticon is redundant.

TAGGING, *REDUX*

Thus, one scenario suggested by a glance to the future is of a prison system that occupies a less central space in the landscape of punishment because prisoners are incarcerated in their own homes with GPS-enabled electronic monitoring being used to enforce curfews, track movements, and trigger alarms (e.g. notifying potential victims if an exclusion zone is entered). To date, electronic monitoring has been deployed mostly as a condition of probation or parole, or to allow remands on bail rather than in custody. Its use as a sanction remains underdeveloped although monitored home detention has, on occasion, been substituted for prison custody. The US is to the fore in taking advantage of the possibilities offered by electronic monitoring to tighten surveillance, reinforce social exclusion, gather data, and generate profit for the private sector. Nine US states have gone so far as to introduce life-time GPS monitoring for certain categories of sex offender (Kilgore 2015: 28).

The tags that allow electronic monitoring have the potential to be more than simply surveillance devices. They can be used to gather biometric data, create an audio or video record of the wearer's activities, or check alcohol consumption via transdermal testing. Tags have not been used to inflict pain and such usage is prohibited by the Council of Europe (2014). Nonetheless, it would be unduly optimistic to think that their potential to do so will never be exploited. Some elements of the public (and their political representatives) would no doubt support the introduction of a device that could deliver a debilitating electric shock should a known paedophile stray too close to a school, or a domestic abuser too close to an ex-partner's home, or should an offender quit their place of confinement during curfew hours. (If an attempt to escape from prison custody in the US can be met with lethal force it would hardly be considered disproportionate to respond to an escape from home confinement with pain delivered through a tag.) Given the huge costs of prisons and their obvious harms, and widespread antipathy towards offenders, who can be certain that electronic monitoring will not morph into electronic custody or even electronic punishment?

One of the inventors of the tag believed that it had the potential to empty the world's prisons (Schwitzgebel 1970). This potential has not been realized. Indeed, Nellis (2014) observed that electronic monitoring has not had a transformative effect on penal practice in any of the numerous jurisdictions where it has been introduced. He noted that across Europe where monitoring has been underpinned by human rights principles, embedded in state agencies, and used to support the delivery of community sanctions, it has served to complement rehabilitative efforts. When offered as a stand-alone measure, or a tracking device, or a method of home confinement, its use is more ethically, and administratively, problematic. When there are commercial pressures to expand usage, these problems are exacerbated. Private sector involvement in the penal system brings in its wake another novel feature, namely the creation of shareholder value out of human suffering, with profitability becoming an essential goal of punishment. This was unheard of 50 years ago.

Those who are subject to electronic monitoring are required to pay a setup charge and daily tariff in addition to meeting the recurring costs of their confinement including food, shelter, heat, and light (Kilgore 2015: 20). As well as taking responsibilization to an extreme level these user fees generate a significant revenue stream for the operators. If the profit margin associated with decentring the prison and dispersing its inmates is greater than for the existing model of institutions that must be built and staffed and whose occupants must be sheltered, fed, and kept occupied, this will no doubt act as a stimulus for further 'progress' in this direction.

PERSONALIZING PAIN

Another prediction for the coming 50 years is that greater attention will be devoted to individual differences in the subjective experience of punishment. It has long been recognized that prison sentences do not have a uniform impact, their effects varying according to the antecedents, disposition, age, and physical condition of the offender (Kolber 2009). From time to time, solutions have been offered to this threat to equitable treatment. Jeremy Bentham, for example, was concerned that the administration of corporal punishment could vary according to the strength and inclination of the man wielding the whip as well as the ability of the afflicted person to pay for softer treatment. To solve this problem he proposed the following:

> A machine might be made, which should put in motion certain elastic rods of cane or whalebone, the number and size of which might be determined by the law: the body of the delinquent might be subjected to the strokes of these rods, and the force and rapidity with which they should be applied, might be prescribed by the Judge: thus everything which is arbitrary might be removed.
>
> (Bentham 1830: 104)

More recently, Graeme Newman (1983) advocated electric shocks as an alternative to imprisonment because they were cheaper, did not rupture family ties or leave scars, and were fairer. By controlling the intensity and duration of the shock, each offender would feel the same amount of pain. A machine which allowed shocks to be calibrated to take account of individual differences in the offender's physical robustness would eradicate disparities in the felt experience of punishment. Newman (1983: 139) argued that for some violent criminals, where it was deemed appropriate to add humiliation to the punitive mix, public whipping should be considered.

Neither Bentham's whalebone rods nor Newman's shocking (in every sense of the word) machine became part of the penal imaginary and it is unlikely that traumatic bodily punishments will regain a foothold in countries where they are recalled as barbaric curiosities that belong to less civilized times or places. But advances in neuroscience and brain imaging create a context for measuring pain in an objective way that might be congruent with public sensibilities as long as the mode of administration of the associated punishment is not deemed cruel or excessively degrading.

It is possible to imagine a twenty-first century scheme of punishment where pain is administered so that there is equality of impact (as measured through neuroimaging rather than self-report) even if the amounts delivered vary. Wager et al. (2013) describe how individuals have their own 'neurologic signature' for physical pain and this can be read from patterns of activity across specific regions of the brain. While this work is at an early stage, and there are serious concerns regarding the reliability and validity of neuroscientific findings in general (Perlin and Lynch 2016), progress is rapid and the identification of a reliable biomarker for pain intensity would allow the administration of punishment to be individualized as never before. This creates the opportunity for a new sanction, an alternative to prison that, because it does not damage the body, will not be equated with the crude forms of corporal punishment for which public acceptance is unlikely to be forthcoming. (A non-lethal injection, perhaps? Or exposure to intense heat, light, or sound?) Further advances might also allow for the more precise quantification of the pains associated with imprisonment so that sentence lengths could be varied in order to equalize their effects.

CONCLUSION

If a shift away from incarceration in institutions and towards remotely monitored home captivity gains momentum, what are the implications for prisoner adaptation and coping? Clearly the role of the prison subculture will wane further if geographical separation from other prisoners becomes the norm. The degree to which the experience of electronic custody is a solitary one will depend on whether the offender shares his or her living space and whether there are opportunities to receive visitors or travel outside for the purposes of leisure or employment. If little in the way of meaningful human engagement is permitted, mastery of some or all of the seven Rs of survival will be necessary.

Electronic custody will mean that offenders are not exposed to a threat from other prisoners but they may be vulnerable to attack from community residents or cohabitants. Time will pass slowly without the distraction provided by other like-situated individuals or the numbing effects of a rigid timetable which, however unwelcome, adds structure and momentum to the day. If internet connectivity is allowed this will lighten the burden of incarceration and provide a way of whiling away time. In short, the pains of confinement will not be eliminated but they will be different.

A new problem will arise if punishments are calibrated to take account of individual differences in resilience. If the punishment is repeated, and the individual has learned to cope, the dosage will be increased so that the level of pain—as assessed by reading the individual's neurologic signature—is kept constant. Considering imprisonment specifically, the imposition of terms that vary according to their impact on the offender, rather than being proportionate to the harm done and the individual's intent, will raise thorny jurisprudential questions about the propriety of aligning penalties with their subjective effects. It also means that successful adaptation will become elusive, if not impossible.

Is there anything that criminologists can, or should, do to address such a turn of events? Are we content to be cartographers, plotting the various upheavals on the penal landscape or should we be attempting to shape the environment that is central to our concerns? Some of the attendant risks seem obvious. There is a clear danger of penal expansionism given the huge financial advantages associated with the decentring of imprisonment, especially if prisoners are required to carry the costs of their own sentence administration. One challenge for the academy is to identify appropriate safeguards to place around new and emerging technologies so that the net of penal control is not widened or its mesh thinned. This is where an Oxford criminology, characterized by thorough empirical work, cautious interpretation of findings, attentiveness to policy impact, and integration into networks of influence, surely has a role to play. Finally, and returning to Crewe's idea of 'tightness' as an apt metaphor for the contemporary experience of imprisonment, it might be plausible to suggest that if the prison is decentred along the lines suggested the result will be a carceral experience that is shallow and light but suffocatingly tight.

REFERENCES

American Civil Liberties Union (2012), *At America's Expense: The Mass Incarceration of the Elderly*, New York: ACLU.

Bentham, J. (1830), *The Rationale of Punishment* (edited by J.T. McHugh 2009), New York: Prometheus Books.

Cavallaro, J. (1997), *Police Brutality in Urban Brazil*, New York: Human Rights Watch.

Council of Europe (2014), *Recommendation of the Committee of Ministers to Member States on Electronic Monitoring*, Strasbourg: Council of Europe.

Crewe, B. (2005), 'Prisoner Society in the Era of Hard Drugs', *Punishment & Society*, 7, 4: 457–81.

Crewe, B. (2011), 'Depth, Weight, Tightness: Revisiting the Pains of Imprisonment', *Punishment & Society*, 13, 5: 509–29.

Downes, D. (1988), *Contrasts in Tolerance: Post-War Penal Policy in the Netherlands and England and Wales*, Oxford: Clarendon Press.

Edgar, K., O'Donnell, I., and Martin, C. (2012), *Prison Violence: The Dynamics of Conflict, Fear and Power*, London: Routledge (first published in 2003 by Willan).

Garland, D. (1985), *Punishment and Welfare: A History of Penal Strategies*, Aldershot: Gower.

Johnson, R. (2005), 'Brave New Prisons: The Growing Social Isolation of Modern Penal Institutions', in A. Liebling and S. Maruna (eds), *The Effects of Imprisonment*, Cullompton: Willan.

Kilgore, J. (2015), *Electronic Monitoring Is Not the Answer: Critical Reflections on a Flawed Alternative*, Urbana, IL: Urbana-Champaign Independent Media Center.

King, R.D. and McDermott, K. (1995), *The State of Our Prisons*, Oxford: Clarendon Press.

Kolber, A.J. (2009), 'The Subjective Experience of Punishment', *Columbia Law Review*, 109, 1: 182–236.

Luyt, W.F.M. (2013), 'Preventing and Managing Sex Crimes inside Correctional Centres', *Acta Criminologica*, 26, 2: 30–63.

Mumola, C.J. (2005), *Suicide and Homicide in State Prisons and Local Jails*, Bureau of Justice Statistics Special Report, Washington, DC: US Department of Justice.

Nellis, M. (2014), 'Understanding the Electronic Monitoring of Offenders in Europe: Expansion, Regulation and Prospects', *Crime, Law and Social Change*, 62, 4: 489–510.

Newman, G. (1983), *Just and Painful: A Case for the Corporal Punishment of Criminals*, New York: Macmillan.

O'Donnell, I. (2004), 'Prison Rape in Context', *British Journal of Criminology*, 44, 2: 241–55.

O'Donnell, I. (2014), *Prisoners, Solitude, and Time*, Oxford: Oxford University Press.

O'Donnell, I. (2016), 'The Aims of Imprisonment', in Y. Jewkes, B. Crewe, and J. Bennett (eds), *The Handbook on Prisons*, 2nd edn, London: Routledge.

O'Sullivan, E. and O'Donnell, I. (2007), 'Coercive Confinement in the Republic of Ireland: The Waning of a Culture of Control', *Punishment & Society*, 9, 1: 27–48.

O'SULLIVAN, E. and O'DONNELL, I. (2012), *Coercive Confinement in Ireland: Patients, Prisoners and Penitents*, Manchester: Manchester University Press.

PAKES, F. and HOLT, K. (2015), 'The Transnational Prisoner: Exploring Themes and Trends Involving a Prison Deal with the Netherlands and Norway', *British Journal of Criminology*, Advance Access, 8 October.

PERLIN, M.L. and LYNCH, A.J. (2016), '"In the Wasteland of your Mind": Criminology, Scientific Discoveries and the Criminal Process', *Virginia Journal of Criminal Law*, 4, 2: 304–60.

ROSS, J.I., DARKE, S., ARESTI, A., NEWBOLD, G., and EARLE, R. (2014), 'Developing Convict Criminology beyond North America', *International Criminal Justice Review*, 24, 2: 121–33.

SATTAR, G. (2001), *Rates and Causes of Death among Prisoners and Offenders under Community Supervision*, Home Office Research Study 231, London: Home Office Research, Development, and Statistics Directorate.

SCHWITZGEBEL, R.K. (1970), 'Behavioral Electronics Could Empty the World's Prisons', *The Futurist*, April: 59–60.

SYKES, G.M. (1958), *The Society of Captives: A Study of a Maximum Security Prison*, Princeton, NJ: Princeton University Press.

WAGER, T.D., ATLAS, L.Y., LINDQUIST, M.A., ROY, M., WOO, C.-W., and KROSS, E. (2013), 'An fMRI-based Neurologic Signature of Physical Pain', *New England Journal of Medicine*, 368, 15: 1388–97.

13

STRIVING TO ABOLISH THE DEATH PENALTY: SOME PERSONAL REFLECTIONS ON OXFORD'S CRIMINOLOGICAL CONTRIBUTION TO HUMAN RIGHTS

Roger Hood

INTRODUCTION

Sometimes one enters a field of research by chance. Out of the blue, in June 1987, I was approached by Eric Prokosch, the leader of Amnesty International's campaign for worldwide abolition of the death penalty. He had been asked by the United Nations Secretariat to help locate a criminologist who would be prepared to undertake research for a report requested by the UN Economic and Social Council (ECOSOC) 'on the question of the death penalty *and new contributions of the criminal sciences in the matter*' (my emphasis). The previous surveys, carried out for the UN by Marc Ancel and Norval Morris were now outdated, taking the account of developments only so far as 1965.[1] Very little interest had been shown by British academic criminologists in international aspects of capital punishment once it had been abolished for murder in this country in 1965 and confirmed in 1969. In the US, where the vast bulk of empirical criminological research on the death penalty was carried out, the focus was almost entirely on the compatibility of capital punishment with its own constitution, not with the issue as a universal human rights goal.[2]

After the report had been presented and favourably received at the UN it was published as *The Death Penalty: A Worldwide Perspective* (Hood 1989). Following this, I was appointed as consultant on three occasions by the UN to design the questionnaire,

[1] United Nations (1962, 1967).

[2] An exception had been *Capital Punishment and the American Agenda* by Franklin Zimring and Gordon Hawkins (1986), which began with the consideration of international developments and recognized 'The human rights linkage' (p. 23).

analyse the returns and prepare the draft for the Secretary-General's fifth, sixth, and seventh quinquennial surveys of *Capital Punishment and the Implementation of the Safeguards Guaranteeing the Protection of the Rights of those Facing the Death Penalty*, covering the years up to 2004. Further extensive research from international, governmental, non-governmental, and academic sources led to the publication of the second and third editions, and, with Carolyn Hoyle, the fourth and fifth.[3] The second edition was translated into Japanese, the third and fourth editions into Chinese, and the fourth also into Farsi. Translations of the fifth edition are to appear in Spanish and Chinese.

This work led to productive collaboration with a number of other inter-governmental bodies, such as the Council of Europe, the European Parliament,[4] NGOs and academic institutions, as a consultant and to carry out empirical research. The Oxford Centre joined forces in research projects with the Great Britain-China Centre, the Max Planck Institute for Foreign and International Criminal Law in Freiburg, Germany, and most frequently with the Death Penalty Project in London.[5] The UK Foreign and Commonwealth Office (FCO) and the European Union supported studies on how the mandatory death penalty was administered in Trinidad and Tobago and what surveys of public and professional opinion would reveal about the claim made by China, Trinidad, Malaysia, and Taiwan that abolition of capital punishment was not possible to achieve because a large majority of their citizens strongly supported it.

As requested by the editors, this chapter reflects on the achievements and disappointments in carrying out this body of research. Any reader interested in following the wider debates about abolition of the death penalty is referred to the fifth edition of Hood and Hoyle (2015). Nevertheless it may prove helpful to place this chapter in context by sketching the main changes that have taken place internationally in the approach towards, and the application of, capital punishment.

SETTING THE SCENE

The Universal Declaration of Human Rights (UDHR), adopted in 1948, made no mention of capital punishment in Article 3, which declared that 'every human being has an inherent right to life'. And when the European Convention on Human Rights

[3] Hood (1996, 2002); Hood and Hoyle (2008, 2015). The fifth edition also made use of the eighth and ninth UN Surveys, prepared by Professor William Schabas. Various editions benefited from the assistance of Sarah Cohen, Lucia Zedner, Timothy Besley, Anja Spindler, Jessica Skinns, Martina Feilzer, Lucy Tulloch, Ravinder Thukral, William Berry III, Sophie Palmer, Chloe Deambrogio, Michelle Miao, Daniel Pascoe, Sylvia Rich, Marion Vannier, and Gabrielle Watson.

[4] See the Introductions to Council of Europe (1999, 2004) and the briefing report prepared for the European Parliament (Hood 2012).

[5] Including assisting the Executive Directors of the Death Penalty Project, Saul Lehrfreund and Parvais Jabbar, by writing an Affidavit on the mandatory death penalty in the case of Lennox Boyce and others before the Inter-American Court of Human Rights (Case 12.480 in 2007), which found it to be a violation of the convention; a submission to the Ghana Constitutional Review Commission whose report recommended complete abolition of the death penalty; and submissions to the Constitutional Review Commission of Grenada and to the Prime Minister of St Vincent and the Grenadines. Also speaking at conferences organized by the Death Penalty Project in several countries, including Barbados, Trinidad, Malaysia, Japan, Taiwan, China, and Uganda.

(ECHR) was adopted in 1950, Article 2(1) stated that 'everyone's right to life shall be protected', but made an exception where capital punishment was provided by law.[6] The International Covenant on Civil and Political Rights (ICCPR), which was approved by the UN General Assembly (UNGA) in 1966,[7] had also not excluded capital punishment. Rather, it had restricted it: the 'inherent right to life' proclaimed in Article 6(1) had been qualified with the words, 'No one shall be *arbitrarily* deprived of his life', and Article 6(2)—which began with the words 'In countries that have not abolished the death penalty'—restricted its infliction to an undefined and therefore disputed category of 'most serious crimes'.[8] Article 7 banned 'torture or... cruel, inhuman and degrading treatment or punishment', but there was nothing to indicate that the death penalty would be so defined. There was simply insufficient support for abolition. In 1953, when Article 6 had been agreed by the drafting committee, only nine countries had abolished the death penalty completely in peacetime and wartime and another ten had abolished it for murder: a total of nineteen. However, Article 6(6) of the ICCPR had indicated the direction that the drafters of the Covenant wished to move. It declared: 'Nothing in this article shall be invoked to delay or prevent the abolition of capital punishment by any State Party.' In support, the UNGA declared by Resolution in 1971, which was repeated in 1977, that its ultimate objective was the 'desirability of abolishing this punishment in all countries'.[9] The *Declaration of Stockholm*, issued following a conference convened by Amnesty International in 1977, was a milestone. It declared unambiguously that 'The death penalty is the ultimate, cruel, inhuman and degrading punishment and violates the right to life' and called on the UN to state unambiguously that 'the death penalty is contrary to international law'.[10]

Although the death penalty has yet to be declared unlawful throughout the world, concern for protecting human rights has become a powerful dynamic over the past quarter of a century since the Berlin Wall came down and the UN added Protocol Number 2 to the ICCPR, which banned the death penalty and committed ratifying states not to reintroduce it.[11] This 'new dynamic'[12] challenged the view that each nation has the sovereign right to retain the death penalty as a repressive tool of criminal justice on the grounds of its purported deterrent utility or the cultural preferences and expectations of its citizens. Instead it aimed to persuade retentionist countries that a system of capital punishment inevitably, and however administered, is prone to error including conviction of the innocent, and punishment which is arbitrary, cruel, and inhumane, all of which violate the rights of all human beings.

At year-end 2015, 108 nations had abolished the death penalty: 102 of them completely, so that only six retained it solely for crimes against the state and in time of war:

[6] Marc Ancel, the distinguished French jurist felt justified in 1962, in his report for the Council of Europe, to write that 'even the most convinced abolitionists realize that there may be special circumstances or particularly troublous times, which justify the introduction of the death penalty for a limited period'. See Ancel (1962: 3).

[7] The ICCPR came into force in 1976.

[8] Under the ICCPR the only categories of persons for whom the death penalty could not be imposed were those convicted of crimes committed by persons below 18 years of age and pregnant women (Article 6(5)).

[9] UN Resolutions 28/57 and 32/61.

[10] Appendix A to *The Death Penalty: Amnesty International Report* 1979. See the Preface by Thomas Hammarberg.

[11] Hood (1996: 10).

[12] Hood and Hoyle (2009).

an extraordinary change since 1966. A further fifty countries retained capital punishment in law and although most of them still imposed death sentences, they had not carried out an execution for at least ten years, and often for much longer. Only thirty-nine of 196 nations had executed anyone within the past decade and most of these had done so infrequently and sporadically. There were only seven or maybe eight countries that had enforced death sentences by execution every year over the past decade: in Asia, China and probably North Korea; in the Middle East and North Africa, Iran, Saudi Arabia, Iraq, Somalia, and Yemen; and in the West solely the USA, although recently at a much reduced rate and confined to fewer and fewer states.[13] However, while capital punishment still exists in law some states that had been regarded as abolitionist de facto (such as Chad) and others that appeared to be moving towards abolition (such as India, Pakistan, and Jordan) have recently bowed to internal pressure to resume executions in response to acts of violence resulting from political conflict and the employment of terrorist methods.

It has needed political leadership on a transnational scale to create and sustain the movement to abolish capital punishment in all countries. Since 2007 abolitionist countries have gained majority acceptance of a resolution at the UNGA in favour of establishing a moratorium on death sentences and executions throughout the world. The number of countries supporting the resolution increased from 54 per cent in 2007 to 61 per cent in 2014, when only 20 per cent voted against—the others abstaining. Perhaps even more significant was the decline from fifty-seven to twenty-seven countries over the same period that signed a *Note Verbale* to the UN Secretary-General protesting that the vote had been an interference with their sovereign right over their system of criminal justice and insisting that capital punishment was not a matter of human rights.[14] Instead of abolitionists being on the weaker flank, as they were until the late 1980s constantly being called upon to justify their position, now the retentionists are on the defensive.[15]

THE GLOBAL SURVEYS

The report prepared in Oxford for the UN in 1987 set out to analyse which countries, in relation to the major regions of the world, had abolished capital punishment in the previous 25 years and the factors that appeared to have influenced the change in policy; to chart the extent to which executions had been carried out in retentionist nations and for which crimes; to try to investigate whether the *Safeguards Guaranteeing the Protection of the Rights of those Facing the Death Penalty*—established by a resolution of ECOSOC without dissent in 1984—were being implemented; and to review the

[13] Those readers who would like to follow these developments in more detail in relation to different areas of the world are referred to: Garland (2010) on the USA; Johnson and Zimring (2009) on Asia; Karimunda (2015) on Africa. Also Scherdin (ed. 2014) more generally.

[14] UN Doc A/69/993. Twenty-one of the twenty-seven were among the thirty-nine 'actively retentionist' nations that had executed within the past 10 years.

[15] See Schabas (2013).

relevant legal and criminological literature relating to arbitrariness and discrimination in enforcement of the death penalty; any evidence relating to its disputed general deterrent effect; and the influence of public opinion.

There was clearly an issue of establishing authenticity. Thus, while Amnesty International would be the source of much factual information, the review would only be taken seriously by all nations if it were presented as an independent 'academic assessment' and not as an 'abolitionist tract' written by a member of Amnesty, to which several nations were hostile. Yet the work was 'naturally orientated' towards assessing the extent to which the abolitionist policy objective of the United Nations Resolutions of 1971 and 1977 was being achieved and what impediments there were to bring it to fruition. As the work progressed it became clear that a 'factual' approach would not suffice. The changes in the orientation of countries towards capital punishment also needed to be interpreted within a normative framework.

The first edition of *The Death Penalty: A Worldwide Perspective*, published in 1989, put forward the view that 'no one can embark upon a study of the death penalty without making the commonplace observation that from a philosophical and policy standpoint there appears to be nothing new to be said'.[16] However, as indicated above, by the third edition (2002) the 'nature of the debate had moved on'. It was argued that the human rights perspective had 'added greatly to the moral force propelling the abolitionist movement' and that 'the case for retaining the death penalty—and thus resisting the movement to make its abolition an international norm—cannot rest solely on moral, cultural or religious arguments'. Countries that still favoured capital punishment 'in principle' were being faced with yet more convincing evidence of the abuses, arbitrariness, discrimination, mistakes, and inhumanity that 'appear inevitably to accompany it in practice'.[17]

As regards methodology, successive editions revealed a major problem in trying to assess international trends and practices by seeking information from governments though a questionnaire distributed by the UN. The majority of countries that retained the death penalty and continued to carry out executions did not respond and, among those that did, information on the number of death sentences and executions was not always supplied, nor on the outcome of appeals or clemency petitions. Answers to questions seeking information on conformity to the safeguards were more likely to be a reflection of the official position as regards criminal procedure, rather than the reality of law enforcement practices as reflected in responses from criminal justice NGOs. The first and subsequent editions of *The Death Penalty* therefore recommended that all countries should provide Annual Returns of death sentences imposed and executions carried out and the UN responded with Resolution 1989/64, which urged member states to publish this information.[18] Regrettably the true scale of death sentences and executions remains unknown in many countries, even to Amnesty International and the recently established Cornell University website (http://www.deathpenaltyworldwide.org), because of state secrecy or inadequate data collection and analysis. This includes many of those suspected of executing the most prisoners.

[16] Hood (1989: 6). [17] Hood (2002: 8); Hood and Hoyle (2015: 9).
[18] Hood (1989: 55–6); Hood and Hoyle (2015: 174–6).

The first edition had revealed that between 1965 and 1988 progress towards global abolition had been disappointing. The number of completely abolitionist countries had increased on average by about one a year: at that rate it would take 150 years for all nations to be totally abolitionist. It had concluded pessimistically that 'In many regions of the world there is little sign that abolition will occur soon.'[19] No nations in continental Africa or in the Middle East or Far East had shown signs of responding to the UN resolutions calling for abolition. In at least fifty-four retentionist countries there had, in fact, been an expansion in the number of crimes subject to the death penalty, most notably for drug trafficking and offences against state security. Indeed the definition of 'most serious crimes', which the UN Safeguards of 1984 had defined more precisely in the hope that it would restrict the scope of capital punishment still further until it was abolished completely, had yet to make its mark. It had become clear that the wording of Safeguard 1, which referred to 'crimes with lethal or other extremely grave consequences', was open to be interpreted as if to permit different national and cultural interpretations. The third and subsequent editions therefore recommended that the wording should be changed so as to make it clear that pending abolition it could only be imposed 'for the most serious offences of culpable homicide (murder), but it may not be mandatory for such crimes' (Hood 2002: 77).[20]

On the criminological front, each edition of *The Death Penalty* brought to international attention research that supported the abolitionist agenda. An example was the ground-breaking study by David Baldus and others (1990) which had demonstrated the failure of the new statutes enacted in 1976 in the US to eliminate the arbitrariness and discrimination that the Supreme Court had found to be unconstitutional in the famous *Furman* decision in 1972.[21] The first edition also demonstrated that it would not be prudent to accept the 'findings', widely quoted at the time, on the basis of Isaac Ehrlich's econometric analysis, that each execution for murder 'saved lives' through its general deterrent effect, Indeed, it concluded that 'such proof is unlikely to be forthcoming'. This assessment has stood the test of time, as subsequent editions have reviewed yet further attempts to prove a marginally greater deterrent effect of execution over life imprisonment.[22] Failure to prove that the death penalty deters more than a life sentence has been widely referred to by Amnesty International, the United Nations, the Council of Europe, and other bodies as an authoritative argument against its retention. Another positive outcome was the evidence provided of wide-scale disregard or failure to implement effectively the fair trial Safeguards established to protect persons under threat of conviction and execution. As a result, ECOSOC introduced several further safeguards in 1989 and again in 1996: to provide for counsel 'at every stage of the proceedings, above and beyond the protection afforded in non-capital cases'; for *mandatory* appeal against or for review of death sentences and consideration of clemency and or pardon in all cases; and to eliminate the death penalty

[19] Hood (1989: 159).

[20] It was encouraging to note that the UN Special Rapporteur, Philip Alston, came to a similar conclusion in 2007, recommending that capital punishment where still practised should be available only where it could be proved that there was an 'intention to kill which resulted in loss of life'. See Hood and Hoyle (2008: 132).

[21] The research by Baldus and his colleagues, as well as other similar—mostly US-based studies—is reviewed in Hood (1989: 98–116) and Hood and Hoyle (2015: ch. 8).

[22] Hood (1989: 98–116); Hood and Hoyle (2015: 389–425).

'for persons suffering from mental retardation (as it was then called) or extremely limited mental competence, whether at the stage of sentence or execution'.

One of the other contributions was to chart throughout the series of surveys the general decline in the number of judicial executions carried out worldwide and in the number of countries that continued to execute regularly each year at a substantial level. It became obvious that this data would only have some meaning if it were to be related at least to the size of population. Bringing this to light in the third edition appears to have had a marked effect on Singapore, where, during the period covered by the sixth survey (1994–8) the average rate of executions had been 13.57 per million of its population, by far the highest in the world (Hood 2002: 90–2). This data was subsequently used by Amnesty International in 2004 to castigate Singapore. The negative image it conveyed of this thriving city state may well have been the reason why the annual rate of executions fell to 1.2 per million in the following years.[23] The fourth and fifth editions added new perspectives brought about by the expansion of research on the issue of public opinion and on the implications of abolition for penal systems, especially the expansion of sentences of 'life imprisonment without parole', or 'whole life sentences' as they are called in the UK.

THE IMPORTANCE OF DISSEMINATION

For books to have an impact, authors need allies among the institutions which wish to use the evidence provided, sufficient resources to travel, and the goodwill and interest of the authorities and non-governmental and academic bodies in the countries to which the evidence and arguments are to be conveyed. As an 'outsider', particularly one from a former imperial power, it was vital to obtain the confidence due to an expert in the field, especially to diffuse the accusation that one was seeking to interfere in an 'internal affair'. Very rarely was there a hostile reaction when explaining how the abolition of capital punishment has come to be regarded as an international human rights goal and to encourage retentionist countries to recognize that their objections and concerns regarding abolition have been overcome by so many nations of the world. Beginning with Moscow, Kiev, and the USA in the 1990s, the opportunities for disseminating this message spread from 2001 onwards to China, the Philippines, Barbados, Trinidad, Taiwan, Japan, India, Uganda, Malaysia, Vietnam, and Pakistan, and at meetings of various international bodies and conferences.[24]

[23] Hor (2013: 159–63). In 2012 Singapore also made the application of the death penalty for drug trafficking discretionary rather than mandatory for persons who could convince the authorities that they had been mere couriers and had 'substantially assisted' the prosecutions. The scope of the mandatory death penalty for murder was also restricted. See Hood and Hoyle (2015: 347–8). See also Zimring et al. (2010).

[24] Such as Amnesty International USA (Hood 1995); EU-China human rights seminars; as consultant to the European Parliament on Asia (Hood 2013); at the Commonwealth Lawyers Conference in Jamaica (Hood 2008); at meetings of the International Commission against the Death Penalty; at meetings organized by the Office of the UN High Commission on Human Rights in China and in New York (Hoyle and Hood 2015); at World Congresses Against the Death Penalty; and in widely read publications (see Hood 2001, 2004, 2007, 2009; Hood and Deva 2013; and Hood and Hoyle 2009).

The opportunity to disseminate the outcome of the surveys with the Chinese government and academics first arose in 1999 when the Chinese delegation to the UK-China human rights dialogue in London agreed that a small group from the Foreign Secretary's Death Penalty Panel should be invited to make a presentation. Such was the scepticism of the leader of the Chinese delegation on hearing my views on abolition that he proclaimed that whatever I knew about other countries, I knew nothing about conditions in China or its culture or the reasons why it must retain capital punishment. We needed to be properly informed. As a result, in 2001 a visit was arranged by the Chinese Ministry of Justice with the FCO and the British Embassy in Beijing for me to go to Beijing with Peter Hodgkinson, Director of the Centre for Capital Punishment Studies at Westminster University, and Saul Lehrfreund, Executive Director of the Death Penalty Project. A series of polite, frank but non-confrontational, meetings with officials, lawyers, and academics left us in no doubt that although abolition was perhaps a long-term goal, it was not considered desirable or possible in China while, in their view, public opinion demanded the death penalty and while it was regarded as a necessary deterrent to control crime during a period of rapid socio-economic change. We were reminded that the process of abolition in the UK had taken well over 100 years. On our part we concentrated on two issues: the necessity to remove the barrier of state secrecy from data about the scope and frequency of the application of capital punishment; and the need to ensure that all the procedures for applying the death penalty from arrest to final appeal should be carried out in conformity with the standards for fair trial enshrined in the UN Safeguards and the ICCPR, which China had signed in 1997, but as yet has not ratified. The visit was regarded as a success by officials from both sides and although a subsequent proposal for a joint research project with the Chinese Academy of Social Sciences did not come to fruition, in 2003, Liu Renwen, a young professor at the Chinese Academy was able to spend three months in Oxford, supported by the Foreign Office, to study the issue of the death penalty. Not only did he undertake the Chinese translation of the third edition of *The Death Penalty* and arrange for its publication by the People's Security University Press, he has since become, as the Director of the Criminal Law Division of the Chinese Academy, one of the most outspoken figures in the movement to reform China's death penalty practices.[25]

The ice had been cracked. Invitations followed to contribute an article to a forward-looking Chinese publication with the optimistic title *The Road of The Abolition of the Death Penalty in China*;[26] and to speak, along with Saul Lehrfreund, (as the only 'Anglos') at an 'Anglo/China seminar' on the death penalty at Renmin University in 2005. We were astonished to find that the agenda had been transformed from the former emphasis on defensive justification for China's policy to a much more open investigation of how China might learn from other countries and proceed to eventual abolition.

In 2007 the opportunity to have a more significant impact on the developing reformist debate in China arose through an invitation to be the consultant to a major project funded by the EU and led by the Great Britain-China Centre in London (which

[25] Liu (2013). See also Liang and Lu (eds, 2015). [26] Hood (2004).

had built up a bank of goodwill with the Chinese authorities). Under the title, *The Death Penalty: Moving the Debate Forward*, it was carried out in partnership with the Max Planck Institute for Foreign and International Criminal Law in Freiburg, Germany which, through its Director Hans-Jörg Albrecht had established a research partnership with the Chinese Academy[27] and which now was to be responsible for conducting the first major public opinion survey on capital punishment in China; the Irish Centre for Human Rights, whose Director at the time, William Schabas, is a leading authority on international human rights law and the death penalty;[28] and the Death Penalty Project, which had a track record of training judges and lawyers and for very successful litigation on behalf of death row inmates in the Caribbean. The essential ingredient to make this project viable was the enthusiastic collaboration of Beijing Normal University College of Criminal Law Science and Wuhan University School of Law, under the direction of Professor Zhao Bingzhi and Professor Mo Hongxian respectively.

A major aim of this project was to inform Chinese scholars, legislators, and Supreme Court Justices, through conferences and workshops, of the advances in death penalty reform throughout the world. One important task was to counter the argument that reform must go slowly in stages by demonstrating that the pace of reform had, since the end of the 1980s, advanced swiftly elsewhere from executions to complete abolition within a few years. We also emphasized that reform of capital punishment procedures would never be sufficient because the evidence demonstrated that the death penalty could not be administered without it being imposed arbitrarily and prone to error and thus in violation of the right not to be arbitrarily deprived of life and the right not to be subjected to an inhuman or degrading form of punishment. These ideas were communicated to a wider audience at a Public Forum held in the cities of Dalian and Wuhan, and papers given by the European contributors at the project seminars were published in the conference papers by Beijing Normal University, thus helping to open up a debate that had been so long repressed and ill-informed.

It was of great significance that reforms to China's death penalty procedures had begun to take root at this time, most notably the return of review of all death sentences to the Supreme People's Court in 2007 in order to restrict and bring more uniformity to the infliction of executions.[29] Regrettably no statistics have yet been published but informed academics have reported a substantial decline in the number of executions since this time. Perhaps even more significant was the fearless endorsement by Professor Zhao Bingzhi, the most politically influential Chinese academic criminal lawyer, of the major message that we had sought to convey through our presentations and publications based on our international surveys of the changes in practices and ideas that had fuelled the abolitionist movement worldwide. He proclaimed:[30]

> The fast headway of abolition in the globe is amazing and exciting. These latest changes present a clear signal to us: abolition is an inevitable international tide and trend as well as a signal showing the broad-mindedness of civilised countries . . . it is now an international obligation.

[27] Published in Albrecht (2006). [28] See e.g. Schabas (2002).
[29] Liu (2013). [30] Bingzhi and Shuiming (2009: 37).

In several of the other countries mentioned above, there is reason to believe that the academic input has also had an impact in helping to overcome some initial resistance to consideration of reform. For example, in 2001 I was invited by the Free Legal Assistance Group (FLAG) to the Philippines, with the support of the British Embassy and the Philippines Coalition against the Death Penalty, to help, through a series of presentations, to 'kick-start' FLAG's campaign to return the Philippines to its former abolitionist status. With only a few exceptions, the response was very positive and when complete abolition was achieved in 2006 FLAG graciously acknowledged my contribution to their campaign. The response in India was also very positive at a conference held in Delhi in 2011 by the O.P. Jindal Global University, attended by Supreme Court Justices, Senior Counsel, and human rights advocates. Four years later, the Chair of the Law Commission of India, in preparation for the finalization of its Report Number 262 on *The Death Penalty* (the first since 1967), invited me to Delhi to give a public lecture on the theme 'World-wide Abolition of Capital Punishment: a Human Rights Imperative', under the joint auspices of the O.P. Jindal Global University and the National Law University in Delhi, and to take part (as the only foreigner) in the Law Commission's national consultation with judges, lawyers, and parliamentarians. In August 2015 the Law Commission recommended the abolition of the death penalty for all 'ordinary' crimes such as murder, as the first step to the complete abolition of the death penalty.[31] The fifth edition of *The Death Penalty* was frequently cited in the report. In Vietnam a speech on the same topic at the invitation of the National University and the Norwegian government in September 2014 apparently assisted the reformers in obtaining a further restriction of the number of capital crimes during 2015. As a result of the public opinion research undertaken in Malaysia (see below), I was appointed by the Attorney-General in 2014 as the consultant to the International Centre for Law and Legal Studies (I-CeLLS), which had undertaken at the request of the Cabinet 'a comprehensive study on the proposal to abolish the mandatory death penalty under relevant legislation'. The final report was completed in 2016 and sent forward for consideration.

EMPIRICAL RESEARCH

The absence of empirical criminological and socio-legal research in all but a very few retentionist jurisdictions other than the US has been a serious impediment to greater knowledge about how the death penalty is administered.

In 2003 the Death Penalty Project invited me to undertake an empirical study of the use of the death penalty in Trinidad and Tobago (T&T), a country with an exceptionally high homicide rate which still retained the mandatory death penalty for murder, despite the fact that the Judicial Committee of the Privy Council had held this to be a cruel, inhuman, and degrading punishment.[32] Financial support was forthcoming from the EU and the UK FCO, and the Faculty of Law of the University of the West Indies took the study under its auspices. Without local sponsorship such research by

[31] See also Batra (forthcoming 2016).

[32] Hood (2007); Hood and Seemungal (2006).

foreigners, especially those from the former colonial power, could not have hoped to make progress. A further advantage was that the fieldwork was carried out by a Trinidadian citizen, Dr Florence Seemungal, a former research officer and then an Associate of the Oxford Centre.

The T&T research followed up until December 2005 the outcome of 633 incidents recorded by the police as murder during the five-year period from January 1998 to December 2002, as well as the decisions on proceedings taken against 297 persons who had been committed for trial over the same period. The findings were striking. The proportion of all reports of murder that led to a conviction for murder and a mandatory death sentence was only 5 per cent and none were subsequently executed, the last executions having taken place in 2000. Furthermore, the conviction rate for 'gang and drug-related' murders and those where the body was found 'dumped', the category of murder that had increased the fastest over the five-year period, was extremely low. By the end of 2005, only two of the 208 recorded murders of this kind had resulted in a conviction for murder and two for manslaughter—2 per cent altogether, although they had made up 33 per cent of the recorded killings. By contrast, 16 per cent of murders committed in the domestic situation, the easiest to detect but the most likely to have mitigating factors, resulted in a conviction for murder. Such a low certainty of punishment proved that the mandatory death penalty was not only very unlikely to be an effective general deterrent, it was also arbitrarily inflicted and only rarely on the 'worst of the worst' cases. Furthermore, murder charges were more likely to result in a verdict of manslaughter because the prosecutor was willing to accept a guilty plea; witnesses were unwilling to provide testimony and jurors unwilling to convict persons of murder when the only punishment would be death. The report was given an appropriate title: *A Rare and Arbitrary Fate*.[33] This was followed by a survey of the experiences and perceptions of sentencing under a mandatory system among fifty-one judges, prosecutors, and counsel in T&T, which confirmed that hardly any of them (only four) supported the status quo.[34] Yet despite the strong evidence bringing to light the realities of the infliction of capital punishment, the findings in relation to the arbitrariness of the mandatory death penalty were ignored by the government and their significance not appreciated by the press, which concentrated on reporting the failure to bring so many murderers to justice.

What stood in the way in Trinidad was the argument that public opinion was so strongly opposed to abolition of the mandatory death penalty that it would be politically impossible to abolish it. Building upon the experience and findings of the public opinion survey conducted in China by the Max Planck Institute, in collaboration with the Peking University Research Centre for Contemporary China and Wuhan University, which had revealed that public opinion was not so strongly committed to capital punishment as those in authority had assumed,[35] public opinion surveys, focusing on the mandatory death penalty, were carried out for the Death Penalty Project in Trinidad,[36] and in Malaysia, with the strong support locally of the Malaysian Bar Council and the Human Rights Commission of Malaysia.[37] Opinion surveys have

33 Hood and Seemungal (2006). 34 Hood et al. (2009).

35 For details of the findings see Bakken (2013); Hood (2009); and Oberwittler and Qi (2009).

36 Hood and Seemungal (2011). 37 Hood (2013).

also been conducted recently in Taiwan and Ghana, both after consultation with the Oxford Centre.[38] In every country it has been essential to employ survey agencies of high repute to undertake the fieldwork.[39]

The Trinidad and Malaysia surveys, as in China, found that only a small minority of respondents were very well informed about the death penalty (see also on Japan, Sato 2011); that while a high proportion of the population in Trinidad and Malaysia (around 90 per cent) said they were in favour of the death penalty, when presented with scenarios where there were mitigating circumstances less than half chose death as the appropriate punishment. As regards the mandatory death penalty only a small minority chose the death penalty for *all* the case scenarios they judged. In China, Trinidad, and Malaysia when respondents were asked whether they would still favour the death penalty if it were proven to their satisfaction that an innocent person had been executed, the proportion changing their minds was such as to bring the total favouring the death penalty down from 58 per cent to 25 per cent in China, in Trinidad from 89 per cent to 35 per cent, in Malaysia from 91 per cent to 33 per cent for murder, and from 75 per cent to 26 per cent for drug trafficking. This was extraordinarily consistent proof that support for the death penalty rested on a belief that the system will and can be administered without error. Furthermore when respondents were asked in T&T and Malaysia to say which of five social and criminal justice policies were the 'most likely to reduce very violent crimes leading to death', greater number of executions was ranked last. Indeed, taken as a whole, this body of research on public opinion in retentionist countries suggested that the argument that the death penalty cannot be abolished because of public demand for it and opposition to its abolition is so strong is very likely to be a myth.[40]

The response to and impact of empirical research has been very different in the countries concerned, depending on whether powerful organizations have been willing to use the findings as a platform for reform. Despite the strong support for the public opinion survey in China by the local universities concerned, the findings have been treated with much scepticism by the authorities and with only lukewarm support by other Chinese scholars, probably because of the high media profile of 'netizens' who publish 'online' objections when death sentences are not imposed in certain high-profile cases, often, but not only, those involving high-ranking 'officials' charged with corruption.[41] The research in Trinidad has so far made no impact in moving either government or opposition parties towards abolition of the mandatory death penalty. The finding that, at the most, only about a quarter of respondents approved of the mandatory death penalty, and that it had almost no support among judges, prosecutors, and criminal lawyers was largely ignored. The lack of a Human Rights Commission and only a small Criminal Bar has not helped. In contrast, the strong support for the research in Malaysia from the Bar Council and human rights bodies

[38] TAEDP (forthcoming 2017); Tankebe et al. (2015).

[39] In Trinidad by Market Facts and Opinions Ltd, and in Malaysia by IPSOS Malaysia, in both cases using a questionnaire designed by Roger Hood. No criticism was received of the survey instrument or of the sample.

[40] For instance, when asked whether they thought that China should 'speedup' towards abolition of the death penalty, only 53% were opposed to this view.

[41] Even though the public opinion survey had shown that only a minority favoured the death penalty for corruption.

has brought the findings to the fore in political debate on the abolition of the mandatory death penalty.

CONCLUSION

The point has been reached where there is now a decreasing number of countries that defy the majority view that the death penalty cannot be practised without a breach of the principles embraced by almost all nations after the Second World War; namely that states should protect the right to life and human dignity of all persons and ensure that their criminal justice systems are free from torture and cruel, inhuman, and degrading punishments. Fewer and fewer countries now seek to stigmatize the abolitionist movement as a product of Western imperialist culture. Only a minority now claim that retention of capital punishment can be justified because it is demanded by religious precepts as interpreted by clerical authority or because it is necessitated by popularly supported cultural norms and values that demand 'a life for a life'. In particular, the argument that capital punishment is a 'domestic criminal justice issue' not a 'human rights issue' is based on a false antithesis. Whatever system of criminal justice a country may choose there must be limits to the power that the state can be permitted to exercise over persons accused of and convicted of crimes, however serious: limits defined by universal human rights principles which apply to all human beings. One key contribution of criminologists and lawyers has been to show that the death penalty cannot be administered in a way that meets the standards of humanity consistent with these principles and that states should not defer to public opinion. In the end, the abolition of capital punishment is decided in the political arena. Although there appears to be no possibility of acceptance of the abolitionist message in those countries that remain committed to Sharia law in the Middle East while political power continues to lie with clerically dominated regimes that are hostile to the concept of universal human rights,[42] abolition of the cruel and inhumane punishment of death has now become the litmus test in all countries that purport to respect international human rights norms.

The body of research briefly described above, conducted over almost 30 years at the Oxford Centre for Criminology, in collaboration with human rights and criminal justice organizations, continues to develop under the direction of Carolyn Hoyle. Along with her colleagues and students she will ensure that the Centre will endeavour to demonstrate further the valuable contribution that academic criminologists can make to the global movement to abolish the death penalty for ever.

REFERENCES

Albrecht, H.-J. and Research Unit of the Death Penalty Cases Survey, Institute of Law, Chinese Academy of Social Sciences (2006), *Strengthening the Defence in Death Penalty*

[42] See Scherdin (2014).

Cases in the People's Republic of China: Empirical Research into the Role of Defence Councils in Criminal Cases Eligible for the Death Penalty, Freiburg: Max Planck Institute for Foreign and International Criminal Law.

ANCEL, M. (1962), *The Death Penalty in European Countries*, Strasbourg: Council of Europe.

BAKKEN, B. (2013), 'Capital Punishment Reform, Public Opinion and Penal Elitism in the People's Republic of China', in R. Hood and S. Deva (eds), *Confronting Capital Punishment in Asia: Human Rights, Politics and Public Opinion*, Oxford: Oxford University Press: 187–204.

BALDUS, D., WOODWORTH, G., and PULASKI, C.A. (1990), *Equal Justice and the Death Penalty*, Boston, MA: Northeast University Press.

BATRA, B. (forthcoming 2016), *The Death Penalty in India*, Delhi: Oxford University Press.

BINGZHI, Z. and SHUIMING, W. (2009), 'Development Trend in Death Penalty in Contemporary Era and its Inspiration for China', in *Proceedings of the Workshop on Trends of Death Penalty Reform and Applicable Standard: Experience of International Society and Chinese Practice*, Guangzhou, China: 37–9.

Council of Europe (1999), *The Death Penalty: Abolition in Europe*, Strasbourg: Council of Europe Publications.

Council of Europe (2004), *Death Penalty: Beyond Abolition*, Strasbourg: Council of Europe Publications.

GARLAND, D. (2010), *Peculiar Institution: America's Death Penalty in an Age of Abolition*, Oxford: Oxford University Press.

HOOD, R. (1989 1st edn), (1996 2nd edn), (2002 3rd edn), *The Death Penalty: A Worldwide Perspective*, Oxford: Oxford University Press.

HOOD, R. (1995), 'The Injustice of the Death Penalty', in E. Harlow, D. Matas, and J. Rocamora (eds), *The Machinery of Death*, Amnesty International USA: 175–80.

HOOD, R. (2001), 'Capital Punishment: A Global Perspective', *Punishment and Society*, 3, 3: 331–54.

HOOD, R. (2004), 'From Restriction to Abolition of the Death Penalty: An Historical and Comparative Note', in Z. Bingzhi (ed.), *The Road of the Abolition of the Death Penalty in China*, Beijing: Chinese Security University Press.

HOOD, R. (2007), 'Attacking the Death Penalty in the Anglophone Caribbean: A Criminological Contribution', in H. Müller-Dietz, E. Müller, K.-L. Kunz, H. Radtke, G. Britz, C. Momsen, and H. Koriath (eds), *Festschrift für Heike Jung*, Baden-Baden: Nomos: 313–30, reprinted (2010) in L. Arroyo, P. Bigling, and W.A. Schabas (eds), *Towards Universal Abolition of the Death Penalty*, Valencia: Tirant lo Blanch: 241–64.

HOOD, R. (2008), 'Capital Punishment: The Commonwealth in World Perspective', *The Commonwealth Lawyer*, 17, 3: 30–5.

HOOD, R. (2009), 'Abolition of the Death Penalty: China in World Perspective', *City University of Hong Kong Law Review*, 1, 1: 1–20.

HOOD, R. (2010), 'Towards Global Abolition of the Death Penalty: Progress and Prospects', in L. Arroyo, P. Bigling, and W.A. Schabas (eds), *Towards Universal Abolition of the Death Penalty*, Valencia: Tirant lo Blanch: 419–41.

HOOD, R. (2012), *Enhancing EU Action on the Death Penalty in Asia*, European Parliament Briefing Paper, EXPO/B/DROI/2011/22.

HOOD, R. (2013), *The Death Penalty in Malaysia: Public Opinion on the Mandatory Death Penalty for Drug Trafficking, Murder and Firearms Offences*, London: The Death Penalty Project.

HOOD, R. and DEVA, S. (eds) (2013), *Confronting Capital Punishment in Asia: Human Rights, Politics and Public Opinion*, Oxford University Press.

Hood, R. and Hoyle, C. (2008 4th edn), (2015 5th edn), *The Death Penalty: A Worldwide Perspective*, Oxford: Oxford University Press.

Hood, R. and Hoyle, C. (2009), 'Abolishing the Death Penalty Worldwide: The Impact of a "New Dynamic"', *Crime and Justice: A Review of Research*, 38, 1: 1–63.

Hood, R. and Seemungal, F. (2006), *A Rare and Arbitrary Fate: Conviction for Murder, the Mandatory Death Penalty and the Reality of Homicide in Trinidad and Tobago*, Oxford: Centre for Criminology.

Hood, R. and Seemungal, F. (2011), *Public Opinion on the Mandatory Death Penalty in Trinidad*, London: The Death Penalty Project.

Hood, R., Seemungal, F., Mendes, D., and Fagan, J. (2009), *A Penalty Without Legitimacy: The Mandatory Death Penalty in Trinidad and Tobago*, Oxford: Centre for Criminology.

Hor, M. (2013) 'Singapore's Death Penalty: The Beginning of the End', in R. Hood and S. Deva (eds), *Confronting Capital Punishment in Asia: Human Rights, Politics and Public Opinion*, Oxford University Press: 141–67.

Hoyle, C. and Hood, R. (2015), 'Deterrence and Public Opinion', in *Moving Away from the Death Penalty: Arguments, Trends and Perspectives*, New York: UN Human Rights: 68–83.

Johnson, D.T. and Zimring, F.E. (2009), *The Next Frontier: National Development, Political Change, and the Death Penalty in Asia*, New York: Oxford University Press.

Karimunda, A.M. (2015), *The Death Penalty in Africa: The Path Towards Abolition*, Farnham: Ashgate.

Liang, B. and Lu, H. (eds) (2015), *The Death Penalty in China: Policy, Practice, and Reform*, New York: Columbia University Press.

Liu, R. (2013), 'Recent Reforms and Prospects in China', in R. Hood and S. Deva (eds), *Confronting Capital Punishment in Asia: Human Rights, Politics and Public Opinion*, Oxford University Press: 107–22.

Oberwittler, D. and Qi, S. (2009), *Public Opinion on the Death Penalty in China: Results from a General Population Survey Conducted in Three Provinces in 2007/08*, Forschung Aktuell/research in brief 41, Freiburg: Max Planck Institute for Foreign and International Criminal Law.

Sato, M. (2011), *The Death Penalty in Japan: Will the Public Tolerate Abolition?*, Weisbaden: Springer VS.

Schabas, W.A. (2002), *The Abolition of the Death Penalty in International Law*, 3rd edn, Cambridge: Cambridge University Press.

Schabas, W.A. (2013), 'Hard-Core Executioners', in L. Arroyo Zapatero, W.A. Schabas, K. Takayama, and M. Muñoz de Morales (eds/coord), *The Death Penalty: A Cruel and Inhuman Punishment*, Cuenca: University of Castilla-La Mancha Press: 23–7.

Scherdin, L. (ed) (2014), *Capital Punishment: A Hazard to a Sustainable Criminal Justice System?*, Farnham: Ashgate, chs. 11, 12, and 15.

Taiwan Alliance to End the Death Penalty (TAEDP) (forthcoming 2017), *Survey of Taiwanese Attitudes toward the Death Penalty and Related Social Values*, Taipei: TAEDP.

Tankebe, J., Boakye, K.E., and Atupare, P.W. (2015), *Public Opinion on the Death Penalty in Ghana*, Accra: Centre for Criminology and Criminal Justice.

United Nations (1962), *Capital Punishment*, New York: UN.

United Nations (1967), *Capital Punishment: Developments 1961 to 1965*, New York: UN.

Zimring, F.E. and Hawkins, G. (1986), *Capital Punishment and the American Agenda*, Cambridge: Cambridge University Press.

Zimring, F.E., Fagan, J., and Johnson, D.T. (2010), 'Executions, Deterrence and Homicide: A Tale of Two Cities', *Journal of Empirical Legal Studies*, 7: 1–29.

14

RESEARCHING THE DEATH PENALTY IN CLOSED OR PARTIALLY CLOSED CRIMINAL JUSTICE SYSTEMS

Daniel Pascoe

INTRODUCTION: STATE SECRECY AND THE DEATH PENALTY

For an abolitionist academic, it is fortunate that the possibilities for conducting a transnational comparative study of the use of the death penalty are becoming more difficult to come by, as actively retentionist nations are reduced to a small but intransient minority.[1] Many of those nations which do continue to utilize capital punishment, shamed by the international human rights movement and by the media elsewhere, have maintained complete or partial secrecy about their death penalty practices. They tend to guard their death sentence, death row, commutation, and execution statistics. These numbers are the quantitative building blocks upon which transnational academic studies of capital punishment ought to be based. When combined with the confusing conceptual overlap with 'extra-judicial' killings, the restricted interpretative material caused by state and self-censorship of the media and the academy, the silencing of local civil society in authoritarian states, and fieldwork safety issues, it is understandable why criminal justice scholars have preferred to tackle less controversial subjects in more transparent jurisdictions.

However, for death penalty scholarship to move forward and to continue to contribute meaningfully to the global abolitionist movement in the twenty-first century, scholars must learn to work with decreasing amounts of official data, shifting their focus from the United States and Japan to less well-documented sites where death penalty information is difficult to come by (Hood and Hoyle 2015; Johnson and Zimring 2009). In the past, such jurisdictions have commonly been cast into the 'too hard basket'. Today they

[1] By the end of 2014, the number of actively retentionist states, using Amnesty International's definition of states that had executed at least one prisoner over the past ten years, had fallen to fifty-eight (of 198) (Amnesty International 2015). In 2015, Fiji, Suriname, Congo, and Madagascar joined the expanding list of abolitionist de jure states (Death Penalty Information Center 2015).

are imperative targets for our study, even as the methodological problems in covering them remain significant.

In Amnesty International's most recent report on the global use of the death penalty, retentionist states performing executions in 2014 where complete execution statistics were *unavailable* outnumbered executing retentionist states where complete information was available by thirteen to nine. For prisoners *sentenced* to death in 2014, Amnesty International possessed incomplete data for thirty-three jurisdictions, as compared with its reliable statistics on twenty-one jurisdictions (Amnesty International 2015). Turning back the clock to 2008, nations where incomplete statistics were available outnumbered nations with complete disclosure by seventeen to eight for executions, and twenty-five to sixteen for death sentences (Amnesty International 2009).

Similarly, Amnesty International's death penalty report in 1989 outlined forty-four jurisdictions where comprehensive execution totals were unavailable for the period 1985–8, compared with thirty-one jurisdictions with complete data (death sentence figures were only provided on a piecemeal basis) (Amnesty International 1989). Notably, nine of the thirteen nations where complete execution figures were unavailable in 2014 had been secretive about their death penalty practices both six years previously and, earlier still, in 1989 (China, Iran, Iraq, Yemen, Egypt, Somalia, Vietnam, Malaysia, and North Korea).[2] These nations have carried out the vast majority of executions since 1989.

The pattern is clear. Although the nations withholding data from Amnesty International might vary from year to year, states with 'minimum' totals of executions and death sentences listed always outnumber those with exhaustive totals.[3] Moreover, most of those places that remain secretive today have *never* been open about the extent to which they use the ultimate punishment. Even as numerous jurisdictions have abolished the death penalty in law (sixty-nine nations from 1990 to 2015), the most prolific executioners (with the exceptions of the USA and Japan) have either refused to make death penalty statistics publicly available, or do not collect these figures in the first place (e.g. because of civil strife). Death penalty scholars cannot afford to ignore nations that comprise more than half of the field of study, particularly given evidence that the abolitionist movement has started to slow during the twenty-first century (Anckar 2014).

Drawing from my fieldwork in Indonesia, Malaysia, Singapore, and Thailand (four jurisdictions evincing various levels of opacity in their criminal justice practices, even if they do not all appear in the above list) together with the collection of data on Vietnam (where death penalty statistics are a state secret) (International Commission Against the Death Penalty 2013), this chapter begins by critiquing the limited breadth of comparative death penalty scholarship today. I then outline methodological problems in dealing with quantitative and qualitative information that is absent, unrelia-

[2] No country data at all was provided for Somalia in 2008, possibly owing to ongoing instability inside the country. Compare Hood and Hoyle (2015), who instead recognize the most secretive jurisdictions as those which have never published official data via the United Nations Quinquennial Survey of member states: Bangladesh, China, Iran, Malaysia, and Vietnam.

[3] Amnesty International's notation where complete death penalty statistics are unavailable is to list a 'minimum' figure, signified by a + sign (Amnesty International 2012).

ble, or difficult to obtain, before suggesting how these problems might be overcome in future, comparative, studies of capital punishment.

SHORTCOMINGS OF COMPARATIVE SCHOLARSHIP ON THE GLOBAL DEATH PENALTY

Comparative methodology plays an important role in scholarship on state responses to serious crime and is especially valuable in death penalty research (Johnson and Zimring 2009). There are three main benefits to analysing criminal justice trends comparatively. First, without information about otherwise similar jurisdictions, we have no way of knowing what is 'normal' or what is 'exceptional' within any criminal justice system (Nelken 2011). Comparative study is also crucial in 'the search for systematic regularities and generalizable laws' (Øyen 1990; Steinmo 2008). While individual cases and specific historical events may make for intriguing reading, it will take a number of comparable events or cases espousing similar characteristics to provide a broader explanation, and perhaps even a cautious prediction, of social and historical phenomena (Kohli et al. 1995; Steinmo 2008). Finally, comparison enables us to learn from the experience of otherwise similarly situated states who have developed markedly different criminal justice policies: in other words relying on the study's results to effect policy transfer (Pakes 2015).

To date, many transnational comparative studies of the death penalty have analysed worldwide retention and abolition trends through qualitative or quantitative methods.[4] The aim has commonly been to explain the socio-political attributes of states that retain or abolish capital punishment, together with the historical processes through which they have achieved abolition. To enrich this literature, researchers should also consider comparing various *retentionist* jurisdictions with each other, including research on *procedurally* or *operationally* specific topics in retentionist countries. These kinds of study would examine why certain crimes possess a capital or non-capital status, or the structural and cultural determinants of high or low death sentence totals, the number of prisoners on death row, the length of time they spend there, yearly execution totals, and judicial appeal or clemency 'success' rates (Johnson and Zimring 2006).

Despite the success of Roger Hood at the Oxford Centre since the 1980s in opening up comparative death penalty scholarship to jurisdictions beyond the United States, there remains much work to do. It is only rarely (and relatively recently) that

[4] The major transnational comparative academic studies of the death penalty to date include those texts authored or collections edited by Karimunda (2016), Johnson and Miao (2016), Hood and Hoyle (2015, 2009, 2008), Anckar (2014, 2004), Scherdin (2014), Futamura and Bernaz (2014), Novak (2014a, 2014b), Hodgkinson (2013), Hood and Deva (2013), Arroyo Zapatero et al. (2013), McGann and Sandholtz (2012), Garland (2010), Johnson (2010), Hammel (2010), Johnson and Zimring (2009), Neumayer (2008a, 2008b), Yorke (2008), Greenberg and West (2008), Bai (2007), Chenwi (2007), Miethe et al. (2005), Boulanger and Sarat (2005), Council of Europe (2004, 1999), Hodgkinson and Schabas (2004), Hood (2002, 1996, 1989), Schabas (1997), Prokosch (1997), and Hodgkinson and Rutherford (1996), following on from the original study of the graduated processes of abolition by French scholar Marc Ancel (1962).

scholars have included some of the most secretive but currently prolific death penalty jurisdictions of East Asia (China, North Korea), the Middle East (Iran, Saudi Arabia, Iraq, Yemen, Palestine), and Africa (Sudan, Somalia) within case-study-based comparative studies, rather than within a quantitative regression sample or a more broadly thematic piece.[5] Most notably—notwithstanding some thematic coverage within Karimunda (2016), Hood and Hoyle (2015, 2009, 2008), Novak (2014b), Chenwi (2007), Hood (2002, 1996, 1989), Simon and Blaskovich (2002), and Schabas (1997)—Iran, Yemen, Saudi Arabia, Sudan, and Somalia *never* appear to have been included as case studies within a comparative study of death penalty practices in the English language, even though they have carried out executions for each one of the past five years. At a very minimum, this suggests that the next generation of comparative death penalty researchers should consider focusing on the Islamic-majority states of the Middle East and North and East Africa, so as to expand the existing academic literature, to influence domestic public opinion, and to focus international attention on understudied but prolifically executing states (Hood and Hoyle 2015).

Of course, in addition to the academic studies mentioned above are the reports authored by NGOs or international organizations.[6] Frequently these fact-based reports, compiled by archival researchers, media monitors, and interviewers, are drawn upon by scholars as a source of death penalty statistics, primary legal materials, and prisoner case studies. However, although the death penalty practices of *all* retentionist states (whether highly secretive or not) are documented at a level of superficial detail in these reports, they do not form part of a truly comparative analysis, generally failing to explain the *reasons* for national similarity and difference. Accounting for similarity and difference is what sets apart comparative academic analysis (Nelken 2002).[7] In the death penalty context, explaining similarity and difference speaks to two of the three goals of comparative analysis described above: finding universal patterns and predictive 'laws' amongst retentionist states, together with formulating policy solutions by recommending the changes a society will need to undertake to successfully abolish capital punishment, or at least to reduce executions and human suffering on death row.

[5] These are the nations that, to Amnesty International's knowledge, conducted executions in each of the past five years, with the number of executions unknown in at least one of those years. For comparative case studies involving these countries, see Johnson and Miao (2016) (China, North Korea); Futamura and Bernaz (2014) (Iraq); Scherdin (2014) (China); Hood and Deva (2013) (China); Johnson and Zimring (2009) (China, North Korea); Yorke (2008) (China); Boulanger and Sarat (2005) (Palestine, China); and Hodgkinson and Rutherford (1996) (China). China has received much recent attention in the academic sphere, and with good reason: over 90% of global annual execution totals in recent decades have been carried out there (Johnson and Zimring 2009).

[6] In particular, the United Nations (which has conducted five-yearly surveys of death penalty usage since 1975); Amnesty International; Harm Reduction International; Hands off Cain; Human Rights Watch; Reprieve; the International Federation of Human Rights (FIDH); as well as reports by local or regional NGOs, and Cornell Law School's online database Death Penalty Worldwide.

[7] On the contrary, perhaps it is also time to acknowledge the academic value in collecting data itself. As Pakes observes, criminal justice statistics: 'require a great deal of interpretation... That requires intimate knowledge about the acquisition of the data itself and a thorough understanding of both the system and the society that produced them' (Pakes 2015: 6).

CLEMENCY AND PARDONS IN SOUTHEAST ASIAN DEATH PENALTY CASES

From 2010 to 2013, I analysed differences in death penalty clemency practice among Southeast Asian jurisdictions, in an inductive and comparative search for plausible hypotheses explaining why some countries have made use of executive clemency and pardons far more often than others since the end of the Vietnam War and the beginning of the regional anti-drug 'paradigm' in 1975 (Pascoe 2014, 2016). Briefly, the findings of the study were that, over the period of study, three cumulative factors contributed to the incidence of death penalty clemency and pardons in Indonesia, Malaysia, Singapore, and Thailand:

1. the amount of *lenient discretion* exercised at earlier stages within the criminal justice system;
2. the extent to which granting clemency enhances or detracts from *political power*, which is closely related to the *type of government* granting clemency; and
3. the usual *length of time capital prisoners spend incarcerated* before execution (Pascoe 2014).

Although the four countries chosen were not amongst the world's most secretive executioners, running what are better described as 'semi-closed' capital punishment systems,[8] the research design offers an example of the benefits and methodological difficulties of conducting transnational comparative studies in this field. In particular, obtaining primary data on the numbers of prisoners granted clemency or pardon over a 35-year period (1975–2009) in four national jurisdictions and the official *reasons* for those grants led to many of the dilemmas that this chapter seeks to resolve: the necessary triangulation of sources, interview-based fieldwork safety and access, and drawing viable conclusions from patchy data. In the following section, I pass on some key lessons learned.

MEETING THE METHODOLOGICAL CHALLENGES

Extending the field of comparative death penalty scholarship to focus on those nations where death penalty statistics are largely unavailable causes the researcher to encounter a number of methodological hurdles. Among the significant challenges researchers have previously faced are:

- the lack of data, or major sampling problems present within the available data;
- data that is of questionable validity or reliability;
- non-equivalent data between the countries forming a comparative study;
- language and visa barriers to collecting data through fieldwork; and
- threats to the researcher's own safety, in some jurisdictions.

[8] Further methodological lessons are taken from remote data collection relating to Vietnam, a country that I did not include in the final doctoral study due to its significant political and legal differences with its ASEAN neighbours.

How is it possible to conduct rigorous scholarship while missing some of the factual building blocks upon which quantitative or qualitative studies are initially based, and without compromising the author's own life or liberty? Drawing on my experiences, I recommend a few simple methodological steps available to researchers, in order to shed light on the death penalty practices of the most secretive executioners in East Asia, the Middle East, and Africa, whilst also remaining within the limits of acceptable scholarly inference.

JUDICIAL, ARBITRARY, SUMMARY, AND EXTRA-JUDICIAL EXECUTIONS AND THE DEATH PENALTY PARADIGM

The first point to note in conducting *any* form of death penalty scholarship, but particularly that involving authoritarian states for which data collection will be problematic, is to be clear on the definition of judicial punishment. While undoubtedly constituting an even more serious violation of human rights that is sometimes more prevalent than judicial killing (Johnson and Zimring 2009), *extra-judicial* executions fall outside the death penalty paradigm and are excluded from consideration in the studies forming the subject of this chapter. While there are already two studies that attempt to ascertain the relationship between judicial and extra-judicial killing (Johnson and Zimring 2009; Miethe et al. 2005), scholars struggling for data equivalence between nations in a comparative study can exclude, in the words of Amnesty International:

> unlawful and deliberate killing carried out by order of a government or with its acquiescence. Extrajudicial killings are killings which can reasonably be assumed to be the result of a policy at any level of government to eliminate specific individuals as an alternative to arresting them and bringing them to justice. These killings take place outside any judicial framework.
>
> (Amnesty International 2001)

Within my own research in Southeast Asia, important examples were the mass killing of alleged communist sympathizers, regional separatists (Bourchier 1990; Imparsial 2010) and petty criminals (Amnesty International 1987; Bourchier 1988) within Suharto's 'New Order' regime in Indonesia (1967–98), together with legally unsanctioned killings of suspected drug traffickers by Thai police from the 1970s onwards (Freedom House 2002; *The Economist* 4 December 2008).

Greater definitional difficulties arise when the killings concerned are clearly conducted as part of an established government policy, yet they only take place after 'sham' trials designed to disguise their predetermined nature. Prominent examples of this practice in Southeast Asia were the ad hoc 'People's Courts' convened in South Vietnam after the fall of Saigon in 1975 to try former South Vietnamese soldiers and collaborators. Here, prosecutors doubled as judges in most cases, accused persons were not entitled to a legal defence nor to an appeal, were convicted regardless of the available evidence, and were often given a death sentence and summarily executed following the demands of onlookers (*The Economist* 14 June 1975; *The Milwaukee Journal* 6 June 1975; Vo 2004).

Nevertheless, such 'summary' executions do remain part of the death penalty paradigm, whereas 'extra-judicial' executions, committed outside the judicial process, do not (Schabas 2002). Even the executed victims of trials breaching the fair trial requirements of Articles 6 and 14 of the International Covenant on Civil and Political Rights are still deemed *judicially* executed, once they have been tried in any way at all (Schabas 2002). For many of the traditional units or themes of analysis within comparative studies of the death penalty—death sentences, appeal attrition rates, the death row population, judicial/prosecutorial discretion and arbitrariness, vulnerable populations, deterrence, public opinion, clemency, and so forth—there is no principled reason why death penalty scholarship should limit itself to 'fair' trials only. Indeed, neglecting 'sham' trials compromises one of the instrumental reasons for publication: to improve the present system for defendants during investigation, trial, and appeal. As such, comparative scholars should continue to embrace a broad definition of capital punishment.

However, whether this more open definition extends to *arbitrary* executions, which prima facie conform to the domestic law of the executing state, yet do not take place after trials at all (Schabas 2002), is more controversial and will arguably depend on the study's aims and scope. The power of the Thai Prime Minister to order targeted killings within Thailand's various military constitutions was a pertinent example within my own research.[9] I chose to exclude these non-judicial killings from my comparative analysis given the phenomena for comparison was executive clemency, which may only be granted in cases involving the *judicial* death penalty in Thailand and other jurisdictions. Nevertheless, there will undoubtedly be other project designs, particularly involving execution rates and vulnerable populations, where including 'arbitrary' executions enables a more complete story to be told.

DEALING WITH DATA SHORTCOMINGS AND FIELDWORK SAFETY

After designing the comparative study, settling on a definition of the 'death penalty', and developing a theoretical framework through which to interpret the data (Bottoms 2007; Flyvbjerg 2001; McConville 2007), comes the challenge of collecting sufficient data relating to the closed or partially closed jurisdictions under study. In an ideal world, the primary material relied upon in completing academic research on a criminal justice topic would emerge from official (government) sources only, to maximize its reliability and authenticity.[10] However, capital punishment is a highly politicized and sensitive criminal justice issue. Researchers are often left to rely on incomplete data sets, speculative recounts and interpretations of factual events, unclear reasoning behind official decisions, and apathy or even downright hostility from potential interview subjects. As Hood and Hoyle have observed:

[9] See *Constitution of Thailand* 1959, Article 17; *Constitution of Thailand* 1972, Article 17; *Constitution of Thailand* 1976, Article 21; *Constitution of Thailand* 1977, Article 27; *Constitution of Thailand* 1978, Article 200; *Interim Constitution of Thailand* 1991, Article 27.

[10] Of course, merely because statistics come from a government source does not necessarily mean that they are a reliable factual measure, especially in the case of authoritarian states. In such cases, the researcher should still cross-reference official data against unofficial estimates.

> It will be impossible to present an accurate picture of capital punishment until all retentionist states take seriously their obligation to collect statistical data on this subject systematically and to report their practice, as requested, to the United Nations.
>
> (Hood and Hoyle 2015: 2)

The accepted academic means of overcoming defects and omissions within official sources is an epistemological technique known as 'triangulation of proof', which involves cross-referencing various official and non-official, quantitative and qualitative sources of data, in the hope that the aggregate of a number of flawed sources will reveal the 'true' picture on sensitive topics (Davies 2001; Johnson and Zimring 2009; Merriam 1995). The triangle metaphor relates to the overlap of (1) first-hand or documentary sources; (2) secondary, interpretative materials; and (3) interview-based information (Lilleker 2003; Merriam 1995). While official data must still be the researcher's first choice, employing this technique is often the best option available in the circumstances (Hood and Hoyle 2015).

Accordingly, death penalty researchers can rely upon available official sources (such as government archives, press releases and reports, speeches, and autobiographies), non-official sources (such as independent media reports and foreign and local NGO publications), together with 'elite' interviews. Nevertheless, any unofficial sources relied upon must be treated with caution. NGO-sourced statistics are often themselves based upon incomplete government data, eyewitness accounts, or media reports of individual executions, and they best serve as reliable *minimum* estimates for executions in systems that are otherwise 'closed' to the outside world (Amnesty International Staff Member 2011: personal communication 3 November; Johnson and Zimring 2009).[11] As for media sources themselves, in my own experience researching Southeast Asia, newspaper reports sometimes confused death sentences with executions, listed sentences and executions imposed pursuant to *mandatory* death penalty crimes only or narcotics offences only rather than for all death-eligible crimes, or else reported arbitrary or extra-judicial executions undifferentiated from judicial executions. Triangulation's promise is that the aggregate of individually flawed sources (including extrapolation from smaller provincial or city-based samples (Johnson and Zimring 2009)) will point to a more accurate estimate, rather than simply choosing the least unreliable source as sole authority. If providing estimates through triangulating multiple sources still proves impossible, *adjectival* description of death penalty trends is the next best substitute (ibid), before the researcher descends into pure speculation.

The third element of triangulation comprises unstructured or semi-structured 'elite' interviews (Davies 2001; Peabody et al. 1990). Interviews with relevant experts on capital punishment including academics, criminal defence lawyers, journalists, opposition politicians, and NGO staff, together with key decision-makers in the political and criminal justice systems such as judges, bureaucrats, prison staff, prosecutors, and government politicians have the potential to provide:

[11] E.g., 'Amnesty [International] bends over backward not to overestimate execution numbers' (Johnson and Zimring 2009: 21–2).

> insights into events about which we know little: the activities that take place out of the public or media gaze, behind closed doors... interviews can provide immense amounts of information that could not be gleaned from official published documents or contemporary media accounts.
>
> (Lilleker 2003: 208)

My own study of clemency comprised sixty-four in-country and off-site interviews, plus many more spurned approaches. Importantly however, 'elite' interviewing is not a panacea for inaccessible official data: as a data collection method it is also challenging. Care must be taken in identifying an individual as a relevant 'elite' or 'expert' (Nelken 2002; Smith 2006). Information gleaned from interviews should mainly be used to corroborate data taken from existing *archival* sources (Davies 2001; Lilleker 2003; Seldon 1996). In secretive jurisdictions, it is likely that a greater number of non-government interviewees (possibly favouring abolition or death penalty reductionism) are willing to speak on the record, thereby creating a sampling bias. As a result it is difficult, if not impossible, to obtain a 'representative' sample of views on a contentious political issue (Richards 1996), yet the researcher must seek to achieve a balance: if not numerical, at least evincing a plurality of political opinions (Pakes 2015).

Even if the researcher manages to enlist a balance of government and non-government participants, 'elite' interviews pose unique problems of reliability and validity. As Nelken describes:

> The issue 'whom can you trust?' is therefore as relevant to the process of doing research as it is to understanding criminal behaviour and responses to it... Who is 'authorised' to speak for a given legal system or specific practice?
>
> (Nelken 2010: 91)

For participants drawn from the government side, there will usually be an 'official' line to be promulgated (ibid). Yet, as Smith admits, it is not always clear 'how easy it is to identify the people who influence "important decisions"' (Smith 2006: 645), especially decisions made many years before. Who is the correct decision-maker to interview, for example when considering political or bureaucratic issues such as prosecutorial policy, executive clemency decisions, patterns of voting at the United Nations, as well as constitutional or legislative proposals for abolition? For these and other reasons, even interview responses from prominent civil servants or serving politicians must be treated with caution, with best practice requiring a minimum of two interviewees in agreement before accepting any otherwise unsubstantiated assertion as fact (Davies 2001; Singleton and Straits 2010).

As for foreign language sources, travel, and research safety difficulties, it is best to rely on remotely accessible material, local collaborators, interpreters (for interviews), and translators (for written material) to aid empirical studies. Ideally, scholars should 'live there', to learn the local language and legal and political culture, when conducting research, as opposed to merely 'researching there', to employ Nelken's taxonomy for fieldwork in comparative studies (Nelken 2010). Yet, long-term residence is often impractical, and the researcher will have to undertake one or more short in-country fieldwork trips (Zedner 1995) (all the while stressing before immigration authorities and interviewees the author's institutional affiliation and the academic value of the study, lest he or she be mistaken for a foreign spy or activist). This was the approach I took with my own research, spending one or two months in Singapore, Kuala Lumpur, Bangkok, and Jakarta. My visa status in each jurisdiction was in reality quite unclear, as I was neither a salaried academic, nor a student at a local university, nor a journalist. Certain precautions, such as only publishing on sensitive topics after returning home from fieldwork,[12] or avoiding interviews with high-level government officials, may be necessary in cases where the nature of the research is not initially brought to the immigration authorities' attention.

The least preferable but sometimes necessary alternative, being 'virtually there' (Nelken 2010), involves relying on materials available remotely, interviewing expatriates or exiles from the country under study, and employing email or telephone interviews. Collaboration with a local scholar, if publishing on the topic does not threaten their life, liberty, or future career, is another possible option, and may even represent a more efficient division of labour, and an opportunity for more widespread dissemination of the findings (Techera 2014). Even if the security situation in one of the countries under study has deteriorated to such an extent that none of these measures are safe, ethical, and reliable means of obtaining qualitative and quantitative data representative of the entire jurisdiction, the researcher may be able to rely less on empirical data collection. Although the *judicial* death penalty will likely have been far eclipsed in importance as a means of state killing in totalitarian, failed, or failing states, remaining options for comparative death penalty scholarship include a strictly doctrinal comparison of capital laws 'in the books', a comparison of policy statements by political leaders, and research comparing voting records and treaty accession within the UN and its agencies. Even the governments of several secretive retentionist nations facing civil strife and secessionist movements (Iraq, Yemen, Sudan), plus North Korea as a closed state, have still submitted responses to the UN Human Rights Council's Universal Periodic Review mechanism in recent years. At a very minimum, such reports contain basic information on death penalty laws and practices,[13] and can of course be supplemented by unofficial sources.

STATING CONCLUSIONS CAUTIOUSLY

Finally, in analysing triangulated data, the researcher can only come to *tentative* conclusions based on the limited information available. If the findings derive from a particular set of four Southeast Asian jurisdictions, or from a specific historical period (i.e. 1975–2009), the author must not attempt to extrapolate to a non-representative case outside these parameters (Heidensohn 2007; Kohli et al. 1995), despite one of the

[12] In my own study, potentially falling foul of Thailand's *lèse-majesté* laws prohibiting criticism of the Royal Family or Malaysia's colonial-era anti-sedition laws remain the most troubling consequences stemming from publicizing findings.

[13] See UN Human Rights Council 2014b: 21–2 (Iraq); UN Human Rights Council 2013: 20 (Yemen, although this report was submitted before the start of civil war there in 2015); UN Human Rights Council 2011: 25 (Sudan and South Sudan); UN Human Rights Council 2014a: 6 (North Korea). Additionally, the Palestinian Authority (not yet a part of the Universal Periodic Review procedure) completed the UN Secretary-General's quinquennial survey on the death penalty relating to the period 2009–13 (UN Secretary General 2015: 6 n3).

stated aims of comparison being to discover generalized death penalty norms. It is important not to overplay the significance of the findings, but rather, to provide qualified conclusions and provide guidance for further analysis from what is an already low knowledge base. Future studies can then build on and enrich the data, to present a gradually more complete picture (Johnson and Zimring 2009), especially after democratization and an improved security environment in the country concerned results in new information coming to light.[14]

As Johnson and Zimring have observed:

> Research on the death penalty... [is] so thick in some parts of the subject that no one can master it, yet so thin in others that storytellers are 'reduced to guesswork, weaving great swatches of narrative from little rags of data'... research on capital punishment outside the USA is so thin that [even] guesswork must sometimes be considered progress.
>
> (Friedman 1993: ix, cited in Johnson and Zimring 2006: 94)

While engaging in frivolous 'guesswork' (to employ the above term) would not produce an academically rigorous thesis, some liberties must be taken and inferences drawn, as the two authors note. In this context, even a heavy reliance on independent media reports, NGO-authored documents, and 'elite' interviews as quantitative and qualitative data still allow for tentative conclusions to be made. So long as the research is an improvement on what has gone before, and the appropriate caveats are made explicit to the reader, the results will be well worth publishing.

CONCLUSION: THE FUTURE OF COMPARATIVE DEATH PENALTY RESEARCH

In this chapter I have offered a number of methodological tips for criminal justice scholars interested in studying those nations whose capital punishment practices remain opaque. As McConville has noted, scholars should provide 'a full account of the natural history of research projects, including the ethical and political dimensions, so that those who come after can be better prepared' (McConville 2007: 213). Importantly, while the methodological recommendations in the latter part of this chapter are primarily directed towards death penalty scholars, they may also be adapted for research on any criminal justice topic in closed or partially closed jurisdictions. My own research on clemency and pardons in Southeast Asian death penalty cases forms just one example of comparative criminal justice work beset by the data-collection hazards associated with opaque jurisdictions. Far more difficult challenges await death penalty researchers over the next few years, especially when comparing retentionist states with each other.

[14] There are also cases where, despite future democratization and stability, the requisite statistical data will probably never be available to academic researchers, due to its implications for national security, or the fact that it was never collected in the first place. In this case, the solution is to explicitly acknowledge where the problems lie and to allow the reader to make his or her own judgement on the limited data presented (Academic Expert on Capital Punishment 2011: personal communication, 7 November).

While the authors of international or regional death penalty studies have already dealt thoroughly with the various jurisdictions comprising the United States, with Japan, and are increasingly tackling the People's Republic of China,[15] the most prolifically executing nations still tend to be the most secretive about their death penalty practices. Exposing and juxtaposing the death penalty practices of these jurisdictions which include China, North Korea, Iran, Saudi Arabia, Iraq, Yemen, Palestine, Sudan, and Somalia[16] offers yet another means of 'chipping away' at the death penalty over time, along with scholarship covering more universal issues such as international human rights law standards, public executions, the mandatory death penalty, the reinterpretation of religious texts, and victim support and compensation. However, to expand the comparative capital punishment field in this manner requires careful definition of the death penalty itself, using unconventional sources of data, and a humble approach to stating conclusions, all of which must be explicitly brought to the reader's attention at the writing-up phase. It would be a shame if future scholarship ignored closed or partially closed jurisdictions altogether until further data becomes available. To do so would betray the contemporary realities of global death penalty usage.

REFERENCES

Academic Expert on Capital Punishment (2011), personal communication, 7 November.

Amnesty International (1987), 'Recent Executions in Indonesia and the Application of the Death Penalty', in *Law and Political Liberty in Indonesia*, Lanham-Seabrook: Indonesia Publications.

Amnesty International (1989), *When the State Kills: The Death Penalty*, New York, NY: Amnesty International Publications.

Amnesty International (2001), *Israel and the Occupied Territories: State Assassinations and Other Unlawful Killings*, AI-Index MDE 15/005/2001.

Amnesty International (2009), *Death Sentences and Executions in 2008*, AI-Index ACT 50/003/2009.

Amnesty International (2012), *Death Sentences and Executions in 2011*, AI-Index ACT 50/001/2012.

Amnesty International (2015), *Death Sentences and Executions in 2014*, AI-Index ACT 50/0001/2015.

Amnesty International Staff Member (2011), personal communication, 3 November.

Ancel, M. (1962), *The Death Penalty in European Countries*, Strasbourg: Council of Europe.

Anckar, C. (2004), *Determinants of the Death Penalty*, Abingdon: Routledge.

Anckar, C. (2014), 'Why Countries Choose the Death Penalty', *The Brown Journal of World Affairs*, 21, 1: 7–25.

Arroyo Zapatero, L., Schabas, W., and Takayama, K. (eds) (2013), *Death Penalty: A Cruel and Unusual Punishment*, Cuenca: Ediciones de la Universidad de Castilla-La Mancha.

[15] See note 5, above. [16] See note 5 and associated text, above.

BAE, S. (2007), *When the State No Longer Kills: International Human Rights Norms and Abolition of Capital Punishment*, Albany, NY: State University of New York Press.

BOTTOMS, A. (2007), 'The Relationship between Theory and Empirical Observations in Criminology', in R.D. King and E. Wincup (eds), *Doing Research on Crime and Justice*, 2nd edn, Oxford: Oxford University Press.

BOULANGER, C. and SARAT, A. (eds) (2005), *The Cultural Lives of Capital Punishment*, Stanford, CA: Stanford University Press.

BOURCHIER, D. (1988), 'Behind Indonesia's Courts', *Inside Indonesia*, 14: 10.

BOURCHIER, D. (1990), 'Crime, Law and State Authority in Indonesia', in A. Budiman (ed.), *State and Civil Society in Indonesia*, Melbourne: Monash University Centre of Southeast Asian Studies.

CHENWI, L. (2007), *Towards the Abolition of the Death Penalty in Africa: A Human Rights Perspective*, Pretoria: Pretoria University Law Press.

Council of Europe (1999), *The Death Penalty: Abolition in Europe*, Strasbourg: Council of Europe.

Council of Europe (2004), *The Death Penalty: Beyond Abolition*, Strasbourg: Council of Europe.

DAVIES, P.H.J. (2001), 'Spies as Informants: Triangulation and the Interpretation of Elite Interview Data in the Study of the Intelligence and Security Services', *Politics*, 21, 1: 73–80.

Death Penalty Information Center (2015), *Abolitionist and Retentionist Countries*, available at: http://www.deathpenaltyinfo.org/abolitionist-and-retentionist-countries.

Economist, The (1975), 'Vietnam: Two in One Won't Go Yet', 14 June.

Economist, The (2008), 'Thailand's King and its Crisis', 4 December.

FLYVBJERG, B. (2001), *Making Social Science Matter*, Cambridge: Cambridge University Press.

Freedom House (2002), *Freedom in the World: Thailand*, available at: http://www.freedomhouse.org/report/freedom-world/2002/Thailand.

FRIEDMAN, L.M. (1993), *Crime and Punishment in American History*, New York, NY: Basic Books.

FUTAMURA, M. and BERNAZ, N. (eds) (2014), *The Politics of the Death Penalty in Countries in Transition*, Abingdon: Routledge.

GARLAND, D. (2010), *Peculiar Institution: America's Death Penalty in an Age of Abolition*, Oxford: Oxford University Press.

GREENBERG, D.F. and WEST, V. (2008), 'Siting the Death Penalty Internationally', *Law and Social Inquiry*, 33, 2: 295–343.

HAMMEL, A. (2010), *Ending the Death Penalty: The European Experience in Global Perspective*, Basingstoke: Palgrave Macmillan.

HEIDENSOHN, F. (2007), 'International Comparative Research in Criminology', in R.D. King and E. Wincup (eds), *Doing Research on Crime and Justice*, 2nd edn, Oxford: Oxford University Press.

HODGKINSON, P. (ed.) (2013), *Capital Punishment: New Perspectives*, Farnham: Ashgate.

HODGKINSON, P. and RUTHERFORD, A. (eds) (1996), *Capital Punishment: Global Issues and Prospects*, Winchester: Waterside Press.

HODGKINSON, P. and SCHABAS, W. (eds) (2004), *Capital Punishment: Strategies for Abolition*, Cambridge: Cambridge University Press.

HOOD, R. (1989), *The Death Penalty: A World-Wide Perspective: A Report to the United Nations Committee on Crime Prevention and Control*, Oxford: Clarendon Press.

HOOD, R. (1996), *The Death Penalty: A World-Wide Perspective*, 2nd edn, Oxford: Clarendon Press.

Hood, R. (2002), *The Death Penalty: A Worldwide Perspective*, 3rd edn, Oxford: Oxford University Press.

Hood, R. and Deva, S. (eds) (2013), *Confronting Capital Punishment in Asia: Human Rights, Politics, and Public Opinion*, Oxford: Oxford University Press.

Hood, R. and Hoyle, C. (2008), *The Death Penalty: A Worldwide Perspective*, 4th edn, Oxford: Oxford University Press.

Hood, R. and Hoyle, C. (2009), 'Abolishing the Death Penalty Worldwide: The Impact of a New Dynamic', *Crime and Justice*, 38, 1: 1–63.

Hood, R. and Hoyle, C. (2015), *The Death Penalty: A Worldwide Perspective*, 5th edn, Oxford: Oxford University Press.

Imparsial (2010), *Inveighing Against Death Penalty in Indonesia*, Jakarta: Imparsial.

International Commission against the Death Penalty (2013), *The Death Penalty and the 'Most Serious Crimes'*, available at: http://www.icomdp.org/cms/wp-content/uploads/2013/02/Most-serious-crimes_final_6Feb2013.pdf.

Johnson, D.T. (2010), 'Asia's Declining Death Penalty', *The Journal of Asian Studies*, 69, 2: 337–46.

Johnson, D.T. and Miao, M. (2016), 'Chinese Capital Punishment in Comparative Perspective', in B. Liang and H. Lu (eds), *The Death Penalty in China: Policy, Practice, and Reform*, New York, NY: Columbia University Press.

Johnson, D.T. and Zimring, F.E. (2006), 'Taking Capital Punishment Seriously', *Asian Criminology*, 1: 89–95.

Johnson, D.T. and Zimring, F.E. (2009), *The Next Frontier: National Development, Political Change, and the Death Penalty in Asia*, Oxford: Oxford University Press.

Karimunda, A.M. (2016), *The Death Penalty in Africa: The Path Towards Abolition*, Abingdon: Routledge.

Kohli, A., Evans, P., Katzenstein, P.J., Przeworski, A., Hoeber Rudolph, S., Scott, J.C., Skocpol, T. (1995), 'The Role of Theory in Comparative Politics: A Symposium', *World Politics*, 48, 1: 1–49.

Lilleker, D.G. (2003), 'Interviewing the Political Elite: Navigating a Potential Minefield', *Politics*, 23, 3: 207–14.

McConville, M. (2007), 'Development of Empirical Techniques and Theory', in M. McConville and W.H. Chui (eds), *Research Methods for Law*, Edinburgh: Edinburgh University Press.

McGann, A. and Sandholtz, W. (2012), 'Patterns of Death Penalty Abolition, 1960–2005: Domestic and International Factors', *International Studies Quarterly*, 56, 2: 275–89.

Merriam, S.B. (1995), 'What Can You Tell from an N of 1?: Issues of Validity and Reliability in Qualitative Research', *PAACE Journal of Lifelong Learning*, 4: 51–60.

Miethe, T.D., Lu, H., and Deibert, G.R. (2005), 'Cross-National Variability in Capital Punishment: Exploring the Sociopolitical Sources of Its Differential Legal Status', *International Criminal Justice Review*, 15, 2: 115–30.

Milwaukee Journal, The (1975), 'PRG to Eliminate "Enemies of the People"', 6 June.

Nelken, D. (2002), 'Comparative Criminal Justice', in M. Maguire, R. Morgan, and R. Reiner (eds), *The Oxford Handbook of Criminology*, 3rd edn, Oxford: Oxford University Press.

Nelken, D. (2010), *Comparative Criminal Justice: Making Sense of Difference*, Los Angeles: Sage.

Nelken, D. (2011), 'Why Compare Criminal Justice', in M. Bosworth and C. Hoyle (eds), *What Is Criminology?*, Oxford: Oxford University Press.

Neumayer, E. (2008a), 'Death Penalty Abolition and the Ratification of the Second Optional Protocol', *The International Journal of Human Rights*, 12, 1: 3–21.

Neumayer, E. (2008b), 'Death Penalty: The Political Foundations of the Global Trend towards Abolition', *Human Rights Review*, 9, 2: 241–68.

Novak, A. (2014a), *Comparative Executive Clemency: The Constitutional Pardon Power and the Prerogative of Mercy in Global Perspective*, London: Routledge.

Novak, A. (2014b), *The Death Penalty in Africa: Foundations and Future Prospects*, New York, NY: Palgrave Macmillan.

Øyen, E. (1990), 'The Imperfection of Comparisons', in E. Øyen (ed.), *Comparative Methodology: Theory and Practice in International Social Research*, London: Sage.

Pakes, F. (2015), *Comparative Criminal Justice*, 3rd edn, London: Routledge.

Pascoe, D. (2014), 'Clemency in Southeast Asian Death Penalty Cases', *Centre for Indonesian Law, Islam and Society Policy Papers*, No. 1, available at: http://law.unimelb.edu.au/__data/assets/pdf_file/0003/1547094/ALC-CILISPolicyPaper_Pascoe_web2.pdf.

Pascoe, D. (2016), 'Singapore and Thailand: Explaining Differences in Death Penalty Clemency', in J. Lu, M. Travers, and L. Chang (eds), *Comparative Criminology in Asia*, New York, NY: Springer.

Peabody, R.L., Webb Hammond, S., Torcom, J., Brown, L.P., Thompson, C., and Kolodny, R. (1990), 'Interviewing Political Elites', *Political Science and Politics*, 23, 3: 451–5.

Prokosch, E. (1997), 'Death Penalty Developments', in W. Schabas (ed.), *The International Sourcebook on Capital Punishment*, Boston, MA: Northeastern University Press.

Richards, D. (1996), 'Elite Interviewing: Approaches and Pitfalls', *Politics*, 16, 3: 199–204.

Schabas, W.A. (1997), 'African Perspectives on Abolition of the Death Penalty', in W. Schabas (ed.), *The International Sourcebook on Capital Punishment*, Boston, MA: Northeastern University Press.

Schabas, W.A. (2002), *The Abolition of the Death Penalty in International Law*, 3rd edn, Cambridge: Cambridge University Press.

Scherdin, L. (ed.) (2014), *Capital Punishment: A Hazard to a Sustainable Criminal Justice System*, Farnham: Ashgate.

Seldon, A. (1996), 'Elite Interviews', in B. Brivati, J. Buxton, and A. Seldon (eds), *The Contemporary History Handbook*, Manchester: Manchester University Press.

Simon, R.J. and Blaskovich, D.A. (2002), *A Comparative Analysis of Capital Punishment: Statutes, Policies, Frequencies, and Public Attitudes the World Over*, Lanham, MD: Lexington Books.

Singleton, R.A. and Straits, B.C. (2010), *Approaches to Social Research*, 5th edn, Oxford: Oxford University Press.

Smith, K.E. (2006), 'Problematising Power Relations in "Elite" Interviews', *Geoforum*, 37, 4: 643–53.

Steinmo, S. (2008), 'Historical Institutionalism', in D. Della Porta and M. Keating (eds), *Approaches and Methodologies in the Social Sciences*, Cambridge: Cambridge University Press.

Techera, E.J. (2014), *Challenges and Opportunities for Cross-Jurisdictional Collaborations: Building Research Linkages between Australian and Chinese Law Schools*, paper presented at the 4th Sino-Australian Law Deans' Meeting, Zhejiang University Guanghua Law School, Hangzhou, 28–9 September.

UN Human Rights Council (2011), *National report submitted in accordance with paragraph 15 (a) of the annex to Human Rights Council resolution 5/1—Sudan*, UN Doc A/HRC/WG.6/11/SDN/1, 11 March.

UN Human Rights Council (2013), *National report submitted in accordance with paragraph 5 of the annex to Human Rights Council resolution 16/21—Yemen*, UN Doc A/HRC/WG.6/18/YEM/1, 8 November.

UN Human Rights Council (2014a), *National report submitted in accordance with paragraph 5 of the annex to Human Rights Council resolution 16/21—Democratic People's Republic of Korea*, UN Doc A/HRC/WG.6/19/PRK/1, 30 January.

UN Human Rights Council (2014b), *National report submitted in accordance with paragraph 5 of the annex to Human Rights Council Resolution 16/21—Iraq*, UN Doc A/HRC/WG.6/20/IRQ/1, 22 August.

UN Secretary General (2015), *Capital punishment and implementation of the safeguards guaranteeing protection of the rights of those facing the death penalty*, UN Doc E/2015/49, 13 April.

Vo, N.M. (2004), *The Bamboo Gulag: Political Imprisonment in Communist Vietnam*, Jefferson, NC: McFarland & Company.

Yorke, J. (ed.) (2008), *Against the Death Penalty: International Initiatives and Implications*, Farnham: Ashgate.

Zedner, L. (1995), 'Comparative Research on Criminal Justice', in L. Noaks, M. Levi, and M. Maguire (eds), *Current Issues in Criminology*, Cardiff: University of Wales Press.

15

BORDER CRIMINOLOGY: HOW MIGRATION IS CHANGING CRIMINAL JUSTICE

*Mary Bosworth**

INTRODUCTION

Well before the mass arrival of refugees in the summer of 2015, Europe had expended considerable effort to secure its external borders, making it harder and harder for people from large sections of the globe to enter legally. Policies associated with so-called 'Fortress Europe' have prioritized internal freedom of movement for EU and EEA citizens over the entry of others, creating a geographically restricted labour marketplace for all but the most highly skilled (De Giorgi 2010). With the exception of students or tourists, the only other routes in require successful human rights-based claims for protection as refugees or the right to family life.

As part of their attempt to 'manage migration', most member states including Britain, have integrated aspects of their criminal justice and immigration policy, thereby reshaping border control and systematically reorienting the criminal justice system around matters of citizenship. Actions that were previously immigration violations such as working with false documents, failing to produce a passport, or overstaying a visa have become criminal offences, while remaining immigration offences as well. These dual powers, as Aliverti (2012, 2013) has observed in the UK and as others have noted elsewhere (Chacón 2012; Stumpf 2006) offer governments considerable flexibility in managing foreign nationals. In Britain, the Home Office may handle such matters administratively or the police may pass cases to the Crown Prosecution Service.

Under these arrangements, police have acquired new roles and responsibilities related to border control within and beyond the borders of the nation state (on the UK see Aliverti 2015; on elsewhere see, inter alia, Aas and Gundhus 2015; Mutsaers 2014;

* I would like to thank a series of organizations for supporting the research on which this chapter draws, including the British Academy who funded the original 2010–12 fieldwork under BARDA Grant 10060 along with the University of Oxford John Fell Fund. Since 2012 my research has been funded by my ERC Starter Grant 313362.

Weber 2013). In Britain, they may now check for immigration status while conducting routine police work and should, when people are arrested, check their fingerprints against the Home Office database as well as a European database (EURODAC) and other transnational databases. In a parallel development, evident in a number of jurisdictions, immigration officers may arrest those suspected of violating immigration law at the border and elsewhere.[1] Working alongside the police, these days they regularly conduct workplace and domestic raids within the community. Increasingly citizens too, are required to act as 'border guards', checking the immigration status and whereabouts of their students, tenants, and employees (Aliverti 2015).

Elsewhere in the criminal justice system, other changes have been introduced. Criminal courts may hand down deportation orders as part of a sentence (Aliverti this volume). Prisons must check the citizenship of their inmates, both to determine whether they must, by law, be deported, and to manage their access to aspects of the institutions' regimes (Kaufman 2015). Since the passage of the UK Borders Act 2007, deportation has become mandatory in Britain for those from outside the European Economic Area (EEA) sentenced to 12 months in prison or more, or whose criminal sentences add up to this sum over the past five years, unless they can show that their deportation would violate their human rights (Bosworth 2007). Those from within the EEA are also liable to deportation if their sentences add up to 24 months. All foreign criminals, no matter what punishment they are given, must be considered for deportation.

During their sentence, foreign national prisoners face greater restrictions than citizen prisoners (Kaufman 2015). Since 2006, they have been considered an escape risk and are thus rarely entitled to Category D, open prison conditions. They are treated differently to those born in Britain in other ways as well, overlooked in the allocation of rehabilitative programmes, or gathered together in foreign-national only penal establishments (Warr 2016). Other countries, from Norway (Ugelvik 2012) and Sweden (Barker 2013a) to Australia and the US are pursuing similar policies (Bosworth and Kaufman 2011; Grewcock 2011).

Alongside these criminal justice initiatives, countries around the world have opened new sites of administrative detention specifically for foreign nationals (Flynn 2014; Guild 2006). In the UK, these sites, known as Immigration Removal Centres (IRC), are primarily used for foreigners awaiting removal or deportation,[2] although a small number of people may also be held for identification purposes, or while their asylum claim is underway (Bosworth 2014; Wilsher 2011). In Australia, similar institutions have been built offshore, to house those who arrive by boat, seeking sanctuary (Lloyd and Mountz 2014). In the US, immigration detention facilities are filled with people who have crossed the Mexican border (Hernandez 2012).

[1] In the UK powers of arrest set out in the 1971 Nationality Act have been amended and extended by subsequent legislation, including the 1999 Immigration and Asylum Act and the 2002 Nationality, Immigration and Asylum Act.

[2] Though leading to the same outcome—expulsion from the British territory, removal and deportation differ in their legal status and effect. Those who are deported may not return until and unless the deportation order is lifted. Those who are removed, may apply to come back after the passage of a certain number of years.

Finally, and like many other countries, Britain has also expanded its powers of expulsion (De Genova 2002; Golash-Boza 2015; Hasselberg 2016). While the system aspires to deport from the prison gates, many of those with a deportation order spend an interim period in detention with others on a removal order, awaiting or contesting their departure. Those who leave may be assisted by British taxpayer-funded programmes aimed at their reintegration in places they may not have lived for years.[3] Some serving prisoners will be transferred to penal institutions in their country of origin during their sentence, under mandatory or voluntary prisoner transfer agreements (Bosworth 2017). Some of those deported return to the UK, and the whole process starts again.

Despite such extensive and significant overlaps between migration control and crime control (not to mention foreign policy and development), most criminologists have, until recently, paid little attention to these sorts of developments, continuing to present crime, justice, and punishment within national frameworks, often limited to one jurisdiction. Matters, however, are changing. In the sections below I explore the contours and effects of a new subfield of the discipline, known as 'border criminology', in which, alongside colleagues in criminal law, sociology, migration studies, and beyond, criminologists have started to ask whether our existing categories of analysis and concepts work in a 'world in motion' (Aas 2007). What does punishment mean, scholars in this field ask, when it includes expulsion (Kaufman 2015; Kaufman and Weiss 2015)? What is the effect on policing, when the matter under investigation is immigration status (Weber 2013)? How do people, who may have lived among us for many years, understand their role, identity, and treatment, when they are forced to leave the country (Barker 2013b; Bosworth 2012; Kaufman and Bosworth 2013)? What are the implications for how we do criminology and for our understanding of crime, justice, victims, and punishment?

BORDER CRIMINOLOGY: A GENEALOGY

Issues of migration and border control are high on the political agenda. Governments around the world are struggling to manage the growing numbers of people on the move. The vast majority of people who leave their home country remain nearby; most Syrian refugees have fled to Jordan and Lebanon for instance. Yet, as the numbers displaced by war, famine, poverty, and climate change expand (UNHCR 2015), economically prosperous states such as Britain and France, as well as the USA, Australia, and Canada have made it clear that they will offer only limited succour to those seeking protection. In addition to their reluctance to welcome refugees, these states have also made it more difficult for foreign students, workers, and their family members to enter legally or to remain.

As such matters climb to the top of the political agenda they have intersected with and been amplified by concerns about integration, economics, and security. Some of

[3] Or at all—since they may be deported to countries where they hold passports but in which they have never lived.

these issues are long-standing. As former colonies gained their independence, similar fears were articulated about the capacity of former colonial powers to absorb culturally or economically their erstwhile subjects (Gilroy 2002). Strategies like the White Australia Policy, which favoured immigrants from English-speaking countries and the north of Europe, were explicitly designed to keep out those who looked and sounded different (Jupp 2002). The USA has long sought to regulate migration from its southern borders.

Other issues are, however, more recent. As many have observed, concerns over security and its connections to migration were irrevocably shaped by the terrorist events of 2001 in the USA, when 2,977 people were killed (Bigo 2008; Bosworth and Guild 2008). Subsequent attacks in Bali, Madrid, and London ushered in new laws, greater powers of surveillance, and incarceration targeted at suspect foreigners, even when many of the assailants were actually citizens of the country they attacked (Zedner 2005). As a result, immigration law is a key part of counter-terrorism policy (HM Government 2015).

While the field of border criminology is primarily interested in contemporary events, it is also attendant to long-standing debates and practices. Thus, although earlier accounts of migration can be found within criminology, such as in the Chicago School sociology (Park and Burgess 1921), or in literature on the scale of crime committed by immigrants (Bucerius and Tonry 2014), such work is only weakly connected to current scholarship (Pickering et al. 2015). Instead, in its attention to the constitutive nature of borders and migration control, their racialized nature and effect, and implications for understanding sovereignty and rights, border criminology owes far more to the sociology of punishment and security studies than to these earlier bodies of work (Aas and Bosworth 2013).

To understand these developments, scholars in border criminology draw on a range of concepts from feminist theory, refugee and immigration studies, postcolonial studies, human rights, immigration and refugee law, politics, and international relations. Work by Foucault on governmentality (1991) and biopolitics (2004), Bauman on modernity (2001), as well as Agamben's (2004) notion of the 'state of exception' have been particularly influential (see e.g. Aas 2007, 2013; Eriksson 2016). Elsewhere, Ahmed's account of 'the stranger' (2000), and Butler's (2004) consideration of why some people are considered 'grievable' while others are not, have also illuminated aspects of current policy and public attitudes (Bosworth 2014). Although the field has been slow to integrate issues of race and ethnicity fully, despite the clearly racialized nature of most border controls (Bhui 2016), Hall's (2001) work on colonial amnesia and Gilroy's (2002, 2006) study of Empire have both shaped the field (Bowling 2013; Kaufman 2015).

Deploying this conceptual literature, border criminologists revisit the relationship between state sovereignty and criminal justice through the lens of citizenship. It is not just crime that the sovereign state cannot fully control, authors point out, but also mobility (Bosworth 2008). Under these conditions, it is less surprising, as Barker puts it that 'membership matters most' (Aas 2014; Barker 2013b). Certain activities, from using the National Health Service, to taking up the offer of a job without a visa, are only criminal when committed by non-citizens.

The theoretical engagement of border criminology can be invigorating. Yet, for some, like Bhui, there are dangers in taking a purely conceptual approach to migration control because 'a theoretical approach that fails sufficiently to incorporate human experience or to connect with . . . lived experience can lead to flawed understanding' (2013: 11). Studying border control can be difficult. By definition, those subject to it are hard to locate, pushed to the margins by their precarious legal status. So, too, the border is not always self-evident (Loftus 2015). Rather, state practices push it further back, to the sending countries, while symbolically bringing it forward to the bodies of foreigners themselves. Non-citizens, wherever they are located, carry the border with them. Finally, in sites of immigration control, such as the port, airport, or detention centre, the state and its partners from the private sector are often reluctant to permit researchers to study their activities.

While drawing theory and practice together can be a challenge, much of border criminology is trained on the lived experience of those subject to or engaged in border control. In this, they must navigate the considerable social distance that exists between the researcher and the participants. The undocumented or those awaiting expulsion are particularly vulnerable. Yet, they are also part of the polity and have long been so. Acknowledging their abjection, while recalling their agency, is critical.

Methodologically the field is shaped by a wide range of disciplines including anthropology, geography, visual studies, as well as sociology, criminology, and law. It is primarily qualitative, based on interviews and observations with migrants and state and private sector agents. In a bid to maintain contact with those who are precarious, or who have been deported, some scholars turn to social media as a means to communication. To bridge the gap in language, others have experimented with photographic methods and other visual material.

In my own work, I have focused for many years on immigration detention. Notwithstanding the fact that most of those subject to border control will never be detained, IRCs, like prisons in the criminal justice system, represent the symbolic heart of the border control system (Bosworth 2007, 2012, 2013, 2014). Without them, ideas and justifications of control would founder. Intrigued initially by their apparent similarities to prisons, my interest in detention has endured because of their differences. My early questions were primarily descriptive. What are these places like, and what are they for? As it turned out, even these most basic questions evade straightforward answers, raising challenging methodological and epistemological questions of their own. In the sections below, I outline some of the issues that arise from these characteristics. First, however, I offer a brief overview of the detention estate.

IMMIGRATION DETENTION

At the time of writing, around 3,500 people are held across nine IRCs. The Home Office contracts out all of these sites to private custodial firms (currently Mitie, G4S, Serco, and GEO) and the prison service. While daily life in them must abide by the guidelines set out in the Detention Centre Rules 2001, the national operating standards

(UKBA 2008), and by a range of Detention Service Orders (DSOs), each establishment is shaped by the terms set out in the confidential contracts the government signs with the providers.

In their design and regulation, IRCs resemble more familiar penal institutions. They are secure institutions, located behind razor wire, with considerable interior surveillance and security. Detention Custody Officers (DCOs) wear uniforms and carry keys. Senior staff who run and design policies for these institutions have all worked in the prison service. The regimes and purpose of IRCs, however, are distinct. Most of those detained have not been found guilty of a criminal offence; nobody is serving a sentence.[4] While there is talk of the 'risk' detainees pose to the community, it is rarely apparent what this danger might involve, other than flight. Although IRCs are evidently part of the government's stated aim to make Britain a 'less attractive place to come and work illegally' (Cameron 2015), the numbers of irregular migration swell and diminish unrelated to these sites; their deterrent effect hard to discern.[5] Finally, detainees may be held indefinitely (Bosworth and Vannier 2016). In all these ways, detention fits uneasily into existing criminological explanatory paradigms about custody (Bosworth 2013).

There are not just conceptual barriers to understanding detention, but also methodological ones. It is extremely difficult to gain access to these places. Governments around the world have refused to allow rigorous academic study of these institutions or those who stay or work in them. I have been, for many years, the only independent academic researcher in the UK with permission to enter them. Once inside, the methodological challenges continue. Many detainees speak only limited English. They hale from countries with an array of cultural, religious, and traditional norms and practices that may be difficult for researchers to understand. Some are held overnight, most only for weeks or months, others for several years;[6] it is not always clear how to capture the range of experiences under these circumstances.

How then, can we approach immigration detention? Given their administrative rationale, should IRCs even fall into the purview of criminology? Do they fit into existing theoretical frameworks within punishment and society, or might they open up new ways of thinking about punishment? Finally, what do such institutions suggest about 'doing' criminology.

On the surface, matters may not seem so difficult. I have been conducting fieldwork since 2009 and, to some extent, I have deployed strategies similar to those in prison sociology (Bosworth 1999; Crewe 2009; Phillips 2010). That is to say, I use mixed

[4] Precise statistics are difficult to obtain. According to the most recently available ones set out in the 2016 *Review into the Welfare in Detention of Vulnerable Persons*, 1,050 out of 3,532 women and men in detention in March 2015 had been referred by the police under Operation Nexus or by the Criminal Case Directorate (Shaw 2016: 34–5). While not all of the former will have been convicted of a crime, those in the latter would have been.

[5] It is worth noting that the evidence for the efficacy of deterrence in respect of punishment is also thin (von Hirsch et al. 1999).

[6] Though the government reports general figures, a breakdown is harder to find. According to the Shaw review (2016: 36), there is considerable variation in duration of detention. Although the national average in March 2015, for those currently detained, was 65 days, for those who were detained via Operation Nexus, duration was nearly twice as long (116 days), with those detained via the criminal case directorate close behind at 109 days.

methods. I conduct formal and informal interviews. I have developed two survey instruments—one for detainees and another for staff (Bosworth and Kellezi 2013; Bosworth et al. 2016). Yet, IRCs are not prisons. Fieldwork in them feels entirely different from prisons research. Its purpose and impact is less clear. It is even more painful to do, and the ethics of commenting on such places rather murkier.

First of all, IRCs are far more politicized than prisons. It took me 12 months to obtain permission to do my research and, while I encountered few barriers, I was warned explicitly by a senior civil servant: 'We don't want your research to embarrass us' (see also Bosworth and Kellezi 2016). Such official reluctance to permit research is difficult to explain as the centres are, in most respects, no worse than prisons in terms of staff culture, safety, cleanliness, etc. Notwithstanding the occasional inflammatory claim in the media to the contrary, there are no hidden subterranean punishment cells, nor, as far as I have seen, evidence of systematic physical abuse.[7] Yet, these are places of intense suffering, with well-known deleterious effect on mental health (Shaw 2016).

The key distinction between the two systems springs from their purpose. Whereas prisons have a range of justifications from rehabilitation to deterrence or simply incapacitation (Zimring and Hawkins 1997), the point of IRCs is rather less clear. Various reasons are put forward, yet rarely agreed. Policy makers and politicians, for instance, claim they are part of generalized deterrence. They serve the goal of making Britain hostile to irregular migrants. They are also simply a means of ensuring removal; the Home Secretary argued in 2015: 'Immigration detention is a vital tool in helping ensure those with no right to remain in the UK are returned to their home country' (May in Wintour 2015).

Custodial staff sometimes claim that they are protecting the community 'We provide a service and intelligence, e.g. in relation to terrorism', Juba[8] stated proudly. 'Immigration officers don't know that stuff. We monitor them on the phone, internet etc. We can say we need to move, remove, or imprison someone. Most of them are asylum seekers but with a mission. You don't see with your eyes but with your ears. Some of them are into child trafficking etc. We make a big contribution. We, who've worked here for long, know how important the job is. We do a public service by protecting the community' (DCO, Harmondsworth). At other times they claim to be assisting a vulnerable population, housing them in a care home, a boarding school, a hospital. 'It's a bit like a school, really, isn't it? A boarding school', one experienced officer suggested. 'You know, there's people held here. They're learning stuff. They've come from all different backgrounds. You're kind of thrown together like you would be in a school, with people you might get on with, you might not get on with' (Joyce, DCM, Colnbrook).

Charlie, a colleague who had worked at the same institution for many years, took a different view. While talking specifically about local changes that had recently been

[7] There are some exceptions. In 2014, for instance, it became clear that some staff members at Yarl's Wood IRC had been having sexual relations with some of the detained women. While subsequent investigations by Her Majesty's Inspectorate of Prisons (HMIP 2015) and by an independent inquiry (Lampard and Marsden 2016) found no evidence of systematic wrongdoing, staff members were fired and Serco has instituted a series of reforms to minimize the risk of this kind of abuse occurring again.

[8] This is not his real name. All participants have been allocated pseudonyms.

introduced in the regime, he captured the problem caused by lack of clarity over the institution:

> I think the staff need to know: are we a prison or are we a detention centre?... Are we a relaxed detention centre or are we a borderline prison, okay? We're swapping and changing so many times. One minute we're a high, high-risk detention centre. We're secure; we don't have, we don't have problems with this; we don't have problems with that. The next minute, we've opened all the doors, people walking all over the place, people are randomly being sick on drugs, on spice, where they're freely getting a hold of it, probably five, six times a day—different individuals.
>
> (DCM, Colnbrook)

Detainees, as might be expected, have a bleaker outlook. 'I am in a prison', one man in Harmondsworth stated sadly, in words I have heard from many others before and since, 'though I have committed no crime. I see cells, bars, barbed wire... It's always a prison. This is a prison' (Fabio, Italy, Harmondsworth). They believe detention is designed to break their spirit and force them to go. 'They do not beat us or hurt us', Sanjeewa acknowledged, 'but they wear us down' (Sri Lanka, Campsfield House). In this aspect, the centres are greatly assisted by the lack of an upper statutory time limit. After a few weeks, women and men start to worry, not without reason that they may be there for much longer. 'What if I'm here for one year?' Raj anxiously asked me, after he had been in Colnbrook for a few weeks. 'One year! I can't cope. This place no good for me. I used to be fresh. Now look at me. Outside I eat good food, every day, good food. Here just rice. No good for me' (India, Colnbrook). As this man had slowly realized, notwithstanding the fact that around two-thirds of detainees are returned or released within 28 days, Colnbrook, like every other centre had people who had been detained for over 12 months (Bosworth and Vannier 2016).

Only about half of those in detention are actually removed or deported. The rest are, eventually, released back into the British community. They may be detained again, or they may simply be asked to report regularly to the police and the Home Office. For this section of the incarcerated population, detention primarily seems designed to disrupt their lives, and to impress upon them their unwelcome and precarious status within British society.

Conducting fieldwork under these conditions is challenging. Staff and detainees are often suspicious, confused, or ill at ease. 'Who are you?' 'Why are you here?' 'Why should I talk to you?' many demand. In setting people at ease, researchers encounter numerous and considerable language barriers and cultural and religious differences that have to be overcome. Unsure how long they will be detained, and often extremely fearful of where they will be sent, since some are not returning at all but being sent to countries of which they hold passports but may never have visited or at least not for many years, detainees are usually anxious and depressed (Shaw 2016). Their capacity to give 'informed consent' to participate in research under these circumstances is attenuated.

Unlike prisons, where for the most part, people's sentences are determinate, in detention matters are far more fluid. Although the government has significantly reduced the capacity to appeal an immigration decision, or to lodge a new claim, detainees still expend considerable efforts in doing so. In these attempts they must tell their story over and over again. Under these circumstances, being asked to share their experiences with a researcher as well can simply be too much. While some appreciate the attention from an outsider, others remain suspicious, angry at the inability of academics to assist them in their case.

Finally, these institutions need to be understood in the wider legal context of generalized restrictions on those born outside Britain to access the welfare state and the current influx of refugees across Europe. So too, IRCs exist in the shadow of the rise of nationalist parties like United Kingdom Independence Party (UKIP) to those on the far Right. Detention centres here, as elsewhere, are located in multicultural, multi-ethnic societies with long-term migrant populations where questions of belonging and criminal justice intervention take many forms. These aspects generate specific intellectual and ethical challenges. They also raise questions about the novelty of border control practices like detention that targets similar populations to those managed by the criminal justice system. IRCs are, after all, heavily racialized sites of confinement, populated almost entirely by citizens from the global south. While staff are usually careful to withhold racist views, they evidently differentiate between those in their care by nationality, which often stands in as a proxy for race. Some are direct: 'South Africa has been ruined by the Natives', Gertrude told me angrily, 'and England is going the same way!' (DCO, Colnbrook).

Under these circumstances, the goal of conducting research in IRCs needs careful consideration. Whereas prisons research has ameliorated many aspects of prison conditions, it is not always clear that a similar aspiration should or could animate IRC research. Seeking to improve conditions within sites that play a role in denying sanctuary to other human beings is not straightforward. Further ethical questions are raised by the role of detention in blocking access to the UK job market and welfare protections for those from the global south.

To some extent, criminologists always have to deal with such matters. Prison studies are not without critics (Foucault 1991; Sim 1990). But, in detention, the stakes are higher. Forcibly returning people to endemic poverty and violence, or simply extinguishing their hopes, separating them from their families, and denying their past is very hard to justify. It is painful to observe. Without a clear research outcome, it often feels voyeuristic. Is understanding and documentation enough?

Such fears about legitimating the system are difficult to manage. They are compounded by the sensitivity of the government and the private contractors to criticism which means that research access is always provisional. Offering meaningful critique without 'embarrassing' them can be difficult.

In managing this research environment, authors often fall back on affective language, referring to the imperative of bearing witness (Kaufman 2015) and acknowledging humanity (Bosworth 2014), reminding the IRCs, the Home Office, and detainees, that people are watching and that they care. While alone such actions may do little, they are imperative for building a body of evidence. A certain degree of pragmatism is also important. Immigration detention centres are not going away, and their continuation will not depend on academic research. They are a political choice. Any improvements that can be generated by writing about them are worth pursuing. We cannot hope to solve global inequality. Yet we should consider how global inequality and governmental policies in respect of the mass mobility that global inequality generates affects our scholarship and our discipline.

CONCLUSION

As states around the world put the criminal justice system to work in managing migration, criminologists need to adapt their ideas and strategies. Traditional distinctions between criminal law and immigration law, and between criminal justice and immigration institutions and practices are eroding. These days, sentences passed in a criminal court may have effects felt far beyond the borders of the nation state. Institutions like the police and the prison, previously bound to the nation state, these days extend well beyond its borders. Prison and policing policies, implemented in our communities, shape the experiences of those we have never met. As more foreigners are imprisoned and as states pursue more vigorously confinement in immigration detention as an adjunct to removal and deportation, the distinct justifications of punishment and administrative penalties blur.

The intellectual ramifications of these developments are complicated. Other than those drawn from just beyond the borders of Europe to the east, most of the targets of these new practices are from the global south. The ties of border control to post-colonialism are strong. Yet, for many, with whom we identify and where we live are fluid matters. Thus, the rise of multiculturalism and the removal of internal borders within Europe jostle against resurgent nationalism and localism. We are all always located somewhere even as many of us have emotional and historical ties elsewhere as well.

As citizenship (or lack thereof) increasingly underpins differential treatment under law (Zedner 2010), many of the fundamental concepts and methods of criminology have been reshaped. Unless matters shift radically, in the criminal justice system as in other areas of public policy, a dual system is becoming entrenched. Those born elsewhere already face additional repercussions to their policing, their sentence, and their incarceration, purely on the basis of their accident of birth. Criminologists are well-placed to hold up these developments to critical scrutiny. We are adept at gaining research access to hidden sites. We are familiar with navigating and analysing coercive practices. It is time to pay attention to where we are heading and to the costs of carving out rights for citizens while denying them to others.

REFERENCES

Aas, K.F. (2007), 'Analysing a World in Motion: Global Flows Meet "Criminology of the Other"', *Theoretical Criminology*, 11, 2: 283–303.

Aas, K.F. (2013), 'The Ordered and the Bordered Society', in K.F. Aas and M. Bosworth (eds), *The Borders of Punishment: Migration, Citizenship, and Social Exclusion*, Oxford: Oxford University Press: 21–39.

Aas, K. (2014), 'Bordered Penality: Precarious Membership and Abnormal Justice', *Punishment & Society*, 16, 5: 520–41.

Aas, K.F. and Bosworth, M. (eds), (2013), *The Borders of Punishment: Citizenship, Crime Control, and Social Exclusion*, Oxford: Oxford University Press.

Aas, K.F. and Gundhus, H. (2015), 'Policing Humanitarian Borderlands: Frontex, Human Rights and the Precariousness of Life', *British Journal of Criminology*, 55, 1: 1–18.

Agamben, G. (2004), *The State of Exception*, Chicago, IL: University of Chicago Press.

Ahmed, S. (2000), *Strange Encounters: Embodied Others in Post-Coloniality*, London: Routledge.

Aliverti, A. (2012), 'Exploring the Function of Criminal Law in the Policing of Foreigners: The Decision to Prosecute Immigration-Related Offences', *Social & Legal Studies*, 21, 4: 511–27.

Aliverti, A. (2013), *Crimes of Mobility: Criminal Law and the Regulation of Immigration*, Abingdon: Routledge.

Aliverti, A. (2015), 'Enlisting the Public in the Policing of Immigration', *British Journal of Criminology*, 55, 2: 215–30.

Barker, V. (2013a), 'Nordic Exceptionalism Revisited: Explaining the Paradox of a Janus-Faced Penal Regime', *Theoretical Criminology*, 17, 1: 3–23.

Barker, V. (2013b), 'Democracy and Deportation: Why Membership Matters Most', in K. Aas and M. Bosworth (eds), *The Borders of Punishment: Criminal Justice, Citizenship and Social Exclusion*, Oxford: Oxford University Press.

Bhui, H.S. (2013), 'Introduction: Humanizing Migration Control and Detention', in K.F. Aas and M. Bosworth (eds), *The Borders of Punishment: Migration, Citizenship, and Social Exclusion*, Oxford: Oxford University Press: 1–17.

Bhui, H.S. (2016), 'The Place of "Race" in Understanding Immigration Control and the Detention of Foreign Nationals', *Criminology & Criminal Justice*, 16, 2: 267–85.

Bigo, D. (2008), 'Globalized (in)Security: the Field and the Ban-Opticon', in D. Bigo and A. Tsoukala (eds), *Terror, Insecurity and Liberty: Illiberal Practices of Liberal Regimes after 9/11*, Abingdon: Routledge: 10–48.

Bosworth, M. (1999), *Engendering Resistance: Agency and Power in Women's Prisons*, Aldershot: Ashgate.

Bosworth, M. (2007), 'Immigration Detention in Britain', in M. Lee (ed.), *Human Trafficking*, Collumpton: Willan Publishing: 159–77.

Bosworth, M. (2008), 'Border Control and the Limits of the Sovereign State', *Social & Legal Studies*, 17, 2: 199–215.

Bosworth, M. (2012), 'Subjectivity and Identity in Detention: Punishment and Society in a Global Age', *Theoretical Criminology*, 16, 2: 123–40.

Bosworth, M. (2013), 'Can Immigration Detention Be Legitimate?', in K. Aas and M. Bosworth (eds), *The Borders of Punishment: Migration, Citizenship, and Social Exclusion*, Oxford: Oxford University Press: 149–65.

Bosworth, M. (2014), *Inside Immigration Detention*, Oxford: Oxford University Press.

Bosworth, M. (2017), 'Penal Humanitarianism? Punishment in an Era of Mass Migration', *New Criminal Law Review*, 20, 1.

Bosworth, M. and Guild, M. (2008), 'Governing through Migration Control: Security and Citizenship in Britain', *The British Journal of Criminology*, 48, 6: 703–19.

Bosworth, M. and Kaufman, E. (2011), 'Foreigners in a Carceral Age: Immigration and Imprisonment in the U.S.', *Stanford Law and Policy Review*, 22, 1: 101–27.

Bosworth, M. and Kellezi, B. (2013), 'Developing a Measure of the Quality of Life in Detention', *Prison Service Journal*, 205: 10–15.

Bosworth, M. and Kellezi, B. (2016), 'Getting In, Getting Out and Getting Back: Access Ethics and Emotions in Immigration Detention Research', in S. Armstrong, J. Blaustein, and A. Henry (eds), *Reflexivity and Criminal Justice: Intersections of Policy, Practice and Research*, London: Palgrave Macmillan.

Bosworth, M. and Vannier, M. (2016), 'Comparing Immigration Detention in Britain and France: A Matter of Time?', *European Journal of Migration and Law*, 18, 2: 157–76.

Bosworth, M., Aitken, D., and Gerlach, A. (2016), *Understanding Staff Culture: Results from the Heathrow IRC Survey*, Oxford: Centre for Criminology.

Bowling, B. (2013), 'Epilogue: The Borders of Punishment: Towards a Criminology of Mobility', in K.F. Aas and Bosworth, M. (eds), *The Borders of Punishment: Migration, Citizenship, and Social Exclusion*, Oxford: Oxford University Press: 291–306.

Bucerius, A. and Tonry, M. (eds) (2014), *The Oxford Handbook of Ethnicity, Crime and Immigration*, New York: Oxford University Press.

Butler, J. (2004), *Precarious Life: The Powers of Mourning and Violence*, London: Verso.

Cameron, D. (2015), The Queen's Speech, 21 May 2015.

Chacón, J. (2012), 'Overcriminalizing Immigration', *Journal of Criminal Law & Criminology*, 102, 3: 613–52.

Crewe, B. (2009), *The Prisoner Society: Power, Adaptation and Social Life in an English Prison*, Oxford: Oxford University Press.

Eriksson, A. (ed) (2016), *Punishing the Other: The Social Production of Immorality Revisited*, Abingdon: Routledge.

Flynn, M. (2014), 'How and Why Immigration Detention Crossed the Globe', *Global Detention Project Working Paper Series* [Online], Geneva: Global Detention Project, available at: http://www.globaldetentionproject.org/publications/working-papers/diffusion.html.

Foucault, M. (1991), 'Governmentality', in G. Burchell, C. Gordon, and P. Miller (eds), *The Foucault Effect: Studies in Governmentality*, Chicago, IL: University of Chicago Press: 87–104.

Genova, de, N. (2002), 'Migrant "Illegality" and Deportability in Everyday Life', *Annual Review of Anthropology*, 31: 419–47.

Gilroy, P. (2002), *There Ain't No Black in the Union Jack: The Cultural Politics of Race and Nation*, Abingdon: Routledge.

Gilroy, P. (2006), *After Empire or Postcolonial Melancholia*, New York: Columbia University Press.

Giorgi, de, A. (2010), 'Immigration Control, Post-Fordism, and Less Eligibility: A Materialist Critique of the Criminalization of Immigration across Europe', *Punishment & Society*, 12, 2: 147–67.

Golash-Boza, T. (2015), *Deported: Policing Immigrants, Disposable Labour and Global Capitalism*, New York: NYU Press.

Grewcock, M. (2011), 'Punishment, Deportation and Parole: The Detention and Removal of Prisoners under Section 501 of the Migration Act 1958', *Australian and New Zealand Journal of Criminology*, 44, 1: 56–73.

Guild, E. (2006), *Briefing Paper: A Typology of Different Types of Centres for Third Country Nationals in Europe*, Brussels: European Parliament, available at: http://www.europarl.europa.eu/RegData/etudes/note/join/2006/378268/IPOL-LIBE_NT(2006)378268_EN.pdf.

Hall, S. (2001), 'Conclusion: The Multicultural Question', in B. Hesse (ed.), *UN/Settled Multiculturalisms: Diasporas, Entanglement, Transruptions*, London: Zed Books: 209–41.

Hasselberg, I. (2016), *Enduring Uncertainty: Deportation, Punishment and Everyday Life*, London: Berghahn Books.

HERNANDEZ, C.C.G. (2012), 'The Perverse Logic of Immigration Detention: Unravelling the Rationality of Imprisoning Immigrants Based on Markers of Race and Class Otherness', *Columbia Journal of Race and Law*, 1: 353–64.

HIRSCH, VON, A., BOTTOMS, A.E., WIKSTROM, P.-O., and BURNEY, E. (1999), *Criminal Deterrence and Sentence Severity: An Analysis of Recent Research*, Oxford: Hart Publishing.

HM Government (2015), *National Security Strategy and Strategic Defence and Security Review 2015*, Cm 9161, London: HMSO, available at: https://www.gov.uk/government/uploads/system/uploads/attachment_data/file/478933/52309_Cm_9161_NSS_SD_Review_web_only.pdf.

HMIP (2015), *Report on an Unannounced Inspection of Yarl's Wood Immigration Removal Centre by HM Chief Inspector of Prisons, 13 April–1 May 2015*, London: HMIP.

JUPP, J. (2002), *From White Australia to Woomera: The Story of Australian Immigration*, Cambridge: Cambridge University Press.

KAUFMAN, E. (2015), *Punish and Expel: Border Control, Nationalism, and the New Purpose of the Prison*, Oxford: Oxford University Press.

KAUFMAN, E. and BOSWORTH, M. (2013), 'Prison and National Identity: Citizenship, Punishment and the Sovereign State', in D. Scott (ed.), *Why Prison?*, Cambridge: Cambridge University Press: 170–88.

KAUFMAN, E. and WEISS, S. (2015), 'The Limits of Punishment', in K. Reiter and A. Koenig (eds), *Extreme Punishment*, London: Palgrave: 32–49.

LAMPARD, K. and MARSDEN, E. (2016), *An Independent Investigation into Concerns about Yarl's Wood Immigration Removal Centre*, London: Verita.

LLOYD, J. and MOUNTZ, A. (2014), 'Managing Migration, Scaling Sovereignty on Islands', *Island Studies Journal*, 9, 1: 23–42.

LOFTUS, B. (2015), 'Border Regimes and the Sociology of Policing', *Policing & Society*, 25, 1: 115–25.

MUTSAERS, P. (2014), 'An Ethnographic Study of the Policing of Internal Borders in the Netherlands: Synergies between Criminology and Anthropology', *British Journal of Criminology*, 54, 5: 831–48.

PARK, R. and BURGESS, E. (1921), *Introduction to the Science of Sociology*, Chicago, IL: University of Chicago Press.

PHILLIPS, C. (2010), *The Multicultural Prison*, Oxford: Oxford University Press.

PICKERING, S., BOSWORTH, M., and AAS, K. (2015), 'The Criminology of Mobility', in S. Pickering and J. Ham (eds), *The Routledge Handbook on Crime and International Migration*, Abingdon: Routledge.

SHAW, S. (2016), *Review into the Welfare in Detention of Vulnerable Persons*, Cm 9186, London: HMSO.

SIM, J. (1990), *Medical Power in Prisons: The Prison Medical Service in England 1774–1989*, Basingstoke: Open University Press.

STUMPF, J. (2006), 'The Crimmigration Crisis: Immigrants, Crime, and Sovereign Power', *American University Law Review*, 56, 2: 367–419.

UGELVIK, T. (2012), 'Imprisoned on the Border: Subjects and Objects of the State in Two Norwegian Prisons', in S. Ugelvik and B. Hudson (eds), *Justice and Security in the 21st Century: Risks, Rights and the Rule of Law*, London: Routledge.

UKBA (2008), *Operating Standards for Immigration Removal Centres*, London: Home Office.

UNHCR (2015), 'Worldwide Displacement Hits All Time High as War and Persecution Increase', available at: http://www.unhcr.org/558193896.html.

WARR, J. (2016), 'The Deprivation of Certitude, Legitimacy and Hope: Foreign National Prisoners and the Pains of Imprisonment', *Criminology & Criminal Justice*, 16, 3: 301–18.

Weber, L. (2013), *Policing Non-Citizens*, Abingdon: Routledge.

Wilsher, D. (2011), *Immigration Detention: Law, History, Politics*, Cambridge: Cambridge University Press.

Wintour, P. (2015), 'Theresa May Announces Review of Immigration Detainees' Welfare', *The Guardian Online*, 8 February 2015, available at: http://www.theguardian.com/uk-news/2015/feb/08/theresa-may-immigration-detention-welfare-review.

Zedner, L. (2005), 'Securing Liberty in the Face of Terror: Reflections from Criminal Justice', *Journal of Law and Society*, 32, 4: 507–33.

Zedner, L. (2010), 'Security, the State, and the Citizen: The Changing Architecture of Crime Control', *New Criminal Law Review*, 13, 2: 379–403.

Zimring, F. and Hawkins, G. (1997), *Incapacitation: Penal Confinement and the Restraint of Crime*, Oxford: Oxford University Press.

PART IV

VICTIMS IN, AND OF, THE CRIMINAL JUSTICE SYSTEM

16

RECLAIMING JUSTICE: THE CHALLENGES POSED TO RESTORATIVE AND CRIMINAL JUSTICE BY VICTIM EXPECTATIONS

Joanna Shapland

The questions of what is 'just' and what is 'justice' partly depend upon social and legal cultures, which have long historical roots (Shapland 2008). What is seen as or pronounced to be a 'just' solution to a conflict is not simply dependent upon the outcome: the solution. Rather, as Tyler (2006) has shown, views of a 'just' outcome are intertwined with ideas about the process that has produced that solution.

This chapter aims to examine victims' perspectives on what is 'just' in processes and outcomes in response to crime. In doing so, it considers both criminal justice and restorative justice. The aim is not to follow the well-trodden path comparing criminal justice and restorative justice in terms of what 'they do for victims', but to start to put together what victims value in that justice process, and their needs and expectations, as seen through the results of empirical research: what might be seen as 'good justice' by victims. In doing this, we need to examine not only 'traditional' forms of criminal justice, but also more recent innovations, like problem-solving courts, and also to consider victims' views on justice in different national settings. Because responding to crime has been primarily a nation state responsibility, the processes of criminal justice and restorative justice tend to take particular national cultural forms. By comparing countries, it may be possible to distinguish national cultural views about what is 'good justice' from those specific to the role the participant is playing (e.g. victims).

Victims or any other participants in justice do not develop their view in isolation from their surroundings. The activities of justice occur in front of audiences, including the media and the general public. For some, a properly appointed judge, for example, has and should have unfettered power under the law. Under the terms of a separation of executive and judicial powers, whatever a judge legally does cannot immediately result in his or her expulsion by government (or worse). However, judges are also enmeshed within their societies and are usually very aware that their audiences are judging them. Disputes and crime will cause ripples of unease to spread throughout the local community (and in these instant news days, often far beyond). What judges and other authorities, such as the police (Innes 2014), try to do is to ensure that appropriate signals about what action is being taken follow those ripples to signify that the authorities are taking action. I will argue the appropriateness of that action will be judged in terms of both its processes and its outcomes, by victims as well as the general public.

In this chapter, I shall set out some of the parameters of the social and legal cultural contexts in which criminal justice occurs and explore public views on what is 'right', 'just', and 'proper' in criminal justice. Taking on board the interaction between outcome and process, victims' views specifically will then be explored. By comparing and contrasting what happens in criminal justice and in restorative justice, it may then be possible to set out what might be termed 'good' justice for these times. Research has gone a long way towards describing what is considered today as a 'good' prison environment (Liebling 2004) and a 'good' police custody suite (Skinns 2012). It is time to start conceiving what would constitute 'good' at the core of criminal justice, between police and prison—in other words, in the courts at sentence. Are current ideas of either criminal justice or restorative justice producing what would be seen as 'good' justice? If not, how may they need to be melded to achieve this?

THE SOCIAL AND LEGAL CULTURAL CONTEXTS OF CRIME AND JUSTICE

The deeply embedded legal culture of a society is closely linked to its political and cultural history. France, for example, with its tradition of a 'strong' state, actively rebuts any idea of an intermediate body, such as a local community, becoming involved in justice matters and so breaking the direct link between the state and its citizens (Milburn 2008). Indeed, the direct translation into French of the word for 'community' (*communauté*) implies such an intermediate grouping, possibly along ethnic or other group lines, which in France would be seen as implicitly against the state or interfering in the state's prerogatives (Wyvekens 2008). Is it possible, then, for justice to be administered separately to local areas, particularly local areas which may feel themselves less favoured by state action (such as the *banlieux*)? The compromise is that the idea of localized justice, translated as 'proximity justice' is allowed, as long as it only means a local manifestation of the state's justice (locally based prosecutors, *maisons de justice*), rather than different forms or institutions of justice being provided in different areas, or resulting in different outcomes (Milburn 2008). In contrast, many countries with a common law tradition of justice, such as the UK, Canada, Ireland, or the US, look fondly on local communities being involved in justice matters and accept some local variation as in, for example, neighbourhood policing, local courts bound to their communities, community courts, and so on.

Where there has been political conflict, whether recently or even several centuries ago, justice processes may still be felt to be tinged with political overtones. In Canada, for example, First Nations peoples have argued that federal and provincial justice systems have overridden their ways of 'doing justice', to create an excessively 'Europeanized' justice (Bartkowiak and Jaccoud 2008). In response, the state judicial system has sought to (literally) take national justice processes from the main population centres out to local communities, through, for example, flying in judges and prosecutors, and developing methods of restorative justice in conjunction with local elders. Results include the circle sentencing processes, in which local people meet with the state-appointed judge to discuss sentencing of a local offender (Stuart and Pranis 2007), and the use of local panels, with locally trained judges, to hear cases.

However, Bartkowiak and Jaccoud (2008) have pointed to the tensions which can confront local leaders who become state-trained local judges. Will their state-assigned role lead to them losing legitimacy in local people's eyes, essentially being seen as state 'stooges'? Similar tensions can affect community restorative justice initiatives where there is a history of conflict between different community groups or between the state (seen as essentially a colonizing power) and local people. In Northern Ireland, for example, the route to establishing community restorative justice schemes (such as Alternatives and CRJI—Community Restorative Justice Ireland) and building links to state criminal justice institutions has been difficult (McEvoy and Eriksson 2008). The state has sought to control the work of community groups, partly because it was worried about justice matters and decisions being taken away from its authority, partly because of the risk of double jeopardy if offenders are sanctioned by both state and community. Interestingly, however, these tensions have been mitigated by both state and community restorative justice schemes finding common ground by stressing the need to follow international human rights principles, thereby moving their ground towards a higher international rights plane.

There is no doubt that many of these conflicts concern the power of the state to impose what it would like to see in terms of justice processes, either in relation to local communities or to lay participants. Where there has been a history of unrest, the state has often sought to make overtures to local groups or communities to show that it has heard local concerns, which may involve softening the homogeneity of state-wide justice. However, as the immediate need to pacify recedes (less unrest on the streets, fewer protests from community groups), state criminal justice professionals may return to the ways they were operating before. The upsurge in and subsequent withdrawals from *maisons de justice* in France in the period 1999–2005 illustrate this dynamic well (Wyvekens 2008). State prosecutors who were initially outsourced into offices in poor suburbs where there had been disturbances and riots after a while drew back to their old offices in city centres, leaving their former offices to become advice centres for residents. Residents were no longer provided with state personnel to take decisions on their cases, but with aids to learn how to deal with the state institutions in the centre of the towns (Milburn 2008). The state-funded new employees changed from mediators using restorative justice to mediate disputes in the outlying areas, to ex-police officers employed in city centre offices to take the strain off overworked prosecutors—again a move back to the traditional criminal justice ways.

Similar tensions to those between the central state and local justice have occurred between state criminal justice officials and lay participants. Many have documented the change over the last century or more from victims prosecuting their own cases—

with the time, trouble, and expense, but also power to decide that this brought—towards courts being inhabited primarily by professionals, there to represent the state or the defendant (see e.g. Sebba 1996). Rock's (1993) study of the Crown Court in England and Wales has shown how even the architecture of courts is shaped by power relations, with the judiciary and the professionals centrally placed and made separate from both lay participants and the local community by having separate corridors, rooms, and entrances.

In the wake of the change to state prosecutors throughout Europe and more widely, the role of victims has come into question, with some seeing the lack of regard for victim needs and victims' wishes in criminal justice as only remediable if victims have procedural rights to intervene at relevant points.[1] Indeed, the trend has recently been, in many countries, to grant victims more procedural rights. So, the limits for using the *partie civile* process in the Netherlands, France, Germany, etc. have been increased, so that such proceedings are now available to more victims.[2] In England and Wales, victims can now speak in person about the effects of the offence on them before sentence, in place of a written victim personal statement (Ministry of Justice 2015).

VICTIM VIEWS

When victims are asked about what they would prefer in terms of decision-making, findings from empirical research over the last 30 years or so have been unequivocal that victims, at least in England and Wales, want to be heard about certain matters, and to be consulted, but do not want to be made to take decisions on the case (Shapland et al. 1985; Victim Support 1995). So, victims in criminal justice want courts and prosecutors to know about the effects of the offence on them, and may even wish to advise courts on sentence,[3] but they do not desire decision-making power: to take away from prosecutors and judges decisions on whether to prosecute and what sentence to give.

Yet, where there is statutory restorative justice conferencing, as for example in Northern Ireland or in New Zealand in young offender cases, victims are happy to participate in discussions on outcome agreements which go to the judge and in the majority of cases form the sentence (Campbell et al. 2005; Morris and Maxwell 2003). These are not diversionary cases, but ones in which restorative justice occurs as part of criminal justice processes. Similarly, victims in mainland European countries who wish to meet the offender welcome talking with him or her in victim–offender

[1] See Fenwick (1997) for a valuable discussion of the difference between service rights and procedural rights for victims.

[2] The *partie civile* process involves victims being able to register their civil claim for compensation with the state, so that they become full parties to criminal justice proceedings, with the ability to see the prosecutor's file, question witnesses, and have their civil claim adjudicated by the criminal judge.

[3] In England and Wales, victims are prevented by a Practice Direction (see Consolidated Criminal Practice Direction, also *Perks* [2001] 1 Cr App R (s) 19) from putting any specific suggestions on sentence in their victim personal statement, and are discouraged in criminal justice proceedings from doing so.

mediation about restitution, with some of those discussions being passed on to the judge and forming part of the 'dossier'.[4]

Why is there this apparent contradiction in victims' wishes regarding participation in procedures around sentencing? Is it because so little attention has been paid by criminal justice practitioners to victims' wishes to have service rights, such as being given information about the progress of the case, or stating the effects of the offence on them (Ashworth 1993), that the only way they can influence anything or be consulted is to essentially 'go the whole distance' and participate in decisions which influence sentence? Or is it that there are subtle differences between victims' wishes and abilities to intervene in different cultural and legal traditions? Or is there a nuanced explanation which is capable of reconciling victims' reluctance to take decisions in traditional criminal justice proceedings, with their desire to participate actively in restorative justice?

In an evaluation of pre-sentence restorative justice conferences in England and Wales in 2001–4, which involved primarily adult offenders and more serious offences, the conference process involved three stages: discussion about the offence itself, discussion about the effects of the offence, and then discussion about what might happen in the future, including what elements the sentence might contain. When the conference participants (which included victim, offender, and their supporters) were asked by the facilitator to turn to talking about what should happen in the future to improve matters, there was sometimes a pause before all started discussing items which then were included in the outcome agreement (Shapland et al. 2011). It was as though participants needed to be given permission to address these matters—that they were not sure initially that they dared to do so. However, with even slight encouragement from the facilitator to turn to the third phase of the conference about the future, participants, including victims, were very happy to do so. In interviews afterwards, there was no concern from victims (or offenders) that they should not have been talking about programmes the offender might undertake, or the payment of restitution (though appetite for restitution was rare), or conditions on community sentences. There was no hesitancy or unhappiness about signing the outcome agreement, or everyone having a copy of it to keep, with the signatures on it—either at the time, or reflecting back in interviews afterwards.

There was, however, one key difference between those restorative justice discussions and decisions taken in criminal justice sentencing: the outcome agreements were given to the sentencer before sentence was passed, but they were not the sentence themselves. In other words, outcome agreements were (strong) advice to the sentencer, but the sentencer was left to consider them and pass judgment. A similar process occurs in Northern Ireland youth conferencing: the outcome agreement is likely to form the sentence (the legislation refers to making a 'youth conference order' (Justice (Northern Ireland) Act 2002 s. 60)), but it is first reviewed by the judge at the

[4] The dossier is the bundle of evidence used by judge, prosecutor, and defence. In some mainland European countries, e.g. Belgium, victim–offender mediation is the normal form of restorative justice and takes place either pre-charge or post-charge, often in parallel with the criminal justice proceedings (van Camp 2014). In others, such as Poland, the result of the victim–offender mediation is provided to the judge and intended potentially to influence sentence.

time of passing sentence. The restorative justice conference is hence not given full responsibility for the sentence, nor is the victim. Given that sentencing is properly a public matter and needs to reflect the public interest, this must be correct, as it enables accountability to the public, as well as the victim and community (ibid).[5]

One difference between most restorative justice processes and criminal justice sentencing, therefore, is that the person representing the public view and the state (i.e. the judge) reviews the restorative justice outcome before the public sentence is pronounced. In Northern Ireland, this review element was introduced to ensure that outcomes were not wildly disproportionate to the offence.

KEEPING VICTIMS, FAMILIES, AND COMMUNITY AWAY FROM SANCTIONS

The pause we witnessed in the conferences in England and Wales, before discussion flowed, has always tantalized me. Why the pause, given that participants were subsequently very happy to discuss forms of sentence? Did they initially feel unprepared or ill-equipped to comment? Certainly, there was sometimes a lack of information as to whether specific programmes were available in particular prisons, or, for example, whether appropriate substance abuse schemes existed in the area. Contributions on this from professionals attending, or the facilitator, were welcomed. But the pause signified to me something more—as though the lay participants, victims, and offenders, were not sure they were allowed to talk about these matters. If so, this seems to be a sorry state of affairs.

We know that, even though process is important to both victims and offenders in terms of their confidence in the justice system and its legitimacy (Tyler 2006), outcomes also have an effect. 'Crime talk' on the street and in pubs and neighbourhood gatherings, is not just about what offences have occurred in the locality, but also about what people think about recent sentences passed. If, in restorative justice or criminal justice processes, we have separated lay people from the procedure of sentencing so far that they think contributing at the time of sentencing is a matter only for the professionals (which is what the pause may imply), then we have removed justice away from those lay people and the public. We have also, potentially, separated the community into which offenders will need to be reintegrated following sentence from any means developed to create such reintegration—because that community (and key parts of it, such as victims) do not see themselves as relevant to the sentencing process. At present, in the criminal justice system in England and Wales, there are no such reintegrating opportunities following sentence, because there are no formal post-sentence meetings arranged for the community (including the victim), judge, and offender. The only mechanisms which can carry that reintegrating task are those

[5] The discussion of 'balance' in sentencing in Edwards (2004) is also helpful here—as is the fact that conferencing includes both victim and offender agreeing on the outcome agreement.

during the sentencing process (e.g. the judge's homily,[6] or pre-sentence reports) and during sentences themselves. If sentencing and penal processes do not relate to local communities, but instead are divorced from them, then criminal justice appears to have few ways to reintegrate offenders; instead, as Braithwaite (1989) originally commented, stigmatizing and potentially 'othering' offenders. Did we mean to push offenders away in this way?

Separating offenders and sentencing into a realm occupied by professionals[7] also puts all the onus for promoting desistance onto relevant professionals and the offender. Desistance is, after all, learning to lead a non-offending life in the community (Bottoms and Shapland 2016). This separation does not allow communities (or indeed victims, should they wish to do so) to play any part. It is not at all clear that our current practices in prisons and probation/licence supervision create good outcomes in terms of desistance. Recidivism rates remain stubbornly high, particularly after release from custody. This appears to be the case in many countries, whether they have very high, high, or relatively low rates of imprisonment, and whatever the dominant legal culture. Could this be partly, as Lero Jonson and Cullen (2016) argue, because most correctional work focusing on re-entry is poorly funded and targeted, with little throughcare between prison and community corrections? In an emphasis on deriving the 'right' sentence, have sentencers and probation services put too much emphasis on the past, the offence, and too little on the future and aiding potential desistance? It would be ironic if criminal justice systems had put so much into achieving proportionate and legitimate processes to determine the sentence, focusing on the offence, that they have lost sight of the aim of preventing reoffending and helping offenders to turn their lives around. Victims often have a variety of aims in relation to their participation in justice processes, such as restorative justice, but high up in their priorities is often preventing reoffending, to help the offender change his or her life (Shapland et al. 2011; van Camp and Wemmers 2013).

The growing body of research on desistance indicates that, in order to desist, offenders need not only to wish to desist, but also to have help in overcoming many practical obstacles. As perceived by the offenders themselves, these obstacles include earning money legitimately, securing affordable accommodation and reducing debts, getting help for substance abuse, and finding support to continue on a hard desistance path (Shapland et al. 2016). It may be that the individualist and responsibilizing agendas which have dominated penal policy-making in Western countries over the last few decades have inadvertently knocked away some of the potential props to maintaining desistance. So, for example, if offenders who are trying to desist are seen solely as individuals, on a personal journey to try to stop offending, then probation staff and others will not contact or enlist families, partners, or others in that process. Yet we know that many offenders in their 20s or even 30s rely on their families (as well as their partners) as support, and many male offenders, at least, live with their parents or other relatives when released from prison (Bottoms and Shapland 2011). McNeill (2016) argues that

[6] The homily is the judge's remarks when passing sentence.

[7] In England and Wales, panels of lay magistrates sentence many cases in the magistrates' court, though this kind of lay input is rare in other countries. Lay magistrates are, however, selected by the state and highly trained to operate as professionals, so they cannot really be seen as representatives of the community.

supporters should be brought into supervision practice to maximize the chances of starting and maintaining desistance. Seeing sentencing and desistance as solely about the state and the offender does not only exclude victims, but also partners, families, and the community.

DO PROBLEM-SOLVING COURTS SUPPORT DESISTANCE EFFORTS?

The term 'Good Courts' has been used by Berman and Feinblatt (2015) as the title of their book on problem-solving courts in the US. They bring together experiences with community courts, domestic violence courts, mental health courts, and drug courts, to argue that what is key is to focus on the underlying problems that bring people to court, offering a more effective response to crime. There is no doubt that, at least in the US, problem-solving courts reduce reoffending for some kinds of offence, particularly drug-related crime (Belenko 1998). The same court personnel, particularly the judge, preside over the case throughout its progress, reviewing what has happened. There have been some negative reactions, though, with critics arguing that this configuration of actors, where judge, prosecution, and defence counsel sit 'on the same bench' sharing responsibility to seek solutions, undermines defence rights, even though the defendant has to opt in specifically to take part in the problem-solving process. Once the defendant opts in, the key aims are to address the underlying problems of the defendant, according to what these key actors think is in the defendant's interests, and bearing in mind the interests of the community at large.

Defendants have more active involvement in problem-solving courts than in traditional courtroom procedures. Would they then be a model which could be expanded to cover all offences, including those with individual or corporate victims? One difficulty is that victims rarely feature in the problem-solving process. Problem-solving courts are often silent on victims, not deliberately I suspect, but because, with the exception of domestic violence, the kinds of problems they were developed to address do not have readily identifiable victims, whether individuals or corporate. Problem-solving courts also have a philosophy that the key issue is to address the problem presented by the defendant and the difficulties the defendant is facing, whether those are substance misuse, mental disorder, or simply causing community concern and complaints. Their primary ethos, in other words, is to change the defendant, with a subsidiary goal being to involve the community as a whole, through restitution to the community and engagement in advisory boards, meetings, and community mediation. Although problem-solving courts aim to involve the community, they do not seem to intend that the community should acquire any power over what happens to the defendant, but rather that the community should be provided with information, with the aim that it will then be supportive. Power still resides with the judge—this is about the 'active use of judicial authority to solve problems and to change the behaviour of litigants' (Berman and Feinblatt 2001). A key impetus in developing community courts—and other problem-solving courts—beyond the initial pilots has been the wish for greater judicial activism and influence on what is done with defendants, driven by concerns over the excessive routinization and processing in 'normal' courts.

Problem-solving courts, therefore, feature active judicial work with defendants. They have been less radical in relation to community input. So for example, the pilot that brought community courts to the UK (Mair and Millings 2011) only involved the community through surveys and meetings to define local problems. Members of the community had no power to propose or decide upon solutions to those problems. This minor role for local community people contrasts with more restorative community processes, also intended to solve problems, such as circle sentencing and community meetings (Shearing 2001), which involve members of the community actively debating possible solutions.

Domestic abuse is the one type of offence dealt with by problem-solving courts in the US in which there are clear individual victims. Research on domestic abuse problem-solving courts has concentrated upon the judicial role and the effect on offenders (see e.g. Burton 2006). Relevant outcomes are seen as 'improving victim safety and ensuring perpetrator accountability' (ibid: 370). In these courts, however, it seems as though the paternalistic, offender reform-oriented ideology of problem-solving courts has been prioritized over the possibility of lay community or victim involvement. Victims of domestic abuse in problem-solving courts do not seem to be seen as survivors, or people who need to be empowered by the court, but as weak creatures who need to be protected from the defendant until he or she is changed/reformed. A key element of the domestic abuse problem-solving court in the US is the provision of victim advocates, who provide safety planning to victims, explain court procedures, and refer victims to social services—but their role is not to help the victim to speak but to speak *for* the victim (ibid). Interestingly, evaluation of the first domestic violence courts in England and Wales showed that there was no slowing in rates of withdrawal of testimony by victims when a problem-solving court format was used (Cook et al. 2004). Whether the victim withdrew her testimony or not, however, the courts, through having gathered evidence from sources other than the victim, were able to continue to work with defendants, so retaining their emphasis on reforming the defendant. This is in no way to deny the work that has been done, under the problem-solving umbrella in the US, to bring together under one roof services needed by survivors of domestic abuse (Burton 2006). So, too, there is no doubt that a coordinated response is needed to provide any kind of solution for survivors and perpetrators (Hester and Westmarland 2005).

The 'problem' that problem-solving courts has sought to address is a multiplicity of appearances by the defendant before the court for new offences stemming from that defendant's ongoing difficulties (substance abuse etc.) or continuing proximity to the victim (domestic abuse). It is thus seen as a 'court–defendant' problem, rather than one which needs to actively involve victims (or the local community). It is less clear, though, whether the necessary kinds of threat and activism embodied in the work of judges in problem-solving courts (to get perpetrators to take the court proceedings seriously and to bring the necessary social welfare agencies on board) need entail an entirely welfare, rather than empowering, approach to victims.

Moving away from the kinds of recurrent offences typically seen in problem-solving courts, could the idea of a 'good court' be further expanded to embody and allow both problem-solving and empowering victims? Typically, empowerment of victims, as well as facilitating accountability in defendants through communication, has occurred in restorative justice, particularly conferencing. Here, direct communication between the parties is facilitated in a safe space and the lay parties particularly are encouraged to create the outcome agreement, rather than it being imposed by a judge (Shapland et al. 2011). As we have seen, one of the deficits of this arrangement is that participants (especially lay participants) may not know about the kinds of support and services available in the area—a problem found in the original evaluation of family group conferencing in New Zealand (Morris and Maxwell 2000), and in more recent evaluations in England and Wales (Shapland et al. 2011), as well as in the use of mediation in France (Milburn 2008). In Northern Ireland, the deficit has been met by training the police officers who are required by statute to attend youth conferences to know about such services and provide this information to the conference (Campbell et al. 2005). It is, however, a strange task for the police, particularly given their contested role in Northern Ireland.

Surprisingly, even in an age of partnership in community safety and multi-agency initiatives, we do not seem to have developed any professional role which could signpost judges or conferences to available services, let alone one which could then actively engage those services in the aftermath of a conference, during the sentencing process in court, or propose a bundle of solutions for a problem-solving court—what one might call a 'resource person' for justice. We still seem to be relying on workers from each agency coming together to liaise periodically, rather than creating such a role. As the criminal justice and social welfare systems become more fissured in their composition in terms of delivery of services (with statutory agencies joined by voluntary sector bodies, private providers, and indeed hybrids, as in the new community rehabilitation companies in England and Wales), 'resource people' are likely to become essential to meet the very different needs of both defendants and victims in justice processes and outcomes. A model for such a person may be seen in the 'resource people' adopted in some previous Probation Trusts,[8] where one member of the probation staff of each area would specialize in keeping up to date with resources on accommodation, one on training and education, etc. (Robinson et al. 2014). This was one of the key ways to provide what was seen as 'real quality' in one-to-one supervision by probation staff. A similar service is needed for courts and restorative justice.

WHAT MIGHT 'GOOD JUSTICE' LOOK LIKE?

We have seen that 'justice' in relation to criminal offences is not some abstract entity, but situated in its societal and legal cultural context. Victim expectations, like public

[8] Probation Trusts were replaced by a mixture of Community Rehabilitation Companies and the National Probation Service in England and Wales in 2014/15.

expectations of justice, relate to both processes and outcomes. Much has already been written about how processes need to be seen as procedurally just—to be seen as fair, to be seen as involving all those they should. It has been shown that both restorative justice and criminal justice (at least at the police/prosecution stage) can meet those standards (Tyler et al. 2007). For many years now we have known that, for victims, this procedural fairness needs to involve respect, being kept informed, having a voice (being consulted, being able to input relevant information), and fair decision-making (lack of bias). What has been less clear is whether such fair, 'just', or 'good' processes can be achieved solely by providing excellent services to victims, or whether they also mean that victims need to be able to participate actively in justice. Do they imply, for example, that the participatory model of restorative justice is necessary?

The debate between those advocating solely service rights and others promoting additional procedural rights for victims has been, in academic terms, fierce (see e.g. Ashworth 1993; Erez and Laster 1999; Pemberton and Reynaers 2011). Looking more closely at the chief battleground, the process between conviction and sentence, it may be that the battle has been fought over the wrong front lines. For onlookers, such as the public or even victims, this is not about what role each party plays, but about the essence of the debate. In other words, what may be important to the public and victims may include processes *and* outcome, rather than primarily processes.

Victims do not want ultimate decision-making power over key criminal justice decisions, though many do want to be informed and consulted and have opportunities to make an input. But they are prepared to help to attain what they see as 'good justice'. This good justice requires consideration of the harm that has been done, the ability to ask questions about and understand the offender's current situation (including what tends to lead to that offender offending), and appreciation of what help needs to be offered to the victim. It does not minimize the past, whether in terms of the seriousness of the offence or the harm done to the victim. But it would also have a future-oriented phase which aims to solve problems linked to offending and thereby to aid desistance. Moreover, though the ultimate decision on sentencing is for the judge, many victims are prepared and indeed wish to take part in this consideration of what harm has been caused and conversation about the offender's situation.

Dissatisfaction with the current purposes and processes of sentencing has been linked to the growth of problem-solving courts. Where reoffending seems likely, judges themselves have turned their backs on the traditional criminal justice process and its focus on the past offence, in order to develop problem-solving courts which have their emphasis on preventing reoffending in the future. They have started working more rigorously with the offender to tackle problems and aid desistance. However, in several ways they may be trying to do so with their hands tied behind their backs, because they are seeing the process solely in terms of the judge and offender working together. Problem-solving courts are not usually an inclusive process, involving others close to the offender—or the victim.

Victim views about what is 'good justice' have many similarities with what would be seen as desistance-focused justice, aimed at enabling offenders to stop offending. For many reasons, this good justice needs to be inclusive justice. It needs properly to acknowledge the past (and allow victims to ask questions), in order to show respect to the victim and acknowledge the breach of the state's criminal law. But it is not a matter of replacing judge with victim. Both need to participate, in a safe way, so that victim views are heard and respected, yet the public interest is prime, and it is judges who take sentencing decisions.

Good justice, for victims, needs not only to mark the seriousness of the offence but to take action to reduce the likelihood of its reoccurrence. To do that, through strengthening the offender's wish to desist and aiding that desistance, all the help that criminal justice system, family, friends, and victim can provide are likely to be necessary, at least for more persistent offenders. Good justice choreographs all those inputs and strengths into a fair and future-oriented process which is also appropriate to that legal cultural tradition.

REFERENCES

Ashworth, A. (1993), 'Victim Impact Statements and Sentencing', *Criminal Law Review*: 498–509.

Bartkowiak, I. and Jaccoud, M. (2008), 'New Directions in Canadian Justice: From State Workers to Community "Representatives"', in J. Shapland (ed.), *Justice, Community and Civil Society: A Contested Terrain*, Cullompton: Willan.

Belenko, S. (1998), 'Research on Drug Courts: A Critical Review', *National Drug Court Institute Review*, 1, 1: 1–42.

Berman, G. and Feinblatt, J. (2001), 'Problem-Solving Courts: A Brief Primer', *Law and Policy*, 23, 2: 125–40.

Berman, G. and Feinblatt, J. (2015), *Good Courts: The Case for Problem-Solving Justice*, New York: Quid Pro Books.

Bottoms, A.E. and Shapland, J. (2011), 'Steps towards Desistance among Male Young Adult Recidivists', in S. Farrall, M. Hough, S. Maruna, and R. Sparks (eds), *Escape Routes: Contemporary Perspectives on Life After Punishment*, London: Routledge: 43–80.

Bottoms, A.E. and Shapland, J. (2016), 'Learning to Desist in Early Adulthood: The Sheffield Desistance Study', in J. Shapland, S. Farrall, and A.E. Bottoms (eds), *Global Perspectives on Desistance: Reviewing What We Know, Looking to the Future*, London: Routledge: 99–125.

Braithwaite, J. (1989), *Crime, Shame and Reintegration*, Cambridge: Cambridge University Press.

Burton, M. (2006), 'Judicial Monitoring of Compliance: Introducing "Problem Solving" Approaches to Domestic Violence Courts in England and Wales', *International Journal of Law, Policy and the Family*, 20, 3: 366–78.

Camp. van, T. (2014), *Victims of Violence and Restorative Practices: Finding a Voice*, London: Routledge.

Camp, van, T. and Wemmers, J.-A. (2013), 'Victim Satisfaction with Restorative Justice: More Than Simply Procedural Justice', *International Review of Victimology*, 19, 2: 117–43.

Campbell, C., Devlin, R., O'Mahony, D., Doak, J., Jackson, J., Corrigan, T., and McEvoy, K. (2005), *Evaluation of the Northern Ireland Youth Conference Service*, NIO Research and Statistical Service Report No. 12, Belfast: Northern Ireland Office.

Cook, D., Burton, M., Robinson, A., and Vallely, C. (2004), *Evaluation of Specialist Domestic Violence Courts/Fast Track Systems*, London: Crown Prosecution Service and Department for Constitutional Affairs.

Edwards, I. (2004), 'An Ambiguous Participant: The Crime Victim and Criminal Justice Decision-Making', *British Journal of Criminology*, 44, 6: 967–82.

Erez, E. and Laster, K. (1999), 'Neutralizing Victim Reform: Legal Professionals' Perspectives on Victims and Impact Statements', *Crime & Delinquency*, 45, 4: 530–53.

Fenwick, H. (1997), 'Procedural "Rights" of Victims of Crime: Public or Private Ordering of the Criminal Justice Process?', *Modern Law Review*, 60, 3: 317–33.

Hester, M. and Westmarland, N. (2005), *Tackling Domestic Violence: Effective Interventions and Approaches*, Home Office Research Study 290, London: Home Office.

Innes, M. (2014), *Signal Crimes: Social Reactions to Crime, Disorder and Control*, Oxford: Oxford University Press.

Lero Jonson, C. and Cullen, F. (2016), 'Prisoner Re-Entry Programs', *Crime and Justice*, 44, 1: 517–75.

Liebling, A. (2004), *Prisons and Their Moral Performance: A Study of Values, Quality and Prison Life*, Oxford: Oxford University Press.

McEvoy, K. and Eriksson, A. (2008), 'Who Owns Justice? Community, State and the Northern Ireland Transition', in J. Shapland (ed.), *Justice, Community and Civil Society: A Contested Terrain*, Cullompton: Willan.

McNeill, F. (2016 forthcoming), 'The Fuel in the Tank or the Hole in the Boat? Can Sanctions Support Desistance?', in J. Shapland, S. Farrall, and A.E. Bottoms (eds), *Global Perspectives on Desistance*, London: Routledge.

Mair, G. and Millings, M. (2011), *Doing Justice Locally: The North Liverpool Community Justice Centre*, London: Centre for Crime and Justice Studies.

Milburn, P. (2008), 'How Civil Society Is on the Criminal Justice Agenda in France', in J. Shapland (ed.), *Justice, Community and Civil Society: A Contested Terrain*, Cullompton: Willan.

Ministry of Justice (2015), *Code of Practice for Victims of Crime*, October 2015, London: Ministry of Justice.

Morris, A. and Maxwell, G. (2000), 'The Practice of Family Group Conferences in New Zealand: Assessing the Place, Potential and Pitfalls of Restorative Justice', in A. Crawford and J. Goodey (eds), *Integrating a Victim Perspective Within Criminal Justice*, Dartmouth: Ashgate.

Morris, A. and Maxwell, G. (2003), 'Restorative Justice in New Zealand', in A. von Hirsch, J. Roberts, A.E. Bottoms, K. Roach, and M. Schiff (eds), *Restorative Justice and Criminal Justice*, Oxford: Hart.

Pemberton, A. and Reynaers, S. (2011), 'The Controversial Nature of Victim Participation: Therapeutic Benefits in Victim Impact Statements', in E. Erez, M. Kilchling, and J.-A. Wemmers (eds), *Therapeutic Jurisprudence and Victim Participation in Criminal Justice: International Perspectives*, Durham, NC: Carolina Academic Press.

Robinson, G., Priede, C., Farrall, S., Shapland, J., and McNeill, F. (2014), 'Understanding "Quality" in Probation Practice: Frontline Perspectives in England & Wales', *Criminology and Criminal Justice*, 14, 2: 123–42.

Rock, P. (1993), *The Social World of an English Crown Court*, Oxford: Clarendon Press.

Sebba, L. (1996), *Third Parties: Victims and the Criminal Justice System*, Columbus, OH: Ohio State University Press.

SHAPLAND, J. (ed.) (2008), *Justice, Community and Civil Society: A Contested Terrain*, Cullompton: Willan.

SHAPLAND, J., FARRALL, S., and BOTTOMS, A.E. (eds) (2016 forthcoming), *Global Perspectives on Desistance*, London: Routledge.

SHAPLAND, J., ROBINSON, G., and SORSBY, A. (2011), *Restorative Justice in Practice*, London: Routledge.

SHAPLAND, J., WILLMORE, J., and DUFF, P. (1985), *Victims in the Criminal Justice System*, Aldershot: Gower.

SHEARING, C. (2001), 'Transforming Security: A South African Experiment', in H. Strang and J. Braithwaite (eds), *Restorative Justice and Civil Society*, Cambridge: Cambridge University Press.

SKINNS, L. (2012), *Police Custody: Governance, Legitimacy and Reform in the Criminal Justice Process*, London: Routledge.

STUART, B. and PRANIS, K. (2007), 'Peacemaking Circles: Reflections on Principal Features and Primary Outcomes', in D. Sullivan and L. Tifft (eds), *Handbook of Restorative Justice: A Global Perspective*, Abingdon: Routledge: 121–33.

TYLER, T. (2006), *Why People Obey the Law*, 2nd edn, Princeton, NJ: Princeton University Press.

TYLER, T., SHERMAN, L., STRANG, H., BARNES, G., and WOODS, D. (2007), 'Reintegrative Shaming, Procedural Justice, and Recidivism: The Engagement of Offenders' Psychological Mechanisms in the Canberra RISE Drinking-And-Driving Experiment', *Law and Society Review*, 41, 3: 553–86.

Victim Support (1995), *The Rights of Victims of Crime*, Policy Paper, London: Victim Support.

WYVEKENS, A. (2008), '"Proximity Justice" in France: Anything but "Justice and Community"?', in J. Shapland (ed.), *Justice, Community and Civil Society: A Contested Terrain*, Cullompton: Willan.

17

DOMESTIC VIOLENCE AND THE UNITED STATES' CRIMINAL JUSTICE SYSTEM

Michelle Madden Dempsey

In the late 1970s, we reached into the shadows to retrieve physical abuse from the canon of 'just life'. Now it appears, we did not reach nearly far enough.

(Stark 2007: 16)

This chapter explores the changing contours of domestic violence in the United States criminal justice system throughout the past 50 years, and considers shifts that will likely inform the criminal law's approach to domestic violence in the next few decades. In so doing, it offers a US perspective on the themes identified in this collection about the changing contours of criminal justice. As scholarship from the Centre for Criminology in Oxford has amply demonstrated, taking an international perspective often illuminates aspects of local policy and practice. Though the US functions with a particular legal structure, on which this chapter will focus, elements from my argument apply also to Britain and to British criminology more generally.

The touchstone that organizes this chapter's exploration of domestic violence is the US Violence Against Women Act (VAWA), originally enacted in 1994. It is difficult to underestimate the importance of VAWA's influence on the understanding of and approach to domestic violence in the US. Yet, as suggested in the final section, it seems that VAWA—with all of its promise, compromises, and limitations—may hinder more than help when it comes to addressing the root causes of domestic violence in the US.

The discussion that follows is organized in three parts. It begins with a retrospective account of the emergence of the concept of domestic violence in political discourse and criminal law enforcement practices in the US in the decades prior to VAWA's enactment. It then explores the impact of VAWA during its first two decades. In conclusion, this chapter considers whether the US criminal justice system has a significant role to play in addressing domestic violence in the coming decades. While the future of domestic violence in the US remains uncertain, there is growing momentum to reject law enforcement intervention in favour of restorative justice practices outside the criminal justice system (Various 2015). This shift, if broadly realized in practice, will go far beyond the 'victim empowerment' model of domestic violence prosecution advocated in the UK (Hoyle and Sanders 2000) and will reject criminal law as the default response to domestic violence (Coker et al. 2015).

THE EMERGENCE OF DOMESTIC VIOLENCE (1960S–1990S)

Feminists in the US and UK began to organize around the issue of domestic violence in the late 1960s and early 1970s.[1] The establishment of shelters for victims was key to laying the groundwork for feminist political advocacy around domestic violence. Following the example of Erin Pizzey, who established the first battered women's shelter in Chiswick, England in 1971 (Pizzey 1974: 44), the first domestic violence shelter in the US opened in St Paul, Minnesota, in 1974 (Schneider 2008: 21). Soon thereafter others opened in Boston, Massachusetts, and Ann Arbor, Michigan (Stark 2007: 28).

During this time of early political organizing around domestic violence, an influential understanding of domestic violence emerged in Duluth, Minnesota. The 'Duluth Model', as it has come to be known, is grounded in the belief that battering is a pattern of intentional conduct designed to exert power and control over the victim, and that effectively addressing domestic violence requires changes to unjust social conditions which enable men to subordinate women. Central to the Duluth model's account of domestic violence is its 'power and control wheel' (Pence and Paymar 1993), an illustration of the physical, emotional, economic, and other forms of power and control that constitute domestic violence.[2] The original power and control wheel is shown in Figure 17.1.

While the Duluth model's conception of domestic violence informed some early empirical research in this field (Dobash and Dobash 1979), it differed considerably from the model which informed early national studies of domestic violence in the US (Straus et al. 1980). The two different theoretical models for understanding the nature, causes, and extent of domestic violence arrived at vastly different findings regarding whether domestic violence was primarily a matter of men battering women, or whether there was a hidden epidemic of 'battered husbands' in the US (Steinmetz 1977). The latter research relied on a theoretical model that obscured the context and meaning of violence within intimate relations, conflating violence grounded in power and control (what Michael Johnson (1995) later coined, 'patriarchal terrorism' or 'intimate terrorism') with a distinct, and more common form of intimate partner violence (coined by Johnson as 'common couple violence' or

[1] Prior to this decade, many criminal courts followed the English common law doctrine, according to which husbands had a legal right to physically discipline their wives, 'with a stick as thick as his own thumb' (*James v Commonwealth* (1825) WL 1899, at p. 6 (para. 1825)).

[2] The power and control wheel has been adapted into nearly 100 variations, addressing a variety of forms and context for interpersonal abuse (NCDSV 2016). The original wheel, created by the Duluth Abuse Intervention Project in collaboration with more than 200 battered women, documents 'the most common abusive behaviors or tactics that were used against these women' (DAIP 2016).

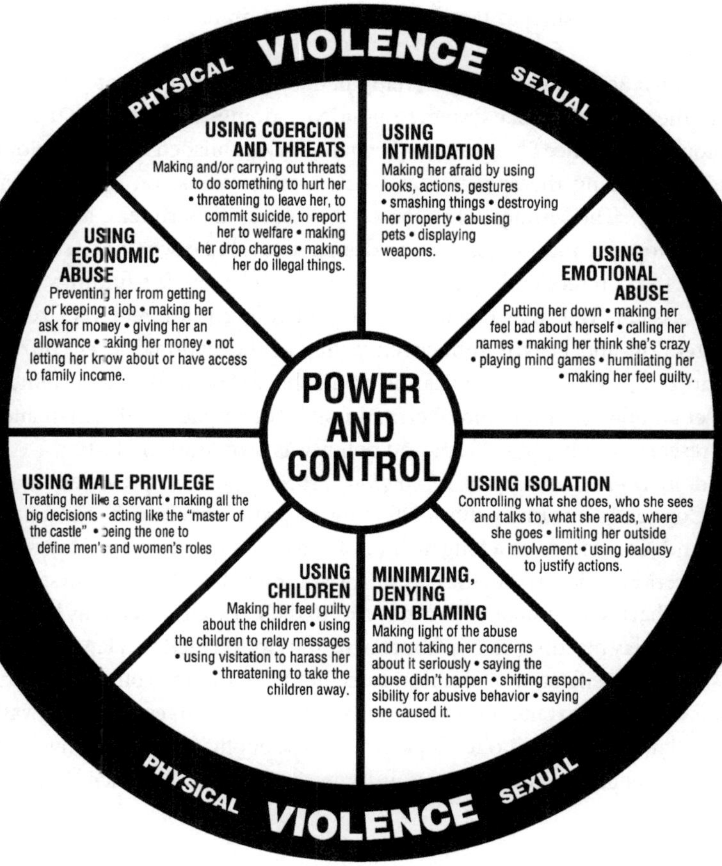

Figure 17.1 Power and Control Wheel

'situational violence').[3] Not only did Johnson's richer theoretical model provide American criminologists with 'a gracious exit from two decades of methodological back-biting' in the empirical study of domestic violence, it suggested that these forms of violence 'have different dynamics and qualitatively different outcomes and so... require a different response' (Dempsey 2009: ch. 6; Stark 2007: 104).

Despite increasingly sophisticated understandings of domestic violence in social science research and mounting political activism aimed at 'taking domestic violence seriously' (Whitebread et al. 1984: 1411), during this period the US criminal justice system largely continued to treat domestic assaults as an occasion for 'cooling off', rather than an occasion for arresting the abuser. Indeed, in many police departments, 'policies for domestic "disputes" actively discouraged arrest, focusing instead on

[3] Johnson subsequently changed the names of his key concepts from 'patriarchal terrorism' to 'intimate terrorism' and from 'common couple violence' to 'situational couple violence' so as not to 'beg the question of the connections with patriarchy that are so clear in heterosexual relationships (but not so clear in same-sex relationships in which there is an intimate terrorist)... and [to avoid] the risk of trivialization [inherent in the term] common couple violence' (email from Michael Johnson, Pennsylvania State University, to Michelle Madden Dempsey, Oxford University (13 September 2004) (on file with author)).

alternative responses such as family crisis intervention or counselling for batterers' (Fagan 1996: 4).

In the mid-1980s, however, two developments ushered in a major transformation in the way the criminal justice system responded to domestic violence in the US. First, criminologists Lawrence Sherman and Richard Berk published the first major empirical study measuring the specific-deterrent effect of arrest on domestic violence offenders (1984). The Minneapolis Domestic Violence Experiment, as it came to be known, employed a randomized study design to evaluate whether arrest had any significant effect on reoffending in domestic violence cases. The findings, that arrest for minor assaults did indeed reduce future offending rates, received tremendous media attention and heavily influenced policy at the national level (Buzawa and Buzawa 2002: 95). While later replication studies have produced inconsistent findings (Garner et al. 1995; Schmidt and Sherman 1996), the impact of Sherman and Berk's original research on shaping US law and policy was profound and lasting.

Second, in *Thurman v City of Torrington*[4] Tracey Thurman prevailed in a lawsuit against a Connecticut municipality for its failure to protect her from her estranged, abusive husband, Charles. After a long history of abuse and numerous attempts to secure police protection, officers from the City of Torrington Police Department stood by and watched as Charles, who stabbed Tracey prior to their arrival, repeatedly kicked her in the head as she lay bleeding on her front lawn. The Court ruled that law enforcement's administrative classification of domestic assaults as 'less serious offenses' contributed to the officers' failure to take action during the attack, and thus established a valid constitutional claim against the police department.[5] The publicity surrounding this case set the stage for sweeping reforms to the way domestic violence was policed in the US.

THE 'VAWA ERA' (1990S–2013)

After four years of political advocacy, VAWA was signed into law in September 1994. The enactment of VAWA was widely regarded as a 'watershed, marking the first comprehensive federal legislative package designed to end violence against women' in the US (Legal Momentum 2016). As VAWA's chief architect observed upon the occasion of VAWA's twentieth anniversary:

> Even just 20 years ago, few people wanted to talk about violence against women as a national epidemic, let alone... do something about [it]. No one... denied that kicking your wife in the stomach, or smashing her in the face, or pushing her down the stairs in public was repugnant. But our society basically turned a blind eye. And hardly anyone ever... directly intervened...
>
> (Somanader 2014, quoting then-Senator Joseph Biden)

[4] *Thurman v City of Torrington* 595 F Supp 1521 (1984).

[5] To be clear, the court's ruling in the Thurman case did not involve a determination or review of the factual allegations. Rather, the court ruled that Tracey Thurman's factual allegations stated a cause of action under the 14th Amendment, and thus denied the City of Torrington's motion to dismiss.

Key features of VAWA 1994 included 'funding for women's shelters, a national domestic abuse hotline, rape education and prevention programs, and training for federal and state judges' (Schneider 1995: 371). Moreover, VAWA provided for criminal enforcement of interstate orders of protection, reformed laws to better protect immigrant women experiencing domestic violence, and established a federal civil rights remedy to enable victims of gender-based violence to sue their abusers in federal courts. Although the civil remedy, perhaps VAWA's most progressive and innovative provision, was struck down by the US Supreme Court in *US v Morrison*,[6] the other provisions of VAWA 1994 remained intact (Goldfarb 2000).

Two of the most prominent aspects of VAWA have been (1) the amount of money it has funnelled into the criminal justice system, and (2) the funding stream's influence on the development of criminal justice policies regarding domestic violence. Since funding became available in 1996, more than $4 billion in discretionary grants have been awarded under VAWA (Legal Momentum 2016). The majority of these grants continue to encourage 'pro-arrest programs and policies in police departments' at the state, local, and tribal level (Department of Justice, Office of Violence Against Women 2015: 7). In sum, VAWA's funding structure has incentivized a shift towards a more aggressive stance on arrest and prosecution in domestic violence cases.

While VAWA is not without its problems, it has had some positive impacts on how domestic violence is addressed in the US. Notably, the rate of domestic violence homicides dropped considerably during the 'VAWA era', and the rate of non-fatal intimate partner violence declined 53 per cent between 1993 and 2008 (Catalano et al. 2009: 2). For a richer, albeit anecdotal account of how attitudes in the US criminal justice system shifted during this time, consider the transformation in one small county in the middle of the US—Champaign County, Illinois. In 1989, before the revolution leading up to the 'VAWA era', the prosecuting authority's standard procedure in domestic violence cases in this county was to pursue charges if, and only if, the victim fully cooperated in the prosecution. If the victim withdrew her support, prosecutors dismissed charges and frequently adopted a hostile, dismissive attitude toward the victim. In one case where the victim was hospitalized from serious injuries suffered in an exceptionally violent beating by her partner, the prosecutor promptly dismissed the charges when the victim failed to cooperate. The prosecution's motion to dismiss, summarily granted by the trial court, stated:[7]

1. THAT the 'victim' in the above-entitled case is Susan James, 52 years of age.
2. THAT People's Exhibit 1 [depicting the badly battered victim], truly and accurately portrays the physical condition of Susan James on September 17, 1989 at Burnham City Hospital.
3. THAT on September 17, 1989, a Deputy of the Champaign County Sheriff's Office interviewed the 'victim' who claimed that her injuries resulted from being hit in the left eye by the defendant, Thomas Franklin, her live-in boyfriend.

[6] *US v Morrison* 120 S Ct 740 (2000).

[7] The names of the parties have been changed to protect the identity of the victim(s).

4. THAT subsequent to the initial statement, the 'victim' signed People's Exhibit 2 [a sworn statement recounting the battery] in the Champaign County State's Attorney's Office.
5. THAT the 'victim' now claims not to recall what happened to her or what she told the police.
6. THAT the 'victim' either likes being battered or has reconciled with her boyfriend and has therefore chosen to protect the defendant at the expense of her own dignity.
7. THAT, as an officer of the Court, Assistant State's Attorney Janice Blakely cannot endorse the credibility of this 'victim' or condone a further waste of judicial and State resources in the prosecution of this case.

WHEREFORE, the People pray that this Honorable Court dismiss the above-entitled cause.

(Champaign 1989)[8]

Approximately eight years later, after the political, social, and legal revolution of VAWA had taken hold, a strikingly different understanding of the dynamics of domestic violence appeared in Champaign County. At the sentencing of a defendant who had been convicted of his third serious domestic battery against his wife, in violation of a no-contact order, the defendant argued in mitigation that the victim had 'contributed' to the violent episode by agreeing to see him. By 1997, however, this county's criminal justice system was decidedly less hostile to victims. As the court explained:

> Domestic battery presents society and this Court with... [a] complex... multi-faceted problem... and while perhaps it would weigh heavily on this Court's decision if, in a stranger-to-stranger battery, the victim, after being battered, seeks out the perpetrator, that [fact] has much less if any impact on the Court, quite frankly, in the situation of domestic battery... [S]imply because a victim feels compelled by circumstances to accept and even initiate contact with her abuser, quite frankly, doesn't alter the facts of the abuse at all. If anything, perhaps it makes those circumstances more acute and more telling.
>
> (Champaign 1997)

The apparent transformation in attitudes toward domestic violence from the demeaning, ridiculing tone of the 1989 motion to dismiss, to the more empathic, insightful conceptualization of the crime articulated in the 1997 sentencing order, demonstrates the sense in which the 'VAWA era' created palpable and practical change in addressing domestic violence in the US.

This sort of practical change was fuelled in large part by a dramatic increase in empirical research regarding domestic violence—research made possible by funding from VAWA and administered through the National Institute of Justice (NIJ). Crucially, this research was grounded in the belief 'that the expertise needed was frequently outside of NIJ, and so convening a body of experts—researchers, practitioners, and policymakers, along with key government officials—was the route to gaining the most useful ideas, getting buy-in from all stakeholders, and building relationships with potential collaborators' (Auchter and Backes 2013: 717).

More controversially, the Minneapolis Domestic Violence Experiment (Sherman and Berk 1984), discussed above, sparked a shift toward mandatory arrest and

[8] The Champaign County sources were obtained during my time as a prosecutor (Dempsey 2009: 3–6).

'no-drop' prosecution policies throughout the US during the 'VAWA era' (Hanna 1996). In comparison, as 'no-drop' policies were proliferating throughout the US in the late 1990s, the practice in the UK was rare until the mid-2000s (Ellison 2003; Hoyle 2000; see discussion below for possible explanations as to why the UK's move toward so-called 'victimless prosecution' gained momentum in the mid-2000s).

While at least one study found that the formal adoption of 'no-drop' prosecution policies in the US often failed to have any substantial impact on how domestic violence cases were prosecuted (Rebovich 1996: 183), mandatory arrest and 'no-drop' prosecution policies have nonetheless faced considerable criticism, due to the rise in 'dual arrests' of both victim and offender, and concerns that such policies play into what Linda Mills characterizes as the prosecutors' 'impulse to play God' (Mills 2009: 5).[9]

THE PROBLEM OF DUAL ARRESTS

One significant problem with VAWA's encouragement of mandatory arrest policies was the dramatic increase in the number of domestic violence victims subjected to arrest (Dasgupta 2002). When faced with limited discretion to decide whether, or whom, to arrest when called to a 'domestic disturbance', police officers who previously might have left the scene without making any arrests began to arrest anyone who engaged in physical violence. The practice of dual arrest plainly led to an increase in the arrests of women at domestic disturbance calls (Miller 2001), yet it remains unclear what truly motivated these arrests: officers' good faith efforts to implement the new policies, efforts to undermine the potentially radical effect such policies might have if effectively implemented solely against batterers, a genuine inability to differentiate victims from abusers, or a fear of facing a lawsuit if they failed to arrest everyone involved in a domestic altercation (Martin 1997).

In response to the dual arrest problem—and, specifically, the problem of victims being arrested along with, or instead of, the primary batterer—states began to adopt laws that required officers to attempt to identify the 'primary aggressor' in a domestic disturbance. A Missouri statute, for example, instructs officers as follows:

> When an officer makes an arrest he is not required to arrest two parties involved in an assault when both parties claim to have been assaulted. The arresting officer shall attempt to identify and shall arrest the party he believes is the primary physical aggressor. The term 'primary physical aggressor' is defined as the most significant, rather than the first, aggressor. The law enforcement officer shall consider any or all of the following in determining the primary physical aggressor: (1) The intent of the law to protect victims of domestic violence from continuing abuse; (2) The comparative extent of injuries inflicted or serious threats creating fear of physical injury; (3) The history of domestic violence between the persons involved.
>
> (Missouri. Ann. Stat. § 455.085(3) (West))

[9] Indeed, even those researchers who at first recommended a more aggressive criminal justice response to domestic violence soon came to endorse 'victim-directed arrest' and prosecution (Sherman et al. 1992: 256–7). Moreover, recent work by Sherman and Harris has concluded that 'arrests for domestic common assault apparently increased premature death for their victims, especially African-Americans' (2015: 1).

While such laws may ameliorate the harsh effects of mandatory arrest policies resulting in dual arrests, they can prove difficult to implement, and thus, the evidence of their effectiveness in avoiding dual arrests remains 'murky' at best (Miller 2005: 133).

THE PROBLEM OF 'NO-DROP' POLICIES

A related problem identified by commentators regarding the pro-criminalization policies advanced by VAWA concerns 'no-drop' prosecution policies. In jurisdictions with 'no-drop' prosecution policies, a victim's request to dismiss does not necessarily result in dismissal (Dempsey 2009: 3–6). As such, victims are deprived of the opportunity to decide whether and when to engage with the criminal justice system in prosecuting their abuser. Commentators such as Leigh Goodmark have argued forcefully for an approach to domestic violence that allows for greater victim control over the criminal justice response:

> If empowerment is... *the* goal of the battered women's movement, we must accept that women subject to abuse have the right... not to participate in a prosecution that could cause an intimate partner to go to jail, or be deported, or be removed from the family.
>
> (Goodmark 2012: 135, emphasis added)

In previous work, I argued the matter is somewhat more complicated, since victims' stated wishes do not always reflect their genuine views on whether a criminal prosecution should proceed. In cases involving what I called, 'performative withdrawal' by victims, they 'make a public showing of requesting dismissal and/or recanting their statements of abuse in order to appease their abusers'. In some such cases, victims will 'covertly acknowledg[e] to the prosecutors the truth of their original statements of abuse and their continued desire to see their abusers prosecuted'—but in other cases, victims may remain too frightened or intimidated to make their true wishes known (Dempsey 2009: 17–20).

Yet, Goodmark's point is valid. Certainly empowerment is an important goal of the battered women's movement. It is not, however, the only goal. As Goodmark (2012: 134) and I (Dempsey 2009: 220) recognize equally, there are consequential risks of serious harm on both sides of the equation:

> The choices made by women subjected to abuse will certainly have consequences, sometimes overwhelmingly negative consequences, for the women who make them. Some women who ask that their partners not be arrested will be abused again; some will die. Some offenders will be free to abuse again as a result of dismissed prosecutions.
>
> (Goodmark 2012: 134)

The point of weighing these consequences is not to suggest that the state is in a better position to judge these consequences than victims themselves, or that the risk of negative consequences unequivocally trumps the value of empowering women who have experienced abuse. Far from it. Rather, it is simply to observe that consequences matter. To that extent, I take exception both with Goodmark's (2012: 135) suggestion that empowerment is the only goal of the battered women's movement, and with her assumption that the goal of empowering women is necessarily inconsistent with a general policy to prosecute domestic violence without victim support (Dempsey 2009: ch. 9).

However, Goodmark and I do agree about the inadvisability of prosecutors employing so-called 'hard no-drop' policies (Hanna 1996), whereby victims are indiscriminately subpoenaed to testify and the subpoenas are enforced against them if they refuse to appear at trial. Even at the risk of making 'no-drop' policies less effective (ibid), there is wide agreement that the use of such 'hard no-drop' policies tends to undermine the proper goals of domestic violence prosecution. As I have argued previously, 'prosecutorial enforcement measures taken against domestic violence victims to secure their testimony has a tendency to sustain and perpetuate patriarchy and thus defeats the project of feminist prosecutorial action more broadly' (Dempsey 2009: 210). Put somewhat more forcefully by Linda Mills, '[f]eminist political practice—even in the name of gender warfare—should not mimic patriarchy through . . . the use of threat tactics . . .' (Mills 1999: 568).

DOMESTIC VIOLENCE BEYOND CRIMINAL JUSTICE: A 'POST-VAWA ERA'?

While VAWA improved the way domestic violence has been addressed in the US to some extent, it has not been without its problems. While there is hope that some of the problems discussed above may be ameliorated to some extent through criminal justice reforms, a deeper problem remains: VAWA's approach to domestic violence over the past 20 years has been, fundamentally, crime-focused. This fact is reflected in VAWA's funding structure, which funnels vast resources into the criminal justice system at the expense of victim services and civil legal remedies (Bettinger-Lopez et al. 2012).[10]

VAWA's focus on crime control is a result of both an idealistic hope that treating domestic violence as a crime might provide some measure of safety and justice for its victims, and a pragmatic compromise between feminists and conservative crime-control politicians in the early 1990s:

> By aligning themselves with the state, feminist activists in the battered women's movement have had to compromise their political analyses of battering and transform their grassroots activism in to a more state-controlled enterprise . . . Rather than challenging male privilege and prioritizing broad social transformations that would increase women's well-being and make available the resources needed for them to survive away from a violent relationship, the conservative crime-control model sacrifices [such] goals . . . in order to shore up law enforcement powers.
>
> (Miller 2005: 140–1)

[10] VAWA's crime-focused funding programmes (STOP (Services, Training, Officers, Prosecution) and Grants to Encourage Arrest and Enforce Protection Orders) total $295 million, as compared with only $39 million in funding for shelters (Bettinger-Lopez et al. 2012).

In a society where the criminal justice system is merely in need of reform, where feminists are powerful agents of change, and where the tools of the criminal justice system can be used to transform the state and broader community in positive ways, it makes sense to think that a crime-focused approach to domestic violence can prove effective, at least in theory (Dempsey 2009). If, however, a society's criminal justice system is irretrievably unjust—in need of abolition rather than reform—then expanding law enforcement powers will merely serve to reinforce the very structural inequalities that feminists seek to dismantle, the very structural inequalities that sustain and perpetuate domestic violence.[11] The question is, what kind of society is the US—and what role, if any, can its criminal justice system play in ending, rather than perpetuating, these unjust structural inequalities?

Some are rightly concerned that the US criminal justice system may prove irretrievably unjust because crime-control policies during the 'VAWA era' have disproportionately targeted African Americans, establishing what Michelle Alexander characterizes as a 'new racial caste system' through 'mass incarceration' of African Americans (Alexander 2012: 3). The concern here is not only that the US criminal justice system is irretrievably unjust and racist—but, moreover, that VAWA's emphasis on criminal law enforcement to address domestic violence has exacerbated the racially unequal impact of the criminal law. As Beth Richie observes:

> [W]omen of color in the antiviolence movement have [long] warned against investing too heavily in arrest, detention, and prosecution as responses to violence against women. Our warnings have been ignored, and the consequences have been serious: serious for the credibility of the antiviolence movement, serious for feminist organizing by women of color, and, most important, serious for women experiencing gender violence who fall outside of the mainstream.
>
> (Richie 2000: 1136)

Amplifying these concerns, a 2014 conference in Miami, Florida, 'CONVERGE: Reimagining the Movement to End Gender Violence', featuring Beth Richie as keynote speaker, emphasized that the crime-centred approach to addressing domestic violence has largely failed. In its place, the participants at the CONVERGE Conference of 2014 urged the US to address domestic violence through 'innovative strategies ... that are *not* focused on criminal intervention or [at least] are focused on a *reimagined* criminal justice response' (Coker et al. 2015: 254). The key goal of the CONVERGE Conference was to 'change the structural inequalities ... that create and strengthen gender violence':

> Fundamental to that change is to replace the criminal justice system as the default response to gender violence ... [since] the criminal justice response to domestic violence is not only failing to provide satisfying solutions for many people subjected to abuse, but ... is affirmatively harming those it is meant to protect (ibid).

Indeed, several domestic violence victim advocates at the CONVERGE Conference reported they no longer advise women facing an immediately violent confrontation to

[11] To be clear, here I mean to refer to what I have labelled 'domestic violence in its strong sense' (Dempsey 2007, 2009: ch. 6).

'call 911', since criminal law enforcement interventions often proved 'more dangerous than the immediate threat posed by an abusive partner' (ibid).

The CONVERGE Conference marked an important turning point in the US response to domestic violence: one that may ultimately prove as impactful as Seneca Falls Convention of 1848. The key paradigm shift urged by conference participants echoes a growing recognition in the US: criminal law enforcement is ill-suited to addressing domestic violence and the structural inequalities upon which it is grounded. In rejecting a state-centred, crime-control focused approach to domestic violence, the US is witnessing a resurgence of grassroots progressive activism, which makes opposition to mass incarceration central to its commitments and work (Coker and Macquoid 2015), and promises to reimagine whether the criminal justice system should play a lead role in addressing domestic violence in the US in the future.

In closing, it is worth asking why the US is shifting away from criminal law responses to domestic violence (Kohn 2010), while criminal prosecution remains the default response in the UK (CPS 2015). Two points may partially explain the difference. First, since the hearsay exceptions enacted in the Criminal Justice Act 2003 (especially sections 114 and 116) came into effect, it has become increasingly easy to prosecute domestic violence cases without the victim's cooperation in the UK. In comparison, since the US Supreme Court decision in *Crawford v Washington*,[12] it has become increasingly difficult for such prosecutions to take place in the US. Second, the increasing political will to end (or at least reduce) 'mass incarceration' in the US (Alexander 2012) has gained some political traction (Hulse and Steinhauer 2015)—making criminal justice solutions to social justice problems far less attractive than they once appeared (Coker and Macquoid 2015). While, perhaps because it has not experienced US levels of mass incarceration (Walmsley 2015), recent policy initiatives in England have focused on prison reform rather than alternatives to imprisonment (BBC 2016). Thus, while the emergence of domestic violence as a criminal justice concern took similar paths in the US and UK during its early decades, it seems possible the US and UK approaches may be growing ever more distant: with the UK increasing the range of domestic violence subject to criminal penalty in the Serious Crime Act 2015, and the US shifting even further away from the criminal justice system as the default response to domestic violence.

REFERENCES

Alexander, M. (2012), *The New Jim Crow: Mass Incarceration in the Age of Colorblindness*, New York: The New Press.

Auchter, B. and Backes, B.L. (2013), 'NIJ's Program of Domestic Violence Research Collaborative Efforts to Build Knowledge Guided by Safety For Victims and Accountability of Perpetrators', *Violence Against Women*, 19, 6: 713–36.

BBC (2016), 'Prisons "overhaul" announced by David Cameron', *BBC News*, 8 February 2016, available at: http://www.bbc.com/news/uk-35518477.

[12] *Crawford v Washington* 541 US 36 (2004).

Bettinger-Lopez, C., Coker, D., Goldscheid, J., Goodmark, L., Kalei Kanuha, V., Ptacek, J., Weissman, D. (2012), *VAWA Is Not Enough: Academics Speak Out about VAWA*, available at: http://blogs.law.columbia.edu/genderandsexualitylawblog/2012/02/28/vawa-is-not-enough-academics-speak-out-about-vawa.

Buzawa, E.S. and Buzawa, C.G. (2002), *Domestic Violence: The Criminal Justice Response*, 3rd edn, Thousand Oaks, CA: Sage.

Catalano, S., Smith, E., Snyder, H., and Rand, M. (2009), *Female Victims of Violence*, Washington, DC: US Bureau of Justice Statistics.

Champaign County, Illinois (1989), Motion to Dismiss, on file with author.

Champaign County, Illinois (1997), Transcript of Proceedings, on file with author.

Coker, D. and Macquoid, A. (2015), 'Why Opposing Hyper-Incarceration Should Be Central to the Work of the Anti-Domestic Violence Movement', *University of Miami Race & Social Justice Law Review*, 5: 585–618.

Coker, D., Goodmark, L., and Olivo, M. (2015), 'CONVERGE! Reimagining the Movement to End Gender Violence', *University of Miami Race & Social Justice Law Review*, 5, 2: 249–56.

CPS (2015), *Violence Against Women and Girls Crime Report (2014–2015)*, London: Crown Prosecution Service.

DAIP (2016), *Duluth Abuse Intervention Project*, http://www.duluth-model.org.

Dasgupta, S.D. (2002), 'A Framework for Understanding Women's Use of Nonlethal Violence in Intimate Heterosexual Relationships', *Violence Against Women*, 8, 11: 1364–89.

Dempsey, M.M. (2007), 'What Counts as Domestic Violence?: A Conceptual Analysis', *William and Mary Journal of Women and the Law*, 12, 2: 301–33.

Dempsey, M.M. (2009), *Prosecuting Domestic Violence*, Oxford: Oxford University Press.

Department of Justice, Office of Violence Against Women, (2015), *OVW Fiscal Year 2015 Grants to Encourage Arrest Policies and Enforcement of Protection Orders Program Solicitation*, Washington, DC: Department of Justice.

Dobash, R.E. and Dobash, R. (1979), *Violence Against Wives: A Case Against the Patriarchy*, New York: Free Press.

Ellison, L. (2003), 'Prosecuting Domestic Violence without Victim Participation', *Modern Law Review*, 65, 6: 834–58.

Fagan, J. (1996), *The Criminalization of Domestic Violence: Promises and Limits. National Institutes of Justice Research Report*, Washington, DC: National Institutes of Justice.

Garner, J., Fagan, J., and Maxwell, C. (1995), 'Published Findings from the Spouse Assault Replication Program: A Critical Review', *Journal of Quantitative Criminology*, 11, 1: 3–28.

Goldfarb, S. (2000), 'No Civilized System of Justice: The Fate of the Violence Against Women Act', *West Virginia Law Review*, 102, 3: 499–546.

Goodmark, L. (2012), *A Troubled Marriage: Domestic Violence and the Legal System*, New York: NYU Press.

Hanna, C. (1996), 'No Right to Choose: Mandated Victim Participation in Domestic Violence Prosecutions', *Harvard Law Review*, 109, 8: 1849–910.

Hoyle, C. (2000), *Negotiating Domestic Violence*, Oxford: Oxford University Press.

Hoyle, C. and Sanders, A. (2000), 'Police Response to Domestic Violence', *British Journal of Criminology*, 40, 1: 14–36.

Hulse, C. and Steinhauer, J. (2015), 'Sentencing Overhaul Proposed in Senate with Bipartisan Backing', *New York Times*, 1 October 2015.

Johnson, M.P. (1995) 'Patriarchal Terrorism and Common Couple Violence: Two Forms of Violence against Women', *Journal of Marriage and the Family*, 57, 2: 283–94.

Kohn, L. (2010), 'What's So Funny about Peace, Love and Understanding? Restorative Justice as a New Paradigm for Domestic Violence Intervention', *Seton Hall L. Rev.*, 40, 2: 517–95.

Legal Momentum (2016), *History of the Violence Against Women Act*, available at: https://www.legalmomentum.org/history-vawa#sthash.wLsJCPAW.dpuf.

Martin, M.E. (1997), 'Double Your Trouble: Dual Arrest in Family Violence', *Journal of Family Violence*, 12, 2: 139–57.

Miller, S.L. (2001), 'The Paradox of Women Arrested for Domestic Violence: Criminal Justice Professionals and Service Providers Respond', *Violence Against Women*, 7, 12: 1339–76.

Miller, S. (2005), *Victims as Offenders: The Paradox of Women's Violence in Relationships*, New Brunswick, NJ: Rutgers University Press.

Mills, L.G. (1999), 'Killing Her Softly: Intimate Abuse and the Violence of State Intervention', *Harvard Law Review*, 113, 2: 550–613.

Mills, L.G. (2009), *Insult to Injury: Rethinking our Responses to Intimate Abuse*, Princeton, NJ: Princeton University Press.

NCDSV (2016), 'Wheels Adapted from the Power and Control Wheel Model', National Center on Domestic and Sexual Violence Website, http://www.ncdsv.org/publications_wheel.html.

Pence, E. and Paymar, M. (1993), *Power and Control: Tactics of Men who Batter*, Duluth, MN: Domestic Abuse Intervention Program.

Pizzey, E. (1974), *Scream Quietly or the Neighbors Will Hear*, Harmondsworth: Penguin Publishing.

Rebovich, D.J. (1996), 'Prosecution Response to Domestic Violence: Results of a Survey of Large Jurisdictions', in E. Buzawa and C. Buzawa (eds), *Do Arrests and Restraining Orders Work?*, Thousand Oaks, CA: Sage: 176–91.

Richie, B.E. (2000), 'A Black Feminist Reflection on the Antiviolence Movement', *Signs*, 25, 4: 1133–7.

Schmidt, J.D. and Sherman, L.W. (1996), 'Does Arrest Deter Domestic Violence?', in E. Buzawa and C. Buzawa (eds), *Do Arrests and Restraining Orders Work?*, Thousand Oaks, CA; Sage: 43–53.

Schneider, E.M. (1995), 'Introduction: The Promise of the Violence Against Women Act of 1994', *Journal of Law and Policy*, 4, 2: 371–6.

Schneider, E.M. (2008), *Battered Women and Feminist Lawmaking*, New Haven, CT: Yale University Press.

Sherman, L.W. and Berk, R.A. (1984), 'The Specific Deterrent Effects of Arrest for Domestic Assault', *American Sociological Review*, 49, 2: 261–72.

Sherman, L.W. and Harris, H.M. (2015), 'Increased Death Rates of Domestic Violence Victims from Arresting vs. Warning Suspects in the Milwaukee Domestic Violence Experiment (MilDVE)', *Journal of Experimental Criminology*, 11, 1: 1–20.

Sherman, L.W., Schmidt, J.D., and Rogan, D.P. (1992), *Policing Domestic Violence: Experiments and Dilemmas*, New York: Free Press.

Somanader, T. (2014), *'Even One Case Is Too Many': Vice President Biden Marks the 20th Anniversary of the Violence Against Women Act*, available at: https://www.whitehouse.gov/blog/2014/09/09/.

Stark, E. (2007), *Coercive Control: How Men Entrap Women in Personal Life*, Oxford: Oxford University Press.

Steinmetz, S.K. (1977), 'The Battered Husband Syndrome', *Victimology*, 2, 3–4: 499–509.

Straus, M.M.A., Gelles, R.J., and Steinmetz, S.K. (eds) (1980), *Behind Closed Doors: Violence in the American Family*, New Brunswick, NJ: Transaction Publishers.

Various (2015), 'Symposium: CONVERGE! Reimagining the Movement to End Gender Violence', *University of Miami Race & Social Justice Law Review*, 5, 2: 249–671.

Walmsley, R. (2015), *World Prison Population List*, London: Institute for Criminal Policy Research.

Whitebread, C.H., Heilman, J., and Zeisel, H. (1984), 'Increasing Our Effectiveness against Crime: Expanding the Limits of Law Enforcement', *Yale Law Journal*, 93, 7: 1339–413.

18

ADOLESCENT TO PARENT VIOLENCE AND THE CHALLENGE FOR YOUTH JUSTICE

Rachel Condry and Caroline Miles

This chapter examines violence committed by adolescents towards their parents and the way in which it is managed within the youth justice system. It shows how adolescent to parent violence (APV) has only recently been recognized by British policy makers and the public. Academic research, including the first UK large-scale study by members of the Centre for Criminology at the University of Oxford (Condry and Miles 2014), has contributed to this recognition. Drawing on this research, this chapter explores the place of APV within youth justice work and the views of youth justice practitioners.

Since the nineteenth century there have been a raft of legislative and policy developments in youth justice in the UK. However, most have only recognized the young person as an offender *outside* the home. Crimes within the home have remained relatively hidden from view. At the same time, there has been a growth in understanding of, and responses to, other forms of intra-familial crime and violence. Under these circumstances, it is worth reflecting on why it has taken so long for violence from young people towards their parents to be recognized by the youth justice system in England and Wales.

WHAT DO WE KNOW ABOUT APV?

Offences committed by young people within the home can include criminal damage, theft, and more rarely sexual offences. APV ranges in severity, from lower level physical assault such as pushing, throwing objects, slapping, pinching, or pulling hair, to punching, pushing down stairs, and threatening or assaulting with knives and other weapons. APV rarely involves a single isolated incident, and is more likely to include a pattern of sustained behaviour across time. It usually has a profound impact upon the parent victim.

A body of international research has attempted to gauge the extent of the problem of APV, but tends to vary in how it defines the problem, the age, and relationship parameters. There is considerable methodological variation. Some studies use criminal justice datasets of incidents reported to the police (e.g. Evans and Warren-Sohlberg 1988; Howard 2011; Kethineni 2004; Routt and Anderson 2011; Snyder and McCurley 2008; Strom et al. 2010; Walsh and Kreinert 2007, 2009) while other studies utilize self-report data from large, often dated, retrospective datasets (e.g. Agnew and Huguley 1989; Brezina 1999; Calvete et al. 2013a, 2013b; Ibabe et al. 2013; Kratcoski 1985; Pagani et al. 2004; Peek et al. 1985; Ulman and Straus 2003). As a result, estimates of the extent of APV vary widely, from 7 per cent (Peek et al. 1985) to 21 per cent of families in the US (Kratcoski 1985) and 21 per cent of families in Spain (Ibabe et al. 2013).

Smaller, qualitative studies of APV tend to focus on its aetiology and the impact of the violence and abuse upon parents (e.g. Bobic 2004; Cotrell and Monk 2004; Eckstein 2004; Gallagher 2004; Howard and Rottem 2008; Jackson 2003; Stewart et al. 2007). These accounts find multiple, contextual circumstances in families experiencing APV, which go beyond notions of power and control associated with more conventional domestic violence theories. Cottrell and Monk's (2004) research in Canada, for example, identifies a variety of pathways including socialization of male power, previous history of victimization and/or witnessing domestic violence, poverty, parenting styles, peer influences, mental health problems, and substance abuse problems. These studies demonstrate that existing theories of family violence are insufficient for explaining the complexity of APV and its causes.

While research on APV in the UK is under-developed, there have been a number of studies that have reported evidence of it in interviews, while broader parenting surveys suggest that many parents experience violence from their children (Biehal 2012; Browne and Hamilton 1998; Holt 2009; Hunter et al. 2010; Mirrlees-Black et al. 1996; Parentline Plus 2008, 2010; Smith et al. 1992). Specific studies of APV in the UK have almost all been published since 2009. This literature has recognized the difficulty of locating APV within existing policy frameworks and has opened a debate over how best to respond to it (e.g. Holt 2009; Holt and Retford 2012; Hunter et al. 2010; Hunter and Piper 2012; Nixon 2012; Wilcox 2012).

THE OXFORD APV STUDY

Our own research, funded by a grant by the Economic and Social Research Council for 2010–13, sought to map the contours of APV, and to explore how it was being addressed within criminal justice and how families managed the problem. In 2008, when our study began, APV did not appear at all in any government policy. It was not the concern of domestic violence organizations, and had not been the subject of criminological research in the UK. There were no specialist programmes and no guidance for practitioners working with these families.

The Oxford study was the first major criminological study of APV in the UK. We deployed a range of methods including statistical analysis of Metropolitan Police data;

analysis of 100 police case files across two police force areas; and 117 in-depth interviews with parents, adolescents, police officers, youth justice workers, and expert practitioners, all of whom had encountered APV.

Prior to our study, there were no official data available on APV in the UK. Because of the restrictive definition of domestic violence, APV was not 'flagged' in police databases, making it a complex process to uncover and analyse cases. No other services—including youth justice—had counted the cases they managed.

As a first step in estimating the size of the problem, we analysed data provided by the Metropolitan Police over a one-year period from April 2009 to March 2010, finding 1,892 incidents of violence from adolescents (aged 13–19) towards their parents had been reported to the police—and defined as offences—across the thirty-three London Boroughs. Within these recorded cases, 66 per cent were son-to-mother violence, 87 per cent of suspects were male, and 77 per cent of victims were female. However, it should be noted that these figures might also represent reporting patterns rather than actual patterns of experience. That said, our findings suggest that APV—like other forms of family violence—is gendered (see Condry and Miles 2014).

Other methods deployed in the study included interviews with experts and practitioners, and with parents and adolescents, across the country. In addition to youth justice case workers, we interviewed expert practitioners working across a variety of community-based support, training, and consultancy services including a domestic violence helpline, a children's Independent Domestic Violence Advocacy (IDVA) service, a clinical psychology forensic service, parenting support services, training services for domestic violence support workers, and a number of independent charities specializing in APV and other forms of family violence. These interviews helped us to understand more about the ways in which APV is experienced by families, how it is conceptualized and responded to in the UK, and its place within criminal justice.

From our interviews we found that parents experiencing violence from their children find it very difficult to get support. There are only a handful of very small, localized programmes that specifically address APV across the UK. Parents in our study described their desperate search for help, often over several years. Many felt that their plight had been ignored or misunderstood. Parents also found it very hard to speak up about abuse from their own child. They experienced stigma and shame. Many felt as if they were to blame for their child's actions. Such factors suggest that cases reported to the police represent the tip of the iceberg of this form of family violence.

Most parents did not report their child to the police, for fear of the consequences for their child. Furthermore, there are few escape routes for parents experiencing APV. Most of the routes available to victims of intimate partner violence are not appropriate in this situation. A parent is very unlikely, for example, to move away from the child into a refuge and break all ties with that child.

Why children are violent towards their parents is complex. Their actions need to be understood in terms of a variety of factors including psychological development, cultural acceptability, and the specifics of individual cases and range of pathways that lead to the problem. As with all crime, there is no one simple explanation. Parents described a range of other difficulties in which they sought to locate the source of the violence, including substance abuse, mental health problems, learning difficulties, previous family history of domestic violence, and self-harm. There were some families, however, who could not explain why the violence had happened. They had raised other children who had not displayed any of the same problems and were at a loss to know why this had happened in their family.

Finally, APV is a problem that stretches across the social spectrum in society. Some of the families in our study were struggling on benefits and in overcrowded housing, while others had professional jobs and high incomes. This may be even more of a hidden problem for families who can afford to seek private therapeutic interventions.

THE POLICY CONTEXT

One reason why APV has received such scant attention from policy makers is that until 2013, the official definition of domestic violence only applied to perpetrators over the age of 18 (Condry and Miles 2012). In 2013, a new definition came into effect which lowered this age to 16 (Home Office 2013). Perpetrators under 16 remain excluded.

The problem of APV was included in the government-led 'Violence against Women and Girls' (VAWG) strategy, which aims to reduce domestic violence and abuse. The 2014 'VAWG action plan' incorporated an objective to improve local services for domestic violence and abuse victims through developing and disseminating 'information for practitioners working with children and families on how to identify and address the risks posed by adolescent to parent violence' (Home Office 2014: 27).

The Home Office has now published a comprehensive information guide for practitioners across a range of services with advice on how to respond to 'adolescent to parent violence and abuse' (Home Office 2015a). APV has, therefore, only become visible in government policy through its inclusion in the primarily adult-focused domestic violence and abuse agenda (Miles and Condry 2015). APV might potentially increase in prominence with the new offence of 'controlling or coercive behaviour in an intimate or family relationship' under section 76 of the Serious Crime Act 2015, which could potentially be applied to anyone over the age of 10 years old (Home Office 2015b: 9).

The government's VAWG agenda has a specific, gendered discourse of adult-perpetrated domestic violence with clear demarcations of female victim and male offender status. As we have seen, APV is a gendered problem—yet 23 per cent of victims in the cases reported to the Metropolitan Police were male and 13 per cent of perpetrators were female (Condry and Miles 2014), so it is not exclusively a male to female phenomenon. Co-opting APV into this agenda has provided one way to understand the victim status of the parent, through the discourse of women's patriarchal victimization by men. While this view of violence might have utility for recognizing its harm, it pays little attention to the youth of the perpetrator and the specific status of the parent–child relationship. These matters are better understood in the youth justice system.

WHY HAS APV BEEN OVERLOOKED IN THE YOUTH JUSTICE SYSTEM?

All the youth justice practitioners that we spoke to during our research described APV as a matter they routinely encountered in their work. Most could identify families experiencing this form of family violence in their current caseload. One expert in adolescents and domestic violence from a third-sector organization who trains practitioners from a range of fields, including youth justice, reported that she was increasingly being asked for information about APV:

> [Practitioners attending the courses] say that they get so many calls every day, about child to parent violence. And loads of social workers are reporting that's the big issue that they're working on. But no-one really knows how to respond to it, because it doesn't neatly fall into the definition of domestic violence. So I think there's a real gap still in the knowledge around how to deal with it.

The Youth Justice Board (YJB) has begun to address the problem of APV—the Home Office guidance has been sent to every youth offending team in the country—and, at the time of writing, it is considering whether there is anything further that might be done to address the problem. The YJB has also been involved in the production of the Home Office's information guide, records examples of good practice in local responses to APV in its online Effective Practice Library, and has hosted a session discussing APV at its national conference.

Yet, despite the first-hand experience of those who work with young people and their families, APV has taken a long time to come to the fore in youth justice and it still cannot be said to be firmly on the policy agenda. Why might this be so? A number of factors are likely to have contributed to this: underreporting; the exclusion from the official definition of domestic violence and indeed a lack of recognition in any area of government policy; the fact that it falls between the cracks of different services; the dearth of academic research and evidence from the UK; and the absence of an interest group lobbying for its recognition. The restructuring of the youth justice system around the turn of the millennium and the sheer weight of policy issues clamouring for attention and requiring a clearly defined response have also made it difficult for specialist issues to emerge.

Powerful constructions of young people and their parents have held sway in the youth justice system in recent decades and may also have contributed to the lack of policy interest in APV. The youth justice system holds in tension two key principles of welfare and justice (McAlister and Carr 2014; Muncie 2006). At different points in time, the balance between these principles shifts. Yet what remains constant is the construction of young people as offenders outside the home—rather than within it—and as young people lacking in parental control and guidance.

When the Centre for Criminology was established in 1966, youth justice was in the early years of a more progressive and welfare-focused phase. In 1963 the Children and Young Persons Act introduced, among other measures, a rise in the age of criminal responsibility to 10 years old. In 1964, a Labour government came to power, bringing a series of developments that led to a radical rethink of the youth court and youth justice (Gelsthorpe and Morris 1994). Particularly significant was the 1969 Children and Young Persons Act which aimed to decriminalize, to divert, and reduce the number of juveniles appearing before the youth court, and to deinstitutionalize, abolishing borstals and detention centres. The youth court was to become a welfare-providing institution and also one of last resort (ibid).

So it was that, in the second half of the 1960s, in the early years of the Centre, the welfare principle came to prominence. As was described (ibid), the 1969 Act was never fully implemented and welfare measures were added to more punitive measures rather than replacing them, a compromise that sometimes led to the punitive and welfare systems colliding. In the 1970s there was an increase in the use of custody for young offenders—and though this was also alongside the increased use of diversion, the balance tipped again and more punitive measures came to dominate. The rhetoric of the Conservative government in the 1980s directly attacked the welfare perspective, though diversion continued to expand.

1997 brought a New Labour government and with it a raft of reforms that completely restructured the youth justice system and established the YJB and a youth offending team in every local authority. Despite these political and social measures and ebbs and flows in perceptions of and responses to youth offenders, youth offending has always been understood as something that happens outside of the home, and parents—even in families deemed in need of welfare interventions—as responsible agents who should be able to control their child. The parent-as-victim was not visible in legislative or policy developments through these decades.

In the contemporary context, much of youth justice policy and practice has been devolved to the local level and on many topics the YJB provides guidance but not instruction to youth offending teams. Youth offending teams control their own budgets—at a time of austerity and significant cuts to services—which includes determining which projects should receive investment. As a result, the provision of support for families experiencing APV is patchy at best, and programmes that directly address the problem of APV are still relatively few in number. Although APV is now on the radar of youth justice policy makers and service providers, there is still little consistent, coordinated response. The support families receive depends very much on where they live.

There is a long history within youth justice of parents being held accountable for their children's behaviour through measures such as fines, which stands in stark contrast to understanding a parent as a victim of their child's actions. This has strengthened in recent decades with a focus on 'problem families' and a 'parenting deficit' as a cause of youth offending under the New Labour administration of 1997–2010 and in the years since. Throughout this period, a new body of knowledge, and ways of talking and thinking about parenting developed which constructed parents of young offenders and parent–child relationships in very particular ways. Specifically, parents who were thought to be shirking their responsibilities could be made to control their children through measures such as Parenting Orders. As Muncie has argued, this ultimately resulted in criminalizing 'inadequate parenting' (Muncie 1999) and in an individualized analysis which failed to take account of structural inequalities. At the centre of New Labour's youth justice strategy there was: 'a familiar analysis of family breakdown, poor parental control, failing child rearing practices and a dependency culture' (Muncie, 2002) despite repeated research findings that young people in trouble with the law have complex and systematic patterns of disadvantage which lie beyond any incitement to find work, behave properly, or take up the 'new opportunities' on offer (Muncie 2006: 781).

Henricson and Bainham point to the way in which these measures overestimate the ability of parents to control adolescent children: 'the attribution of blame to parents for their children's behaviour up to the age of 16 underestimates children's independence and overestimates the ability of parents to control the behaviour of young people as they grow older' (2005: 103).

Constructions of parental accountability have continued through various measures aimed at parents under the subsequent Conservative-Liberal Democrat coalition and the Conservative administration. The Troubled Families initiative, launched under the Coalition government in 2011 and extended under the current government, has been criticized for continuing to promote a focus on negligent parents who fail to take responsibility (Collins et al. 2014).

As Arthur (2005) has argued, the continuing assumption underlying legal instruments like the Parenting Order is that parents of young offenders have not accepted responsibility and that they can be forced to do so with court orders and financial penalties. These assumptions are particularly problematic in the case of parents being victimized by their adolescent children. One mother we interviewed described how she was vividly aware of the expectation that she ought to be able to control her 14-year-old son and that she would be held responsible for his actions, despite the fact he regularly assaulted her. She had already been taken to court and fined for his non-attendance at school and was terrified that she was at risk of receiving a prison sentence. She kept letters and other records to try to prove that she was doing all she could, including her attempts to force him to get out of bed in the morning to go to school:

> I'm dead scared of being taken back to court... Everything I've tried, it don't work... I've tried pulling him out of bed, I've tried splashing water on his face, I've dragged him out the front door with boxer shorts on and just threw his clothes at him, and nothing has worked. He'll just lay in bed, and when he gets up, he'll sit there wrapped in a quilt watching TV.

It should also be noted that although the language of youth justice is gender-neutral, it is primarily mothers who receive parenting support in the youth justice system and mothers who are given Parenting Orders (Drakeford and Calliva 2009), although there may be practical reasons for this gendered focus in families headed by single mothers, or in circumstances where the mother is the primary carer. However, such policies also entrench enduring assumptions about maternal responsibility and perceptions of mothers as the guardians of family morality. Hunter and Nixon (2001) have shown how gender intersects with responses to the problem of anti-social behaviour, which they say has not been acknowledged by either policy makers or practitioners. Women are more likely to be the recipients of such measures, despite most of the behaviour being committed by men. They are, in this way, routinely blamed for their failure to discipline their wayward sons or partners. At the same time, as we have seen above, women are also more likely to be the victims of violence from their adolescent children.

The politics of blame and culpability are complex in APV and categories of 'victim' and 'offender' may not be clearly defined. Parents experiencing APV can be described as 'paradoxical victims' (Condry 2016). They do elicit sympathy on occasions and there were examples in our study of kindness and supportive actions from friends and family. However, sympathy was often drowned out—or at the very least muffled—by blame. We have seen how parents can be made legally accountable for their children's deviant behaviour, and moral accountability and judgement from others can be strong. Parents often described feeling isolated from friends or other family members and a lack of understanding about the problem of APV in their everyday lives. This may partly be because parents can be reluctant to speak out, given the stigma and shame associated with this problem, as this youth justice worker explained:

> So stigmatizing, isn't it, for them? Because…They, if they tell their family or friends, they don't really get it. And it's a bit like, 'why are you putting up with that? Why don't you do [this]?' Yeah, so there's no empathy about what they're actually experiencing.
>
> (Youth justice worker 12)

In the case of APV, parents may be held accountable for behaviour of which they are also the victim. They are therefore paradoxical victims, condemned for their failures while simultaneously suffering often quite significant harm. Powerful countervailing constructions of parental accountability and the paradoxical victim status of parents have left little room for the problem of APV to emerge and may continue to stymie the prospect of a systematic youth justice response to APV.

WHAT WOULD A COHERENT YOUTH JUSTICE RESPONSE TO APV LOOK LIKE?

Youth justice practitioners report that APV occurs frequently in their work with young people and their families. Some young people are prosecuted for violence towards their parents but APV also emerges in work with other young people who are in the system after other kinds of offences. APV is a complex phenomenon and requires a focused and specific response that keeps the age of the adolescent and their kin relationship—as the child of the victim—firmly in focus.

There is considerable criticism of the age of criminal responsibility in England and Wales. A strong case exists that it should be raised on a number of grounds including capacity, human rights, incompatibility with other countries in Europe and elsewhere, social harm, and the need to ensure best outcomes for children in conflict with the law and the wider community (Goldson 2013). Such matters are relevant for thinking about how best to respond to APV.

Children who commit crimes of familial violence should not be held accountable in the same way as adult perpetrators. Their circumstances are different—their histories and the explanations for why they have become violent, their adolescent developing brains and level of maturity, and the more positive prospect as they mature into adulthood that they might actually grow out of violence—all the more likely with the use of diversionary processes in youth justice and with support and appropriate intervention. It may therefore be apposite to employ diversionary measures such as a caution if a child is arrested for violence towards their parent.

A child who is violent towards a parent will have shared a history with the victim. At one point, the child will have been completely dependent upon the parent for their very existence, needing the parent to provide care in order to survive. Gradually some independence will have developed as the child slowly begins to separate from the parent during adolescence. In 'normal' or non-violent circumstances the adolescent child will remain dependent on the parent, though to a diminishing degree, and the parent will retain control of finances, important decisions, and so on, and this might be pictured as a continuous negotiation across the years until the child finally becomes an independent adult. In the case of APV something might be awry with this process and the balance of power can look quite different.

Families experiencing APV may have complex histories. In some families there may be a history of previous violence. A child might have witnessed domestic violence and seen his or her parent (often the mother) as a victim in the past. Children might themselves have experienced violence either from the parent who is now the victim, or from another adult in the family, or might have experienced sexual abuse, or neglect. Children might be violent towards a parent in defence, or to protect a non-violent parent. The violence might also be explained by other factors such as emerging mental health problems, learning difficulties, substance abuse, and so on.

In light of these complexities, interventions for families experiencing APV therefore need to be designed to take account of these complex histories. Practitioners and experts in our study frequently spoke of the need for programmes specifically tailored to address the problem of APV. Cognitive behavioural parenting programmes that focus on changing a parent's responses to an adolescent child in situ are not able to address the particular dynamics of APV and what might be deep-rooted problems, as one consultant psychologist working within youth justice explained:

> So I think you need a much more unique family-focused approach. You know, there's not a 'one size fits all'. And that's the difficulty with your Triple P parenting [programmes] and things like that; they're not really taking into account family history, family structure, how it operates. All those things are coming down over the generations. [These programmes are] saying 'This is a behaviour that needs to be changed. If you change the contingencies, you change the behaviour'. And that of course doesn't happen.

In his experience, parents experiencing APV were often exhausted and at 'breaking point' and some of the changes demanded by these programmes required considerable personal resources:

> What's really interesting for me is that in the cases that we do tend to see it is often the mums in the families who are completely burnt out, you know. And so the strategy, and what people are trying to teach them—to be consistent, to sort of be doing the same thing all the time, to apply the same strategies—they can't do it. They just can't, you

know, they get too tired, they just, you know, over time it just degrades to a position where actually the intervention is no longer any use, because they just can't maintain it.

Parents experiencing violence therefore need their own support, which is unlikely to be met through generic parenting programmes within youth justice. Interventions for families experiencing APV will need to be designed to assist parents in safety planning and responding to violent episodes; explore and address the reasons underlying the violence; and help young people to specifically address their use of violence in family relationships and their understanding of domestic abuse.

There are some excellent examples of programmes that achieve these aims in novel ways. Break 4 Change in Brighton and Hove, for example, was created from a partnership between youth justice and domestic violence services. It works with both parents and young people from families experiencing APV in separate groups that take place in the same building but with their own facilitators and programme of work. The young people's group has a creative focus and the programme uses a film dialogue process that enables communication between young people and parents. However, these specific programmes are few and far between—in many local authorities, specific responses to APV are non-existent and work within youth offending teams with families experiencing APV is on an ad hoc, case-by-case basis.

There is, therefore, a need to provide specifically tailored support to parents experiencing APV in every youth offending service in the country. These programmes should take account of the complex circumstances of families experiencing APV and should connect with other services outside of criminal justice to ensure a multi-agency approach and the possibility of early intervention. Now that the problem of APV has been recognized in the youth justice system, the challenge will be to tailor specific interventions—in a time of austerity and cuts—that keep the youth of the perpetrator in the foreground, capitalize where possible on potential opportunities to divert the young person from criminalization, and address the complex histories of families experiencing this form of violence.

REFERENCES

AGNEW, R. and HUGULEY, S. (1989), 'Adolescent Violence toward Parents', *Journal of Marriage and the Family*, 51, 3: 699–711.

ARTHUR, R. (2005), 'Punishing Parents for the Crimes of Their Children', *The Howard Journal*, 44, 3: 233–53.

BIEHAL, N. (2012), 'Parent Abuse by Young People on the Edge of Care: A Child Welfare Perspective', *Social Policy and Society*, 11, 2: 251–63.

BOBIC, N. (2004), 'Adolescent Violence towards Parents', *Australian Domestic and Family Violence Clearinghouse*, Topic Paper: 1–15.

BREZINA, T. (1999), 'Teenage Violence toward Parents as an Adaption to Family Strain: Evidence from a National Survey of Adolescent Males', *Youth and Society*, 30, 4: 416–44.

BROWNE, K.D. and HAMILTON, C.E. (1998), 'Physical Violence between Young Adults and their Parents: Associations with a History of Child Maltreatment', *Journal of Family Violence*, 13, 1: 59–79.

Calvete, E., Orue, I., and Gamez-Gaudix, M. (2013a), 'Child-to-Parent Violence: Emotional and Behavioural Predictors, *Journal of Interpersonal Violence*, 28, 4: 755–72.

Calvete, E., Gamez-Gaudiz, M., Orue, I., Gonzalez-Diez, Z., Lopez de Arroyabe, E., Sampedro, R., Pereria, R., Zubizarreta, A., and Borrajo, E. (2013b), 'Brief Report: The Adolescent Child-to-Parent Aggression Questionnaire: An Examination of Aggression against Parents in Spanish Adolescents', *Journal of Adolescence*, 36, 6: 1077–81.

Collins, A., Cox, J., and Leonard, A. (2014), '"I Blame the Parents": Analysing Popular Support for the Deficient Household Social Capital Transmission Thesis', *The Howard Journal of Criminal Justice*, 54, 2: 135–56.

Condry, R. (2016 forthcoming), 'The Parent as Paradoxical Victim: Adolescent to Parent Violence and Contested Victimization', in D. Spencer and S. Walklate (eds), *Reconceptualizing Critical Victimology: Interventions and Possibilities*, Lanham, MD: Lexington Books.

Condry, R. and Miles, C. (2012), 'Adolescent to Parent Violence and Youth Justice in England and Wales', *Social Policy & Society*, 11, 2: 241–50.

Condry, R. and Miles, C. (2014), 'Adolescent to Parent Violence: Framing and Mapping a Hidden Problem', *Criminology and Criminal Justice*, 14, 3: 257–75.

Cottrell, B. and Monk, P. (2004), 'Adolescent to Parent Abuse: A Qualitative Overview of Common Themes', *Journal of Family Issues*, 25, 8: 1072–95.

Drakeford, M. and Calliva, K. (2009), 'Working with Parents in the Youth Justice System: Compulsory Help and "Doing Good"', *Practice*, 21, 4: 215–27.

Eckstein, N. (2004), 'Emergent Issues in Families Experiencing Adolescent-to-Parent Abuse', *Western Journal of Communication*, 68, 4: 365–88.

Evans, E.D. and Warren-Sohlberg, L. (1988), 'A Pattern Analysis of Adolescent Abusive Behaviour towards Parents', *Journal of Adolescent Research*, 3, 2: 201–16.

Gallagher, E. (2004), 'Parents Victimised by their Children', *Australian and New Zealand Journal of Family Therapy*, 25, 1: 1–12.

Gelsthorpe, L. and Morris, A. (1994), 'Juvenile Justice 1945–1992', in M. Maguire, R. Morgan, and R. Reiner (eds), *The Oxford Handbook of Criminology*, Oxford: Clarendon Press.

Goldson, B. (2013), '"Unsafe, Unjust and Harmful to Wider Society": Grounds for Raising the Minimum Age of Criminal Responsibility in England and Wales', *Youth Justice*, 13, 2: 111–30.

Henricson, C. and Bainham, A. (2005), 'The Child and Family Policy Divide: Tensions, Convergence and Rights', London, Family and Parenting Institute, available at: https://www.jrf.org uk/sites/default/files/jrf/migrated/files/1859353312.pdf.

Holt, A. (2009), 'Parent Abuse: Some Reflections on the Adequacy of a Youth Justice Response', *Internet Journal of Criminology*: 1–11, available at: http://www.internetjournalofcriminology.com.

Holt, A. and Retford, S. (2012), 'Practitioner Accounts of Responding to Parent Abuse—A Case Study in ad hoc Delivery, Perverse Outcomes and a Policy Silence', *Child and Family Social Work*, 18, 3: 1–10.

Home Office (2013), *New Government Domestic Violence and Abuse Definition*, Home Office Circular 003/2013, available at: https://www.gov.uk/government/publications/new-government-domestic-violence-and-abuse-definition.

Home Office (2014), *A Call to End Violence Against Women and Girls: Action Plan*, HM Government, available at: https://www.gov.uk/government/uploads/system/uploads/attachment_data/file/287758/VAWG_Action_Plan.pdf.

Home Office (2015a), *Information Guide on Responding to Adolescent to Parent Violence and Abuse*, London: Home Office, available at: https://www.gov.uk/domestic-violence-and-abuse#adolescent-to-parent-violence-and-abuse.

Home Office (2015b), *Serious Crime Act (2015)*, Legislation.gov.uk, available at: http://www.legislation.gov.uk/ukpga/2015/9/section/76/enacted.

Howard, J. (2011), 'Adolescent Violence in the Home: The Missing Link in Family Violence Prevention and Response', *Australian Domestic & Family Violence Clearinghouse*, Stakeholder Paper 11.

Howard, J. and Rottem, N. (2008), 'It All Starts at Home: Male Adolescent Violence to Mothers', Research Report, Inner Couth Community Health Service Inc and Child Abuse Research Australia, Monash University. http://ischs.org.au/content123/uploads/2012/08/It_all_starts_at_home1.pdf.

Hunter, C. and Nixon, J. (2001), 'Taking the Blame and Losing the Home: Women and Anti-Social Behaviour', *Journal of Social Welfare and Family Law*, 23, 4: 395–410.

Hunter, C. and Piper, C. (2012), 'Parent Abuse: Can Law Be the Answer?', *Social Policy and Society*, 11, 2: 217–27.

Hunter, C., Nixon, J., and Parr, S. (2010), 'Mother Abuse: A Matter of Youth Justice, Child Welfare or Domestic Violence?', *Journal of Law and Society*, 37, 2: 264–84.

Ibabe, I., Jaureguizar, J., and Bentler, P.M. (2013), 'Risk Factors for Child-to-Parent Violence', *International Research on Aggression and Violence*, 28, 5: 523–34.

Jackson, D. (2003), 'Broadening Constructions of Family Violence: Mothers' Perspectives of Aggression from their Children', *Child and Family Social Work*, 8, 4: 321–9.

Kethineni, S. (2004), 'Youth-on-parent Violence in a Central Illinois County', *Youth Violence and Juvenile Justice*, 2, 4: 374–94.

Kratcoski, P. (1985), 'Youth Violence Directed toward Significant Others', *Journal of Adolescence*, 8, 2: 145–57.

McAlister, S. and Carr, N. (2014), 'Experiences of Youth Justice: Youth Justice Discourses and their Multiple Effects', *Youth Justice*, 14, 3: 241–54.

Miles, C. and Condry, R. (2015), 'Responding to Adolescent to Parent Violence: Challenges for Policy and Practice', *British Journal of Criminology*, 55, 6: 1076–95.

Miles, C. and Condry, R. (Dec. 2015, online first) 'Adolescent to Parent Violence: The Police Response to Parents Reporting Violence from their Children', *Policing and Society*.

Mirrlees-Black, C., Mayhew, P., and Percy, A. (1996), *The 1996 British Crime Survey England and Wales*, Home Office Statistical Bulletin, London: Home Office.

Muncie, J. (1999), 'Institutionalised Intolerance: Youth Justice and the 1998 Crime and Disorder Act', *Critical Social Policy*, 19, 2: 147–75.

Muncie, J. (2002), 'A New Deal for Youth? Early Intervention and Correctionalism', in G. Hughes, E. McLaughlin, and J. Muncie (eds), *Crime Prevention and Community Safety: New Directions*, London: Sage: 142–62.

Muncie, J. (2006), 'Governing Young People: Coherence and Contradiction in Contemporary Youth Justice', *Critical Social Policy*, 26, 4: 770–93.

Nixon, J. (2012), 'Practitioners' Constructions of Parent Abuse', *Social Policy and Society*, 11, 2: 229–39.

Pagani, L., Tremblay, R., Nagin, D., Zoccolillo, M., Vitaro, F., and McDuff, P. (2004), 'Risk Factor Models for Adolescent Verbal and Physical Aggression toward Mothers', *International Journal of Behavioural Development*, 28, 6: 528–37.

Parentline Plus (2008), *Aggressive Behaviour in Children: Parents' Experiences and Needs*, London: Parentline Plus.

Parentline Plus (2010), *When Family Life Hurts: Family Experience of Aggression in Children*, London: Parentline Plus.

PEEK, C.W., FISCHER, J.L., and KIDWELL, J.A. (1985), 'Teenage Violence toward Parents: A Neglected Dimension of Family Violence', *Journal of Marriage and the Family*, 47, 4: 1051–8.

ROUTT, G. and ANDERSON, L. (2011), 'Adolescent Violence towards Parents', *Journal of Aggression, Maltreatment & Trauma*, 20, 1: 1–18.

SMITH, S., BAKER, D., BUCHAN, A., and BODIWALA, G. (1992), 'Adult Domestic Violence', *Health Trends*, 24, 3: 97–9.

SNYDER, H.N. and MCCURLEY, C. (2008), 'Domestic Assaults by Juvenile Offenders', *Juvenile Justice Bulletin*, U.S. Department of Justice: Office of Justice Programs.

STEWART, M., BURNS, A., and LEONARD, R. (2007), 'Dark Side of the Mothering Role: Abuse of Mothers by Adolescent and Adult Children', *Sex Roles*, 56, 3: 183–91.

STROM, K.J., WARNER, T.D., TICHAVSKY, L., and ZAHN, M.A. (2010), 'Policing Juveniles: Domestic Violence Arrest Policies, Gender, and Police Response to Child-Parent Violence', *Crime and Delinquency*, DOI: 10.1177/0011128710376293.

ULMAN, A. and STRAUS, M. (2003), 'Violence by Children against Mothers in Relation to Violence between Parents and Corporal Punishment by Parents', *Journal of Comparative Family Studies*, 34, 1: 41–60.

WALSH, J.A. and KRIENERT, J.L. (2007), 'Child-to-Parent Violence: An Empirical Analysis of Offender, Victim, and Event Characteristics in a National Sample of Reported Incidents', *Journal of Family Violence*, 22, 7: 563–74.

WALSH, J.A. and KRIENERT, J.L. (2009), 'A Decade of Child-Initiated Family Violence: Comparative Analysis of Child–Parent Violence and Parricide Examining Offender, Victim and Event Characteristics in a National Sample of Reported Incidents, 1995–2005', *Journal of Interpersonal Violence*, 24, 9: 1450–77.

WILCOX, P. (2012), 'Is Parent Abuse a Form of Domestic Violence?', *Social Policy and Society*, 11, 2: 277–88.

19

VICTIMS OF THE STATE: RECOGNIZING THE HARMS CAUSED BY WRONGFUL CONVICTIONS

Carolyn Hoyle

INTRODUCTION

Fifty years ago, as Nigel Walker founded the Centre for Penal Studies at the University of Oxford, the first results from victims' surveys established by the 1965 USA President's Commission on Law Enforcement and the Administration of Justice were published. These data inspired academic, political, and public interest in the experiences, needs, and latterly the rights of victims of crime. From the establishment of compensation schemes in the 1960s, through the development of support services in the 1970s, and rights of allocution and rights to information in the 1980s and 1990s, crime victims found a powerful voice in policy-making and the politics of crime control. Over the same period, they have become a key subject of academic enquiry. By 1985—the year of the influential UN Declaration of Basic Principles of Justice for Victims of Crime and Abuse of Power ('UN Basic Principles')—Britain had its own victims' survey, and over the next 30 years British politicians of all persuasions found the victims' lobby to be a useful ally in their pursuit of the popular vote.

Throughout these developments, however, one class of victim has been marginalized: victims of wrongful conviction by the criminal court. These individuals, who have arguably been mistreated by the state, unlike those who have suffered at the hands of individual offenders, have struggled to find a collective voice. They are poorly represented by politicians and policy makers, and have received little official support or academic attention.

There was, in the early 1990s, a short but potent burst of interest in wrongful convictions, when some journalists[1] and academics[2] turned their attention to the fallibility of the criminal process. As the convictions of the 'Guildford Four' were overturned by the UK Court of Appeal in 1989, followed by the 'Birmingham Six', 'Tottenham

[1] For example, Woffinden 1987; Rozenberg 1994; Rose 1992, 1996.

[2] See e.g. Walker and Starmer 1993, 1999; McConville and Bridges 1994

Three',[3] and other high-profile cases, critical attention turned to flaws in criminal procedure. The Royal Commission on Criminal Justice (1993) took evidence from criminologists and lawyers, and it commissioned and published various research reports on police, prosecutors, and the Court of Appeal.[4] While this period saw a new more critical (some thought 'pessimistic', Dixon 1995) criminological scholarship (e.g. McConville et al. 1991),[5] by the start of the new millennium British criminology seemed to be losing interest. In short, while our knowledge of victims of crime expanded, academic and public understanding of wrongful conviction remained underdeveloped.

This chapter considers why victims of wrongful conviction have been overlooked. Arguing that those who are wrongfully convicted experience similar injuries to crime victims, it makes a case for their recognition as 'victims' and for the appropriate statutory responses that should accompany such recognition. While there are different academic approaches to defining wrongful convictions (Naughton 2013; Walker 1999), this chapter focuses on those whose convictions are overturned by the Court of Appeal (Criminal Division) of England and Wales, following a referral by the Criminal Cases Review Commission (CCRC).[6] While the overturning of their conviction does not prove that they are innocent—given that the Court is concerned only with the *safety* of the conviction (Hoyle 2016)—these are appellants who have been wrongfully convicted and failed to have their cases considered by the Court of Appeal under the direct right of appeal, or whose convictions were upheld at their first appeal. The chapter considers wrongful conviction as a form of state harm and explores the potential of restorative justice processes to enable the state to make amends.

THE RISE OF THE CRIME VICTIM

The field of victimology in Britain has expanded rapidly since the UK published the UN Basic Principles in 1985. British criminology has demonstrated the need for improved services to victims and provided evidence of the efficacy of measures introduced by government. Research conducted by the Oxford Centre for Criminology explored victims' experiences of the criminal justice system (Maguire 1985; Shapland et al. 1985) and of victim support services (Maguire and Corbett 1987), and charted the increasing political attention towards victims (Maguire and Pointing 1988). From early work on victims of burglary (Maguire 1980, 1982), Oxford researchers focused increasingly on marginalized or vulnerable groups of victims, including: child victims (Morgan and Zedner 1992); victims with learning difficulties (Sanders et al. 1997); victims of domestic violence (Hoyle 1998, 2008; Hoyle and Palmer 2014; Hoyle and

[3] See Rozenburg 1994 for a discussion of these cases.

[4] See http://discovery.nationalarchives.gov.uk/browse/r/h/C3042

[5] For a review of this body of critical scholarship, see Sanders, Young and Burton 2010.

[6] http://www.ccrc.gov.uk/. Other research being conducted within the Oxford Centre explores the experiences of those who claim to be innocent but whose convictions are yet to be overturned; see https://www.law.ox.ac.uk/research-and-subject-groups/miscarriages-justice

Sanders 2000; Madden Dempsey 2009), hate crime (Walters and Hoyle 2012), sex trafficking (Hoyle et al. 2011), genocide and other crimes against humanity (Hoyle and Ullrich 2014; Viebach 2014); and victims' participation in restorative justice schemes (Hoyle et al. 2002; Young and Hoyle 2003). From evaluation of the early Victim Charters (Hoyle et al. 1998), it also focused critical attention on the dangers (Ashworth 1993; Hoyle 2011) as well as the potential (Roberts 2009) of victim participation in criminal justice.

While government attention to victims coincided with the emergence of scholarship in the mid-1980s, since the introduction of the Victims Charter in 1990, victims' 'rights' have moved towards centre stage in criminal justice policy. The government has issued multiple policy statements, purportedly reflecting its aim to improve the experiences of victims in the criminal justice system; to treat victims and witnesses with respect; to take account of their rights; to secure victim participation; to communicate effectively with, and provide timely information to victims and witnesses; to provide reparation and opportunities for restorative justice; and to strengthen the protection for vulnerable and intimidated victims and improve consistency and take-up of special measures. The UK, like all EU member states, must demonstrate that it has modified domestic laws to establish minimum standards on rights, support, and protection of victims; this includes giving victims a key role in criminal proceedings under an EU Directive of 2012.[7] The UK easily meets these standards. Yet were it asked to demonstrate minimum standards on rights, support, and protection of victims of wrongful convictions, it would not be able to do so. This one class of victim remains marginalized or excluded from academic study and official support. What accounts for this exclusion?

THE WRONGFULLY CONVICTED: YESTERDAY'S PROBLEM?

Crime victims serve as a potent rhetorical device to argue for populist criminal policy, as many criminologists have observed. Indeed, Garland describes 'the projected, politicized, image of "the victim"... as an all-purpose justification for measures of penal repression' (2001: 143). In the UK, proliferating government policy on crime victims has—over the past two decades—run concurrent with ever more punitive criminal policy. However, with a few notable exceptions,[8] politicians see no benefit to taking up the cause of miscarriages of justice. But this cannot fully account for the continued marginalization of victims of wrongful convictions; there must be systemic factors at play. Changes to criminal procedure, evolutions in forensic science, and the

[7] Directive 2012/29/EU of the European Parliament and of the Council of 25 October 2012 establishing minimum standards on the rights, support, and protection of victims of crime, and replacing Council Framework Decision 2001/220/JHA at: http://ec.europa.eu/justice/criminal/files/victims/guidance_victims_rights_directive_en.pdf.

[8] Particularly the tireless campaigner Chris Mullin, MP for Sunderland South 1987–2010, and Claire Curtis-Thomas, MP for Crosby 1997–2010.

establishment of a statutory appeals review body (the CCRC), may have persuaded those in politics, criminal justice, and the academy that the problem that seemed so pressing just 25 years ago has been solved; in other words, that miscarriages of justice are relics of an imperfect past.

Until the 1960s, the broad consensus was that British criminal justice could be trusted. The Confait case and the Royal Commission on Criminal Procedure (1977–81)[9] demonstrated that this was not the case and produced changes to balance the investigative needs of the police with the rights of suspects. For some time, the Police and Criminal Evidence Act of 1984 (PACE) and the PACE Codes of Practice were thought by many[10] to have introduced adequate due process safeguards to prevent most of the egregious miscarriages of justice of the earlier decades. This confidence was misplaced. While the English courts are today much less likely to see suspects whose confessions have been beaten out of them,[11] my review of CCRC referrals to the Court of Appeal shows that not all police mischief was eliminated by PACE. Many cases from the last decade or two feature non-disclosure of exculpatory evidence and other forms of malpractice by police,[12] even if this is not the main reason for their referral to the Court (Hoyle and Sato forthcoming). Furthermore, police and prosecution powers have increased since PACE (not least through the Criminal Procedure and Investigations Act 1996 and the Criminal Justice Act 2003) and suspects' rights have been eroded, particularly the right to legal aid. As Cape put it recently, 'Defence rights are being managed out of the investigative stage of the criminal process, and the danger is that miscarriages of justice are being managed back in' (2013: 17).

The string of wrongful convictions that surfaced in the late 1980s led to a crisis of confidence in the British criminal justice system in general, and in the appeals process in particular. In 1991, following the quashing by the Court of Appeal of the convictions for murder of the 'Birmingham Six', the then Home Secretary established the Royal Commission on Criminal Justice to examine the effectiveness of the criminal justice system in securing the conviction of the guilty and the acquittal of the innocent. The Royal Commission's Report (1993) recommended the removal of the Home Secretary's power to review wrongful convictions and the creation of a new independent body to investigate these cases where appropriate, and to refer meritorious, apparently unsafe cases to the Court of Appeal. These recommendations gave birth to the CCRC.

Almost simultaneously, after a 'golden age' when aspects of the media devoted considerable resources to investigating and reporting wrongful convictions, there was a notable decline in media attention (May 2013). When the CCRC was established 'it was assumed the requirement for investigative journalists to be involved in cases had more or less ended' (O'Neill 2012) and others also thought that the problem was solved. Meanwhile, it has become clear that the CCRC is impeded in its work

[9] http://discovery.nationalarchives.gov.uk/details/r/C3028.

[10] Academics associated with the 'Warwick School' were notable exceptions, sceptical of the likely success of the recommendations of the Royal Commission from the start (see McConville and Bridges (eds) 1994).

[11] Though there are some alarming experiences, such as that of Babar Ahmad http://www.theguardian.com/uk-news/2016/mar/12/terror-suspect-babar-ahmad-scotland-yard-met.

[12] For example, the 'Rigg Approach' cases and some West Midlands Drugs Squad cases referred back to the Court by the CCRC were post-PACE; see Elks 2008. Warren Blackwell is one of the more nefarious CCRC cases: *R v Blackwell* [2006] EWCA Crim 2185.

by inadequate funding (House of Commons Justice Committee 2015: 6) and has acknowledged that some victims of wrongful conviction fall through its safety net (Newby 2014). Furthermore, advances in forensic science, which had raised the prospects of exculpatory evidence at both the investigation and review stages, have not proven to be the remedy for all criminal justice ills. Indeed, even DNA evidence is now recognized as fundamentally probabilistic and prone to uncertainties at each stage of its production (Aronson and Cole 2009).

RECOGNIZING THE WRONGFULLY CONVICTED AS 'VICTIMS'

The limited academic literature on wrongful convictions has focused on causes. Less attention has been paid to how victims experience injustice or how they fare upon release from their sentence; still less has it explored whether or not the state meets, or attempts to meet, their various needs.

While crime rates in the UK have been falling, the number of those applying to the CCRC is rising, to around 1,500 each year (CCRC 2015). Since its inception in 1997, the Commission has referred over 600 cases back to the Court of Appeal: approximately 400 appeals were successful.[13] Many of these quashed convictions were for very serious crimes that had attracted long sentences, including life sentences for murder in about a fifth of cases. How do the experiences of such people compare to those of crime victims?

Surveys show that the vast majority of crime victims are emotionally affected by their experience of being victimized (Flatley et al. 2010). Typical effects include 'shock and loss of trust/faith in society', 'guilt at having become a victim', 'financial loss', and 'psychological effects, including fear, anger and depression' (Shapland and Hall 2007: 178), but a significant minority experience more severe symptoms such as depression and panic attacks (Walker et al. 2009), and some are diagnosed with Post-Traumatic Stress Disorder (PTSD) (Boccellari et al. 2007). There would appear, a priori, to be sound reasons to expect victims of wrongful convictions to be similarly affected and indeed the literature demonstrates this to be the case.

Traumatic as the experiences of crime victims are, with the exception of domestic abuse, victimization is typically experienced as a discrete event, or a time-limited set of events, the pains of which will be alleviated by a network of support. Those who are wrongfully convicted experience anxiety, anger, frustration, and despair as an ongoing condition, for years or even decades. There are, in typical cases, a series of landmark occasions when the original injustice represented by the trial verdict will be reinforced: for example, for those who are given custodial sentences, the beginning of imprisonment, with its myriad humiliations; the loss of a first appeal; or a setback

[13] See http://www.ccrc.gov.uk/case-statistics/ for up-to-date statistics. The majority are Crown Court convictions quashed by the Court of Appeal, but a small proportion are magistrates' convictions overturned by the Crown Court.

in the search for fresh exculpatory evidence. Even without such milestones, each day the wrongfully convicted prisoner wakes up, he or she will be confronted by the realities of a seemingly impossible situation: the absence of choice and freedom; separation from loved ones; and, above all, a lack of power, a sense of being at the mercy of an impersonal, adamantine state. How this is experienced differently to the 'regular' pains of imprisonment, when the wrongfulness of the conviction serves as an aggravating feature, is not yet fully understood.[14]

To cope with prison, some become aggressive, others isolated, withdrawn, and depressed. Studies from North America show that 'wrongful incarceration compounds these typical effects of imprisonment in ways that are only beginning to be understood' (Delaney et al. 2010). The 'deleterious effects of [prisoners'] confinement are further exacerbated by the unjust nature of their incarceration' (Campbell and Denov 2004: 145), and their experiences of unjust stigmatization (Campbell and Denov 2004; Clow and Leach 2015: 161; Westervelt and Cook 2010). Violence plays a 'part of daily existence inside' 'to ensure their survival in the hostile prison environment' (Campbell and Denov 2004: 141–8) and most contemplate suicide during their incarceration (ibid: 149). However, American and Canadian prisons and justice systems differ in some key respects to the British system and local research needs to explore how people in the UK experience wrongful imprisonment.

One similarity may be the implications of protesting innocence. On both sides of the Atlantic, research suggests that prison staff withhold privileges from those who claim to be innocent. In the UK, for example, some such prisoners are denied access to the Incentive and Earned Privileges Scheme (Campbell and Denov 2004; Evans 2012; Vollen and Eggers 2005). They are less likely to be moved to a lower category prison and the term they serve in prison may be significantly longer, as parole boards are reluctant to release those who have not 'acknowledged' their guilt (Medwed 2008; see also Naughton with Tan 2010). Those convicted of sexual offences face particular challenges if they continue to maintain their innocence as this may be interpreted as 'denial', considered to be a typical trait of sex offenders. They are also ineligible for treatment programmes that are a prerequisite for parole in many jurisdictions (Medwed 2016 forthcoming).

Post release, psychological harms do not dissipate. Rightfully convicted inmates completing their sentences anticipate release and are provided with services to prepare for it. The wrongfully convicted may be set free suddenly, after years of struggle, with no support or preparation, creating further practical and emotional difficulties (Delaney et al. 2010). They 'often must deal with long-term personality change, post-traumatic stress and other psychiatric disorders, and the difficulties of coping with stigma, grief and loss' (Norris 2012: 355). Indeed, their experiences have been likened to victims of torture (Weigand 2009; Westervelt and Cook 2010). British research (Grounds 2004) on eighteen men 'referred for systematic psychiatric assessment after their convictions were quashed on appeal and they were released from long-term imprisonment' found evidence of 'a pattern of disabling symptoms and

[14] Research comparing the experiences of the wrongfully convicted in prison to those who believe themselves to be 'rightfully convicted' is underway in the Oxford Centre (Burtt, current PhD research).

psychological problems that were severe... and similar in all cases' (ibid: 167). Those assessed were found to have endured personality change 'in ways that caused distress to them and their family' (ibid: 168). Twelve met the diagnostic criteria for PTSD, and most 'had intense, chronic, feelings of bitterness, as did some families, and all had strong and unresolved feelings of loss' (ibid: 170; see also Jamieson and Grounds 2005). Lost time was a persistent concern for those who missed the death of parents, family funerals and weddings, and other life events and for those who were 'frozen developmentally', feeling 'psychologically the same age they had been on entry to prison' (Grounds 2004: 172; US research has produced similar data: Weigand 2009: 427).

Media reports and biographies offer further descriptive evidence of psychological trauma. After Gerry Conlon—wrongfully convicted as one of the 'Guildford Four'—was released in 1989, his mental health rapidly deteriorated, presenting symptoms of Complex PTSD: 'Since I came out of prison, I have suffered two breakdowns, I have attempted suicide, I have been addicted to drugs and to alcohol. The ordeal has never left me. I was given no psychological help by the government that had locked me up, no counselling' (Conlon 2009).

Research by the Oxford Centre for Criminology has focused on those wrongfully accused of abuse while in occupations of trust (the majority were subject to 'historical' allegations of sexual abuse of children while in residential institutions; Hoyle et al. 2016). Only one of our thirty participants was prosecuted (though acquitted); the others were investigated, sometimes over years, but insufficient evidence was found to prosecute them. Although the majority were not prosecuted their experiences included depression, suicidal ideation, self-harming, fear, anger, shame, nightmares, and panic attacks. One explained:

> I was very close to suicide on at least three occasions... In my rages I became so angry I would take it out on walls and doors... I have never been a violent person so this was very much out of character for me. I still have nightmares and anger and... I still feel people are looking at me and judging me.

Their wives and other family members also sought counselling or medication for stress, but the impact was wider, affecting social networks and communities:

> My family were, naturally, devastated. They were put through the emotional wringer as well. Some casual friends became close friends and others whom I considered close friends severed their relationship with me.

Many were unable to return to their jobs, either because suspicion remained, even though they were legally innocent, or because their mental health was insufficiently robust. The wrongful conviction impacted on their sense of themselves and their reputation, and for most it took away their faith in the criminal justice system:

> I have no respect for the police at all. They were determined to prosecute me... They chose not to seek evidence, only to search for corroboration... What happened to me was malicious, cruel, vindictive.

These findings suggest that there is a strong case for recognizing the wrongfully convicted as victims, and this raises the question of whether the state should assume some responsibility to make amends and provide adequate support and compensation, as it does to victims of crime.

INADEQUATE SUPPORT AND COMPENSATION FOR VICTIMS OF WRONGFUL CONVICTION

Various CCRC cases demonstrate the inadequate response of the state to the harms caused by wrongful conviction. For example, Sam Hallam, whose conviction was quashed in 2012, was left to cope with his father's suicide 18 months before he was released (Hattenstone and Allison 2013) and has struggled to rebuild his life with little assistance and no compensation from the state.[15] Sally Clark, who was wrongfully convicted in 1999 for the murder of her two infant sons on the tendentious statistical evidence given by a pathologist, Sir Roy Meadow, died just four years after the Court of Appeal overturned her conviction in 2003, having never fully recovered from the compound trauma of losing her children and then being wrongly convicted of their murder. She had, as her solicitor put it 'lost five to six years of her life in what was state-sponsored torture' (Shaikh 2007). Angela Cannings, who served 18 months in prison after being wrongly convicted of killing two of her babies, has spoken out about the complete absence of support from the state which had wrongfully imprisoned her (ibid).

Years of institutionalization away from a rapidly changing society, and the consequential breakdown of support networks, as well as inadequate education and training within prisons, can make it hard to adapt. While 're-entry programmes', probation support, as well as limited funds are provided to others released from prison, these services are not available to those who were wrongfully convicted (Westervelt and Cook 2008, 2010). In the UK, the only state assistance for the wrongfully convicted is provided by the Miscarriages of Justice services at the Royal Courts of Justice Citizens Advice Bureau, established in 2005.[16] However, it is under-funded, 'lacking the resources to ensure that difficulties with housing, employment and money are resolved expeditiously with the minimum stress on the former prisoner'.[17] Most must therefore rely on a handful of charities with enormous goodwill but insecure status and funding.[18] It is small wonder that many of the wrongfully convicted slide into poverty or substance abuse as they struggle to rebuild a life outside prison (Mandery et al. 2013):

> The[y] . . . win their freedom only to find that they are penniless, unemployable, and dependent on others, experience family friction, poverty, and depression. This

[15] Interview with Paul May, miscarriage of justice campaigner working with the Hallam family.

[16] http://www.rcjadvice.org.uk/miscarriages-of-justice/.

[17] Interview with Paul May.

[18] The Glasgow-based Miscarriages of Justice Organization (MOJO), founded by Paddy Hill, is one of the few: http://www.miscarriagesofjustice.org/.

> can result in homelessness, self-medicating with drugs and alcohol, and societal alienation.
>
> (Weigand 2009: 429)

A number of those whose convictions were overturned, following a CCRC referral, have experienced frustration and despair once the celebrations on the steps of the Court of Appeal are over and the news camera crews have gone. Victor Nealon, released from 17 years in prison after DNA evidence showed his conviction to be unsafe, spent his first night of freedom sleeping on a street in Birmingham. Andrew Adams, who was released from prison in 2009 after his case was referred to the Court of Appeal by the CCRC, had spent 15 years in prison wrongfully convicted of murder. He lost significant relationships and employment skills while in prison and, a few years after winning his freedom, he still had no income and no home of his own. He had not been prepared for release by the prison authorities, received no advice about training, education, housing, and employment, and no emotional support.[19] Furthermore, his long battle for compensation from the state has been unsuccessful.

Compensating those whom the state has wrongfully convicted and imprisoned is an obligation of the state.[20] However, in the UK, the last decade has seen the gradual erosion of the state's commitment to compensate the wrongfully convicted and the emergence of what is effectively a 'two tier' standard for exoneration. The Court of Appeal's attempts to distinguish between deserving and undeserving appellants—between those who could prove themselves innocent and those who could not, as established in the Supreme Court's decision in the case of *Adams*[21] and enforced in the more recent case of *Allen*[22]—are odious and flawed.[23] They have left those who cannot prove factual innocence under a cloud of suspicion, and deprived them of compensation for the harms inflicted by the state (Hoyle 2016). Hence, those who have recently had their convictions quashed, following a referral by the CCRC—such as Sam Hallam and Victor Nealon—have been denied compensation despite overwhelming evidence of their innocence.

In 2015, a judicial review of the government's denial of compensation in the cases of Hallam and Nealon—the first challenges to be brought against the narrowing of eligibility for an award—did not find it to be unlawful as the new evidence that persuaded the Court of Appeal to quash their convictions was not considered to prove beyond reasonable doubt that they did not commit the offences.[24] Compensation lawyers believe that most cases will now fail to meet the test for compensation.[25] Despite the manifold harms caused to these victims, in most cases the state does not make amends.

[19] Interviews with his legal defence team and those involved investigating his case.

[20] See Article 14(6) of the UN International Covenant on Civil and Political Rights

[21] *R (Adams) v Secretary of State for Justice* [2011] UKSC 18, para. 9.

[22] *Allen v United Kingdom*, Application no. 25424/09, Grand Chamber Judgment, 12 July 2013.

[23] It is disappointing that the ECtHR has not declared them to be incompatible with the European Convention.

[24] *The Guardian*, 'Wrongfully jailed men lose high court actions in battle for compensation', 8 June 2015, http://www.theguardian.com/law/2015/jun/08/wrongfully-jailed-men-lose-high-court-actions-battle-compensation.

[25] Interview with Alex Bailin QC, Matrix Chambers, London.

JUSTICE AND RESTORATION FOR VICTIMS OF WRONGFUL CONVICTION

The failure to recognize the wrongfully convicted as victims clearly results in inadequate provision of practical and emotional support (see Jenkins 2013).[26] Yet, an extension of victim support services and resources to include the wrongfully convicted is unlikely to be forthcoming in the current climate, and may, in any event, be insufficient. Research shows that the wrongfully convicted want 'their standing as innocent people recognized and the trauma of their conviction acknowledged' by the state (Weigand 2009: 432), as well as assistance with their reintegration and some form of reparation (Hoyle et al. 2016). However, a rationale for expecting the state to provide this has not, as yet, been fully articulated.

Quantitative empirical research on wrongful convictions has provided us with analysis of causes, while qualitative empirical studies, media reports, and biographies have shed some light on the experiences of being wrongfully convicted. However, it has failed to provide rich theoretical understanding of the production and consequences of wrongful conviction (Leo 2007: 213). Recent work by Westervelt and Cook (2010: 261)—drawing on Kauzlarich et al. (2001)—develops a theoretical framework for recognizing the wrongfully convicted as victims of state-produced harms. Like typical victims of 'state crime', they tend to be the least socially powerful actors; are often blamed for their own suffering; are easy target for repeat victimization; their victimizers often fail to recognize the harms they have done; and—in particular—they must rely on their victimizers for redress. Exploring the experiences of those released from death row in America after wrongful conviction, and particularly the role the state plays in creating as well as exacerbating the harms they suffer, Westervelt and Cook (2010) have broadened the reach of the concept of 'state crime' to encompass 'state harm'. This allows them to consider not only acts defined by law as criminal (and committed by state officials in the pursuit of their jobs) but improper behaviours by state agents that, while falling short of criminal actions, result in wrongful convictions. Framing the wrongfully convicted as victims of 'state harms' throws into sharp relief the need for the state to acknowledge and assume *some* responsibility for the harms caused to the wrongfully convicted, and to make amends (we return below to the question of whether this should imply obligations by the state).

Wrongful convictions are typically the product of eyewitness misidentification, false confessions, perjury by witnesses, police and prosecutorial misconduct, bad trial tactics, forensic error, tunnel vision, or ineffective assistance of counsel (Gould and Leo 2010). While human error—whether by victims, lay or expert witnesses, or by defence solicitors—has a role to play, in many cases police and prosecutors breach procedural safeguards and sometimes engage in malfeasance. Hence, just as the wrongfully convicted can be considered to be victims, some state agents are 'perpetrators' of state harm. Justice and redress for harms done is a critical part of 'ordinary'

[26] A new Oxford study focuses on how well the wrongfully convicted fare upon release and what services they receive from statutory and non-profit bodies (Tilt, current PhD research).

victims' recovery (Boom and Kuijpers 2012) and the literature suggests that victims of wrongful conviction also want the state, and criminal justice officials in particular, to take responsibility for the errors that have occurred. Without this, there remains a 'profound cynicism and mistrust regarding the fairness and legitimacy of authority figures' (Campbell and Denov 2004: 155).

Prosecution of police officers for criminal acts that have resulted in wrongful convictions might bring some satisfaction to their victims. Police malpractice was a key factor in many of the high-profile miscarriages of justice that led to the establishment of the CCRC. Yet those who have engaged in malfeasance are almost never prosecuted and when they are put on trial for perjury and conspiracy to pervert the course of justice, juries have typically acquitted them or the case has collapsed because of police or prosecution errors in the process.[27] If victims of wrongful conviction do not receive compensation or see wrongdoers punished, do they at least get an apology? Apologies by the Court of Appeal are not unheard of. At the end of the 'Tottenham Three's' appeal, Lord Justice Farquharson said the Court wished to express its 'profound regret that they have suffered as a result of the shortcomings of the criminal process', adding: 'No system of trials is proof against perjury, but this will be of little consequence to its victims' (quoted in Rose 1992: 220). It is certainly significant that his judgment expressly described the exonerated men as 'victims'. However, while this statement may not have been unique, similar judicial comments are rare. Further, outright judicial statements that an appellant was factually innocent remain very rare,[28] and recent changes to compensation make them less likely.

If conventional routes to redress for victims of wrongful conviction are blocked, restorative justice may be a viable alternative. Restorative processes can be effective in moderating harms to the victims of even the most serious crimes (Shapland et al. 2011), and desire for revenge is considerably reduced after restorative meetings (Sherman and Strang 2011). Yet apart from a limited experiment with restorative processes piloted some years ago to those who complained against the police in Thames Valley (Young et al. 2005), there have been no opportunities for wrongfully convicted persons to meet the police officers or others who investigated the case against them. According to Savage (2007), the prospects of restorative justice for such victims are distant, because the state and its institutions are reluctant to accept guilt or acknowledge failure, will not engage in meetings with the victims, and will not provide reparation. In the absence of a clear rationale for making good the harms they have caused, that may well be the case, but it is not inevitable. Police, as other criminal justice agents, can and do change if persuaded that they should, but at present there is no expectation that they do so, nor opportunities for change. What might therefore be the challenges of introducing restorative processes in the aftermath of wrongful convictions?

[27] One example being the failed attempt to convict the police officers charged with corruption for their handling of the 'Cardiff Three' case, as a result of disclosure failures; *The Guardian*, 'Cardiff Three police corruption case collapsed "due to disclosure failures"', 16 July 2013.

[28] Peter Fell, convicted, largely on the basis of his confession, of murdering two women in 1982, is an exception (*R v Fell* [2001] EWCA Crim 696).

LOOKING FORWARD: CHALLENGES FOR FUTURE RESEARCH ON WRONGFUL CONVICTIONS

Over the past 50 years, British criminologists have played a crucial role in persuading state agencies to provide adequate support and services to crime victims. Yet, as we have seen, there has been little progress on victims of wrongful convictions. Perhaps there is a causal link, with obeisance to victims putting the rights of defendants in second place? This is indefensible. As well as time and money, the wrongfully convicted lose their independence and autonomy, their sense of security and identity, and their positive relations with others, in most cases through no fault of their own but at the hands of the state. Over three decades after the UN Basic Principles focused attention on victims of the abuse of state power, it is time to turn critical attention to victims of wrongful conviction. Criminology needs to pay more attention to the failings of the criminal justice process. This is not to ignore the small number of important studies on wrongful convictions over the past two decades, discussed above, but to acknowledge that criminology as a discipline has failed adequately to map the contours of the problem or propose a normative framework for state responses. What therefore might be the challenges in going forward?

As a start, more rigorous evidence that wrongful convictions are not a product of an imperfect past, but still very much a part of our present fallible criminal justice landscape, might shake criminology from its complacency. Further, more thought needs to be given to the potential to reframe wrongful convictions as 'state harms'. This would raise important questions about the responsibility of the state to make amends; not least, how much responsibility should the state assume and on what grounds? Is 'responsibility' the same as 'duty' or something less? And if the state has a duty to repair the undeniable harms caused by a wrongful conviction, what are the correlative rights asserted by those wrongfully convicted? Do citizens have a right not to be wrongfully convicted, or is error an inevitable part of our system? If the latter, is it sufficient to have a statutory compensation scheme (even based on such restrictive criteria as described above) that pays out compensation not in recognition of a failure of state responsibility but out of sympathy for the plight of those upon whom the burden of the failure falls (as per the rationale of the victim state compensation system; see Miers 2014)? It is hard to make the case that citizens have a right not to be wrongfully convicted, as systems inevitably err. Given that, is it possible to make a claim that the state has a *legal* duty to make amends beyond a statutory compensation system, where the duty to compensate is established by Article 14(6) of the International Covenant on Civil and Political Rights? Failing this, would it be sufficient to assert that it has a *moral* duty? And if so, how might state agents be persuaded to commit resources to meeting that moral obligation if there were no repercussions for failure to do so? Would it be acceptable, given the extent of harms caused by the state in such cases, to promote merely voluntary amends-making by state officials?

Making amends is not simply material restitution or reparation. Indeed, restitution in criminal justice does not require a moral commitment to make amends (Barnett 1977). Making amends requires that something is given to the wronged person by the wrongdoer (and that could simply be an apology or a recognition that a harm was done) and that it is given voluntarily and with the express purpose of healing the damaged relationship. If a robust case could be made for the state to make amends, what might this look like? We might, for the purpose of considering this question, bracket off cases where it can be established that a state official committed a criminal offence that resulted in a wrongful conviction. These cases should remain firmly within the criminal justice process and be prosecuted in the public interest—though persistent failures in that process clearly deserve critical attention too. Instead, we should consider those cases that fall short of criminal acts but nonetheless involve misdeeds or malpractice.

One possible model for establishing the causes of and responsibility for wrongful convictions is the domestic homicide review process, which was established by the Domestic Violence, Crime and Victims Act 2004, and became law in 2011. Domestic homicide reviews are undertaken following a domestic homicide by a review team formed of members of local statutory and voluntary bodies to consider, among other things, failings in the state's response to the victim: what went wrong and what lessons can be learnt to reduce the risk of further cases. The reviews produce detailed reports and an action plan to ensure that any recommendations made in the report are acted upon. In other words, a wrongful conviction review could identify failings in the police, defence, prosecution, or another part of the criminal process and recommend structural or cultural changes in those organizations as well as specific reparative or reintegrative gestures towards the victim. While this process might be run along restorative (case conference) lines, and provide a voice for all those affected by the wrongful conviction, it could also make a recommendation for a further restorative meeting of the victim with the particular individuals who have caused the harm.

Whereas criminologists have typically focused on restorative justice as a response to criminal behaviour, moral theorists are interested in the broader moral concept of 'making amends' for wrongdoing and the harms it causes (Adler 1992). A Case Review following a wrongful conviction, modelled on restorative justice values and processes, as well as a specific restorative encounter for the victim and the wrongdoer, could be helpful in considering harms caused by moral agents employed by the state, as well as those working in a private capacity (such as defence counsel), who could be considered to be morally obliged to make amends (Radzik 2007). Making amends through restorative processes may have considerable scope for reparation and reconciliation. Restorative encounters provide opportunities for the rebuilding of damaged relationships, which could restore the legitimacy of agencies whose reputations were damaged following a wrongful conviction, and rehabilitate and re-educate criminal justice personnel who erred or engaged in malpractice (Eglash 1958), thus potentially reducing the risk of further wrongful convictions.

This is neither the place to establish parameters for such restorative interventions, nor to tackle the principled objections to restorative justice including concerns about proportionality, independence, and impartiality (see Ashworth 2002). Space also precludes consideration of the risk of further harm to the wrongfully convicted by engagement with a 'community' that includes state actors, and that is therefore characterized by significant power imbalances. More thought will need to be given to the apparent tension between the desirability for wrongdoers to make amends, respect for moral agency of the wrongdoer, and the role of a liberal state (Adler 1992: 193). However, restorative processes have evolved mechanisms for dealing with these challenges and well-facilitated encounters can create a safe environment where the powerful can be challenged and held to account (Cunneen and Hoyle 2010). Given that the wrongfully convicted will in any event have been locked into an unequal and unyielding relationship with state agents, and maybe even his or her own lawyer, for some significant time, a restorative process offers some hope of redressing that imbalance. It is at least worth considering. After years of neglect, when academic attention was focused on crime victims, criminologists now should take up the challenge of developing a robust theoretical framework for understanding the wrongfully convicted as victims of state harm and, with the weight of further UK-based research on such victims' experiences, make a coherent and robust normative claim for an adequate state response.

REFERENCES

Adler, J. (1992). *The Urgings of Conscience*, Philadelphia, PA: Temple University Press.

Aronson, J. and Cole, S. (2009), 'Science and the Death Penalty: DNA, Innocence, and the Debate over Capital Punishment in the United States', *Law and Social Enquiry*, 34, 3: 603–33.

Ashworth, A. (1993), 'Victim Impact Statements and Sentencing', *Criminal Law Review*, 498–509.

Ashworth, A. (2002), 'Responsibilities, Rights and Restorative Justice', *British Journal of Criminology*, 43, 3: 578–95.

Barnett, R.E. (1977), 'Restitution: A New Paradigm of Criminal Justice', *Ethics*, 87, 4: 279–301.

Boccellari, A., Alvidrez, J., Shumway, M., Kelly, V., Gregory, G., and Gelb, M. (2007), 'Characteristics and Psychosocial Needs of Victims of Violent Crime Identified at a Public-Sector Hospital: Data from a Large Clinical Trial', *General Hospital Psychiatry*, 29, 3: 236–43.

Boom, A. and Kuijpers, K.F. (2012), 'Victims' Needs as Basic Human Needs', *International Review of Victimology*, 18, 2: 155–79.

Campbell, K. and Denov, M. (2004), 'The Burden of Innocence: Coping with a Wrongful Imprisonment', *Canadian Journal of Criminology and Criminal Justice*, 46, 2: 139–64.

Cape, E. (2013), 'Designing out Defence Lawyers', in J. Robbins (ed), The Justice Gap, *No Defence: Lawyers and Miscarriages of Justice*, Wilmington Publishing: 14–17.

CCRC (2015), Annual Report 2014/2015, available at:http://www.ccrc.gov.uk/wp-content/uploads/2015/07/CCRC-Annual-Report-and-Accounts-2014-15.pdf.

Clow, K.A. and Leach, A.M. (2015), 'After Innocence: Perceptions of Individuals Who Have Been Wrongfully Convicted', *Legal and Criminological Psychology*, 20, 1: 147–64.

Conlon, G. (2009), 'My Ordeal Goes On. For Others the Nightmare Is Just Starting', *The Guardian*, 5 May 2009.

Cunneen, C. and Hoyle, C. (2010), *Debating Restorative Justice*, Oxford: Hart Publishing.

Delaney, M.C., Findley, K.A., and Sullivan, S. (2010), 'Exonerees' Hardships after Freedom', *Wisconsin Lawyer*, 83, 2: 18.

DIXON, D. (1995), 'New Left Pessimism', in M. Levi, M. Maguire, and L. Noaks (eds), *Contemporary Issues in Criminology*, Cardiff: University of Wales Press: 216–33.

EGLASH, A. (1958), 'Creative Restitution: Some Suggestions for Prison Rehabilitation Programs', *American Journal of Correction*, 40: 20.

ELKS, L. (2008), *Righting Miscarriages of Justice? Ten Years of the Criminal Cases Review Commission*, London: Justice.

EVANS, M. (2012), 'Living in Denial', The Justice Gap, available at: http://thejusticegap.com/2012/04/living-in-denial/.

FLATLEY, J., KERSHAW, C., SMITH, K., CHAPLIN, R., and MOON, D. (2010), *Crime in England and Wales 2009/2010: Findings from the British Crime Survey and Police Recorded Crime*, London: Home Office.

GARLAND, D. (2001), *The Culture of Control: Crime and Social Order in Contemporary Society*, Oxford: Oxford University Press.

GOULD, J.B. and LEO, R.A. (2010), 'One Hundred Years Later: Wrongful Convictions after a Century of Research', *Journal of Criminal Law and Criminology*, 100, 3: 825–68.

GROUNDS, A. (2004), 'Psychological Consequences of Wrongful Conviction and Imprisonment', *Canadian Journal of Criminology and Criminal Justice*, 46, 2: 165–82.

HATTENSTONE, S. and ALLISON, E. (2013), 'The Three Women Fighting to Clear Their Loved Ones' Names', *The Guardian*, 16 March 2013.

House of Commons Justice Committee, (2015), *Criminal Cases Review Commission 2014–15*, House of Commons, London: The Stationery Office Limited.

HOYLE, C. (1998), *Negotiating Domestic Violence: Police, Criminal Justice and Victims*, Oxford: Oxford University Press.

HOYLE, C. (2008), 'Will She Be Safe? A Critical Analysis of Risk Assessment in Domestic Violence Cases', *Children and Youth Services Review*, 30, 3: 323–37.

HOYLE, C. (2011), 'Empowerment through Emotion: The Use and Abuse of Victim Impact Evidence', in E. Erez, M. Kilchling, and J. Wemmers (eds), *Therapeutic Jurisprudence and Victim Participation in Justice: International Perspectives*, Durham, NC: Carolina Academic Press.

HOYLE, C. (2016), 'Compensating Injustice: The Perils of the Innocence Discourse', in P. Roberts, J. Hunter, S.N.M. Young, and D. Dixon (eds), *The Integrity of the Criminal Process*, Oxford: Hart Publishing: ch. 16.

HOYLE, C. and PALMER, N. (2014), 'Family Justice Centres: A Model for Empowerment?', *International Review of Victimology*, 20, 2: 191–210.

HOYLE, C. and SANDERS, A. (2000), 'Police Response to Domestic Violence: From Victim Choice to Victim Empowerment?', *British Journal of Criminology*, 40, 1: 14–36.

HOYLE, C. and SATO, M. (forthcoming), *Last Resorts for Wrongful Convictions*, Oxford: Oxford University Press.

HOYLE, C., SPEECHLEY, N.-E., and BURNETT, R. (2016), *The Impact of Being Wrongly Accused of Abuse in Occupations of Trust: Victims' Voices*, Oxford: Centre for Criminology.

HOYLE, C. and ULLRICH, L. (2014), 'New Court, New Justice? The Evolution of Justice for Victims at Domestic Courts and the International Criminal Court', *Journal of International Criminal Justice*, 12, 4: 681–703.

HOYLE, C., BOSWORTH, M., and DEMPSEY, M. (2011), 'Labelling the Victims of Sex Trafficking: Exploring the Borderland between Rhetoric and Reality', *Social and Legal Studies*, 20, 3: 313–29.

HOYLE, C., CAPE, E., MORGAN, R., and SANDERS, A. (1998), *Evaluation of the 'One Stop Shop' and Victim Statement Pilot Projects*, Home Office RDSD.

HOYLE, C., YOUNG, R., and HILL, R. (2002), *Proceed with Caution: An Evaluation of the Thames Valley Police Initiative in Restorative Cautioning*, York: Joseph Rowntree Foundation.

JAMIESON, R. and GROUNDS, A.T. (2005), 'Release and Adjustment: Perspectives from Studies of Wrongly Convicted and Politically Motivated Prisoners', in A. Liebling and S. Maruna (eds), *The Effects of Imprisonment*, Cullompton: Willan Publishing: 33–65.

JENKINS, S. (2013), 'Secondary Victims and the Trauma of Wrongful Conviction: Families and Children's Perspectives on Imprisonment, Release, and Adjustment', *Australian & New Zealand Journal of Criminology*, 46, 1: 119–37.

KAUZLARICH, D., MATTHEWS, R., and MILLER, W. (2001), 'Toward a Victimology of State Crime', *Critical Criminology*, 10, 3: 173–94.

LEO, R. (2007), 'Rethinking the Study of Miscarriages of Justice: Developing a Criminology of Wrongful Conviction', *Journal of Contemporary Criminal Justice*, 21, 3: 201–23.

MCCONVILLE, M. and BRIDGES, L. (eds) (1994), *Criminal Justice in Crisis*, The Justice Gap, Aldershot: Edward Elgar Publishing.

MCCONVILLE, M., SANDERS, A., and LENG, R. (1991), *The Case for the Prosecution*, London: Routledge.

MADDEN DEMPSEY, M. (2009), *Prosecuting Domestic Violence: A Philosophical Analysis*, Oxford University Press, Monographs in Criminal Law and Justice Series.

MAGUIRE, M. (1980), 'The Impact of Burglary upon Victims', *British Journal of Criminology*, 20, 3: 261–75.

MAGUIRE, M. (1982), *Burglary in a Dwelling*, London: Heinemann.

MAGUIRE, M. (1985), 'Victims' Needs and Victims' Services', *Victimology*, 10: 539–59.

MAGUIRE, M. and CORBETT, C. (1987), *The Effects of Crime and the Work of Victim Support Schemes*, Aldershot: Gower.

MAGUIRE, M. and POINTING, J. (1988), *Victims of Crime: A New Deal?*, Milton Keynes: Open University Press.

MANDERY, E., SHLOSBERG, A., WEST, V., and CALLAGHAN, B. (2013), 'Compensation Statutes and Post-Exoneration Offending', *Journal of Criminal Law and Criminology*, 103, 2: 553–84.

MAY, P. (2013), 'What Has the Media Ever Done for Us?', in J. Robins (ed.), *No Defence: Lawyers and Miscarriages of Justice*, Wilmington Publishing: 18–21.

MEDWED, D. (2008), 'The Innocent Prisoner's Dilemma: Consequences of Failing to Admit Guilt at Parole Hearings', *Iowa Law Review*, 93: 408.

MEDWED, D. (2016 forthcoming), "In Denial': The Hazards of Maintaining Innocence after Conviction', in R. Burnett (ed.), *Wrongful Allegations of Sexual and Child Abuse*, Oxford: Oxford University Press.

MIERS, D. (2014), 'Offender and State Compensation for Victims of Crime: Two Decades of Development and Change', *International Review of Victimology*, 20, 1: 145–68.

MORGAN, J. and ZEDNER, L. (1992), *Child Victims: Crime, Impact, and Criminal Justice*, Oxford: Oxford University Press.

NAUGHTON, M. (2013), *The Innocent and the Criminal Justice System: A Sociological Analysis of Miscarriages of Justice*, Basingstoke: Palgrave Macmillan.

NAUGHTON, M. with TAN, G. (2010), *Claims of Innocence: An Introduction to Wrongful Convictions and How They Might Be Challenged*, Bristol: University of Bristol.

NEWBY, M. (2014), 'The Curious Case of Victor Nealon and the Importance of Saying Sorry', The Justice Gap, available at: http://thejusticegap.com/2014/05/curious-case-victor-nealon-importance-saying-sorry/.

NORRIS, R.J. (2012), 'Assessing Compensation Statutes for the Wrongly Convicted', *Criminal Justice Policy Review*, 23: 352–74.

O'Neill, E. (2012), 'Remember the Roots', in Jon Robins (ed.), *Wrongly Accused: Who Is Responsible for Investigating Miscarriages Of Justice?*, Wilmington Publishing.

Radzik, L. (2007,) 'Offenders, the Making of Amends and the State', in G. Johnstone and D.W. Van Ness (eds), *Handbook of Restorative Justice*, Cullompton: Willan: 192–207.

Roberts, J.V. (2009), 'Listening to the Crime Victim: Evaluating Victim Input at Sentencing and Parole', in M. Tonry (ed.), *Crime and Justice*, Vol. 38, Chicago, IL: University of Chicago Press.

Rose, D. (1992), *A Climate of Fear: The Murder of PC Blakelock and the Case of the Tottenham Three*, London: Bloomsbury.

Rose, D. (1996), *In the Name of the Law: The Collapse of Criminal Justice*, London: Jonathan Cape.

Royal Commission on Criminal Justice, (1993), Cm 2263, London: HMSO.

Rozenberg, J. (1994), *The Search for Justice: An Anatomy of the Law*, London: Hodder and Stoughton.

Sanders, A., Creaton, J., Bird, S., and Weber, L. (1997), *Victims with Learning Disabilities*, University of Oxford, CCR, Occasional Paper No. 17.

Sanders, A., Young, R., and Burton, M. (2010), *Criminal Justice*, 4th edn, Oxford: Oxford University Press.

Savage, S.P. (2007), 'Restoring Justice: Campaigns against Miscarriages of Justice and the Restorative Justice Process', *European Journal of Criminology*, 4, 2: 195–216.

Shaikh, T. (2007), 'Sally Clark, Mother Wrongly Convicted of Killing her Sons, Found Dead at Home', *The Guardian*, 17 March 2003.

Shapland, J. and Hall, M. (2007), 'What Do We Know about the Effects of Crime on Victims?', *International Review of Victimology*, 14, 2: 175–217.

Shapland, J., Robinson, G., and Sorsby, A. (2011), *Restorative Justice in Practice: Evaluating What Works for Victims and Offenders*, Abingdon: Routledge.

Shapland, J., Wilmore, J., and Duff, P. (1985), *Victims in the Criminal Justice System*, Aldershot: Gower.

Sherman, L. and Strang, H. (2011), 'Empathy for the Devil: The Nature and Nurture of Revenge', in S. Karstedt, I. Loader, and H. Strang (eds), *Emotions, Crime and Justice*, Oxford: Hart Publishing.

Viebach, J. (2014), 'Alethéia and the Making of the World: Inner and Outer Dimensions of Memorials in Rwanda', in S. Buckley-Zistel, and S. Schäfer (eds), *Memorials in Times of Transition*, Antwerp: Intersentia.

Vollen, L. and Eggers, D. (2005), *Surviving Justice: America's Wrongfully Convicted and Exonerated*, San Francisco, CA: McSweeney's Publishing.

Walker, A., Flatley, J., Kershaw, C., and Moon, D. (eds) (2009), *Crime in England and Wales 2008/09: Findings from the British Crime Survey and Police Recorded Crime*, London: Home Office Statistical Bulletin, 11/09(1).

Walker, C. (1999), 'Miscarriages of Justice in Principle and Practice', in C. Walker and K. Starmer (eds), *Miscarriages of Justice: A Review of Justice in Error*, Oxford: Oxford University Press.

Walker, C. and Starmer, K. (eds) (1993), *Justice in Error*, London: Blackstone Press.

Walker, C. and Starmer, K. (1999), *Miscarriages of Justice: A Review of Justice in Error*, Oxford: Oxford University Press.

Walters, M. and Hoyle, C. (2012), 'Exploring the Everyday World of Hate Victimisation through Community Mediation', *International Review of Victimology*, 18, 1: 7–24.

Weigand, H. (2009), 'Building a Life: The Wrongfully Convicted and Exonerated', *Public Interest Law Journal*, 18: 427–37.

Westervelt, S.D. and Cook, K.J. (2008), 'Coping with Innocence after Death Row', *Contexts*, 7, 4: 32–7.

Westervelt, S.D. and Cook, K.J. (2010), 'Framing Innocents: The Wrongly Convicted as Victims of State Harm', *Crime, Law and Social Change*, 53: 259–75.

Woffinden, B. (1987), *Miscarriages of Justice*, London: Hodder and Stoughton.

Young, R. and Hoyle, C. (2003), 'New Improved Restorative Justice?: Action-Research and the Thames Valley Initiative in Restorative Cautioning' in A. von Hirsch, A. Bottoms, J. Roberts, K. Roach, and M. Schiff (eds), *Restorative Justice and Criminal Justice: Competing or Complementary Paradigms?*, Oxford: Hart Publishing.

Young, R., Hoyle, C., Cooper, K., and Hill, R. (2005), 'Informal Resolution of Complaints against the Police: A Quasi-Experimental Test of Restorative Justice', *Criminal Justice*, 5, 3: 279–317.

INDEX